The Best American
Travel Writing 2003

The Best American Travel Writing 2003

Edited and with an Introduction
by Ian Frazier

Jason Wilson, Series Editor

HOUGHTON MIFFLIN COMPANY
BOSTON · NEW YORK   2003

Visit our Web site: www.houghtonmifflinbooks.com.

ISSN 1530-1516
ISBN 0-618-11881-0
ISBN 0-618-11882-9 (pbk.)

Printed in the United States of America

MP 10 9 8 7 6 5 4 3 2 1

"Pope on a Rope Tow" by Lisa Anne Auerbach. First published in *Outside,* January 2002. Copyright © 2002 by Lisa Anne Auerbach. Reprinted by permission of the author.

"The Happiest Man in Cuba" by Rebecca Barry. First published in *The Washington Post Magazine,* January 27, 2002. Copyright © 2002 by Rebecca Barry. Reprinted by permission of the Wylie Agency, Inc.

"A Cup of Cuban Coffee" by Stephen Benz. First published in *Potpourri,* Vol. 14, No. 2. Copyright © 2002 by Stephen Benz. Reprinted by permission of the author.

"Eternal Winter" by Tom Bissell. First published in *Harper's Magazine,* April 2002. Copyright © 2002 by Thomas Carlisle Bissell. Reprinted by permission of International Creative Management, Inc.

"Stranger in the Dunes" by Graham Brink. First published in *The St. Petersburg Times,* February 10, 2002. Copyright © 2002 by *The St. Petersburg Times.* Reprinted by permission of *The St. Petersburg Times.*

"The Forest Primeval" by Peter Canby. First published in *Harper's Magazine,* July 2002. Copyright © 2002 by Peter Canby. Reprinted by permission of International Creative Management, Inc. Lyrics from "Tattooed Love Boys" by Chrissie Hynde. Copyright © 1979 by Chrissie Hynde. Reprinted by permission of EMI Music Publishing. All rights reserved.

"Over There" by Scott Carrier. First published in *Harper's Magazine,* April 2002. Copyright © 2002 by Scott Carrier. Reprinted by permission of the author.

"The Road from Abalak" by Peter Chilson. First published in *The American Scholar,* Summer 2002. Copyright © 2002 by Peter Chilson. Reprinted by permission of the author.

"They Shoot Poachers, Don't They?" by Tom Clynes. First published in *National Geographic Adventure,* October 2002. Copyright © 2002 by Tom Clynes. Reprinted by permission of the author.

Contents

Contents

Foreword

I would like to share a travel dispatch that was written by Laurel Clark, a mission specialist on the tragic space shuttle *Columbia* that disintegrated upon reentry into the earth's atmosphere on February 1, 2003, killing all seven crew members. Laurel Clark was, by all accounts, an intrepid explorer. Prior to becoming an astronaut, she had been an undersea medical doctor who dove with the Navy SEALS, a submarine officer, and a helicopter pilot — as well as the mother of an eight-year-old boy. The following excerpt is taken from an e-mail, as quoted by the Associated Press, that Clark wrote home to family and friends the day before she died:

Hello from above our magnificent planet Earth. The perspective is truly awe-inspiring. This is a terrific mission and we are very busy doing science round the clock. Just getting a moment to type e-mail is precious and so this will be short, and distributed to many who I know and love.

I have seen some incredible sights: lightning spreading over the Pacific, the Aurora Australis lighting up the entire visible horizon with the cityglow of Australia below, the crescent moon setting over the limb of the Earth, the vast plains of Africa and the dunes on Cape Horn, rivers breaking through tall mountain passes, the scars of humanity, the continuous line of life extending from North America, through Central America and into South America, a crescent moon setting over the limb of our blue planet. Mount Fuji looks like a small bump from up here, but it does stand out as a very distinct landmark.

Magically, the very first day in orbit, we flew over Lake Michigan and I saw Wind Point (Wisconsin) clearly. Haven't been so lucky since. Every orbit we go over a slightly different part of the Earth. Of course, much of the time I'm working back in Spacehab and I don't see any of it. Whenever I do get to look out, it is glorious. Even the stars have a special brightness.

I have seen my "friend" Orion several times. Taking photos of the earth is a real challenge, but a steep learning curve. I think I have finally gotten some beautiful shots the last two days. Keeping my fingers crossed they're in sharp focus.

The space shuttle tragedy happened just before we began making our final selections for this year's anthology. A few weeks later, someone sent me the newspaper account of Laurel Clark's e-mail. I was struck by how well Clark's prose exemplified the beautiful impulse that seizes travelers and moves them to share the experience of their journeys with others.

Consider how precious Clark's time was in outer space, and consider how thoroughly documented *Columbia*'s mission would be. Yet she still felt compelled to take the time to contribute her own personal fragment to the whole. What's incredibly touching about her descriptions is their sheer exuberance and how her joy alone conveys the significance of the journey. Perhaps what haunts me most is Clark's humble admission of her own limitations in trying to document what she's witnessed — and her hope that she might return home with at least a few snapshots that were faithful to the experience.

A travel writer knows these feelings well, and the essays in this anthology reflect that knowledge. The writers collected here have witnessed and experienced things so extraordinary, and at the same time so universal, that they simply must share them with others. They have mustered their skills — often in the brief, stolen moments between travels — in an attempt to express something significant about a place, and about themselves. And most keep their own fingers crossed in genuine hope that they've done justice to the place at hand.

The past twenty-four months have not been easy ones for those who enjoy travel. The essays here do not shy away from war, terrorism, environmental degradation, poachers, slavery, nuclear power — the "scars of humanity," as Clark wrote. But to see these essays solely as field reports on the sad state of the world is to deny them their beauty, their humor, and their benevolence.

As Kira Salak writes in her wonderful essay "Mungo Made Me Do It," chronicling a six-hundred-mile trip to Timbuktu in which she finds all manner of violence and depravity: "It is such a kind yet cruel world. Such a vulnerable world. I'm astounded by it all." And as this anthology proves every year, it's not always necessary to travel to Iraq or Afghanistan or Niger or Cuba or the Canadian Arctic to be astounded by it all.

In his recent bestseller, *The Art of Travel*, Alain de Botton meditates on why we, as travelers, are drawn again and again to the sublime. He writes: "If the world seems unfair or beyond our understanding, sublime places suggest that it is not surprising that things should be thus. We are the playthings of the forces that laid out the oceans and chiselled the mountains. Sublime places gently move us to acknowledge limitations we might otherwise encounter with anxiety or anger in the ordinary flow of events. It is not just nature that defies us. Human life is as overwhelming."

On the evening of the *Columbia* disaster, I found myself in a small village in Italy. It was the same village where I had stayed as a young American on my first trip abroad. It was where I had taken my wife on our honeymoon, and it was the first foreign town our young son had known. It also happened to be the place from which we had tearfully watched the World Trade Center fall. I know this village as well as anywhere I have ever lived.

Yet that night, after I had watched the tragic news of the space shuttle, and as I wandered home from the local café, I experienced something marvelous. For the very first time, I watched a soft, beautiful snow fall from the Italian sky. I lingered for a while in the tiny piazza, watching the snow coat everything — the scooter, the statues, the stacked café tables. By the next morning, all of the snow had melted away. But now the entire village felt transformed for me in some small yet considerable way.

"Whenever I do get to look out, it is glorious," Laurel Clark wrote from her spacecraft. "Even the stars have a special brightness." I hope that all of us who travel remember this, whether we are leaving the atmosphere or simply taking a trip to the other side of town.

For that reason, I want to dedicate this edition of *The Best American Travel Writing* to Clark and her fellow crew members.

*

The stories included in this anthology are selected from among hundreds of stories in hundreds of diverse publications — from mainstream and specialty magazines to Sunday newspaper travel sections to literary journals to in-flight magazines. My eyes are far from perfect, but I have done my best to be fair and representative, and in my opinion the best one hundred travel stories from the year 2002 were forwarded to Ian Frazier, who made the final selections.

With this publication, I begin anew by reading the hundreds of stories published in 2003. I am once again asking editors and writers to submit the best of whatever it is they define as "travel writing." These submissions must be nonfiction, published in the United States during the 2003 calendar year. They must not be reprints or excerpts from published books. They must include the author's name, date of publication, and publication name, and must be tearsheets, the complete publication, or a clear photocopy of the piece as it originally appeared. I must receive all submissions by January 15, 2004, in order to ensure full consideration for the next collection. Further, publications that want to make certain their contributions will be considered for the next edition should make sure to include this anthology on their subscription list. Submissions or subscriptions should be sent to Jason Wilson, The Best American Travel Writing, P.O. Box 260, Haddonfield, NJ 08033.

It was an honor to work with Ian Frazier, and I want to thank him for choosing such a wonderful collection. I would also like to thank Andrea Calabretta for her assistance on this year's anthology, as well as Deanne Urmy, Melissa Grella, and Liz Duvall, among others at Houghton Mifflin.

JASON WILSON

Introduction

I travel for all the usual reasons — to see new places, meet new people, have exciting experiences, etc. Also, I travel just because I like to move. Motion simply for its own sake is often my goal. This is true not only when I travel but anytime. The other night as I was loading the dinner dishes into our freestanding, roll-around dishwasher, my sister-in-law, who was staying with us, observed me carrying each dish individually across the kitchen, and suggested I could save myself some steps by rolling the dishwasher closer to the sink. I told her that I didn't mind, that I was enjoying the walk. I was being kind of glib with her: I know this love of motion must be controlled. When I'm doing research in a library, reading microfilmed newspapers on a microfilm-reading machine, I always have to restrain myself from zipping the whole roll back onto its spool at high-speed rewind, just for the thrill of it, before I'm completely done. The whine of the spinning spool, the accelerating flicker of the speeding days, express my restless disorder perfectly.

I attribute this disorder partly to my being from Ohio, and partly to my dad.

1. Ohio. When I was growing up there, Ohio seemed centrifugal. Some mystical force the place possessed flung people from it, often far. The northern part of the state was a corridor where westbound traffic on the Ohio Turnpike picked up speed on its first real stretch of flat country past the Allegheny Mountains. When we slept with our windows open in the summers, the sound of accelerating traffic on the Turnpike a couple of farm fields away was with us morning and night. I remember Rose Rugan and Kim Gould, two girls I had crushes on, leaning on the railing of the Stow Road bridge over the Turnpike and watching the trucks and cars whoosh past beneath. As I rode by them on the bridge on my bicycle, they turned to look at me over their shoulders; for a moment, a huge concentration of hope and longing and possibility shivered through me invisibly. Not many years afterward I walked to that bridge carrying a small suitcase, hopped the fence, climbed down to the highway, stuck out my thumb, and disappeared, like the taillights of that famously fast local dragstrip racer whose racing name was Color Me Gone.

Ohio seemed not somewhere to be, but somewhere to be from. We knew the Wright brothers, from Dayton, had learned to fly and had flown away, and John D. Rockefeller had departed with his Cleveland-made millions for New York City, and popular local TV personalities had vanished into vague careers in Hollywood, and most Cleveland Indian baseball players didn't get to be any good until they were traded to the Yankees. The high school kids our parents held up for emulation, the brains and athletes, went off to distant colleges and never returned, while everybody's grandparents decamped to Ohioan-filled retirement communities in Florida or Arizona. When we were still in elementary school, some of our fellow Ohioans began to leave the planet entirely. In fifth grade our teacher brought her black-and-white TV to school one morning so that we could watch the launch of the rocket carrying the first American to orbit the earth — John Glenn, of New Concord, Ohio. Ten minutes later, it seemed, Neil Armstrong was walking on the moon. Armstrong came from Wapakoneta, in the less populous western part of the state. We watched on live TV as he stepped from the lunar lander and spoke his historic first words, his rural Ohio accent clearly audible through the staticky vastness of space.

Of course Americans in general like to move, not just those from Ohio. I do know that in almost any far place I go, someone from Ohio either is there already, or was. Recently I've traveled in Siberia, passing through parts visited by George Kennan, of Norwalk, Ohio, back in 1885 and 1886. Kennan nearly destroyed his health getting to end-of-the-earth spots which would more than daunt a traveler today, and the book he later wrote about Siberian prisons helped bring down the czar. And he is only one of the Ohio travelers who went to that region and wrote books about it; in the genre of Siberian travel literature, books by Ohioans make a small but distinct subcategory.

The first time I ever traveled really far from home, thirty years ago, I was walking across a bazaar in Morocco when a man with blond, stringy hair came up to me and said, *"Parlez-vous anglais?"* I looked at him twice and asked, "Where are you from?" "Cincinnati," he replied sheepishly.

2. *My dad.* Like George Kennan, my dad was born in Norwalk. I never knew anyone who loved to ramble more than he. Dad was so restless that he kept on moving even after he had reached his destination, like those longhorn cattle that would walk endlessly round and round in their railyard corrals at the end of the Chisholm Trail. He had a relative who, as a young boy, was discovered one morning at the Norwalk train station sitting expectantly on the cowcatcher of a pausing westbound train. Dad's urge to escape pointed that direction. At first opportunity, he headed west — to California, and Stanford University. After Depression-era Ohio, he could not believe the wonderfulness of California. "Why do people live in Ohio, anyway?" he wrote to his mother. From Stanford he joined the navy and went to China; after the navy, perhaps against his better judgment, he came home.

Having a job and a wife and (eventually) five kids stopped his rambling hardly at all. When we visited my grandparents in Tucson, Arizona, Dad used to take off on walks across the desert on dusty, newly graded roads and return in the evening bright red with sunburn. At gatherings at a family cottage on Lake Erie he often launched the little sailboat he had built himself and sailed beyond the horizon, leaving people to wonder if they'd ever see him again. He took pride in having driven as far as one could drive in America — to the end of the Florida Keys, and to where the road ran out just north of Circle, Alaska. He was proud, too, that he and my mother had done the journeys in a station wagon with all us kids along. At restaurants he used to point us out to the waiters and say, embarrassingly, "These kids have been to both ends of the road!"

After we were grown he and my mother continued onward, to a farther destination every summer. They saw Europe, India, China,

Russia, Japan. Dad had various adventures and rambles-within-rambles everywhere — car wreck in India, encounter with suspicious characters in China, unauthorized explorations in East Berlin — and wrote about the experiences for the magazine at the company where he worked. When his health failed, and he had to stay home, he would pace back and forth by the hour in their condo on the west side of Cleveland. They were on the twelfth floor and could see the lake. He would walk to a window and look out at it, walk to another window and look out again. My mother described this behavior to his doctor, who diagnosed him as suffering from "agitated depression." The term seemed insufficient, somehow, for the urge that had driven him so relentlessly and so far.

Possessing the urge myself, I prefer to leave it unnamed. Even a phrase like "rambling fever," favored by country-and-western songs, pins it down too much. My father's doctor wasn't completely wrong, though, nor are the songs: motion-for-its-own-sake does have a pathological side. Long, almost-incurable spasms of it used to rack me sometimes. When I was a young man I rode Greyhound buses around the midwest (job in Chicago, girlfriend in Iowa, etc.). Often these buses were the opposite of express. Their constant stopping tormented me. At each little station, as the bus sat and sat, as the delays subdivided, as the driver chatted with the baggage guy and finished his cigarette and used it to light another, I gritted my teeth to keep from yelling in pain. But finally the driver would get back in, the bus door would close with a sigh; and then, how indescribably sweet, the moment when the bus began to move! All my sufferings vanished, and I leaned back so soothed with motion as to be narcotized.

A trip that repeated these highs and lows over and over usually delivered me wherever I was going in a basket-case mental condition. Ending the stop-and-go felt worse than going on, and if the people I was visiting seemed not glad enough to see me, or if any awkwardness arose, I would start back to the station. I needed people to slow me down, detain me. Years later, when I was writing a book about the Oglala Sioux Indians of the Pine Ridge Reservation in South Dakota, I heard of journeys harder to stop than any of mine. Some Sioux took journeys that built up a momentum of rambling and drinking and automotive problems and more drinking and more rambling until the velocity made the details blur. Usually at some point in these stories the police would begin to pursue. And usually, of course, the final scene included arrests and/or a car crash. After a while I understood the physics of that: Without an intervening shock from outside, certain journeys might never end.

Here is a maxim to keep in mind: "Reporters, like wolves, live by their paws." I repeat this quotation often to myself when I'm scouting around, working on a story. I came across it in a reminiscence of growing up in Leningrad by the poet Joseph Brodsky. Brodsky's father was a reporter for a nautical newspaper who covered the Leningrad waterfront and who often told this maxim to his son. "Reporters, like wolves . . ." I admire the statement for its succinct, encouraging rhythm, but even more for its accuracy. It reminds me that motion-for-its-own-sake, which I suffer as a low-level neurotic affliction, can be put to good practical use as well. It's the raw material of reporting.

Most reporting is a collaboration between mind and motion. To do it right you have to cover some ground. Your feet and sometimes your physical stamina get you there, while your mind observes. The one can partly fill in for the other, too; when the mind is dull and out of ideas, extra legwork can provide inspiring discoveries, and when the legwork is lazy, the mind can disguise that with embellishments added later.

And if the legwork — the physical accomplishment — is remarkable enough, practically any words you say or write on the occasion stand a chance of being profound. Neil Armstrong's remark about the small step for a man and the giant leap for mankind was pretty good, considering he thought it up himself when he had a lot else going on. We remember it, though, because of where he had gotten to when he said it. Julius Caesar, by all accounts an unpoetic person, went to Gaul, conquered it, and wrote a book about his feat. His *Gallic Wars* was one of the first nonfiction books in the history of the world, with its opening sentence, "All Gaul is divided into three parts," literature's first memorable nonfiction sentence. But the book was written not so much by Caesar's words as by his act of conquering Gaul.

In many nonfiction forms, the author's physical progress from A to B makes the factual spine. No matter how strange and confusing the surrounding reality may be, the writer knows (and, presumably, we believe) that he or she began here, went there, returned here: came, saw, conquered. This is of course true most of all in the special kind of reporting called travel writing, where the basic unit of measure is the author's stride. If the subject is travel, the reader is in the armchair and the author is not; that is, a certain amount of physical participation on the author's part will almost always be required.

Going somewhere and writing about how you got there and what you saw is a more willful thing to do, it seems to me, than it once was. I mean, given our society's rich supply of colorful and convenient virtuality, why bother? No place on the planet is unknown. Satellites hundreds of miles above it gauge and sense and calibrate and monitor and photograph it obsessively. Up-to-the-minute images of it pour from computer screens. On the basis of the images, major decisions about specific places are made by people who have never visited the places and never will. Actually setting foot in them may even seem redundant, or old-technology. Better to stay at the computer and bask in the satellite's reflected glow of olympian serenity.

The hell of it is, though, that many parts of the earth right now look their best only from very far away. Up close a different view is revealed. A traveler propelled by unmedicated agitation or some other personality imbalance actually *goes* to the place in the photo and finds not prettiness but near-catastrophe. Unlike its pictures, the place is, in short, a mess, and when you are up to your ankles in the mess yourself, it loses its serene, theoretical quality. Many magazines today tend not to print troubling stories about the environment, perhaps so as not to upset the cheery commercial mood advertisers want. Travel writing, however, is environmental by definition; the travel writer is unavoidably stuck with relating the sights and smells and general chaos he or she happens to find. Some of the pieces in this volume I regard as important and skillfully done environmental stories put into the form of a traveler's tale.

Offhand I can think of no other nonfiction that's as subversive as writing about travel. In travel writing, expectations are overturned constantly. Travel for diversion is supposed to be fun, but often isn't; stories of nightmare journeys may be more numerous than stories of happy ones. When occasionally the place visited turns out to be uncrowded and welcoming and sublime, and a magazine or book says so, what happens to the place in the sequel is too familiar to describe. Many travelers' accounts revise and dispute previous travelers' writings, and are themselves revised by those who follow. Stories of a "return to" such-and-such a place are an honorable and incxhaustible tradition. And from a larger perspective, we live in an age in which travelers have been puncturing fantasies left over from earlier and perhaps more optimistic generations.

Destinations are less remote and journeys less final than they used to be. You can travel in the most laborious, antique, time-consuming style you choose, knowing that if you get fed up with it you will simply head for the nearest airport and erase the mistake in a matter of hours. With a satellite phone in your pack you can call home from anywhere anytime and find out if the plumber showed up this morning and what was in the mail. In terms of travel fantasy, our world is a theater in which the curtain has just been closed and the house lights turned on. Skepticism descends: everything appears near at hand and too bright, while the hazy charms of distance evanesce away. Despite all that, people still go on journeys and write about them. I can't really explain why. I guess because reality is always beautiful and mysterious, however wise to it we think we are. Or maybe just because we go crazy if we sit around the apartment for too long.

I hoped to choose the pieces in this volume according to an overarching concept of the travel essay. In the end, though, I chose pieces that interested me. I put in a few funny pieces, too, because I liked them. I realize that these methods are feckless and informal. All I can tell you is, there are excellent pieces here. As I read through some of the selections I was at first alarmed: travel writing is about the world, and the world is in worse shape than I'd thought. But then I was amazed at how bizarre and fulsome and endlessly various it is, too. A few of the writers herein accomplished travel sagas of such bravery that I couldn't believe they weren't ten times louder about making it known. It's an honor to include them, and I hope in the future they'll take care. Other writers found fascinating places, or aspects of places, where I would have never thought to look. Each piece has consolations and great pleasures of its own.

People of all sorts, not only reporters, live by their paws. Now and again everybody has to get out, go for a jaunt, look around. At a criminal trial where I was a juror not long ago, a glance passed between the victim and the defendant that changed the course of the trial; the judge, an opponent of allowing TV cameras in the courtroom, later mentioned that moment as an example of what can't be captured on TV. In other words, you had to be there. Technology's fine, but it will never substitute for a person on the scene. The writers in this book, by enterprise and courage and earned happenstance, have managed to be there. They got their stories as travel writers have always done; their writing suggests the alliance between on-site reporting and art, between art and intrepidity. In places beyond our field of vision they've observed wonders and signs the rest of us haven't seen yet. The news they bring is invaluable. You heard it first here.

IAN FRAZIER

The Best American
Travel Writing 2003

LISA ANNE AUERBACH

Pope on a Rope Tow

FROM *Outside*

> God Almighty, you who gave us corporeal life and entrusted us with it, so we
> would honor and care for it, look out for the men and women who ski, may
> they maintain their health and use their free time wisely.
> — Pope John Paul II

I'M SNOOPING AROUND the pope's old bedroom in Kraków, Poland, checking out the gouges on his skis. I confess: I've been in a
lot of bro-dorms, but none nearly as holy. Usually the decor consists of empty beer cans, a PlayStation, and smelly Capilene underwear. But in the tidy one-room pope pad — now part of the
Archdiocesan Museum, located near Wawel Royal Cathedral, where
Father Karol Wojtyla hung his skullcap from 1952 to 1958 —
there's a dainty café table, three chairs, a neat bunk with purple
cushions, and an armoire filled with colorful priestly garb.

But right now I'm more interested in the two pairs of skis leaning
in the corner. One's an old hickory set with spring bindings and
pointy tips, the kind you see hanging over bars in ski towns. The
others, retired more recently, are 195-centimeter Head Pros with
Tyrolia bindings. I can't help myself — I have to touch them. The
undersides are grooved with deep cuts and scratches. The skis
don't quite qualify as sacred relics, but they do serve notice that
when he got away from it all, up in the mountains, Father Wojtyla
wasn't just sticking to the corduroy and cruising the green runs,
like Gerald Ford at Beaver Creek. No — *he skied over rocks!* He
was out there, off-piste. The man who became pope in 1978 might,
in fact, have been a bad-ass. As I clutch the skis, the docent stares,
then quietly reminds me not to take a photograph.

Pope John Paul II is widely known and revered by millions the world over as the spiritual guide and shepherd of the Roman Catholic Church. What is less well known is his history as a trailblazing two-planker. The Man in White ripped the Polish pow from the time the papacy was just a gleam in his eye until his mature years as the toast of the Vatican. In his younger days, JP2 was known as a megahiker, an avid kayaker, and a camper nonpareil. He preached in the woods, ate watery pudding for sustenance while surfing the backcountry, and repeatedly lost his prayer book in the wild. When asked, "Is it befitting a cardinal to ski?" his reply was, "What is unbefitting a cardinal is to ski badly."

One day I heard a tale from a gentleman I met in my neighborhood in Los Angeles. A draftsman who emigrated to the United States during World War II, he insisted he'd once skied with the pontiff back when His Holiness was a seminary student. As evidence, he produced an out-of-focus photo he claimed was him and a grinning Karol Wojtyla. He pointed to a city park on a map of Kraków and mentioned something about reveling in the outdoors.

Not being a student of papal extracurricular activities, this beta came as a shock. Up to this point, my interest in Catholicism had been limited to idle thoughts about sin and the Inquisition, but as a skier I was intrigued by the notion of a sportive pope. So I went to Poland on my own secular quest, to seek the holy trail.

It may come as a surprise to the bourgeois Western skier, raised on a diet of fresh powder in the Rockies or the Alps, but southern Poland is carpeted with mountains, chairlifts, and après-ski huts full of sausages and beer. There are four major ski areas and all have names that would garner triple-digit Scrabble scores: Szczyrk. Zakopane. Szklarska Poreba. The Bieszczady Mountains.

Zakopane (the easiest to pronounce: Zock-o-*pah*-nay) is situated in the Tatra Mountains, a gnarly spur of the Carpathians that crowds the border with Slovakia. Thanks to the mounds of fresh snow that pile up there every year, it is known as the winter sports capital of Poland and a former stomping ground of JP2. Accessible via a well-marked two-lane road, the town lies just a couple of hours south of Kraków, unless you're stuck behind a horse-drawn vehicle, in which case it takes much longer. Joining me on my journey is Witold Krassowski, a dry-witted photographer with a bushy mustache. Witold's usual assignments take him to war zones. He can't understand why anyone would be interested in the pope's sporting past, but he's happy to play along, and as a translator he's invaluable.

As we creep along in our rented Renault, Witold reads aloud from *Papiez, Jakiego Nie Znamy* (roughly "The Pope in Nature"), a paperback we found among the kitschy glow-in-the-dark Jesuses and cards depicting Catholic saints in 3-D at the apartment in Wadowice (thirty miles southwest of Kraków) where the pope was born in 1920. Now, of course, it too is a museum. Young Karol was studious, serious, and religious, but he also dug the outdoors, and it was in Wadowice that he first strapped hickory sticks to his feet and felt the wind whistle through his hair as he slid down farm hills, past chickens and cows. Later, the freedom of downhilling would take on immense spiritual importance. "In the mountains," says Witold, quoting the more mature, philosophical pope, "the ugly hubbub of the city disappears and the quiet of immeasurable distances prevails, which allows a person to more clearly hear the inner echo of the voice of God." Sounds like some hippie telemarkers I know. And yet, JP2 has tapped his ecological veins to add a little more green to a typically anthropocentric religion. He's gone so far as to declare the worldwide environmental crisis an urgent moral problem and has called on Catholics and all humans to show respect for "the hidden, yet perceivable requirements of the order and harmony which govern nature itself." Could it be that the foundations he laid for his own brand of peace-and-earth-loving Catholicism as pope are rooted in his powder-loving past?

Well, it seems totally obvious to me. After he was elected to Rome, enough skis arrived from well-wishers to outfit half the Vatican, but the pontiff resisted the call of the backcountry. "I pray to God to lead me from this temptation," he said in 1979 to an Italian mountain sports club that had presented him with a pair of custom white boards. "I might yet slide into a ravine, and then what?" (Though he did think to add, "God bless skiers and their legs." Amen.) Eight years later he proved he was a regular guy by caving in to that temptation. He donned dark glasses, jumped in an Alfa, and sneaked up to a resort in the Rhaetian Alps. It was the last time he was healthy enough to ski. (Since the early nineties, JP2, who is now eighty-one, has had his gallbladder removed, a hip replaced, and has battled what the Vatican calls "symptoms" of Parkinson's disease.) Still, it certainly lends credence to the Papal Powder Linkage Theory.

Like a lot of post–Cold War Poland, Zakopane is a mélange of communist-era concrete hotels and shops mixed in with traditional wooden buildings. Since the fall of communism, the culture seems to have grown more jumbled in appearance, if not in demeanor. Enterprising locals set up tables in the streets to sell football-shaped lumps of smoked sheep's cheese, which tastes surprisingly like rubber. But the main drag is also packed with restaurants, and a loud Internet café adjacent to a skateboard boutique — two sure signs that capitalist tomfoolery is on the rise — is crammed with malcontent punk rockers playing on-line killing games and kibitzing in chat rooms. These kids, spiky-haired and fashion-conscious, are the closest thing to ski bums I see the whole time I'm in Poland.

From the center of town it's a short taxi ride to the burg of Kuznice, where you catch the cable car to the summit of Kasprowy Wierch, the most popular lift-served peak in the country. Crammed inside the cable car on our first morning in Zakopane, the "inner echo of the voice of God" is drowned out by the complex garbled consonants of tightly sandwiched Poles.

In photos, the Tatra Mountains are breathtakingly beautiful; in person, they're gray and fogbound, magically deep and hobbit-sultry. When we crack through the cloud layer and reach the ski station at the top, the sky is blue, and rocky, snowcapped peaks stretch in every direction.

We pile out of the cable car, 6,500 feet up. Skiers are everywhere, fashionably dressed in understated Eastern European style and carrying the latest equipment. Right out the doors of the station, a modern quad is dropping people off at the top of a gargantuan treeless bowl. The slope is wide open and the icy terrain is crammed with skiers of all levels, though there are no snowboarders in sight. Being a powder-obsessed American, I traverse as far as possible along the ridge, which also happens to be the Poland-Slovakia border. Shuffling past gun-toting, camo-clad guards, I reach the far edge of the bowl, where last night's two centimeters of fresh hasn't been decimated. Then I shove off.

It's a tough crowd on Kasprowy; people take their skiing very seriously. There's no whooping or heckling, even when there's a total crashing yard sale. I've learned that wearing colors other than dark neutrals is a fashion faux pas, but I can't help feeling that people are looking at me suspiciously. Witold claims it's the scrap of pink lining on my navy blue Patagonia jacket — the bright color makes me look freakish and foreign. By the time I reach the bottom, my wave of paranoia has passed. Strange vibes and muted slope excitement are just something else to get used to in this reserved culture.

When Karol Wojtyla was the bishop, and later cardinal, of Kraków, he was still a ripper, and he spent two weeks each winter from 1962 to 1978 with the Sisters of St. Ursula Grey in their convent just down the road from Kasprowy. Witold, who has had to deal with nuns a lot over the years, says they are incorrigible gossips. Don't believe anything they say, he advises, but I believe it all anyhow.

The day after our trip up Kasprowy, we comb our hair and knock on the convent door. We are greeted by two nuns, both named Sister Theresa. Sister Theresa No. 1, pleasant and brisk, introduces us to Sister Theresa No. 2, an older woman eager to talk about the pope. ST2 takes us upstairs to view the pope's old lodgings. It's less of a museum than the other museums, but it's still set up exactly as he left it. The desk, chairs, and table have that behind-the-Iron-Curtain institutional look, all blond wood and modular. Standing here, I realize that at this point I've been in more bedrooms belonging to the pope than to any other man.

In the corner is a black-and-white shot of the then-bishop, skis on his shoulder, wool hat pulled down over his ears. He's wearing a nylon jacket with a broken zipper. ST2 tells Witold that the skiing bishop was a fashion disaster — his goggles were outdated, his clothes mismatched. She tells him this confidentially, in Polish, giggling, saying it's not to be translated. Witold immediately translates for me, happy to prove his point about nuns with wagging tongues.

ST2 is full of dope on the pope, most of which supports my vision of him as a hard-core downhiller. He skied Kasprowy, she says, but preferred the solitude of the Chocholowska Valley, about ten miles to the west. He would drive into the valley, park, climb a mountain, and carve his way to the bottom. "He was critical of skiing as sport," ST2 opines. "And he didn't think taking a cable car up a hill and then going down was sport. The only way he'd go skiing was to carry skis up the mountain and ski down."

Visible through the convent's windows are the slopes of Nosal, a small Zakopane ski hill with poma lifts and a rope tow. ST2 tells me that one night long ago, the bishop arrived at the convent at midnight, couldn't resist the allure of fresh powder, and took off for a run. But then, she adds, he would rarely go into the mountains alone. When I ask why, ST2 explains that to be a prominent Catholic clergyman in a communist country in the midst of the Cold War was dangerous. Police would dress up as sheep in nearby fields as he frolicked, she says. It's hard to tell what she means — were the police masquerading as sheep to spy on him or to protect him? — but I love the idea of fuzzy baaing cops hunched in meadows wearing heavy woolen costumes. Witold doesn't believe a word of it.

As we're about to leave, I ask the sisters if they have a pair of the pope's old boards around. No, all his skis are in the museum in Kraków, they say. "We have his boots, though," ST1 offers. She leaves and comes back with a well-worn pair of leather ski boots, laces up both the front and back. She handles these relics lovingly, setting them on a desk for us to admire. The pope, it turns out, has average-size feet.

In Poland, Pope John Paul II is everywhere — on plaques and posters, in sculptural simulacra, and as the namesake of the Szlak Papieski, a.k.a. the Papal Trail, a hiking and ski route that stretches for three miles in the spruce forests of the Chocholowska Valley. I expected the official Papal Trail to ascend dramatically heavenward, but no dice. In fact, it moseys for most of its length along a creek that meanders through the valley. Trees are marked with the colors of the Vatican, yellow and white, and the trail is dotted with small crosses adorned with tired-looking Jesuses, shivering in the Carpathian wind.

We leave the Renault behind at a Tatra National Park kiosk and jump into a horse-drawn sleigh, the traditional method of accessing the Papal Trail if you're not hiking or skiing. As we plod along, snow starts falling in clumps. Soon it's as misty and atmospheric as a Zeppelin box set. Visibility is so low we can't even make out 6,165-foot Mount Rakon, another of the pope's old haunts. After a mile, our carriage reaches the Papal Trail; we get out and start to walk. Hikers pass us going the other way, and some are on downhill skis, which seems odd, given that the trail is nearly flat. One man trudges by alone. I ask where he's coming from and he replies, sullenly, "From up to down." I brace myself for an uphill rally, but the trail peters out at a makeshift shrine of candles and crosses. It's a bit of a letdown.

The day after, I say good-bye to Witold and decide to follow the pope's footsteps on my own. This means going deeper into the Tatras, to a "refuge," or inn, that lies on the banks of a small alpine lake called Morskie Oko, "Eye of the Sea." There are eight refuges in Tatra National Park, and they're open year-round. In summer they're often filled to capacity, but in winter the trans-Tatra trails get a lot of snow, leaving only the most hardy souls to trek in.

After an hour's drive east to the village of Lysa Polana, I park again and hoof the six-mile trail to Morskie Oko solo. The refuge looks a bit more rickety than I'd been led to expect. On my map there's a photo of a spiffier building perched beside emerald-green waters and surrounded by mountains, but today everything is uniformly white. I walk toward where I think the lake might be until I hear ice creaking beneath my feet. I'm on it.

I turn around and make my way back to the refuge. Downstairs, in a wood-paneled dining room, the proprietress brings out a photo album and shows me snapshots of a surprise visit the pope made in 1997. When she was a little girl, the future pope would visit Morskie Oko for one or two nights at a time during July and August, bringing youth groups to the mountains. She points to a picture of JP2 in '97, standing on the shore. He's wearing white robes and a matching windbreaker. "He remembered my parents," she says in halting English. "Nice man, very nice man."

After the sun sets, the bright white landscape turns to gray and then black. I'm served roast chicken and cabbage salad, which I eat alone in the dining room. There are three other people spending the night, but they are nowhere to be seen.

Outside, the "quiet of immeasurable distances" fills the crisp night air and the Tatras breathe with the solitude and wonderment that nourished the pope during campouts, ski trips, and kayaking adventures. It's my last night in Poland, so I take another walk atop the lake he's paddled across and delivered sermons beside. It's dark, but I can just make out a cross nailed up on a nearby tree — a reminder, I'm guessing, in case visitors become so distracted by the splendor that they forget about the nuts and bolts of the equation. I listen again for that inner echo of the voice of God, but hear only muffled voices, nothing more mystical than my three fellow refugees, out for a late-night smoke.

REBECCA BARRY

The Happiest Man in Cuba

FROM *The Washington Post Magazine*

WHEN MY FATHER was three years old, my grandmother took him to 30th Street Station in Philadelphia. They were a striking pair. My grandmother was a fine-boned woman with dark eyes and wavy black hair. A bout with childhood polio had left her with a slight limp, which gave her beauty a deceptive edge of fragility. My father had her dark hair, his thickly lashed eyes flecked with gold and green, and he held her hand tightly, offering support with his own small body. As my grandmother searched for the right gate, my father caught sight of a train passing on a trestle high above the tracks. It was a freight train, and he began naming the cars in a high, clear voice. "Hopper car, boxcar," he said. "Tank car." By the time he was halfway through, a small crowd had gathered around this little boy, listening to his unflinchingly correct recitation. "Boxcar, gondola car, stock car," he went on earnestly. The last car passed and he took a deep breath. "Caboose!" he said. He turned to his audience and added gravely, "That was a train."

Sixty years later, my father and I are in a rented car near a sugar plantation outside Guines, a small town in Cuba. I am slightly nauseated. My father has rented the car this morning and spent most of the trip from Havana getting used to the gears, the accelerator, and the brakes. The road we're on is narrow and unpaved, flanked on both sides by sugar cane stalks taller than a grown man. My father has spotted some train tracks and is trying to drive and look at them at the same time. "Those look like narrow gauge," he says. "I'll be damned." A man carrying a chicken pedals slowly by on his bicycle, staring into the car. Dad, busy scanning the cane fields for black smoke, swerves and honks the horn by accident.

Then we hear it: a raw, high-pitched whistle, reaching out across the cane fields. "That's a steam engine, by God!" shouts my father. The whistle blows again. "Whooo!" he whistles back. "Whooo! Whoo-whooo!" He waves a hand in his excitement, inadvertently turning on the windshield wipers. "Boy, that's beautiful," he says. "That's just beautiful. There's no other sound like that."

That was a train.

My father loves trains. Not model trains or train memorabilia, but active, working locomotives. He's on the board of directors of the National Association of Railroad Passengers, and spends almost all his spare time working to get the government to earmark funds for improving passenger train service. Over the last decade he's been instrumental in getting about $20 million for improvements in New York state. (This, by the way, is not his day job. He makes his living at a university, researching and shaping community development projects.) He drives a Subaru with a bumper sticker that says, I'D RATHER BE ON THE TRAIN, and has an entire briefcase filled with train schedules, which he's constantly digging through to give unsuspecting dinner guests a cheaper alternative to flying to Florida or Chicago for their vacation.

When he was a young man, my father devoted almost all of his time to chasing trains — steam engines, to be exact. After he graduated from college and before he married my mother, he hitchhiked through Mexico and Central America, primarily to photograph and ride on as many trains as possible. It was a hobby that wasn't that well received once he got married and had kids. After several attempts at dragging the entire family around the country to photograph steam engines, he gave it up to work on saving Amtrak or just riding trains whenever possible.

For the past few years, however, he had been talking about making a trip to Cuba to photograph the steam engines they still use to bring cane from the plantations to the mills. One day, he got a letter from a fellow rail fan urging him to go soon if he was going to go. More than a few of the mills had already started using diesels, and anyone who knows anything about steam engines knows that once diesels are introduced, steam engines go the way of the rotary phone.

I also urged him to go, mostly because I wanted to go along. I was getting married soon and thought this might be one of my last

chances to have an adventure with him. I grew up on stories from
his trips through Mexico — about the time he got arrested, the
time an engineer and fireman got into a fight and tried to push
each other out the windows of a moving locomotive. I always admired and envied that trip, and it seemed like this was a rare
chance for me to recapture some of those experiences with him.

As the trip got closer, however, I began to dread it. It was a two-
week expedition six weeks before my wedding, so the timing wasn't
great. And the itinerary was formidable — packed with visits to
two, sometimes three sugar mills a day. Only one day, a Sunday, was
paced differently. "Relax," my father had typed in on his schedule.
"Organize notes."

Also, no one in Cuba takes credit cards and there are no ATMs,
so we would be traveling with an enormous amount of cash. For
this reason, Dad was aghast when I showed up at the airport with a
purse.

"You don't have a money belt?" he said. "I don't think that's
smart. You need something like this," he gestured toward a slim
pouch that he had tucked neatly into the front of his pants. "I've
also got $300 in each shoe."

That first train we saw outside of Guines was a bit disappointing. It
was rusted and listed to one side, and was being taken out of service to fix a broken spring on the tender. But the crew said there
would be another train nearby, outside the village of San Nicolas,
so we drove off in that direction. We didn't have to wait long before
we heard another whistle.

"By God, there he is!" Dad said (referring to the engineer, not
the engine, which is female). By then we could see a slim black
stripe gliding through the pale green cane. Dad took a picture.
Then he jumped back in the car, and we hurtled on.

We were almost out of breath by the time we reached the station
in Guines. It was closed and had the crumbling beauty that so many
buildings in Cuba do, with high windows and elegant columns,
mottled by missing patches of paint. A tall man named Francisco
was leaning up against one of the pillars, cleaning a thumbnail. He
had a regal nose, proud cheekbones, and sleepy eyes. "I'm the one
you're looking for," he said, after Dad asked a brakeman when the
train was going to leave. "I'm the engineer."

Most steam engines have a crew of at least two: the engineer, who manages the throttle and the reverse lever, and the fireman, who keeps the fire going. Sometimes the brakeman will also ride in the engine. There were six men on Francisco's engine: Francisco; the fireman, who was twenty-three; the fireman's brother, who as far as I could tell was just along for the ride; and three brakemen, who spent most of the time riding on top of the tender. Sitting in the fireman's chair was his sixteen-year-old wife, whom he had invited along so she could see what his job was like. She took turns staring sadly out the window and unsmilingly at me.

Francisco explained this engine — the one he was running — was an experimental locomotive modernized by an Argentine civil engineer who had dedicated much of his life to making a steam engine that was as efficient as a diesel. The result was an engine so complex that Francisco was the only one allowed to run it.

"The Diablo Rojo," my father said with a nod. He had heard of this engine and the Argentinian, and noted with cautious optimism that it was significant that they were using it. After all, most countries on the verge of getting rid of steam wouldn't bother seeing if this engine was indeed more efficient. "If this engine is the one he says it is," Dad said, "he's some engineer. You'd have to be the best in the country to be asked to run this machine."

"We call it Prometeo," Francisco said, clearing a space for me in his seat next to the window. Prometheus, the god of fire.

I was unprepared for the sensory overload of riding in a steam engine. The engines in Cuba burn crude oil, which is heated by steam, then sprayed into the firebox as a black mist. The oil settles everywhere: on your hands, in your hair, under your fingernails. The sound of the steam and wheels is deafening, the engine's vibration seeps into your bones.

This is precisely what gets the men who love steam.

"I know what's going on inside it," Francisco shouted, when I asked him what he liked about steam engines. "If something goes wrong, I can feel it. With a diesel, you just can't tell."

"It's like an animal," my father agreed. "*Vivo,*" he said. It lives. Francisco nodded.

Running a steam engine is hard work. The engineers wear thick gloves to avoid getting burned and clothes they know will never again be clean once the soot, oil, and black smoke get to them. To run the engine, you have to wrestle with levers longer than a man's arm. If the weather is bad and the tracks are slippery, it can take hours to go only a short distance. And the pay is low — eight to ten dollars a month.

Yet it seemed to me that these were the happiest men in Cuba. They waxed poetic whenever I asked about their work. "*Vapores* [steam engines] have been in my blood for generations," said Ernesto, a fireman we met the next day at another mill. "My father worked on them, and my grandfather before him. I have always wanted to run one. Since I was a child."

"They're like cowboys," I said to my father, watching Ernesto swing gracefully onto his engine.

And like cowboys they are often misunderstood by their women. "It's not that she doesn't like them," said Felix, Ernesto's engineer, when asked if his wife liked trains. "I think she just doesn't understand them."

"My wife doesn't like them at all," said Ernesto. "I'm usually on them until one or two in the morning."

"I blow the whistle when I come into town so my wife can start heating up water for my bath," added Felix. "But every night she says, 'I didn't hear any whistle. Draw your own bath.'"

They began to discuss the brake system on their train with my father, and I watched him talk, lulled by the sound of Spanish. My father seems more at ease in Spanish. I don't know exactly why, except that Spanish is a polite, respectful language, and he is a polite, respectful man. But it was also the subject matter.

Once, when I was living in France, my parents took a rare plane trip to visit me. I was staying with a friend in a roomy apartment whose only drawback was that it overlooked the back of the Montparnasse train station. Even on a sunny day, the view was steel gray and gritty. My parents came into the apartment exhausted from the intercontinental flight plus the five-hour train ride they'd taken to the airport. My mother collapsed on the couch. My father headed straight over to the windows, looking ten years younger with every step. "What a beautiful view!" he exclaimed.

Our schedule in Cuba went something like this: We'd get up at seven-thirty or eight and eat breakfast. Then we'd get into the car, drive to a mill, look for a train and chase it. After that we'd find the shop where the engines were serviced. We'd prowl around looking at engines and talking to the men who run them. Then we'd drive to another mill. This would continue until about five or six, when we'd look for a place to spend the night. We did not eat lunch.

It was hard not to notice how funny we looked. My father wore jeans, a button-down madras shirt, and old oxford shoes he'd saved especially for the trip. Around his neck were two cameras: a Canon, and a Rolleiflex he's been using since about 1964. His shirt pocket was stuffed with a notepad, pens, his glasses, and a tire gauge. I wore loose chino shorts, glasses, and puffy running sneakers, and carried a tape recorder and a notepad that I scribbled on constantly.

Dad strode easily, oblivious to people staring as he peered at rusted engine plates and old boilers, patiently explaining the details that fascinated him.

"Those rods control the brakes."

Or, "See that copper pipe that comes from the tender? It goes into a crosshead pump, and when it goes up into that ball, the pressure gets very high, and there's some air in there, and the air gets compressed and pushes the water into the boiler. It's a very antiquated system. I've only seen it on one other railroad."

I'd say, "Hmmm."

"This is the piston. Steam comes out of these holes, pushes it back, and then there's steam that comes out of holes over there that pushes it forward."

"Mmmhmm. I see." In truth, I didn't completely see. It was the same as it's always been around Dad and trains. All those encyclopedic details, all those phrases — crosshead pump, sander pipe, water injector — I could only absorb so much before my mind started to wander to the herd of goats across the street, the little boys who were following us, or why we never ate lunch.

My older sister had warned me this would happen. One night before the trip I went to my parents' house to go over some wedding plans, and my father spent most of the night poring over spreadsheets he'd made with cost estimates of the trip.

"You know it's not going to be a vacation, don't you?" my sister said.

"You know you're just going to spend all your time in a car trying not to be sick, not stopping for lunch, talking about trains, right?"

"It's Cuba," I said. "It will be different. I'm an adult."

"Ha," she said. "Ha ha ha, HAH!"

On our third day in Cuba, we went to a mill called Cai Manalich, which had some old ALCO steam engines, in which Dad was particularly interested.

Most of the Manalich engines were steam, but a few diesels were there waiting for repairs. Diesels are smaller and more streamlined than steam engines. They're quieter, and of course there's no plume of steam. They also have a high-pitched little poot of a horn that has none of the soul of a steam engine's mournful cry.

The chief at Manalich, a man named Jesus, did not smile easily, but he also did not appear to be unfriendly.

"Ingenuity," he said with a shrug, when my father asked how they kept these antique engines running. "We use the old engines for parts, and we invent some parts ourselves."

We passed some men turning a piece of metal on a lathe. "That, for example, is going to go onto that engine over there, the 1312."

The men at the lathe smiled and Dad watched their hands shaping the metal.

Jesus led us to his favorite engine. We stood there and admired it, and I asked my father to ask him if he thought diesel was a threat to steam. He put his hand in his back pocket and frowned. I waited.

We were beginning to chafe at each other. I was frustrated that my Spanish wasn't good enough to ask the questions I wanted to ask, and I could tell he wasn't entirely comfortable asking them for me. He wanted to know how long a particular brake system had been used, or what kind of oil was burned. My questions about whether Ernesto's wife liked trains, how that brakeman lost his front tooth, or what, exactly, the engineers liked about steam were inquiries that bordered on intrusive and slowed down the important talk.

I could see in my father's expression that the question about diesel threatening steam was really trying his patience. These engines, practically extinct everywhere else, seemed to be thriving here. Not only that, but they were cared for by men who understood and loved them, men who still knew the joy and pride of being able to fix their own machines. To bring up the fact that they could soon die out was not only impolite but missed the point.

Jesus didn't seem to mind. "No," he said. "No. These machines have been around for a hundred years. There's no reason they'd stop breathing now."

Everyone feels a connection to them, he went on. The children, the people in town.

In fact, according to the men who work them, you couldn't kill a steam engine in Cuba if you tried.

"The government forbids it," said a steam mechanic at the engine shed at the October the 10th Mill a few days later. "There's even been a proposal that we make our own. *Mira*," he continued, touching my father's arm and pointing to a gutted, rusted engine. "That one will be done by the fall."

Several other men had stopped what they were doing and had gathered around my father, watching him examine the engine. It was a scene I was to see over and over again. My father and I would take our owlish little act into a railroad yard. Eventually someone would approach us, curiously, maybe suspiciously. My father, whose name is Frank, would introduce himself as Francisco Barry. He'd politely explain that he was here to see these steam engines. He would talk about his trip through Mexico forty years ago, and say that with this trip, he was sort of recapturing his youth. Then he'd ask a question. He'd noticed, for example, that those cars sitting over there didn't have couplers. Did they use a link-and-pin system? Very interesting.

These were men who had worked all their lives on steam trains, whose skin and clothes were black from the grease. Most of them had never left their home towns, let alone Cuba, and they probably didn't think they'd have much in common with this white man in a neat button-down shirt, wandering around so far away from home with a tripod hanging from his belt.

"I noticed," my father would continue, "that the steam pipe on the 1418 is crooked. On most engines I've seen, that pipe is straight. Did you make it that way?"

"*Si, si,*" they would say, explaining why they did. My father would nod, listening intently.

Eventually, everyone would get more excited. "*Mira,*" a mechanic would say, taking Dad by the arm, showing him a huge piece of metal they'd shaped to reconstruct a 1910 Baldwin made in Philadelphia. "*Mira!* We made this. See? This way we don't have to use rivets."

"*Muy interesante,*" my father would say. "*Muy impresionante.*"

It was a side of my father I'd almost never seen. At home, he is shy and thinks very carefully before he speaks. He's so quiet that in our family of women (three grown daughters, one wife) he often gets lost in the conversation, or falls asleep. But here, he was the center of attention, talking fluidly and making jokes in a language that somehow seemed to fit him better than the one he speaks at home.

He was so popular, in fact, that at one of the last shops we visited, he was offered a job.

"I could give you a contract," said Solis, the chief mechanic. Solis had a dignified manner and a degree in thermo-something — neither my father nor I could quite make it out. "I think he's in charge of all things hot," my father said, shrugging his shoulders as if to say my guess was as good as his.

"You could take a month to learn how to run a steam engine and work for us during the harvest season," Solis continued.

"That's very nice," said my father.

"That's amazing!" I said as we got into the car. "Are you going to do it?"

"Oh, I don't think so," he said with a sigh. "These are complicated machines. If I were younger, I guess it would be more appealing, but at my age, I'm more and more aware of what I don't know."

I leaned back in my seat, a little defeated. What could he possibly not know? Recently there was a train wreck about an hour's drive from my parents' home, and a TV crew from the local news station showed up at our farmhouse, which is pretty much in the middle of nowhere. The crew members apologized for interrupting dinner, but they needed to talk to someone about the wreck. While they didn't know what made him an authority, exactly, everyone they'd spoken to had insisted they go find Frank Barry. Dad, who is wounded by any bad press about trains, told them about his credentials (on the board of NARP, former president of the Empire State Passengers Association), gave them possibilities for what might have caused the wreck, and then pointed out that statistically trains were still much safer than cars or airplanes. When the segment aired, he appeared in front of the built-in bookshelves in our dining room, with the vague tag line "train expert." ("You see that?" said my mother. "We look like smart people. Aren't you glad I made you put those shelves in?")

Solis offered to show us some good spots for pictures. He climbed in the car and directed us to a railroad crossing on the top of a grade where the engine would be working hard, which would make a dramatic picture. Dad got out and Solis sat back, stretching his long legs out of the car.

"You're very nice," I said, "to spend the day with my father. This is making him very happy."

"*No me molesta,*" Solis said calmly. It doesn't bother me. We looked out the window. My father had climbed up a telephone pole and was peering into the top of his Rolleiflex.

"Your father is a good man," he went on. "*Muy impresionante.*"

He said this without a trace of amusement, and his face wore an expression of such respect and recognition that I felt gently chastised. I was then reminded of our day on the Prometeo. After the first leg of our trip, the train had stopped to take water, and Francisco got out of the engine and came over to the spot where my father was reloading his camera. My father started asking about the Prometeo, and whether or not it was more efficient than the other engines.

To tell the truth, I wasn't sure at that point whether Francisco was enjoying or merely indulging my father. We weren't the only tourists to come to Cuba to photograph trains. Busloads of British, German, and Dutch men pass through these mills on a fairly regular basis with video cameras and tape recorders. They probably all have some kind of story to tell Francisco. They probably all want to ride on his train. Most rail fans know that if an engineer lets you ride on his train, you should give him a few dollars, and although Francisco never did ask us for money, at that point I thought it might be the main reason he was paying so much attention to us.

The conversation moved on to Dad's trip to Mexico, and he began to tell one of my favorite stories. I've heard it so many times I could understand it in Spanish. It starts something like this:

On the trip back from Central America, in the fall of 1962, after I'd worked for the summer in Guatemala, I came back and worked my way up through Mexico as far as Puebla . . .

There were three ways to get from Puebla to Mexico City. One train took about four hours, another train took six hours, and then there was the narrow gauge that took fourteen hours to go the long way around. (There was also a bus that took about two hours, but that was out of the question.) My father wanted to ride the four-teen-hour train, which made so little sense that at first the ticket agent wouldn't sell him a ticket. It took longer, the man said, adding that at thirteen pesos (about a dollar then) it was also the most expensive. Dad tried to explain that he measured the value of a train ride not by how fast it was, but by how many hours on the train he could get for a dollar, and argued that thirteen pesos for four-teen hours was a pretty good deal.

Eventually he got on the train, and for the next twenty-two hours just about everything went wrong. The water injector didn't work, and they had to stop and switch engines. Then there was a rain-storm that made the tracks slippery and the sander pipe clogged. Dad volunteered to sit out on the cowcatcher and pour sand on the tracks by hand.

Francisco looked over at his engine and began drumming his fingers.

After a while, Dad continued, they noticed that the water in the boiler was unnervingly low, and he began to worry about a boiler explosion. He considered getting out of the engine and riding in a passenger car, because he knew that boiler explosions left few sur-vivors.

Finally they reached Ozumba, a water stop, at two in the morn-ing, ten hours late.

"Right beyond Ozumba," my father went on, "was the steepest part of the grade, and as we were working up that grade in total darkness, I looked at the engineer, I looked at the fireman, and I suddenly came to the realization that I was the only one in the en-gine awake."

"Well, you can imagine what a normal person might have done. But I had, as a child, had a fantasy that someday an engine crew on a steam engine would be disabled, and I would heroically take over the train and bring it to its destination. Here I was in that situation. So instead of waking them up, I figured, well, I'd run the engine."

At this point Francisco's regal face opened like a flower. He smiled, showing all of his wide white teeth, as my father finished: Actually nothing much happened, since the engine pretty much ran itself until they got into town and the buildings magnified the sound of the engine, waking the crew.

"That's a great story," Francisco said, clapping my father on the back. We got back in the engine. I gave my father the seat by the boiler with Francisco, and climbed up on the tender where I could watch the scenery. Inside a wooden house, a woman plaited a child's hair. By the roadside, a man appeared to be having a stern conversation with an ox. He looked up long enough to wave at the train, and then continued the discussion.

"Rebecca!" Francisco yelled, "*mira!*" He put a long, muscled arm around my father's shoulders and said something in Spanish. "He says that in Cuba, they have a special name for two men who have the same name," my father yelled. "*Tocayo.* It's like twins who aren't blood related." My father's hair had blown across his face, and his shirt, which he had unbuttoned a little because of the heat in the engine, was blowing open. Francisco smiled. "*Es mi tocayo,*" he said.

I looked at my father, with smudges on his handsome face, black cinders clinging to his graying hair, and the small crowd gathered around him. As he stood there, arm in arm with Francisco, I was gripped by a surge of pride, as well as loneliness, sharp and sudden. I had come on this trip partly to accompany Dad, to console him if the trip was a disappointment or to charm the engineers if they weren't as friendly as they'd been in Mexico. But these men had been waiting for each other all their lives. I was just lucky to be invited along.

STEPHEN BENZ

A Cup of Cuban Coffee

FROM *Potpourri*

AT FIRST I had no idea there was a dearth of coffee in Cuba. The chance to have in the land of its origin a demitasse of café cubano — the ultra-strong bittersweet espresso I had become all but addicted to since moving to Miami — so enticed me I didn't consider the possibility it might not be readily available.

I didn't consider the possibility because for the first few days of my trip I was staying in a tourist hotel, and in Cuba the tourist hotels — long neglected before the Soviet collapse — have now been transformed into lavish islets of conspicuous consumption on an island of privation. No longer supported by Soviet subsidies, the Cuban government has turned to what it once reviled — tourism — as its last best hope for revenue. To attract First World travelers, primarily Europeans and Canadians, the hotels provide everything that is otherwise difficult to find in Cuba — soap, sheets, beef, and good coffee, for example. The hotels offer guests sumptuous mounds of imported food. Foreigners are invited to gorge themselves at buffet tables, while ordinary Cubans go hungry.

I did not stay in the tourist hotel by choice. My Cuban-American colleagues in Miami urged me to avoid the hotels. They told me I could save money staying in private homes. Moreover, the money would go directly to those that needed it, rather than to the Cuban government, which Miami Cubans regard as no better than a syndicate of hooligans.

But when I arrived at Jose Marti Airport, immigration officials refused to let me pass without a "hotel voucher." I had to purchase a voucher for at least three nights in a state-run hotel or face immediate deportation, they explained, smiling. I was given a choice of three hotels, all expensive. For $100 a night, I ended up at the Riviera, a Las Vegas–style hotel built in the 1950s by a mob boss, Meyer Lansky.

It turned out that my voucher included a breakfast buffet. So each of my first three mornings in Cuba, I descended to the hotel basement (the buffet was kept out of sight from ordinary Cubans), where I had my pick of fruit, yogurt, sweet rolls, omelets, pancakes, and sausages and all the strong, frothy coffee I could want.

After three days I left this tower of privilege to take a room in a local residence. Recognizing the need to permit some private initiative, the Cuban government has granted licenses allowing some people (those able to pay a monthly fee of $100) to rent out rooms to foreigners. In order to obtain dollars, those Cubans who have the extra space have partitioned their homes or flats to create boarding rooms. For ten to twenty dollars, they will surrender a bedroom and the family fan for the night.

It's easy for a foreigner to find one of these rooms. In downtown Havana, touts constantly approach with offers for accommodations in a *casa particular* — a private home. On my third day in Havana, a small boy handed me a card with the address of a private pension. His grandfather ran the place, he said, and it was the best in the city. What made it the best? It was the biggest house in Havana, he said.

Bigger than Fidel's?

The boy frowned as though I had said something ridiculous.

"Well, the biggest I've ever seen," he said.

I took a taxi out to see the grandfather's house in Miramar, a suburb of Havana whose stately homes have mostly been taken over by foreign diplomats and the socialist elite. The house was indeed large — four bedrooms, converted into guest rooms, along with a kitchen and a living room. The elderly couple who ran the place confined themselves to the living room and the adjoining sewing room in which they slept. The rest of the place, including the master bedroom and the only bathroom, was surrendered to foreign tourists.

I immediately liked the Colonial Spanish charm of the house — its baroque wooden furniture, the fountain in the patio, the Moorish tile. Still, the private home, however charming, was a far cry from the luxury at the Riviera. The fountain no longer functioned. The tiles were loose and cracked. Water had to be poured into the toilet to get it to flush. There was no soap. The mattress sagged badly. And for climate control, I was given an "Orbita," a small electronic fan of Soviet make, no protective grill, that sputtered and chugged and barely stirred up the musty air of my room.

The innkeeper, learning I was from Miami, wanted to talk all night. He had scores of questions — What about the violence in the United States? Did Americans really hate Cubans and Mexicans? How much would a physics teacher (his former occupation) make in the United States? Were there Cuban baseball players in the major leagues? As with most Cubans I met, he was inquisitive, loquacious, often argumentative. Good talk excited him. Despite his energy in conversation, his face looked gaunt, the eyes oddly hollow, the skin taut and sallow. He, like most everyone else on the island, was showing the strains of hunger.

In the morning, I learned more about the extent of Cuban privations. The innkeeper and the señora set the table for my breakfast: a basket of stale rolls, a bowl of bruised fruit, and a glass of chilled water. They apologized for offering so little and hovered in profound chagrin, hoping I was satisfied.

"You come to Cuba in a bad season," the innkeeper said. "Look here."

He took from his pocket what looked like a tattered receipt book. It was their rations account. He leafed through the pages to show me their monthly allowances for basic items — lard, beans, rice. One item in particular caught my eye: Coffee, though grown in Cuba, was nonetheless rationed.

"We are allowed half a kilo each month," the innkeeper said. But for the last several months they had not collected their coffee. "We have an allowance," he explained, "but that doesn't mean the stores will have anything on the shelves." If I wanted café cubano, I would have to find it elsewhere.

And so, during the next several days, I walked Havana, taking in the sights and searching for my daily dose of coffee — a search that proved more difficult than I had expected. Cafés and corner restaurants abounded, to be sure. Streaming with sunshine and exuberant with salsa music, they seemed pleasant enough — despite peeling paint and threadbare tablecloths and a lack of customers.

The waiters shook their heads, however, at my request for coffee. Or they brought out chipped cups half full of tepid, dun-colored water, the vague coffee flavor masked by the bitter aftertaste of some unidentifiable root or berry used as filler.

Good café cubano, it seemed, was available only in the tourist hotels and restaurants, where a cup of coffee and a sweet roll cost half the monthly wage of the waiter serving it.

Unable to get my coffee fix, I nevertheless found plenty of stimulation on my walks around Havana, a city best explored on foot. It was, I found, a city rich in variations of light: the long morning rays filtering through dust and tropical vegetation; the glare of the midday sun on the city's faded pastels; the chiaroscuro of the evening in the maze of Old Havana where faltering neon and a lambent moon cast shadows on crumbling walls.

It was also a city rich in smells. The saline smell of the sea competed with the heavy perfume of flowers and the musk of tobacco. Over all hung the thick scent of dust and crumbling mortar — the abandoned stage-set smells that contributed to the wistful, voluptuous atmosphere pervasive in the city.

More than anything else, Havana was to me a city of faces. Schoolchildren in their red and white uniforms peered at passersby through the iron bars of a mansion-turned-schoolhouse. An old man sat on a sea wall staring into the bright waves where his fishing line bobbed. A cigar-smoking crone sat on a box outside the cathedral, instructing tourists how best to photograph her. In the marketplace, an entranced vendor kneeled in the corner before a makeshift altar to some Santería deity. At night, I observed a hotel guard yawning and watching the prostitutes across the street, who swayed to the music from the hotel disco. And down the dark street from the hotel, a girl occupied her post at a dimly lit pizza stand; with nothing to do, no pizza to sell, she leaned forward on the counter and stared up at the glowing hotel.

Inevitably, I was drawn each day to the Malecón, Havana's famous seaside promenade, surely one of the more alluring city vistas in the world. The long, broad boulevard curved dramatically between city and sea. Waves crashed against the rocks below and sent sprays of warm water up onto the sidewalk crowded with people dawdling in the sea breeze. Fishermen lingered patiently by their lines. Children sat on the mole, waiting for the splashing waves to douse them. Lovers leaned against each other. Vendors hawked paper cones filled with red peanuts. And then there were the single girls, scores of them in Spandex shorts, tight tops, and platform shoes. Their coffee complexions glistening in the tropical light, they beckoned to foreign men, flashing seductive smiles — a sensuous fantasy until you remembered that hunger and desperation brought them out for your inspection.

In contrast to the packed sidewalk, the boulevard was nearly empty of traffic. A few vintage jalopies — 1950s model Fords, Chevys, and Chryslers — chugged along, occasionally passing sputtering Soviet cars and jammed buses. Across the boulevard, a row of grand old buildings gazed at the sea. Untended for decades, paint peeling, balconies collapsing, walls and decorative columns crumbling, these row houses and tenements merely added to the disheveled romance of the Malecón.

I left Havana on the night train to Camaguey, Cuba's third-largest city, some three hundred miles east of the capital. Cuba is the only Caribbean country that still operates passenger trains. Left over from a long-gone era, the engines and coaches are old but reasonably well kept. Riding the train, like so much else in Cuba, feels like a venture in suspended time. Two hours after the scheduled departure there was still no indication — other than a huge crowd waiting — that the train was ready for a journey. It sat idle on the tracks, no crew in sight.

Suddenly, the crowd murmured and stirred. About a dozen women were parading through the throng, single file. They wore pinstriped blouses, short blue skirts, and fishnet stockings. These were the *ferromozas*, or rail stewardesses, and their appearance touched off a flurry of activity. The engine abruptly roared to life. People grabbed their bags and rushed forward in a madcap rush to funnel through a single gate, where a detached official conducted a slow scrutiny of tickets and identification. For several minutes, I remained pinned against an iron fence while the main current shouted and shoved past me.

Beyond the gate, the scrutiny intensified: The ferromozas, two to a coach, checked tickets and identification on the platform outside the train. Then they passed down the aisle, checking tickets again and entering information on clipboards. Armed guards patrolled the train. A conductor entered the coach to double-check the passengers' tickets. But once the train got rolling, once the industrial sprawl of Havana's outskirts was behind us, things loosened up — considerably. An old man in a boat captain's cap wheeled a cart down the aisle, selling pork sandwiches, peanuts, rum, and beer. Soon blue cigarette smoke filled the coach, several cassette players were turned on full volume, and a group of Cuban passengers gathered up front to talk to the four foreigners on board — two Englishmen, a Spaniard, and me.

The sun set behind the eastbound train, gilding the panorama of cane fields and palm groves. The train rocked languidly along, but inside the pace of conversation was much more energetic. Fortified by rum, cigarettes, and Bucaneros, a strong socialist beer, we touched on a range of subjects — sex, religion, international politics, sports, music, history — in rapid-fire, high-volume chatter. Was it true that the CIA was responsible for killing Kennedy, Martin Luther King, and the singer Selena? Why did Americans call it the World Series when only American teams competed? The guards and ferromozas lost their stern demeanors and joined both the drinking and the conversation.

Night came on. The music, blaring from competing cassette players, reached distorted levels. Several people started dancing in the aisles, their sinuous arms swirling in the cloud of blue smoke. The ferromozas played matchmaker, pulling the foreigners to their feet and handing them over to dancing girls. One of the Englishmen, giddy with the sensuality of the moment, tumbled mid-merengue into the arms of an olive-eyed Cubana, while the ferromozas cheered and clapped.

At Camaguey, well past midnight, I stumbled from the train into the humid tropical night, an unfamiliar station spinning around me. Horn blasting, the train went on its merry way, rocking and rolling down the line, leaving me empty and dizzy and feeling as if I had been expelled from the party. The other departing passengers quickly vanished in the night, and I was left alone.

Well, not quite alone. A fleet of pedicabs — rickshaws affixed to bicycles — waited curbside. A dozen taxi-cyclists offered their services. "Is it possible I could find a pension this late?" I asked one. His ribcage much in evidence, he — like the other cyclists — went shirtless, wearing only running shorts and a pair of worn-out shoes.

"Todo es posible," he said, waving me onto the wooden bench seat

of the rickshaw. "Everything is possible." Over his shoulder he added, "So says Fidel."

I heard many people quote Fidel thus far, and on this occasion, as the others, I couldn't determine the speaker's intention. Was the quotation ironic? Sincere? A reflexive product of indoctrination? Or were Fidel's words ubiquitous and hence quotable in any situation, like an inane pop song in the United States?

The bicycle frame rattled as we cruised the quiet streets of Camaguey, past the Workers' Plaza, then past the flickering fluorescent storefront of the Vietnam Bookstore, where a new collection of Fidel's speeches was on display next to a Spanish translation of *Many Lives, Many Masters*.

The pension, like every other residence, was completely dark. The cyclist knocked several times. I was ready to give up and head to a hotel when the door opened and a middle-aged woman in her nightgown peered out at us. The cyclist explained my situation to the señora. To my surprise, she greeted me like an old friend or lost relative.

The next morning, her hospitality was still keen. For breakfast she served me a ham sandwich on a crusty roll with a plate of tomatoes and cucumbers. I washed it down with a large glass of freshly squeezed orange juice. I hadn't finished the last bite when Caridad — the woman's name meant "charity" — sat down to discuss with me the dinner menu. She was headed to the market and stores to see what she could find.

"Do you like Cuban food?" she asked.

I explained that I lived in Miami, that I was quite familiar with Cuban dishes. More than anything else, I said, I loved Cuban coffee. I told her about Miami's sidewalk espresso stands, the pleasure I took in stopping for a *cortadita*. I was disappointed, I said, not to find real café cubana in Cuba. "There has been such a drought," she said. "Coffee is hard to come by. Even sugar is scarce. Imagine that — sugar scarce in Cuba. It has never been like this."

Caridad left me in the company of her son, Eduardo. Trained as a veterinarian, he now worked construction because it was an easier job and the pay was the same — fifteen dollars a month. He was all too willing to skip work if something interesting came up — a common phenomenon in Cuba — and on this day I was a sufficient diversion. Eduardo volunteered to show me the sights of

Camaguey, including a couple of provincial museums and the houses of Camaguey's famous native sons, the Independence War general Ignacio Agramonte and the internationally renowned poet Nicolas Guillen.

Midday, Eduardo and I bought two TropiColas — an overly sweet soft drink — and sat on a bench in the Plaza of the Workers. Hundreds of bicycles glided the streets around us. With gasoline in short supply, bicycling had become the predominant mode of transportation in Cuba, and the languid pace turned Camaguey, a city of three hundred thousand, into a quaint backcountry town.

Eduardo and I lived only two hundred miles apart, but our conversation revealed the huge difference in our lives. It began when, as I opened my wallet to pay for the TropiColas, Eduardo saw my credit card. Or more precisely, he saw the card's hologram, and when we sat down he wanted to inspect it. He flashed it in the sunlight while I, in vague Spanish, tried to describe the wonders of hologram technology. Which led eventually to an explanation of the purpose of the card — credit being an alien concept to Eduardo — and then to an examination of the rest of my wallet, including an ATM card and my driver's license.

Before long, I was explaining to an increasingly incredulous Eduardo everything from personal checks to Internet shopping. Meanwhile, on the streets around us, people were queuing before storefronts and kiosks, clamoring to see if some necessity had suddenly been made available for purchase.

Eduardo could only shake his head and laugh. "The world has left us behind," he said. "We will be the last ones left in the twentieth century."

In a system of scarcity, Eduardo told me, mere survival required intelligence and guile. You never knew when you would find something you desperately needed — razor blades, a belt, allergy medicine. Dollars were an absolute necessity.

Cubans were paid in pesos, but the Cuban peso could only be used for bus fare and the purchase of sporadically available bulk items like flour. You had to get dollars somehow, either from relatives in the United States or from providing services to tourists. If you had space in your house, you rented out rooms. If you had a car, you moonlighted as a taxi driver. Young women sold their bodies. Anything for dollars.

But dollars were not enough. You needed to barter. If you had access to something like milk, for example, you could trade it for something like gasoline. Eduardo's mother, Caridad, was particularly skillful at this. She worked a vast bartering network with friends and relatives, trading socks for oranges (many farmers kept the best of the crop to sell or trade on the black market) or underwear for quality meat. Eduardo himself played a part in the network: As a construction worker he could obtain trade-worthy goods such as cement and nails.

Foreign tourists, of course, played a big part, too, not only for their dollars but also for the items they left behind, items like clothes and medicine. Once, a German gave Caridad a bottle of five hundred aspirin tablets. Impossible to find in Cuba, aspirin was better than dollars. Caridad wrapped up little newspaper packets of ten tablets each, and for the next few months parlayed those fifty packets into a host of treasures, including a timing belt of Soviet make that, with a little tinkering, got her father's old '58 Ford running again.

When Eduardo and I returned to the house, Caridad and Eduardo's wife, Lydia, were preparing dinner. Caridad called me into the kitchen. "Look what I found for you," she said, pointing to a small burlap bag. She folded down the brim to reveal the contents: dark, shiny coffee beans. She was just about to pulverize the beans by pounding the bag with a wooden mallet.

"Tonight," Caridad sang, "you will have coffee with your dinner. Real Cuban coffee in Cuba!"

Eduardo and I retired to the living room to watch the news on a flickering Soviet black and white. Several reports concerned Castro's decrees of the day. Several more highlighted the latest heinous acts of the U.S. government. Finally, came a lengthy report on the national baseball team. The team's victories, the newscaster said, signaled the inevitable triumph of socialism. All the while, Caridad pounded at the coffee.

Caridad called me to the table, where I was presented with a smorgasbord of Cuban food. She identified each dish — *boniato, tostones, frijoles* — and then the entire family left me to eat by myself. They would wait for the leftovers.

Embarrassed to be left alone at the feast, I ate hurriedly and then went to shower while the family took their turn at the table. After showering, I rifled through my bags looking for items I could give away. I decided to leave behind sunglasses, allergy medicine, aspirin, and extra socks. Eduardo really needed a belt — he constantly hitched his pants while we walked around town — so I also set aside my spare for him.

A knock came at the door to my room. Eduardo and Lydia entered with the coffee service. The pungent biting aroma filled the room, wonderful and tantalizing. We sat around a rickety table. Lydia poured the coffee from a small metal pot into a chipped demitasse. I stirred in a spoonful of brown unrefined sugar crystals and sipped. Even sweetened the brew was sharp and carbon-dominated, with a profound, distinct bite. Nothing mellow about it.

Caridad entered the room, along with her husband and brother-in-law. As usual in Cuba, I was immediately thrust into the midst of an intense, almost frenzied conversation. We touched on everything from the comic frustrations of learning another language to the beauty of a perfectly executed squeeze bunt to the death of those who tried to escape by raft to Florida. Eventually, Eduardo told everyone what he had learned about credit cards and home computers.

"You see what is kept from us," Eduardo said, more sad than indignant.

My question was, Who kept it from them? In all my conversations to date, I had been uncertain whether Cubans were blaming the thirty-seven-year-old American embargo or the socialist system for their problems. Now I asked the family directly. The discussion exploded. They all spoke at once, gesturing, raising their voices, arguing with one another until eventually they reached a consensus and shared it with me.

The revolution, they said, had provided many good things, especially education and health care. But socialism had turned into an unwieldy bureaucracy and, worse, a class system where the few at the top got everything and the masses nothing. As for the United States, it was a great nation with wonderful, creative people. But the actions of the United States government baffled them: Couldn't they see that the embargo did nothing to Cuba's leaders, while the ordinary people suffered tremendously? The answer to my question, then, was that both sides were to blame. The majority of Cubans felt trapped between the incompetence of socialist bureaucrats who used, even relied on, the embargo as an excuse, and the intransigence of an American policy that insisted on punishing them out of fear of something that no longer existed, namely communist expansionism.

Throughout the evening, the conversation moved rapidly from topic to topic, from light to serious, from humorous to tragic. We laughed. We argued. We shook our heads at the strange, ludicrous world we shared. Lydia filled my cup again and again, and I drank Caridad's hard-earned coffee with something bordering on ecstasy. It was a near-perfect travel moment.

Except for one thing: I was the only one drinking.

TOM BISSELL

Eternal Winter

FROM *Harper's Magazine*

> This procedure and this form of execution, which you now have the
> opportunity of admiring, have at present no open supporters left in our
> colony. I am their sole defender, and at the same time the sole defender of
> the legacy of our former commandant. I can no longer contemplate any
> further development of the system; all my energy is consumed in preserving
> what we have.
>
> — Franz Kafka, "In the Penal Colony"

THE DAY I landed in Nukus, 150 miles south of the Aral Sea, the
sky above the city lacked clouds because the day lacked the mois-
ture to provide them. Behind me our plane's engine ticked in the
sunshine, its propellers just stilled. The flight in, on an elderly
Aeroflot prop-jet known as the Yak-40, was all pitches and yaws, as I
had been warned it would be. Foreknowledge had not helped.

Inside the terminal: sparrows. The first seemed as freakish as a
deer wandering the aisles of a suburban grocery store. But another
followed it. Then three, four, as fast as little jets. Five, six. I stopped
counting. They darted across the large, spring-bright terminal and
lifted toward the ceiling, vanishing between girders, muscling into
fissures. No one seemed to notice.

A young man named Manas was supposed to pick me up at the
airport. I waited alone outside for ten minutes, only a little concerned, before he finally arrived. He was not late, I soon realized.
Flights into Nukus were irregular and unreliable. Many were canceled due to fuel shortages. Manas worked across town, and only
when he looked up and saw a plane landing did he bother to make
his way to the airport. Manas was a Karakalpak, a member of one of

Central Asia's least populous peoples. For five hundred years the Karakalpaks have lived as nomads and fishermen along the Aral Sea, in what is now known as Karakalpakistan, a nominally autonomous republic of Uzbekistan. It is a place of almost unimaginable misfortune. Forty years ago the Aral Sea was the fourth-largest inland body of water in the world, its area larger than that of Lake Michigan. Today it has shrunk to a fraction of its previous size and is perhaps the single largest manmade ecological catastrophe in history. The Karakalpaks are nomads with nowhere to go, fishermen with nothing to catch.

The flat khaki-colored buildings beyond the airport's front gate provided little sense of the city's size. Home to one hundred eighty thousand people, Nukus had the pleasant feel of a quiet country city, but the quiet had weight, expectancy, patience. I watched large tidal currents of dust advance down the municipal grid of wide, Soviet-made thoroughfares as well-dressed women covered their mouths with handkerchiefs and children lowered their heads. Silent, squinting young men crouched on every corner, spitting sunflower seeds. Trees lined the streets, their full green foliage shuddering in the dust-swarming wind.

As I walked through the streets of Nukus the dust gathered in my eyes, clogged my mouth and throat, but I was told that what I was experiencing was not a dust storm. Not a real one. For years dust storms have been scouring the region with hundreds of millions of tons of salt and sand from the Aral's exposed seabed, much of which is poisonous, thanks to tons of Soviet insecticides and toxic waste dumped into the sea over the decades. At least five times a year a city-sized cloud of howling sand hits Nukus, an airborne apocalypse that sentences everyone to days indoors and undoes, in hours, months of peasants' work digging irrigation ditches and harvesting what is left of their cotton fields. The Siberian zephyrs that sweep down into Karakalpakistan gather up its loose, poisonous dust and, as though in some lethal travesty of Jesus' mustard seeds, cast it not only upon the Karakalpaks but thousands of miles beyond them. Some of the Aral Sea area's enterprising dust has been found along Georgia's Black Sea coastline, some along arctic Russia's northern shores.

The story of the Aral Sea is a parable of twentieth-century development and industrialization, a parody of Progress. It begins with cotton, of which Uzbekistan is the world's second-largest exporter, a strange accomplishment for a nation that is mostly desert. For this thirsty, ecologically demanding crop, Uzbekistan can thank the American Civil War, which cut off the cotton supply of a powerful northern neighbor, czarist Russia, which in turn began to search for a new, easily accessible agricultural base. In Central Asia, it found that base. The river that runs along Uzbekistan's southern border and feeds into the Aral Sea, the Amu Darya, known in antiquity as the Oxus, was bled into Uzbekistan's vast deserts, and soon "white gold" was blooming on this newly arable but fragile land. The diverting of the Amu Darya was one of the rare czarist policies the Soviets continued. Imperialism was another.

Life around the Aral Sea could never have been easy. The land has few readily exploitable resources, though irrigation-based agriculture had been practiced in the area around the sea for four thousand years. The few Western travelers who visited Khiva, a city in the Amu Darya's delta (the purported birthplace of al-Khwarizmi, the inventor of algebra), have given us early, pristine glimpses of life in the Aral Sea basin. An Englishman named Anthony Jenkinson traveled throughout the delta in 1558 and wrote that "the water that serveth all that country is drawn by ditches out of the River Oxus . . . and in short time all that land is like to be destroyed, and to become a wilderness for want of water."

Soviet hunger for cotton, the strain of a quickly growing population, and an intensifying network of irrigation made Jenkinson's prophecies come true. Shortly after 1960 the Aral Sea began to disappear. Moynaq, my ultimate destination, was once a prosperous seaside fishing town of forty thousand inhabitants and home to a cannery that produced twelve million tins of fish a year; by the late seventies, Moynaq was no longer even near the shore. A place that for so long lived off so little found itself rapidly losing everything. Fishermen, ferry captains, canners, and shipbuilders had to reinvent their lives within a planned economy that could not afford to admit that they existed. The natural world paid an equally appalling price. Of the 178 species of animal life that have historically called the Aral Sea home, only 38 now survive, and the thick desert forests, once unique to the Aral Sea's irreplaceable and distinctive ecosystem, have all but vanished. The climate, too, has suffered. In its unspoiled state, the Aral Sea absorbed the solar equivalent of seven billion tons of conventional fuel, cooling the surrounding

areas during the summers and feeding the stored heat back into
the atmosphere during the winters. Summer temperatures now
regularly surpass 120 degrees, and the commensurately harsh winters doom the irrigation-dependent crops that the sea was drained
to nourish.

With mounting rates of infant mortality, anemia, and tuberculosis, the Karakalpaks began in the 1980s to question publicly, in a
country that routinely crushed dissent, what was happening to
their land and their people. "When God loved us he gave us the
Amu Darya," one poet wrote. "When he ceased to love us, he sent
us Russian engineers."

In the late 1980s, just as glasnost was taking tenuous hold in Soviet society, plans to save the sea were devised and revised; they ac-
cumulated upon the shelves of the Soviet government and well-
meaning international agencies. None were carried out. In 1991
the Soviet Union collapsed. Yet the cotton harvest continued, because the Uzbek economy depended on it. Each year the sea's condition grows worse, and it now shrinks faster than cartographers
can accurately chart. Moynaq sits at least eighty miles from what is
left of the sea, and Karakalpakistan finds its revenues shrinking and
its monstrous medical-care expenditures crippling. It is one of the
sickest places on earth. By 2010, most experts estimate, the Aral
Sea will be completely gone.

I had been to Uzbekistan five years before as a Peace Corps volunteer, though I lasted only seven months. I lived and taught English
in a small regional capital called Gulistan in the central part of the
country, where Karakalpakistan* and the Aral Sea were known simply as "the West" — a place, it was understood, of mythic, limit-
less sorrow. I had read that the Aral Sea was a problem without any
solution, that Karakalpakistan was one of the worst places in the
world. Even the hardier guidebooks warned travelers off the region. "Drab, impoverished, unhealthy, and forlorn," reported one.
But I had seen glimmerings of a different place, a Karakalpakistan that Peace Corps acquaintances had described as the most as-

* Which, let it be known, has nothing to do with Pakistan, an acronym derived from
its regions: "P" for Punjab, "A" for the Afghan border tribes, "K" for Kashmir, "S" for
Sind, and "tan" for Baluchistan.

tounding place they had ever visited. I had returned to experience that Karakalpakistan and to find whatever hope existed for the people of the Aral Sea region, to find an answer to Lenin's great question: What is to be done? I had come looking for hope, not only for the people of Karakalpakistan but for all of us, because what has happened to the Aral Sea, many suspect, is but a dress rehearsal for the global ecological catastrophe commonly known by the deceptively benign terms "global warming" and "global climate change."

I had come looking for hope, but instead, on this my first day in Nukus, I heard warnings of more misery to come, for whispered in Nukus's streets and bazaars were rumors of empty warehouses and withered crops, of delivery-truck drivers suddenly unemployed without explanation. Cure your meat now. Preserve your fruits and vegetables while you can. More drought was coming to an already dry land.

I sat before the enormous desk of Dr. Damir Babanazarov. His hands, a bundle of whitened knuckles, rested atop some open newspapers. He smiled. A good-looking man, with short straight petroleum-black hair and a combed, equally black mustache. He wore fashionable glasses, a shiny red tie. As my translator, Kamal, and I prepared for the interview, I struggled through a long salutation in Uzbek. Dr. Babanazarov looked into his lap, still smiling but clearly puzzled by my error-riddled sentences. Uzbek was the best I could do, even though Karakalpak was his native language and Russian was the language he spoke most comfortably. As I recited my litany of remembered Central Asian pleasantries my eyes journeyed disconnectedly along Dr. Babanazarov's desk. An upright cellular phone. A small steel Eiffel Tower statuette. When I had finished speaking, Dr. Babanazarov's tightly clasped hands burst open. He thanked me in accommodatingly simple Uzbek, then lit the first of many cigarettes. As he spoke, he flitted them around and stabbed the filters into his mouth as though plugging them in. Dr. Babanazarov was Karakalpakistan's minister of health.

In the Soviet Union the Ministry of Health was, famously, a sinecure for bribe-takers. It had been reassuring to hear that Dr. Babanazarov, despite a monthly salary of $25, had a reputation for spurning bribes and was regarded as an open, intelligent man who welcomed journalists and researchers. I had expected an interesting exchange. In preparation I had filled a dozen notebook pages with pointed questions. I asked Dr. Babanazarov about the future of the Aral Sea, the health of Nukus's citizens, the legacy of Soviet rule, the role of international organizations in alleviating the disaster. Dr. Babanazarov responded to my questions with heavy, repetitive Soviet-style speeches that in no way began to answer them. I let his first few evasions go, wrongly believing that Kamal was mistranslating my questions. Finally, I turned to Kamal. Had he put to Dr. Babanazarov the question I asked? Kamal told me that he had. I asked him to repeat the question. He did, and Dr. Babanazarov launched into another oration that bore eerily less relevance to my question. I again turned to Kamal and again asked him if he would repeat my question. Kamal looked almost sorrowful and without shaking his head very softly informed me that while he was really very sorry he simply could not do that.

Dr. Babanazarov was not one of Orwell's fly-swatting, otiose backwater functionaries. He was a good man. But his job was as sensitive as it was difficult. It is commonly believed that plenipotentiaries in the Uzbek government skim from the top of whatever relief Karakalpakistan is fortunate to receive and routinely underfund the region's yearly budgets. But Karakalpakistan's peculiar quasi-independent status means that it relies on Uzbekistan for virtually everything. To an average Karakalpak, the fountainheads of aggravation this arrangement created were innumerable. Dr. Babanazarov, however, was not a civilian. The health of Karakalpakistan was entrusted to him. But the Ministry of Health was not one of the "strong," attention-getting ministries such as Finance or Defense. To what lengths did Dr. Babanazarov have to go to procure for his people the little money and medical supplies they had? His frustration could only be imagined.

But he was not open. Openness is a friendliness dammed by private stricture, an instinctively shallow cordiality that delights tourists and drives journalists mad. The most recent official medical statistics for Karakalpakistan are several years old, and most are worthless. ("Statistics," Lenin said, "must be our practical assistant, and not scholastic.") The actual rates of common Karakalpak afflictions — bronchial asthma, lung disease, infant cerebral palsy, cancers of the stomach and throat, urogenital and endocrine disease — are quite simply anyone's guess. Suffice it to say that all are abnormally high and getting higher. I left Dr. Babanazarov's office, then, with a better appreciation that everyone here, whether peasant or minister, had inherited the tics and secrecy of a regime they neither wanted nor created.

Several blocks from the Ministry of Health I found the Nukus offices of Médecins Sans Frontières, known to English speakers as Doctors Without Borders, which has been working in the Aral Sea area for five years. One of the world's largest humanitarian, nongovernmental medical organizations, MSF provides medical aid for people in crisis situations all over the globe, and it is well known that of all the international convocations to stare the basilisk of the Aral Sea disaster in the eye only MSF has not turned to stone. Just outside the large wooden double doors of MSF's modest, two-story headquarters, foreigners and stylish-looking locals smoked amid a fleet of vehicles parked at hasty angles.

I had hoped somehow to find a ride to Moynaq with MSF, but within the hour I was traveling to Nukus's tuberculosis dispensary with Ed Negus, a tall, crew-cut twenty-eight-year-old Australian obliged to check up on its newly installed medical-waste incinerator. This was one of his main responsibilities, along with assisting medical facilities in their efforts to procure faxes, computers, and medical equipment, and to achieve conditions of acceptable sanitation. When I asked him about his thoughts concerning the people of Karakalpakistan, he grew silent, a silence that seemed funereal, decent. He stared straight ahead. "My translator had an uncle in Moynaq," Negus said finally. "Ten years ago he was told, 'Get out of Moynaq now, because it's just going to end up a hole.' And his uncle said, 'When I'm the last person left in Moynaq, then, and only then, will I leave.' This year, he's leaving."

We parked in a shade-splotched alley behind the TB dispensary because Negus wanted to arrive unannounced. While we made our way past rusty fences and stepped over enormous mounds of cow dung, Negus described the bureaucratic lunacy that installing these incinerators often entailed. To connect the gas line to each incinerator, for instance, you needed permission from the fire department. The fire department would inform you that, in fact, the gas department needed to approve the connection first. The gas department, in turn, would send you back to the fire department. The fire department could now be counted on to give you a form

to take back to the gas department. The gas department, upon seeing the form, would instruct you that nothing of this nature could
be accomplished without the fire department. The fire department
would then be forced to write a letter overruling the gas department's involvement. The gas department would finally declare that
nothing could be done without its approval.

We came to the incinerator, a long narrow Quonset-like concrete
structure, similar to the tandoori ovens in which every Uzbek and
Karakalpak family bakes bread. Negus slowed down so suddenly it
was as though an anesthetic had just taken effect. Small broken
glass bottles were everywhere. The pieces popped underfoot like
heavily shelled insects. The dusty ground sparkled with broken
and, presumably, used needles. The tall narrow pipe in which the
dispensary workers were intended to dispose of needles and glass
was crammed with garbage. The gravelike pit in which the medical
waste's ashes and solely the medical waste's ashes were to be buried
was filled with solids. Much of it looked non-hospital in origin. The
pit was surrounded by footprints, many of them left by barefoot
children. Negus was speechless. He had visited only weeks ago,
drilling the dispensary's workers on the exact procedures needed
to dispose of their medical waste, a time-consuming, sometimes
dangerous operation that was absolutely vital to improving Karakalpakistan's health standards. I could see the frustration in his eyes.
He gathered himself, walked over to the incinerator, and swung
open its creaky iron door.

Clear plastic bags of waste, sanitary napkins, syringes, all tumbled out — a nightmarish landfill in miniature. Proper waste dis-
posal depended on igniting the incinerator and allowing it to heat
up for at least fifteen minutes. Then, and only then, was waste to be
placed inside. This was the best way to assure that the waste would
burn cleanly and thoroughly. The bricks inside the incinerator
should have been clean and white — properly managed, anything
placed inside would ignite almost instantly — but the bricks of this
incinerator were charred, briquette-black. Negus stared forlornly
into the incinerator: "This is not my finest moment."

It may be hard to understand why the dispensary's workers could
not be relied on to dispose of this waste correctly when doing so
would improve their lot immeasurably. But one must remember

the Soviet warlock and the sorcery it had worked upon the minds of all the peoples of its empire. No other industrial society so impartially poisoned its land, water, air, and citizens while at the same time so loudly proclaiming its efforts to improve human health and the condition of the natural world. For decades the Soviet Union was the world's leading producer of oil and steel, held a quarter of the planet's forest resources and fresh water, and was in careless possession of what was probably the most beautiful and varied assortment of landscapes of any nation on the planet. "We cannot expect charity from nature," the Stalinists used to say. "We must tear it from her." Trotsky was more explicit: "The present distribution of mountains and rivers, of fields, of meadows, of steppes, of forests and seashores, cannot be considered final." (Lenin, a nature lover whose brother was a biologist, was a notable exception to this line of sentiment.) By the time of the empire's demise, three-fourths of the Soviet Union's surface water was hopelessly polluted. Its forests were clear-cut. Its mines were stripped of resources. Its people were some of the least healthy in the developed world.

Even a brief catalogue of the former Soviet Union's ecological and health misadventures can stupefy, sicken, silence. The Soviet Union was a nation where one could stand next to a waste-spurting pipe near the town of Chelyabinsk and absorb a lethal dose of radiation in a single hour. Where surgeons were forced by supply shortages to perform appendectomies with safety razors rather than scalpels. Where 40 percent of its medical-school graduates could not read an electrocardiogram. Where the Hippocratic Oath was forbidden, scorned as "bourgeois," and replaced with a pledge "to conduct all my actions according to the principles of the Communistic morale."

Soviet joke: What would happen if the Soviet army conquered the Sahara Desert? For fifty years, nothing. Then it would run out of sand.

The Soviet Union was a nation that placed effluent-spraying factories in residential neighborhoods as a matter of course and once built giant ammonia-storage tanks adjacent to an artillery practice range. Where, until the late 1980s, smokestacks were viewed as symbols of great beauty and progress. Where some cities, such as Magnitogorsk, were so polluted they had "prophylactic clinics" in which children were given regular "oxygen cocktails." Where factory directors guilty of willfully discharging polluted water into the drinking supply were fined fifty rubles, enough for two packs of imported cigarettes. Where people were so enthused over humankind's new technological prowess they named their daughters Elektrifikatsiya and their sons Traktor.

Soviet joke: Two doctors are examining a patient. One doctor looks at the other. "Well," he says, "what do you think? Should we treat him or let him live?"

The Soviet Union was a country whose experts maintained that radiation sickness was basically a mental problem, and called the Aral Sea "nature's error" and hoped it would "die in a beautiful manner." Whose medical personnel were sometimes instructed to wash bandages for a second use. Whose doctors, 66 percent of whom were women, took home 80 percent of the average male factory worker's salary. Whose minister of health in 1989 advised, "To live longer, you must breathe less." The Soviet Union was a country where, in 1990, remembering Nikita Khrushchev's boastful promise to overtake and surpass American standards of living, angry, abused, and exhausted protesters marched past the Kremlin carrying placards that read: "Let us catch up with and surpass Africa."

Some Americans might regard these facts as proof of American capitalism's superiority to Soviet communism in every imaginable way. Such citizens hexed Al Gore as a "radical environmentalist" on the basis of his sensitive and ideologically tame book *Earth in the Balance*. Their organizations have names like The Abundant Wildlife Society of North America. They have wiped from their minds a history in which Ohio's Cuyahoga River periodically burst into flames. They possess crusaderly faith in Le Chatelier's principle, which posits the tendency of the environment to restore itself in the face of destabilizing forces. But the ecocidal histories of the United States and former Soviet Union are startlingly similar. In the years following World War II, Americans cut down vast forests, built thousands of factories, assembled millions of atmospherically toxic automobiles, and filthied the water throughout North America. In 1970 the United States passed the Clean Air Act twenty-one years after the Soviets had decreed their own version. Our Clean Air Act was actually more lenient toward polluters than the Soviet Union's in fixing carbon monoxide limits (not that the Soviet Union, whose environmental pledges were filled with high-minded ideals, actually bothered to obey its own laws). The Pittsburgh of the 1940s and 1950s, to name one locale of acute American environmental shame, bore a ghastly resemblance to the manufacturing leviathans of the Soviet Union.

In 1989, 78 percent of Uzbekistan's polluted water was left untreated. The same year, the EPA found that only 10 percent of America's rivers, streams, and bays were significantly polluted. What achieved this level of relative cleanliness was not the intrinsic munificence of capitalism's better angels but an average of $24.3 billion spent yearly on water protection alone from 1972 to 1987. Without huge monetary efforts to control and ameliorate industry's impact upon the environment, parts of the United States would greatly resemble some of the former Soviet Union's most toxic dumping sites. But another, more gossamer aspect of the American character was as critical to the cleanup as any outlay of capital. From Henry David Thoreau to John Muir to Rachel Carson, there exists in American culture a tradition of reflection upon nature and stubborn activism upon its behalf. The Soviet Union had no comparable tradition.

Ed Negus did not wish to hear any of this at the moment. He needed no education. Here at the dispensary he was staring at failed curricula. What was at stake here but a higher form of hygiene? Manners? A simple problem whose emotional complications ruled out full assault? Negus stood next to the incinerator, hands fused to his hips, a dozen languid flies crawling on his back. Far away, I heard Karakalpak children playing, the drubby kick of a soccer ball. A young man, perhaps a patient, watched us from one of the TB dispensary's windows. With my boot I impotently gathered together a small pile of needles. I stopped when I realized that there was no place to put them. Negus, at last, turned to me, his face malformed by a sun-squinty eye and the dent of a close-mouthed smile. "I think I need to have some more meetings."

Finally I caught a ride to Moynaq, the city that, more than any other, wears the grisly diadem of the Aral Sea disaster. Outside Nukus, the land quickly flattened. Everywhere upon the soil were large white crystallized deposits of salt. As if the extra-strength Soviet pesticides and DDT that befouled the Aral Sea and still maligned its soil were not enough, the soil's salt content had thrust a final stake through Karakalpakistan's agricultural heart. Approximately 90 percent of the soil is now heavily salinated. From the air much of the area looked as if it were covered in snow. Millions of years ago all of Central Asia was a vast, highly saline inland sea (the Aral is its remnant), and ancient groundwater salts were stored in the soil at an unusually shallow level. To irrigate the land was to release those salts, little by little, season by season. The Aral Sea had once harmlessly collected that salt, and the gradual disappearance of the water has left the salt with nowhere to go. And so it has been cooked into the soil, or blown around, or left to seep into the drinking water. The drinking water's pollution, not only by salt but by the herbicides and fertilizers sprayed all over the Aral basin at the height of the cotton boom, would have been a huge problem anywhere. But Karakalpakistan is a closed-system environment without any ocean drainage, and contamination has proved especially pernicious.

The soil not ruined by salt was the color of burnt toast. Salt accumulations drifted like snow into the road. On these highways, it seemed that anything could happen. We passed a parts-shedding bus. A horse-drawn wagon. An aid group's Land Cruiser. A man riding a donkey. A BMW. Laughing children driving a herd of sheep through a pasture of salt.

Only a few miles outside of Nukus, health problems grew brazenly visible. Blind men sat by the side of the road. Children with bulging, malnourished bellies crouched on the berm, flashing siphons to passing cars. They were selling gasoline. This was illegal. Somewhere, nearby, their gasoline cans were stashed. If a policeman happened by, they stuffed the rubber siphons down their pants.

My companions on the way to Moynaq were Johannah Wegerdt, a twenty-seven-year-old British MSF field researcher, and Bahktiyor Madreimov, a twenty-one-year-old half-Russian, half-Karalpak translator. They had driven along these roads more times than either could count. Wegerdt was tracking the health of several dozen children in the hope of determining the respiratory effects of long-term dust-storm exposure. The unprecedented nature of the Aral Sea disaster is not unlike that of Hiroshima after World War II, which allowed scientists a charred ground zero to chart the previously unstudiable effects of widespread radiation poisoning on human beings. Here in Karakalpakistan one could study the similarly vast aftereffects of what happens when an entire ecosystem expires in a single generation. Dust storms are but one way the world ends.

"Up ahead," Wegerdt told me, pointing. Before us lay the Amu Darya. Or what was left of it. That it once was called the "river sea" should provide a sense of its former vastness. Arab geographers were in awe of the river, regarding it as one of the mightiest in the world. It took Alexander the Great's army five days to cross it on inflated tent-skins. More than two thousand years later, we approached the Amu Darya on a gentle glacis, now unnecessary, and crossed on an impressive elevated bridge one kilometer in length. For the kilometer's initial nine-tenths there was nothing below but hard cracked soil furred with ashy vegetation. Near the end of the bridge I saw a powerless thirty-foot-wide braid of dirty blue water slithering along a carved flume of sand.

Before coming to Karakalpakistan, I had spent some time in the Tashkent offices of the World Bank, the Aral Sea disaster's main legatee after the collapse of the Soviet Union. The Bank had been working in Uzbekistan for ten years. Nothing having to do with the Aral Sea had improved in that time, and the Bank was now scaling back on its financial commitment to alleviate the disaster and was backing away from any promises of eventual improvement. Its multilateral compeer, the International Monetary Fund, had just pulled out of Uzbekistan because of the government's refusal to introduce a unified currency exchange and liberalize the Uzbek economy. When the Uzbek government continued to insist on placing large state orders for water-hungry crops its indigent farmers could not hope to fill, much of the Bank's work was pole-axed. Alone in a basement library, I found upon the metal shelves dozens of plastic-spined notebooks containing proposal summaries and pilot-project reports and feasibility studies. I pulled out at random the Bank's "Aral Sea Basin Program Water and Environmental Management Project" from May 1998, which described the fiasco that is Central Asian water management and what could be done about it. As it happened, about $86.4 million worth of things, according to the proposal's recommendation. Again at random I pulled out a directory of the various nongovernmental organizations currently operating in the Aral Sea basin. It was 130 pages long.

Later, upstairs, Ton Lennaerts, the Bank's water-resources con-
sultant, spread before me a map of Uzbekistan and dragged a thick
finger along the Amu Darya. "River deltas," Lennaerts had explained, "are normally the most fertile places in the world. But you
have exactly the opposite situation in Karakalpakistan." Karakalpakistan's canals differed little from those dug a millennium ago.
Virtually no money had been spent to preserve its four million
hectares of irrigated land over the last ten years. The entire region
was entirely without a meaningful infrastructure. The money allo-
cated for better water management had mostly been used to pay
ministry salaries. I remembered now, suspended above the skele-
tally dry bed of the Amu Darya, having studied Lennaerts's map
closely. Along the Amu Darya were numerous green clusters. These
were oases, which meant cities. Near each city dozens of obsolete
pumping stations sucked up the river and spat it out onto outlying,
fundless, and deteriorating collective farms, where up to 40 percent of the water was lost and squandered. To this Lennaerts had
no answers, only terse, frustrated shrugs. It has been an unpleasant
fact of irrigated life since Babylon that downstream communities
always suffer at the expense of upstream communities, especially
when the population of one outnumbers the other by millions. To
bring a spring tide of water back to Karakalpakistan would only
mean transporting disaster somewhere else. Whether by design
or necessity, values had been assigned here, and Karakalpakistan
had fallen beneath the hammer of this calculus. "A cow is being
milked," Lennaerts concluded sadly. "But the cow has died."

After we passed over the Amu Darya, the desert erupted panorami-
cally, and my eyes were overpowered by a dull brown ache. Since returning to Uzbekistan I had learned to dread its highways. All were
staggered with checkpoints and border guards ostensibly looking
to nab any insurgents belonging to the Islamic Movement of Uzbekistan, a group of fanatical Islamists then biding its time in the
Islamic Emirate of Afghanistan. My translator had been strip-
searched at one such roadblock and our driver was hit with a trun-
cheon while I was shoved around, my belongings kicked and scattered along the highway. But here in Karakalpakistan the highways
were empty. They felt large, Nebraskan, existential. Along the
roads, worn little irrigation ditches linked one community to an-

other. Groups of houses were capped with corrugated tin roofs and paired with twiggy side-buildings in which hungry horses were crammed ribcage-to-ribcage. Desperate old women sold Fanta and Coca-Cola beside the roads. Skinny cows tramped along the gravel margin. I had not known cows could be so skinny. Huge tongue slabs dangled from their mouths and clumps of dung hung tangled in their lusterless coats. Along every irrigation ditch were rows of cattailish vegetation. Astonishingly, they were still building canals out here. Large excavators stood abandoned beside half-dug trenches and massive scoops of disinterred soil. Nowhere was the desert's simple splendor. This was a desert turned into an oasis turned into a desert again, a terra-forming tug-of-war that had now been inarguably concluded. As recently as seven years ago, Bahktiyor told me, everything around us had been cotton-field green, living, verdant.

Cotton. In America the thirsty crop at once conjures the whole history of black slavery; here it had murdered the Aral Sea. For a season's growth, cotton typically requires thirty annual inches of rainfall. Uzbekistan receives, at most, fourteen annual inches of rainfall. It was not surprising, then, that the Soviet officials who, in the 1960s, decided to drain the Aral to increase cotton yields knew exactly what they were doing. ("It is obvious to everyone that the evaporation of the Aral Sea is inevitable," a Soviet engineer noted in 1968.) They simply calculated the projected profits from the increase in cotton against those of the fishing industry they were about to destroy. For a while it worked. Between 1960 and 1986, the hectares of Soviet land sown with cotton increased by 60 percent, making the USSR the world's leading cotton exporter. Today cotton accounts for a quarter of Uzbekistan's GDP.* Much of this resplendent yield turned out to be bogus. The Cotton Scandal, as it is known, was an elaborate fraud undertaken by officials at every level of the Uzbek Republic to defraud Moscow into paying one billion rubles for nonexistent cotton. Moscow's subsequent response, a mid-eighties purge led first by Yuri Andropov and later by Mikhail Gorbachev, decimated the Uzbek Communist Party and aggravated Uzbeks' and Karakalpaks' sense of racial exploitation, many of

---

* The adulation of cotton extends so far into Uzbek culture that Tashkent's soccer team is called the Cotton Pickers.

whom wondered, not unreasonably, how they could be taken to task for cheating such consummate cheaters. But Uzbekistan's method of harvesting cotton has only added to its national anguish. The most visible victims of cotton are women and children, whose tiny hands and low centers of gravity, one argument holds, make it easier for them to pick cotton without skinning their fingers or ruining their backs. (Men usually procure the cotton industry's less physically demanding managerial jobs.) During the harvest season, from late summer to late fall, the schools are emptied of children. Poor women are rounded up. All are shipped to the fields and forced to toil beneath the molten Central Asian sun, sometimes without shelter or adequate drinking water. In the late 1980s Uzbek officials made several promises to stop using schoolchildren as harvesters, but every year thousands of little "volunteers" still marched out to the cotton fields. Every night during cotton season, families still huddle around their televisions to learn of the day's harvest. Incidentally, the Russian word for cotton worker is *rabochy*, or *rab* for short. In what few Uzbeks or Karakalpaks accept as an etymological coincidence, *rab* also means "slave."

We came to Porlatau, a small village south of Moynaq that had the gray, isolated air of a lunar settlement. On our way here I had noticed that the closer we drew to the Aral Sea's former shore the fewer road signs we had to guide us. The numerous switchbacks we used to reach Porlatau had not even been marked. I asked Bahktiyor why he supposed this was. "Many reasons," he said, then smiled. We made our way through town, a light floury dust pouring in through our vehicle's vents. We passed a playground outside a school. A dozen boys played basketball on a sandy court. Their ball was multicolored, like a beach ball.

In Porlatau's homes, mothers dragged out their best carpets for us to sit on while their sick children breathed into tubes that measured their lung strength. We were poured cups of tea with camel's milk. Only Karakalpaks use milk in their tea, a subject of anthropological hilarity to Uzbeks who live outside of Karakalpakistan. Karakalpaks use milk in their tea, of course, because without it the tea would taste like boiled seawater.

Later that evening, Wegerdt, Bahktiyor, and I stopped for dinner at a local doctor's home in the village of Raushan. The doctor owned a large plot of land. His nearest neighbor's home was forty yards away. A spacious loose-dirt driveway divided his two broad, flat houses. Wegerdt and Bahktiyor greeted the doctor and walked inside to make sure our sleeping arrangements were in order. I stayed in the car. It had been a long day. I felt as if I had been cudgeled. Could it really be that I had been in Uzbekistan for weeks now and had not heard anyone say anything even guardedly optimistic about the people of the Aral Sea basin? What I had heard were words like "resettlement" and "population transfer." People were already leaving. Roughly fifty thousand Karakalpaks had left their homeland in the last ten years. Maybe one hundred thousand. It was hard to know. Most had vanished, visaless, into Kazakhstan, since Kazakhs are linguistically and culturally closer to Karakalpaks than any other people. The rest were waiting. Moving is not simple here. On every *propiska,* or identity card, one's city of residence is prominently listed, and anyone stopped by the police while not in that city has some explaining to do. To move one needed an intranational visa. Some people waited for money to bribe their way to that visa, some waited for things to improve, and some waited to die. Ton Lennaerts's map appeared again in my mind. How many countries did this problem afflict? When the Soviet Union collapsed, the Aral Sea's last real hope collapsed with it. Instead of one nation's internal problem, it became overnight an international crisis, with the sea's feeder rivers running through five nascent, highly uncooperative nations and providing water for five nascent, highly differentiated economies. How could so many compelling factors — economic, sociological, political, financial — ever be reconciled? One could spend ten years studying ten different disciplines to approach the disaster, and the great question, "What is to be done?" would be no easier to answer.

I sat perched half in and half out of the car. The door was swung open. My chin rested upon the shelf of my hand. The sun was going down, the horizon dyed a Creamsicle orange. I watched a skinny, ravaged-looking dog sniff around various piles of refuse. A dog's life. Then it occurred to me that American dogs have no idea what a dog's life is. Suddenly, two little boys appeared from behind one of the houses and approached me. They were brothers, clearly. One was taller and certainly older. The other was small, perhaps five years old. His head was pumpkin-sized, seemingly twice the circumference of that of his brother, who was regarding me coldly.

The younger boy smiled, his teeth cavitied and yellow, his skinny body completely naked and covered in dust. The dust was spread so evenly over his body that it seemed deliberately applied. His uncircumcised penis looked like an anteater's nose. I smiled back at him. *"Ismingiz nimah?"* I asked. What is your name?

Before the boy could answer his older brother inexplicably struck him from behind. The boy flopped face first into the dust. The blow was two-handed and savage, like something out of provincial hockey. A sound, an involuntary protest, rose in my throat. But I did nothing. The younger boy coughed into the dust. He had landed badly, arms at his sides, and now he tried to get to his feet. His brother placed a foot upon his naked bottom and shoved him, almost tenderly, back into the dirt. He stared down, having satisfied some obscure but insatiable impulse, and then walked away. I waited for tears, the shrieks and cries of fraternal terror. Nothing. The naked dusty child was silent. The dog trotted over, and as the boy picked himself up he searched the ground blindly with a small hand. Finally he stood holding a triangular rock. He turned and threw it at the dog, hitting him full in the ribs; the dog flinched but otherwise took the blow in silence. The boy simply walked away. I made soft kissing sounds to summon the dog, who was understandably skittish. I persisted. I didn't know what else to do. When it slinked over, head lowered and panting, I saw a strange red spider-like creature embedded in its collarless neck. I extended my hand. The dog bit me and staggered off.

Hours later, Bahktiyor and I stood beneath an extravagantly starry Karakalpak sky. Our stomachs were filled with bread and rice, our brains soaked in fermented camel milk. Everywhere around us, but for the occasional tiny peal of cowbells, was a silence as involved as thought. Bahktiyor wore a mesh T-shirt and yellow sunglasses that dangled from his neck on a sporty yellow string. I asked him how he learned to speak English so well. What I was actually asking was why he did not look, speak, or act like anyone else here. He told me that he had received a highly competitive scholarship to study in England in 1998, an experience he said had changed his life. He had seen the world. "And that," he said, "means I have seen everything."

I congratulated him, but even in the darkness I could see Bahktiyor's slender, handsome face twisting. He shook his head. He had come home from England early. While he was on vacation back in Nukus, a gentleman from the Ministry of Education stopped by to inform him that "border problems" with Islamic insurgents fourteen hundred miles away from Karakalpakistan meant that fewer students would be studying abroad that year. Bahktiyor was forbidden to return to England. Later he ran into another gentleman, a young man, in Tashkent, who informed Bahktiyor that he had purchased his scholarship spot for $2,000. "He was too rich," Bahktiyor said to me. Too rich for what? "Too rich to kill."

Bahktiyor was told, soon after the run-in with his usurper, that he was expected to repay the government its scholarship money. He refused and wrote several letters protesting this corruption to the Uzbek government. Those letters never made it past Karakalpakistan's minister of education, who had now effectively blackballed Bahktiyor from attending college even in Nukus. Was this a matter of discrimination? The boy who usurped Bahktiyor's scholarship was an ethnic Uzbek, and Karakalpaks have historically been on the losing end of Uzbekistan's chauvinism. Or did it concern the sense of ethics with which Bahktiyor was either blessed or cursed? How could one know whether to encourage him to fight or plead with him to apologize and bribe everyone with two hands? "My biggest worry," he said, "is that I'll just stay here, which means I'll quit everything, just like everyone else. Many people here make every effort to continue their studies in America. They try and they fail, and they start drinking, they forget everything — all their plans, all those dreams of seeing Las Vegas one day, or going to the Avenue of the Stars. That's the biggest nightmare for me, because if I get to that, it means that I lost my hope."

I stared at my feet. Bahktiyor just shook his head. "My entire life is fucked."

One does not approach Moynaq. Moynaq appears. It appeared to me not as a mirage or a vision but with the same sudden shock of a shipwreck seen through krill-swirling brine or an overturned truck through a blizzard. From a distance it was not unpleasant. In fact, it had the enchanted smallness of a shire or village nestled in a valley. Moynaq's close arrangement was no accident. Forty years ago the entire town was surrounded by water, and anyone wishing to go to Moynaq had to use a ferry to do so. Now the town was engulfed in a dust storm. But it was not so dusty that I failed to see the twenty-foot-high WELCOME TO MOYNAQ sign. Painted on it was a large fish.

We parked somewhere in town. I stumbled from the car and walked slowly through Moynaq's deserted streets. The level of ambient strangeness was so high that when I realized the horizon was on fire several moments passed before it occurred to me that this was worthy of note. "Horizon," I jotted. "On fire." I looked out on huge mile-wide black blossoms of smoke bulbed orange-red at their fuming core. They were burning brush out in the former seabed. Dump trucks filled with brush. Why? The streets were empty. No one could answer me. I simply stared.

I prowled the former seaside on my way to visit Moynaq's museum. The still-lingering maritime feel of the place filled me with disquiet. A pretty thatched fence surrounded each home I passed. The sand beneath my feet was soft beach sand redolent of sunstruck water and oily backs and Sidney Sheldon novels. One could see, even now, why Moynaq was once such a popular vacation site for communist bureaucrats. Moynaq's now moribund airport used to accommodate fifty flights a day during the summer and spring. Now it was home to nothing more than a rusty front gate, which still bore the intaglio of a Soviet hammer and sickle.

Farther into dusty, flat Moynaq, I attracted a retinue of children. There seemed to be an epidemic of shoeless children. Feet were so dirty and beaten they appeared almost cloven. Nearly all the children seemed slightly deranged. Some blew raspberries at me, some shouted, some ran around me in fixated circles and ran off gobbling. Later I was told that severe goiter, a common Moynaq malady, can, when suffered at an early age, lead to mild retardation. A few blocks from the museum a smiling, healthy-looking boy advanced upon me. I returned his *salaam*. He spoke a small, confident amount of English and was delighted when he heard my awkward Uzbek. He was Kazakh. His name was Saghitjan. He had buck teeth, his tiny nose was densely freckled, and his eyes were shiny in the unknowable little-boy way that promised either malice or its utter absence. Despite the heat he wore formal black slacks and a fuzzy maroon sweater. When I told Saghitjan he spoke English well, he said, "Yes, I do." Saghitjan looked to be about eight, maybe nine, years old. He was fourteen.

He accompanied me to the museum. It was a large, teal-walled single room filled with a cube of limpid warm sunlight. Saghitjan looked at the high ceiling, open-mouthed. I asked if he had ever been here before. "Oh, yes," he said, unconvincingly. A large mural on the farthest wall depicted a blissful Karakalpak family. Behind them was the sea, boats, seagulls. A huge, hand-painted aerial map of the Aral Sea next to the mural placed Moynaq happily on the sea's edge.

For a long time one of the most puzzling aspects of the Aral Sea disaster was how little attention it had attracted. But in the end, not even the Soviets could hide a vanishing sea. In the comparatively permissive year of 1987 the Uzbek writer Maruf Jalil published an eyewitness account entitled "The Sea That Is Fleeing Its Shores." A number of Central Asian celebrities, including the Kirgiz novelist Chinghiz Aitmatov, funded a Save the Aral committee. The outcry grew, until the Politburo in Moscow was prepared to divert two Siberian rivers toward the Aral Sea in order to restore it. This unbelievably bad idea was well under way when Mikhail Gorbachev canceled the scheme, having bowed to sensible pressure from Russian environmental groups and what many viewed as nakedly racist pressure from Slavic supremacists. Although Moscow did scale back its demands for Central Asian cotton, it persisted in blaming the Uzbeks and Karakalpaks for wasting water. By 1990 the Save the Aral committee, after reviewing its three years of work, concluded that all had been for naught. Less than naught. The Aral Sea was still shrinking, despite the fact that forty organizations were now at work on the crisis. Amazingly, this had been the zenith of hope for Karakalpakistan.

Saghitjan and I lingered near the exhibits in the room's center. Each item was identified and described on a little placard in Russian, Karakalpak, and English. Together we looked at twenty-five-year-old tins of fish from Moynaq's defunct cannery. Shriveled carp in glass tubes. Model ships. Nets and fishing hooks of notable variety and ingenuousness. Animal skins, too, since the Aral Sea basin was at one time host to a thriving, now extinct, muskrat-fur industry. Anchors. A cracked, carbon-datable butter churn exactly like the equally ancient yet still functional churn I had seen, two days before, in a home in a nearby village. I felt despondent looking at these items, all laid out with such postmortem precision. Saghitjan looked at them, too, his eyes full of sparkling, empty engagement. All of this, I realized, meant nothing to him. The sea was now just a legend, dead before he had teethed.

An older English gentleman also visiting the museum sidled alongside me. "I'm not sure I approve of all this wallowing in nostalgia," he said. "I think I should prefer revolution." He had a point. Karakalpaks are victims of some of the most untrammeled abuse in post-Holocaust history. Why, then, do they not revolt?

Today many Karakalpaks complain bitterly of Uzbek rule, but even though their constitution grants them the theoretical right to secede from Uzbekistan, no one speaks seriously of doing so. Such a tactic might allow the Karakalpaks to throw themselves at the fickle mercies of the international aid community, but it would also make them citizens of one of the most shattered countries on earth. And the Aral Sea is not their only problem. In Soviet times Karakalpakistan served not only as a site for testing Le Chatelier's principle of environment resilience but as the piñata for some of the USSR's most wicked chemical and biological weapons. In the middle of the Aral Sea, for instance, one finds Vozrozhdeniya ("Rebirth") Island — now a peninsula — upon which, a British explorer was told in 1840, stood an enchanted castle guarded by dragons and surrounded by flaming quicksand. The Soviet Union tried to make these stories come true by establishing an anthrax factory there.* What Karakalpakistan is rapidly becoming in its modern, Uzbek incarnation is a huge prison colony. It is estimated that fifteen thousand people, most of them religious Muslims, whom the government fears as seditionists schooled in Taliban tactics, are currently detained in Karakalpakistan in inhuman prison camps. No doubt some of these prisoners are committed Islamists, but the Uzbek government has proved unwilling to distinguish between the fanatical and the merely observant, the violent revolutionary and the peaceful democratic reformer.

The stubborn, indomitable Karakalpak approach to life is difficult to square against the seemingly docile resignation with which they still regard Soviet perfidy. Again and again, when I asked

---

* The island's desperately needed cleanup was, according to the brisk Nukus rumor mill, being handled by the U.S. Department of State, a rumor officially confirmed in October 2001, when Uzbekistan became an official ally in America's war in Afghanistan.

Karakalpaks if they were angry with the Soviets, they merely shrugged and said that in Soviet times they at least had jobs. Perhaps the legacy of the gulag has made social outrage impossible. Who, at any rate, would listen? They have been abused for so long. When Genghis Khan passed near Karakalpakistan in the thirteenth century, he destroyed all livestock and every granary and irrigation ditch, a tactic he called, approvingly, "killing the land." Having their homeland ruined by interlopers is a recurring Karakalpak nightmare.

On the far side of the museum was a sign: PEOPLE, SAVE THE ARAL SEA! The sign was in English. Its chipped, flaking paint suggested that it was quite old, which it would have had to be, since "saving" the Aral Sea in any real sense was now completely impossible. Restoring the Aral Sea to its original volume (disregarding any notion of water quality) would require, according to one estimate, sealing off all the canals in Central Asia for ten years and allowing the sea's feeder rivers to take their original course. All that can be done, then, is to save some small part of the Aral, as Kazakhstan is attempting to do with the decapitated northern part of the sea found within its borders. This is now known as the "Little Aral." Fish have even been reintroduced here, with some success.

We found a wall of black-and-white photos hung on a midroom partition. Saghitjan and I stared at water in photo after photo. In this place it was easy to forget that water, as a bulk phenomenon, still existed. Even black-and-white water seemed exquisite, primally wet. The smiling fishermen in these photos held aloft nets bulging with their haul. Some photos were almost pornographic in their abundance of fish. Overfishing the Aral Sea was a problem long before the amphetamine of Soviet industrialization arrived. The Aral was not a deep sea. It was a desert sea, fragile by definition, vulnerable to heavy fishing. What had these people expected?

A catalogue of Karakalpak denial was not hard to come by. The family with whom I stayed in Nukus, for instance, thought nothing of allowing their leaky spigots to run all day. People washed their cars regularly. Canals kept getting dug. Cotton still grew where it could. Poor water management was rapidly leading the region toward total drought, and average Karakalpaks would not even discuss it, waving their hands or clutching their skulls whenever the topic was broached. Given the magnitude of the catastrophe, most are simply unable to recognize their own culpability in their inescapable misery. Instead, many Karakalpaks choose to believe the old Soviet saw about the Aral Sea's historical tendency to wax and wane. They told me that the sea would return, eventually, that the ecology would improve, eventually, and that Moynaq and Nukus would again come alive. Can one blame them for this failure to confront reality? I, for one, cannot. They have two choices. The first is to completely restructure their cotton-based monoculture and prevent all-but-certain future ecological and economic collapse. The problem with this is that the resultant turmoil would open the doors to some of the worst privation any society has intentionally brought upon itself. The second is to do nothing, to carry on, and watch the same malignant doors magically open themselves.

The road out of Moynaq and into the nonexistent sea was, like everything, covered with thick, salty dust. I bounced around in a blocky white Land Cruiser. The wind had a low constancy, and it came whistling through the tiny slots and cracks in the truck's frame. Outside, along Moynaq's gradually depopulated streets, the wind whipped up a dirty miasma. Children carrying pails walked backward, hands over their eyes, their white T-shirts billowing like parachutes.

The Land Cruiser reached the outermost edge of Moynaq. With a bump and momentary plunge it exited the town proper and entered what was, in living memory, the bed of the Aral Sea. Looking out the window quickly became an exercise in dislocation. Beyond lay not reality but something purely conceptual. The Scene of the Greatest Ecological Crime in History. A land made alien by betrayal. Whatever its nature now, it was threatening and hostile. This was off-planet, a place of low roads and poison flora. Moynaq was gone now, surely, fallen away from the husk of this world as though it were a space shuttle's rocket. I looked out the back window. Moynaq was a hundred yards away. Possibly less. My companion, Ian Small, the head of mission for the MSF Aral Sea Area Program and the man responsible for bringing MSF to Karakalpakistan, wrenched around in his seat and looked at me. He smiled in a way that suggested everything but a smile. The Land Cruiser, I noticed, had stopped. "Ready to go boating?" he asked.

My feet came down on hard, crunchy soil that was, by far, the most chemically transmuted I had yet encountered in Karakalpakistan. My boots left no footprints. This was interesting, but not nearly as interesting as the huge beached trawler to my left. About the size of a baleen whale, this vessel had once been part of Moynaq's considerable armada of fishing boats. At their peak the Aral Sea's fishermen provided a tenth of the entire Soviet catch. In the 1920s their heroism and resolve helped save Russia from widespread famine. In Moynaq alone, ten thousand fishermen plied their trade, a number more than triple its current population. Today every one of the Aral Sea's twenty-four species of fish is dead. I studied the boat. It was encased in a shell of baked, flaky rust that came in six different hues, the whole spectrum of oxidation. The boat was atop a high dune, its bow pushed out over the dune's edge as though recalling the weightlessness with which it once breached the Aral Sea's crests. Dust-speckled sunlight poured through the slots of its missing ribs.

I turned to see half a dozen other boats thirty yards away. From a distance they looked like alien technology, a desert-roaming flotilla of skiffs. I walked toward them atop a dirty white crystallized glaze of salt. Despite the condition of the soil, life had carried on. Growing from the seabed were hundreds of shrubby plants and small, evil-looking trees that seemed to have been conjured from a terrifying children's book. Revenge plants, these were, the helpless counterstrike of a devastated ecosystem. Littering the ground were chunks of cable, bits of fiberglass, strange metal, rusty springs, cigarette butts. When the soil gave way to a boggy patch of mud (only here could mud and desert have existed side by side) I had to walk around a half-submerged propeller as high as my chest.

Ian Small stood near one of the boats on a dune tonsured with gray-green vegetation, his hands in his pockets. I joined him on the dune. We looked at a boat. Half of this boat, for some reason, bore a bright, newish coat of white paint. Small explained that this was the work of a Dutch film crew, who arrived in Moynaq a few years ago to make a documentary. During the shoot, someone decided to slap a fresh overlay of paint on the side they were filming. I couldn't fathom how, precisely, these Dutch filmmakers could have found Moynaq's naval graveyard dramatically or pictorially deficient. Small tamped out a cigarette and shook his head. "They promised the people of Moynaq they'd come back and show the film," he said, "but they didn't. People are still talking about that."

This was a topic of some sensitivity in the Aral Sea area. Experts and journalists and the nuncios of international aid have been piloting their Land Cruisers through Moynaq for more than a decade, and the desert seabed is now larger than Massachusetts. Last year not a single drop of water from the Amu Darya reached the Aral Sea. Two-thirds of the Aral Sea basin's population is now considered, in the simplest medical terms, "sick or unwell." The people have been pummeled into reticence, regarding with indifference the ballpoint pens and tape recorders and television cameras of those who would view and document their decay. Their own doom is of no interest to them. They say that if every scientist and journalist who visited the Aral Sea brought with them a bucket of water, the sea would be filled again.

"I was interviewing this former fisherman," Small told me, "who lives all of two hundred meters that way, and asked him, 'Where's your ship now?' He said, 'Out there, behind the tuberculosis dispensary.' I asked, 'Do you go out to see it sometimes?' He thought that was an absolutely bizarre question. His response was, 'Why would I?'" Small smiled. "To him, there isn't any kind of romantic notion to these ships. This guy was working from five in the morning till nine at night. For him it was a tool, and now that trade is gone. He's not going to cry over his tools."

We decided to visit another batch of grounded ships. The Land Cruiser rumbled far beyond the naval graveyard found at the town's edge along a well-traveled road lined with hundreds of year-old telephone poles. These poles provide power to the oil rigs that are drilling deep in the former seabed. It seems that the withdrawal of the Aral Sea has led to the discovery of oil. Surely, I thought aloud, this will benefit the people of Moynaq. Actually, Small explained, oil is probably the worst thing that could have happened to Moynaq. In Kazakhstan the post-Soviet discovery of vast oil fields has done nothing to improve the lives of average Kazakhs. The Kazakh president, Nursultan Nazarbayev, is believed to have been one of the primary beneficiaries of that country's privatization program. Barring some outpouring of executive goodwill on the part of President Islam Karimov, the discovery of oil near Moynaq would bring nothing to its people but the eerily beautiful diversion of watching the oil rigs flame off at night.

The landscape surrounding this road was huge, yellow, vacant as sky. It looked somehow microwaved. The farther we got from

Moynaq, the more Blakean the terrain became. A stanza from "Holy Thursday" suddenly filled my mind: "And their sun does never shine. / And their fields are bleak & bare. / And their ways are fill'd with thorns. / It is eternal winter there." After a few miles' journey, we jackknifed off the road and jumped along an uneven tire-trenched path. The ships soon appeared. Five of them lay in a careless cluster among erosion-planed dunes. Another half-dozen ships were visible in the heat-distorted distance.

For years after the sea abandoned Moynaq's shoreline, some of the town's more desperate fishermen dug numerous canals out to meet it. Each morning they patiently steered their ships down the narrow, brackish passageways. "Chasing the sea," they called it. In 1986, commonly regarded as the year in which the last of the Aral Sea's native fish expired, the ships were left more or less where they lay. I found I did not want to contemplate the long, difficult walk back to town that these brave, deluded men must have taken the day they realized everything was over.

We came to a large boat half duned-over with sand. *Molodyozh* ("Youth") peeled from its hull. I touched the hull and watched it crumble beneath my palm. I had peeled off a few large pulverous wafers of rust before realizing I could have dismantled the entire craft with little more than my thumb and index finger. We climbed atop one of the ships. I gingerly kicked in the door to the captain's cabin. The narrow space held an ankle-deep accumulation of sand. The meters and gauges were filled with half-moons of sand. The porthole window was spidery with cracks. The walls were grotty with thick, corrosive rust. I placed my hand on the speed control, but it was frozen in place. Before I left, I found a broken teacup in the sand.

Small and I made our way to another ship, hundreds of lizards scrambling beneath our feet. They sounded like mice in drywall, but worse. The lizards were gray-green, their heads as sleek as fingers. When they moved their bodies stayed battened flat but their tails somehow aggressively lifted. Their legs were so blurry they seemed powered by cold-blooded lightning. What was once one of the most interesting and diverse desert ecosystems in the world had devolved into a massive skink preserve.

We strolled along the high edge of a dry, gouged-out canal. The seashells I did not scoop up as morbid souvenirs crunched beneath

our feet. Small fumed about the Bush Administration's recent
hedging over and ultimate miscarriage of the Kyoto Protocol. He
found it a complete failure of any notion of humanitarian law, of
international law, of the conventions of the last hundred years. He
said he found it shortsighted, even criminal. The impact of that decision, he said, was astounding. And yet the United States got away
with it.

We neared another stranded ship. Unlike its more obviously for-
saken sister ships, this one was parked, purposefully, across the des-
iccated canal. This boat was as wide and flat as a pontoon, be-
decked with busted searchlights and pulpits. Why was it bestride
the canal? Was it used to block the other boats in? Why? Violence
had been done to this boat. It had been scavenged, its bolts and
rivets stripped out and the glass in its portholes punched free. The
ship's large, rusty anchor had been heaved onto the canal's de-
clivitous bank.

Everything around me had the same pleading obscurity. What
had happened here? What did these ships want to tell us? Was this
the world's most potent symbol or merely local scrap? It meant everything, nothing. It meant there is still hope for those societies on
the edge of environmental catastrophe, and it meant that all eventually comes to rust. It meant that to remain ignorant of the Aral
Sea disaster is to dodge deliberately its eschatological implications,
and it meant that all the knowledge and attention in the world
prove unable to save the Aral Sea. It meant that placing the needs
of economics over those of the natural world is to invite a near biblical cataclysm in which both are destroyed. Small regarded the
Aral Sea as "a fable of our time," and it is that, too. Indeed, it holds
a fable's multitude of dark, simple, immutable meanings. "Maybe,"
Ian Small told me, "it's time. The Aral Sea's already dead. It's all
about palliative care right now. Maybe it will be a blessing when it's
finally gone, and it will just become this remote post-disaster place
that once had a sea."

The Aral Sea is not coming back, nothing will improve, people like Small will continue their impossible triage, people like
Saghitjan will continue to sicken and die, until, one day, Moynaq
will be spoken of in the doomed, sepulchral tones of Gomorrah,
Pompeii, or one of *The Tempest*'s "still-vexed Bermudas." A luckless
place where angry fates and unwitting human need saw their devas-
tating concussion.

Stranger in the Dunes

FROM *The St. Petersburg Times*

MERZOUGA, Morocco: The sand slams into Zahid's full-length white robe, flattening it against his chest and thighs, blowing the extra material up behind him like a cape. A heavily wrapped scarf covers his head, leaving only a slit for his dark eyes.

He leads the riderless camel through the low-rolling dunes between two ranges of six-hundred-foot peaks. Our footprints begin disappearing, first in minutes, then in seconds. The grains penetrate zippers and chafe exposed skin. Throats scratch. Eyes slowly close with grit.

Gait slowed and head bent low, Zahid pushes on. In comic contrast, the camel seems to smile through his thick lips and bat his huge lashes. We are a couple of hours into a four-day trek through the giant dunes. Four days? I think. Only if we make it through the next four minutes.

Then, the wind vanishes.

No big deal, Zahid announces while shaking a pailful of sand out of his scarf. In the summers, the flying sand blots out the sky, he says. Camels get lost. Nomads sometimes die.

The dunes, named Erg Chebbi, rest in the middle of a plain on the western edge of the Sahara. Chebbi is the largest erg, or sand sea, in Morocco. At about 150 square miles, it's small compared to the Grand Ergs in Algeria and Libya.

Zahid wonders why anyone would travel so far to visit his country's super-sized sandbox. He's not complaining; he just doesn't get it.

"Sandstorms. Not fun. No, no, no," Zahid says.

When I first thought about flying to Morocco last summer, it

seemed a convenient location to live out my desert fantasies —
camels, sand, nomads, brutal weather — my own sanitized version
of *Lawrence of Arabia*.

After September 11, the trip took on new allure. It became what
you don't do. You don't vacation alone in a Muslim country in the
middle of a war on terrorism when many people are scared to visit
grandparents in Omaha. You don't insist on talking religion and
politics in a strange and sometimes volatile land.

In America, we are taught to keep strangers at arm's length. In
recent months, that lesson has grown to "suspect everyone," especially anyone who looks Arab. This was a chance to turn the tables,
to be the stranger, the one suspicion is cast upon.

"I Married My Father"

"You ready to walk?" Zahid asks as I pull my shoes back on and wipe
the remnants of the sandstorm from my cords and long-sleeved
shirt.

Zahid's casual cool is bred from a lifetime of struggle. At fifty-
five, Zahid (like many Moroccans, he uses no last name) has overcome sun blindness, 130-degree temperatures, camel thieves, tribal disputes, disease, and those hellish sandstorms, just to name the
most obvious.

A prolonged drought forced Zahid and his wife off the plains
four years ago and into a remote hamlet called Taboumiat, population thirty. They bought a small house with a view of the dunes, and
Zahid took up handling camels for tourists.

He hasn't had much to do lately.

Even in the desert, Zahid has had to deal with the fallout from
the collapse of the "grand buildings." He wonders if he will have to
return to his life as a herder on the plains, with little money to buy
new camels. Will his wife be forced to give up her new loves — her
stove, her friends, the lights that come on with a flick of a switch?

For Zahid the choice is between convenience and hardship. The
dunes are a living. Me? I'm entranced by the eerie beauty.

Throughout the day, the color of the sand ranges from pink to
red to brown to black. Look one way and the dunes are a washed-
out canvas. Turn around and the sun has transformed them into a
masterpiece of shadows and contrast. With the rising heat, the
smaller dunes appear to move like slow waves.

The wind shapes the dunes quickly, shearing and building peaks, bending razor-straight ridges into S's. The worst storms kick sand high into the sky, sometimes carrying it as far as the Caribbean islands.

The only other person on our trek is Zahid's eighteen-year-old assistant, Hassan. He can cook a tangy Moroccan stew, carry a tune, and speak parts of seven languages. The part of English he knows doesn't include many pronouns. So whether he is talking about the camel or his mother, the sentence begins with "I." As in "I eat a lot of desert plants" or "I married my father in a ceremony near the dunes."

On the first day, he keeps saying we are headed for a "weesis." A weesis? It sounds more like a stifled sneeze than the palm tree–lined "oasis" where we wind up for the first night.

Of Terrorists and Thieves

That evening, we bundle under camel-hair blankets and stoke the fire as the temperature drops into the low 40s. A full moon backlights Zahid's every breath. With his sinewy frame, well-trimmed black mustache, and chiseled features, he looks like a slightly darker version of Burt Reynolds.

The conversation gets going with stupid tourist stories — the winner being Hassan's yarn about a Dutch guy who thought it would be funny to brush his camel's teeth until it bit down, swallowing the brush and the tip of the man's middle finger.

Hassan recalls a myth about how the dunes were created thousands of years ago when the local people refused to help a woman and child who needed food and shelter during a festival. Incensed, God buried the town and its inhabitants in sand.

The story illustrates the importance many Moroccans place on hospitality. In the time it takes to travel only a few miles, a stranger on a bus will offer up a small cup of milk and some smoked sardines, then invite me to his sister's wedding.

At first all the attention makes me suspicious. What scam are they trying to pull? I check my pockets for my money and make sure my bag is still where it should be. Despite my obvious skepticism, the invitations keep coming. I figure the whole country cannot be after my wallet. My guard starts to come down.

Moroccans, it turns out, consider guests to be gifts from Allah.

"We need more gifts," Zahid tells me in Arabic. "Why'd they all go away?"

I'm not sure what to tell him other than that Westerners aren't comfortable and, in some cases, are downright angry with the Arab world. I begin to tell him about the Israeli-Palestinian debacle and Middle Eastern politics, but he gets a perplexed look. It's tough to explain new global realities to someone who has never seen a globe.

A few minutes later, Zahid quietly moves to a flat patch twenty yards away to pray. Zahid is Berber, an indigenous tribe introduced to Islam in the seventh century by the invading Arabs.

Praying is common in a country with twenty-nine million Muslims, 98 percent of the population. No one complains when taxi drivers pull to the side of the highway and drop to their knees on the gravel shoulder. Train passengers switch seats so they face Mecca and quietly whisper *"Allahu akbar"* (Allah is the greatest).

Zahid doffs his sandals and socks. With the dry sand, he washes his hands, forearms, feet, and ankles and runs his hands over his head. He faces east and prays, standing, then kneeling, four times.

Zahid knows that five times a day Osama bin Laden prays the same way to the same God. He smiles when he considers what possible ties a camel herder in the middle of nowhere could have with a Saudi Arabian heir turned terrorist mastermind.

"Are you a terrorist?" I ask jokingly.

No, but you look like you could be, he shoots back with a smile.

The only thing Zahid knows about terrorism is what he's heard from tourists. He knows of the Basques in northern Spain and remembers a Japanese group telling him about poisonous gas in the Tokyo subway.

Zahid has never visited a city. Four months ago, he didn't know what a skyscraper was. But he remembers feeling sad and then angered when he heard about the September 11 attacks. He said toppling a building is like stealing — property, money, and lives — and stealing is never justified.

In the desert when a camel died, any Berber could leave it and the load it was carrying where it fell by simply marking the camel with his brand, Zahid says. No other Berber who happened along would take the load.

Whether it's a dead camel in the desert or a 110-story building, it doesn't matter to Zahid.

"Bin Laden took the load," he said. "There is never an excuse for that."

"Hard to Relax"

Each morning after making tea and toast, Zahid gathers the saddle-bags and ropes and begins a daily battle with our one-thousand-pound camel, named Jimi Hendrix after the rock star who once visited Morocco.

With eight-foot-tall Jimi lying on his belly, Zahid plops the saddlebags over the hump, then digs away the sand under Jimi's belly to affix a rope. He skillfully lassos another rope through Jimi's mouth. With each addition to the load — fifty pounds of bottled water or a towel — Jimi turns his long neck to stare at Zahid, baring his yellowing teeth and mucusy tongue, and lets out a series of long, wet, guttural bellows that echo off the dunes.

In the uneven landscape, Jimi is an uncomfortable, butt-numbing ride. So for most of the trip, he acts as a beast of burden, carrying all the gear as we walk.

With the load secured, our caravan moves out of the dunes onto the hard rocky pan that makes up most of the Sahara. The buttes that mark the Algerian border lie a few miles to our right. Keeping the dunes to our left, we walk past a herd of goats. A big-eared fennec fox eyes us from a distance.

An hour later, we run into a Berber family, their black camel-hair tent pitched on level ground about a mile from the dunes. The family has thirty camels and fifty goats grazing nearby. Two boys kick a soft soccer ball high in the air and give chase barefoot across shards of fossilized rock.

A man dressed in a flowing black and orange robe waves hello.

"*As-salaam 'alaikum* [Peace upon you]," he says.

His name is Abdullah, and while pouring tea for me he explains in so-so English that he is not a nomad, although he was born in the desert. He left when he was fifteen in search of steadier work. Now he sells carpets in Rabat, Morocco's capital city of 1.3 million people, a full day's journey by bus. He has come to visit his sister's family, who own the herds.

He invites us into the tent, which is tall enough to stand up in. In a back corner two baby goats keep warm under the tent flaps. Lately in Rabat, the "worries are more," Abdullah says. In the desert, the rest of the world seems so distant, less important in a way.

"Hard to relax in the city right now," he says. "Don't know what will happen next. What Morocco's role will be."

Abdullah had little formal schooling, but he can read the daily newspapers. He hopes the world situation doesn't destabilize the country, making it even harder for young people to find work. He's read about violent clashes at universities between Islamist student movements and government troops. He wonders how the country's allies will react if terrorist cells are found in Morocco, a country with a reputation as a bridge between Arab and Western countries.

Moroccans like to be thought of as the friendliest people on earth, Abdullah says.

"Everyone is a brother," he says. "But I fear some will take advantage of that."

The Welcoming Committee

The next day, we've been walking for an hour toward the next "weesis" when Jimi starts munching on a shrub. We all stop for a rest.

Hassan wants to know who worked in the World Trade Center and the size of the hijacked planes. His family doesn't have a TV, and he hasn't seen the footage. He's having difficulty fathoming the height of the Twin Towers.

"See that," I say, pointing to a six-hundred-foot dune. "Twice as tall as that."

He pauses a second, looking into the sky above the sandy peak. The tallest building in the biggest town he's visited is just a few stories high.

"How did they not fall down earlier?" he asks.

We arrive at the oasis just after noon. Zahid starts making lunch just for me. Zahid and Hassan cannot eat. Not yet, at least.

We are traveling in the middle of Ramadan, the holy month when Muslims are asked to renew their relationship with God through prayer and fasting. From dawn to dusk, Zahid and Hassan do not eat or drink, not even water.

Zahid seems at ease with the rigor. The younger Hassan, on the other hand, spends the day talking about water, drinking, and thirst.

He asks if Americans drink water right from the tap. What's the biggest lake I've ever seen? Could I drink from it? He explains, with a hint of envy, that a camel's kidneys can concentrate urine until it becomes thick like syrup and saltier than the ocean. Camels also extract so much water from their fecal pellets that they can be used right away for fuel, he says.

In the late afternoon, he wraps himself in a blanket and sleeps away a couple of hours. He says he dreams of eggs and toast and sardines.

Rejuvenated after eating the evening meal of dates, bread, and apples, Hassan convinces us to climb the big dune behind the oasis. With each step up the steep slope, the sand slides away underfoot. It's like climbing on a Stairmaster; our hearts pound and our thighs burn, but we don't really go anywhere. We change to a zigzag pattern and fifteen minutes later reach the peak.

A few lights from Taboumiat and neighboring Merzouga shine in the distance. Behind us, we can see the Algerian desert. The dunes seem dark and moody, all blues and blacks. As the moon rises, long shadows stretch across the sand.

Zahid asks about the mood in the big cities like Casablanca, Fez, and Marrakesh. Are there lots of military patrols? (No.) Do people seem worried? (A little.) Have I been harassed or threatened when people find out I live in the United States? (No.)

The next day we walk back into town, past the makeshift soccer field and the smattering of sand-colored homes with bright blue doors. I'm the one the locals will peer out their windows to see. They smile. I smile back. Are they suspicious, afraid? I have no way to know, but I don't think so. It seems more like curiosity, more like "How was the trip?" than "Don't cause any trouble." They have felt their own reverberations from September 11 but still want to share dinner and tea.

It has become clear to me that they live by a less suspicious ethos. Here, they presume I am okay. Back home, we demand proof.

I say goodbye to my two companions. In the days that follow, Hassan will help buy food for his family by selling some of the fossilized rocks he finds in the desert and later polishes to a shine. Zahid will hope for the knock on his door that signals the start of another trip.

I will cross back over the Atlas Mountains to Casablanca and fly home through New York City, the "grand buildings" missing from the skyline. Before the plane to Tampa takes off, a flight attendant asks if anyone on board knows how to speak Turkish. The heads in front of me pop up or crane down the aisle, eyeballing the tall, dark-skinned man near the door.

The looks say it all. Stranger, don't cause any trouble.

PETER CANBY

The Forest Primeval

FROM *Harper's Magazine*

I'VE JUST REACHED Makao, the most remote village in the Republic of Congo. I'm traveling with Stephen Blake, a British wildlife biologist, in a thirty-foot, outboard motor–powered pirogue — a dugout canoe — following the muddy, weed-clotted Motaba River north from its confluence with the Ubangui River. At first, after leaving the Ubangui, we passed small villages hacked out of the forest, but for a long time we've seen swamp interrupted only by the odd fishing camp: small bird nest–like huts and topless Pygmy women in grass skirts waving their catch forlornly as we motor by.

But now we've arrived at Makao, the end of the line, the last town along the Motaba. Ahead is pure, howling wilderness. Makao has a population of perhaps five hundred, half Bantu and half Bayaka — among the most traditional Pygmy tribes in Africa. The village long had a reputation as a poaching town, one of the centers of the extensive and illegal African "bush meat" trade, which, in the Congo basin alone, still accounts, annually, for a million metric tons of meat from animals that have been illegally killed. But since 1993 the poaching in Makao has all but ceased, and the village has taken on another significance: It is the back door to the Nouabalé-Ndoki forest. Nouabalé-Ndoki is named for two rivers, only one of which actually exists. The name of the existing river — Ndoki — means "sorcerer" in Lingala, the lingua franca of much of the two Congos. Nouabalé doesn't mean a thing. It's a misnomer for another river, the Mabale, inaccurately represented on a geographer's map in the faraway Congolese capital, Brazzaville.

Nouabalé-Ndoki is now a seventeen-hundred-square-mile national park known chiefly for having the least disturbed population of forest life in Central Africa. No one lives in the park, or anywhere nearby. Nouabalé-Ndoki has neither roads nor footpaths. It contains forest elephants, western lowland gorillas, leopards, chimpanzees, forest and red river hogs, dwarf and slender-snouted crocodiles, innumerable kinds of monkeys, and nine species of forest antelope, including the reclusive sitatunga and the supremely beautiful bongo. The southwest corner of the park is home to the famous "naive chimps" that sit for hours and stare at human intruders. Until biologists arrived just over ten years ago, few of these animals, including the chimps, had ever encountered humans.

Blake studies elephants. A self-proclaimed "working-class lad" from Dartford, England, Blake read zoology at the University of London; he is now working on a doctoral thesis about the migratory patterns of Nouabalé-Ndoki forest elephants at the University of Edinburgh. Thirty-six, fit, and lean, Blake is known as a scientist who likes the bush and is not afraid to go where wild animals live. But he's also considered audacious, a biologist who thinks nothing of crossing wild forests clad in sandals and a pair of shorts. Richard Ruggiero, who runs the elephant fund for the U.S. Fish and Wildlife Service and worked with Blake just after the park was established, compares him to nineteenth-century explorers: "He's someone who could walk across Africa, turn around, and then be ready to go back again." Another colleague described encountering him as he emerged from a long stint in the bush. "He was wearing torn shorts and a tattered T-shirt. He had a staph infection but seemed completely happy."

As part of his research, Blake has taken a series of what he calls "long walks" — foot surveys that start in Makao and follow a web of elephant trails up the Motaba and Mokala rivers to the park's northern border, cross the park from north to south, and then emerge from the headwater swamps of the Likouala aux Herbes River below the park's southern border. (The gorillas of the Likouala aux Herbes were the subject of Blake's master's thesis at Edinburgh.) Each of these treks — and Blake has made eight — covers about 150 miles and takes about a month. When I joined him, Blake was preparing to embark on his ninth and final trip along his survey route. I had heard of Blake's work from Amy Vedder, a program director at the Wildlife Conservation Society, which, along with the U.S. Fish and Wildlife Service and the Columbus (Ohio) Zoo, funds his research. Vedder and I had been discussing the toll that the region's wars have taken on its wildlife when she told me about Blake's long walks. I signed on to accompany him on his last one. At the time, it seemed a rare opportunity to see the Earth as it was thousands of years ago, at the moment when humans lived side by side with the great apes from which they evolved.

But now that I've reached Makao, I'm wondering why I made no special preparations for this trip. All the perils, which seemed theoretical before I left, have become disturbingly real. Not only don't we have phones or any means of communication; we also face threats of dengue fever, deadly malaria, the newly resurgent sleeping sickness, and even AIDS and Ebola, which are believed to have emerged from the forests of this region. I'm also afraid of army ants, ticks (eventually one crawls up my nose and inflates just at the top of my nasal passage), swarms of flies, and, above all, snakes. When I let slip that I am particularly nervous about snakes, Blake tells me about the Gabon viper, a fat, deadly poisonous snake with the longest fangs of any snake in the world. It often lies in ambush on Nouabalé-Ndoki trails. "The Gabon viper always bites the third person in line," Blake says glibly. "That's your slot."

The Wildlife Conservation Society maintains a field station in Makao, and we spend several days there assembling a crew. One morning, as Blake and I bathe in the Motaba while a cloud of blue butterflies swarms around us, he explains how his recruiting policy has been determined by local economics. Bush meat, he tells me, was a staple of the Congolese diet and, for many, the only available source of income. In Makao, the WCS provides jobs to people who are now forbidden by law to hunt; Blake himself has also sought to hire the best former hunters in order to keep them off the market. Practically speaking, this means recruiting the Bayaka, who live not just in Makao but also north and east of the park. Unlike Pygmies elsewhere in Africa, who are increasingly removed from hunting and gathering, many of the Bayaka still go into the forest for months, or even years, at a time, living off the land with little more than spears and homemade crossbows. Blake hires them because they know the forest intimately. "I often think every Bayaka should be awarded a doctorate in forest ecology," Blake says. "They know what's going on."

But Makao is ruled by Bantus, who, while dominant, know much less than the Bayaka about the forest. Blake would rather travel only with Bayaka, but, because of the dynamics of the village, he also hires Bantus. The relationship between the groups is complicated. The Bayaka Pygmies are small forest people — the men in Makao seem to average around five feet three — and presumably the original inhabitants of Central Africa. The Bantus, who are taller, are fishermen and slash-and-burn cultivators who migrated to the region several thousand years ago. The Bantus control Bayaka families; the Bayaka are expected to hunt for their Bantu owners and to work their manioc fields. In return the Bayaka get metal implements, notably cooking pots and spear points, made from automobile leaf springs; having acquired these things, they light off to follow a nomadic life in the forest. This arrangement is changing, however, as many Bayaka now live in the village year-round. Not all of the Bayaka still know how to make crossbows, recognize plants, or use spears. They can no longer survive in the forest.

Several of Blake's Bayaka recruits have accompanied him on earlier treks. They include one of Blake's oldest Bayaka friends, Lamba, who is named for a stout vine that winds helix-like up into the canopy trees, and Mossimbo, who is named for an elephant-hunting charm. But this time Blake is excited about a new recruit: Zonmiputu. Zonmiputu comes from one of the most traditional bands of the Makao Bayaka. Blake had met him on one of his early trips after a chance encounter, somewhere outside the park, with Zonmiputu's father's band, which had been living off the forest, following the ancient, intricate Bayaka way of life, for more than a year.

"They were carrying spears and homemade crossbows," Blake recalls. "They had one cooking pot, no water jugs, and a lot of baskets they'd made out of forest vines. Their clothes had worn out, and they'd gone back to wearing bark fabric."

As the first person ever to have employed the Bayaka, Blake is changing their lives. "Before they worked for me, their wives had to scrape for yams using sticks. Almost all their food was baked in leaves. Now one of them works for me for a month and makes enough money to buy a machete, a few clothes, a pot, and some fishhooks." Still, after returning from a month in the forest, Blake has frequently been confronted by Bantu *patrons* demanding the money he is about to pay "their" Pygmy. They react with incredulity when Blake won't give it to them.

As Blake and I talk by the river, I hear what I take for a birdcall. It's soon answered by a similar call — but at a harmonic interval — and then a third. Soon the river valley is full of strange syncopated harmonies. It's as if the trees themselves were singing. "Pygmies," Blake says when he sees my puzzled expression. "They're working the fields."

By the next day we've assembled our team — Zonmiputu, Lamba, Mossimbo, four other Bayaka, three Bantus, Blake, and me. Our walk begins another six hours up the river. We pile ourselves and our gear into the pirogue. Our "tucker," as Blake calls our food, comes from a market in the town of Impfondo along the Ubangui. It consists of sixty cans of tomato paste, two hundred cans of Moroccan sardines, forty cans of Argentine corned beef, twenty pounds of spaghetti, one hundred pounds of rice, several bags of "pili-pili" — the very hot, powdered African peppers — and large quantities of cooking oil, sugar, coffee, and tea. ("What's an Englishman to do in the forest without tea?" Blake asks.) We've topped off our supplies with three fifty-pound sacks of manioc flour and two baskets of smoked Ubangui River fish, bought from a fish merchant in an Impfondo courtyard.

We cast off early one morning. Above Makao, the riverbanks are uninhabited. It's late February — the end of the dry season — but the twenty-foot-wide river courses swiftly between marshy banks. We pass African fish eagles, perched on overhanging branches. Hornbills wing their way overhead, making otherworldly cries and beating the air with a ferocity that evokes the original archaeopteryx. Around ten in the morning an eight-foot, slender-snouted crocodile surfaces next to the boat and glances dispassionately at us. Our disembarkation point, from which the boatman will return the pirogue to Makao and we will begin walking, is near a fallen tree just below the juncture of the Motaba with one of its tributaries, the Mokala. I step ashore, look down at my pale, tender feet clad in rubber sandals, and wonder how I'm going to survive this expedition. In front of me, hearts of palm have been peeled — evidence of gorillas. Behind me Mossimbo spots fresh python skin, assumes the python is nearby, and leaps back in panic. Pythons here can grow to twenty feet; they strangle everything from antelopes to crocodiles. Everyone roars with laughter at Mossimbo's expense. The laughter covers the whir of the pirogue's motor as it pulls away, and when the Pygmies quiet down I hear the pirogue disappearing back downriver. My heart sinks.

Ten years ago the Nouabalé-Ndoki park didn't exist. The land was set aside after a decade of mass slaughter of elephants. During the 1970s a Japanese vogue for ivory signature seals, a consequent tenfold increase in the price of ivory, and a continent-wide collapse of civil authority combined to set off an orgy of elephant destruction. Poachers wielding AK-47s massacred entire herds for tusks, and then sold the ivory through illegal networks presided over by potentates like Jean-Bédel Bokassa, the cannibal emperor of the Central African Republic, and Jonas Savimbi, the murderous Angolan warlord. At the height of the slaughter, poachers were killing eighty thousand elephants annually. In the 1980s almost seven hundred thousand elephants were killed.

In 1989 conservation organizations intervened. The Convention on International Trade in Endangered Species (CITES), a widely supported treaty that regulates trade in endangered species, put African elephant ivory on its list of most-restricted commodities, thus effectively banning its international exchange. The market collapsed and conservationists rallied to save the remaining elephants. Africa has two types of elephants: *Loxodonta africana africana,* the bush elephant of the savannas, and *Loxodonta africana cyclotis,* the forest elephant. Biologists know a great deal about the savanna elephant, the world's largest land mammal, which is easy to spot and easy to monitor. But the forest elephants that Blake studies are smaller, more elusive creatures. Only recently identified as their own species, forest elephants live in Africa's impenetrable jungle, and their behavioral patterns — even their numbers — are almost entirely unknown.

As part of a continent-wide elephant census that began with the conservation efforts, the Wildlife Conservation Society and the European Economic Community contracted to estimate the elephant population in the north of the Republic of Congo. The north was then almost entirely unexplored but had recently been carved into forest blocks designated for European logging interests. Michael Fay, an American botanist and former Peace Corps volunteer who was studying western lowland gorillas, was hired to conduct the survey. Today, Fay is known for having made a twelve-hundred-mile "megatransect," a trek from Nouabalé-Ndoki to the coast of Gabon. But in 1989, Fay was just an adventurous graduate student and Nouabalé-Ndoki merely Brazzaville's name for an unexplored logging concession. Fay traversed Nouabalé-Ndoki with a group of Bangombe Pygmies. In the interior they found large numbers of forest elephants, western lowland gorillas, and chimpanzees that were unafraid of humans. Chimps are hunted everywhere in Africa, and their lack of fear in this instance led Fay to conclude that he and his team were the first humans they had ever seen. He decided that Nouabalé-Ndoki — unspoiled, vast, and teeming with wild animals — would make an ideal national park. Working with Amy Vedder and William Weber, directors of the Wildlife Conservation Society's Africa program, Fay wrote a proposal for a park that WCS, the World Bank, and the U.S. Agency for International Development agreed to fund. In a dramatic gesture that pleased conservationists, the government of Congo withdrew Nouabalé-Ndoki from the list of logging concessions. In December of 1993 it became a national park, with Michael Fay as its first director.

Early in his tenure, Fay recruited Blake to study wildlife at Nouabalé-Ndoki. In 1990, Blake had come to Brazzaville to work in an orphanage for gorillas whose parents had been killed in the bush-meat trade. In those days, Blake hung out with a group of De Beers diamond merchants. His best friend ("a cracking bloke") was an arms trader. He drank a lot of vodka, raced the orphanage car around Brazzaville, and ran a speedboat up and down the Congo River. But by 1993, Blake was ready for a change. When Fay asked him to work in the new park, Blake quickly accepted. He started as a volunteer. Fay remembers that he showed up "clad from head to toe and carrying an enormous green backpack that must have weighed five thousand pounds." In contrast, Fay had evolved a style of jungle travel that involved bringing Pygmies and packing light — one pair of shorts, Teva sandals, no shirt; he would wear the same clothes every day, wash them every night, and wrap blisters and cuts with duct tape. Blake rapidly adopted Fay's style and soon became, as Vedder puts it, Nouabalé-Ndoki's "wild-forest guy."

On his early surveys of the new park, Blake explored an elaborate network of elephant trails that crisscross the forest. Some trails were as wide as boulevards, and each seemed to have a purpose: One led to a grove of fruit trees, another to a river crossing, another to a bathing site. These trails existed only where there were no humans around to disrupt the elephants' lives. Outside the park, where there were human settlements, the trails vanished. Blake became certain that in the trail system was a map of the ecological and psychological mysteries of forest-elephant life. In 1997 he enrolled in the Ph.D. program at Edinburgh and began his thesis on the elephants of Nouabalé-Ndoki. "Elephants are kingpins of forest life," Blake says. "I have come to feel that if you could understand elephants you could really understand what was going on throughout the forest. Here's this bloody great big animal. It's disappearing, and we know bugger all about it."

In the years since he began his study, Blake's work has acquired a new sense of urgency, and this is one of the reasons he's invited me to join him on his long walk. In 1997, just as Blake was beginning his research, a civil war erupted in Brazzaville when the then-president, Pascal Lissouba, sought to disarm a tribal faction from the north. Protracted firefight leveled what had been one of Central Africa's few intact cities; ten to twelve thousand people were killed in Brazzaville alone. The violence also spread to rural areas, where a third of the country's population was displaced and uncounted numbers were killed. Many Congolese fled their villages and hid in the forest, where they died of disease or starvation while trying to subsist off wild game.

"People did a lot of atrocious things and got away with them," Blake says. "Every Tom, Dick, and Harry had an AK-47. You'd go into a tiny village and half a dozen sixteen-year-olds would come strutting down the street with bandannas and automatic rifles." The war led to more hunting. Although the park itself was spared, largely because of its remoteness, the surrounding elephant population, as Blake puts it, "got hammered."

This history has contributed to Blake's conviction that the isolation — indeed the very existence — of places like Nouabalé-Ndoki is imperiled. As we've traveled, I've noticed a certain desperation on his part, as if he were convinced that whatever he doesn't learn about the elephants on this trip will never be learned — and that all there is to know about forest elephants will be irrevocably lost.

"Fresh dung!" Blake exclaims. He sheds his daypack and pulls out his waterproof notebook. With a ruler, he measures the diameter of the dung pile (which looks like an oversized stack of horse manure), cuts two sticks, and begins to separate seeds from the undigested roughage.

We're four days up a wide-open elephant trail along the Mokala River. The trail is thick with dinosaur-sized elephant prints. There are also hoof marks of red river hogs; the seldom seen giant forest hog, which grows to six hundred pounds; and a pangolin, a seventy-five-pound nocturnal consumer of ants and termites that is covered in dark-brown scales that look like the shingles on a roof; as well as leopard prints and both rear foot and knuckle prints of a big gorilla. Overhead, troops of monkeys chatter and scold: spot-nosed guenons, gray-cheeked mangabeys, and the leaf-eating colobus. In spite of all the tracks and animals we've come across, however, we've found little evidence that elephants have been here recently.

We travel each day with one of the Bayaka acting as a guide while the other Bayaka and Bantus, who tend to be boisterous on what for them is a junket into the wilderness, cavort well behind us so that they don't scare away the animals. On this day, Blake's old friend Lamba has taken the lead, followed by Blake, and then me in the Gabon-viper slot. Lamba crouches over the dung pile while Blake isolates four types of seeds in it. Three of the four, he says, are dispersed only by elephants. One of these is the seed of a bush mango.

Lamba tells Blake that we're not seeing elephants along the trail because they've left the river for the hills, where the wild mangoes are bearing fruit.

"Most fruits are produced in fixed seasons," Blake says to me. "But there seems to be no pattern here with mangoes. They fruit whenever. It would be great if we could find lots of fruiting mangoes and lots of elephant signs. That's the kind of thing we're looking for, a few indicators of what moves elephant populations."

The most obvious explanation of what moves elephants is food, and Blake's research involves making a thorough study of the plants we encounter as well as chasing down feeding trails. We stop every twenty minutes so that he can make botanical notes. In order to create a definitive survey, Blake always follows the same route, varying it only when he makes side trips down feeding trails. He carries a Global Positioning System, a handheld device that translates satellite signals into geographic coordinates and which Blake uses to record the exact location of his observations. The Bayaka take care of navigation. Blake also carries a palm-sized computer, into which he enters his data. The use of such technology is new in wildlife biology. As Richard Ruggiero puts it, "[Blake]'s the first to use GPS and satellites to successfully look at the long-term movements of elephants in the forest. He's collected data no one else has looked at before."

But none of this matters if we don't see elephants. Despite Blake's estimate that as many as three thousand elephants use the park, the animals themselves elude us. They're hard to see because they are agile and fast: Forest elephants grow to nine feet at the shoulder and weigh up to eight thousand pounds but move with surprising stealth, thanks to a pad of spongy material on the soles of their feet, which dampens the sound of breaking branches. The elephants also communicate by using infrasound, a frequency below the range of human hearing. Once elephants have determined that intruders are present, they can warn one another over significant distances — without humans detecting the exchange.

Blake has attempted to make elephants easier to find in a number of ways. In the fall of 1998, he received a grant from Save the Elephants, a foundation run by noted elephant conservationist Iain Douglas-Hamilton, to outfit several elephants with GPS collars. Blake and Billy Karesh, a Wildlife Conservation Society field veterinarian, went deep into the forests of Central Africa with a high-powered tranquilizing rifle; they managed to sedate two elephants near Nouabalé-Ndoki and put collars on them. One of the collars never worked, but the second, placed on a female, worked for a month, long enough to trace the elephant's movements outside the protected forest.

The fewer signs we see of elephants, the more restless Blake becomes. "Amazing, isn't it," he muses. "Absolute bugger all."

On the fifth day, as we're walking along a ridge above the Mokala, Blake hears a branch snap. Zonmiputu is our guide. He is a quiet man, about five feet tall, an inch or two shorter than the rest of the Pygmies, and perhaps forty years old.

"*Ndzoko,*" Zonmiputu whispers. Elephant.

Quietly he puts down his pack, indicates the elephant's direction with his machete, and leads us at a crouch through the thick underbrush. After thirty-five yards, Zonmiputu stops and points out a shadowy shape looming twenty yards away. It is a young-looking bull, about eight feet at the shoulder, with deep chocolate-colored skin. I can see its brown tusks waving as it reaches up with its trunk and rips branches out of the surrounding trees. We approach. Blake hands me his binoculars. The elephant is now fifteen yards away, and I'm focused on its eye — a startling sight, sunken in the wrinkled skin, bloodshot; it seems to peer out from another epoch, as if it were looking forward at some huge, unfathomable span of time.

"A young bull," Blake whispers. "Perhaps twenty years old."

The bull senses that we're near, lifts its trunk toward us, and crashes off into the forest.

In the evening, sitting around the camp after dinner, I ask Blake to ask the Bayaka if any of them has ever killed an elephant. I know that Pygmies have traditionally hunted elephants with spears. As Blake relays the question, the Bayaka stiffen. It's illegal to kill elephants. They don't know why I'm asking, and they all say no — unconvincingly. All, that is, except Lamba. Blake refers to Lamba as "Beya," the Bayaka word for giant forest hog, because he has, as Blake puts it, "scabby habits." Having made this trip several times together, Lamba and Blake are perpetually laughing at each other, and, in front of Blake, Lamba doesn't bother to dissemble. He's killed three elephants with his spear, he tells us. He stalked the elephants and speared them in the gut. When necessary, he'd spear one a second time in the foot to prevent it from running.

For one of these elephants, which a Makao Bantu hired him to kill for its tusks, Lamba was paid an aluminum cooking pot. For another, he received a pair of shorts.

"This for a hunt that would have taken him weeks," Blake says hotly.

I ask Lamba whether he has any fear while hunting an elephant.

No, he doesn't, he responds, even though elephants can kill hunters. Gorillas, however, scare him. A mature male — a silverback — can grow to over four hundred pounds. He knows three Pygmies who've been killed while stalking gorillas.

"And do the Bayaka kill *people?*" Blake asks.

This elicits nervous laughter. Cannibalism is not unknown in this region, though no one has ever accused the Bayaka of eating people. But we're not far from Bangui, where, in modern times, Emperor Bokassa is said to have served human flesh at state dinners. Blake tells me that the first Frenchman to arrive in Makao in 1908 was eaten. "We found records of it in the colonial archives in Paris," he tells me. (Later, when looking in vain for a copy of the document at park headquarters, I turn up a similar complaint from another colonist whose son had been eaten in a nearby village.)

When the laughter dies down, we hear a roar in the hills. It's a gorilla beating its chest.

Talking to my fellow travelers requires several stages of translation. Most of our conversation is in Lingala, which Blake, the Bayaka, and the Bantus all speak. In addition to Lingala, however, the Bayaka speak Kaka, the Ubangui language of Makao Bantus, and Sango. Their own language — Bayaka — is Bantu-based, and if the Bayaka ever spoke an independent, non-Bantu language, it disappeared after the Bantu migration into the region thousands of years ago. As we progress farther into the forest, the Pygmies use words for plants and animals that are so specific they may be relics of an older Bayaka, the ancestral language of a forest-based people.

"There are four to five thousand plants in this forest," Blake says one day. "I know the botanical names of perhaps four hundred. Mossimbo knows the Bayaka names for probably twice that. Zonmiputu knows even more."

What the language gap means is that if I want to ask the Bayaka a question, I have to first ask Blake in English, who then translates it into Lingala, which often sets off a discussion in Bayaka, which is summarized in Lingala to Blake, who finally gives it back to me in English. Meaning is distorted — lost — in the process. My frustration rises as I gradually realize that not only do the Bayaka speak several human languages but they can also summon wild animals.

We are walking under a troop of monkeys one day when Lamba begins to whistle, a loud, repeated screech in imitation of an African crowned eagle, a canopy predator. The monkeys are already screaming at us, but Lamba's sound throws them into a state of agitation and draws them down to the trees' lower branches. Soon the forest resounds with the thrashing of limbs and the cracking of branches, as well as grunts, whistles, and alarmed chattering, as the monkeys react to being caught between the imagined eagle above them and the indefinable hominids below.

On another occasion, Lamba crouches down and makes a nasal call that imitates the distress call of a duiker, a type of forest antelope that has adapted to the lack of browse on the tropical forest floor by eating fruit, flowers, and leaves dislodged by canopy monkeys and birds. Immediately a blue duiker — only a foot tall, one of the smallest of the forest antelopes — charges out of the undergrowth. It has big eyes and a small, round nose. When it spots us, it pulls up short, then turns around and bolts. But it can't resist Lamba's call. It returns, stops, bolts again, and comes back — until Lamba finally breaks the spell by laughing at the antelope's confusion.

Later, we come across a herd of fifteen red river hogs rooting and grunting around the forest floor. These hogs grow to 250 pounds and have small, razor-sharp tusks. Our presence makes them skittish, but they don't flee. They may never have seen men before. We stalk until the closest hog is five yards away, just over the trunk of a fallen tree. Mossimbo then begins a wheezing-pig call. The pigs freeze, dash away, and then, spellbound, return nervously, almost compulsively. Mossimbo keeps calling until he has the biggest boars lined up across the trunk from us. Staring, entranced, their faces look extraterrestrial — tufted ears, long snouts, big sensitive eyes ringed with white; they seem unable to fathom just what they're looking at. Mossimbo squeals — an alarm. The pigs' eyes bug out, and they race off into the forest as Mossimbo erupts in laughter.

To me these episodes are fragmentary glimpses of a world in which humans and animals share a symbolic language. The Bayaka take great pleasure in their mastery over the animal world, and nearly every episode of their summoning animals ends in guffaws. It's not benevolent laughter. If Blake and I hadn't been present, each of these animals would certainly have wound up in a Bayaka cooking pot — and there's something about this nasty, exhilarating confidence that is quintessentially human.

We've come to a point where we must ford the crocodile-rich Mokala. The current is swift, the river bottom sandy, and the water up to our chins. We hold our bags above the water level and, shortly after we reach the far shore, wade across a tributary and enter the park. As we climb up the bank, we enter an area of closed canopy forest where the understory is more passable and the butts of the trees are eight and nine feet in diameter, with straight boles that explode into kingdoms of filigree high above. Zonmiputu is again in the lead when he stops stock-still, turns back to us, and whispers, "*Koi.*" Leopard.

Through a gap in the underbrush, we make out a pattern of dark rosettes on a brown background. The impression gradually resolves into the abdomen and haunch of a large leopard. As we watch, it glides out of the frame, its snaky tail trailing behind.

Zonmiputu crouches, clears his throat, and makes a duiker call to try to fool the leopard into coming to investigate. Through another gap, I see the leopard hesitate, then break into a run. It's gone.

Although leopards are not commonly believed to attack humans, the Pygmies claim they do. Several days earlier, Mossimbo had pointed out a pile of leopard scat filled with reddish-brown hair. Blake poked around in it long enough to discover a strange brown cylinder the size and color of a cigar butt. Using a stick, we rolled it over. I leapt back in horror. It was the top half of a finger, the nail still intact.

"Chimpanzee," Blake said.

The eerie discomfort of the forest is beginning to overwhelm me. One night, I'm inside my tent in the grips of a dream. I'm being suffocated by vines, buried until only my face is exposed. Slowly I'm being pulled into the earth. I awake with a start, pull out my flashlight, and check my watch. It's four-thirty in the morning. The air inside the tent is thick and stifling. Outside, water drips from leaves, unseen creatures scurry, branches snap, beasts hoot and squeak. Overhead, I feel the claustrophobic weight of tropical foliage. Tonight's dream is one of a series that has become vivid — houses I used to live in, offices I've worked in, visits with friends — and I wonder if this is what it's like to be dead. My restless spirit is haunting the places I loved.

Dawn is filtering down to the forest floor. I hear the rest of the camp stirring: The Pygmies whack their machetes into dead branches and clang our battered, soot-covered aluminum pots over the fire. I hear Blake yawning in his tent. He calls out to ask how I've slept. I lie and tell him I've slept well. But now, at six in the morning, this trip has become oppressive. Breakfast arrives: a mound of glutinous white rice covered with Moroccan sardines and the leftovers of last night's smoked-fish stew. Gloomily, I tuck in. Blake asks if I find the forest claustrophobic. I lie again and tell him no, but it's a bad line of thinking, because today in fact I do. Neither am I heartened by the fact that today we're not moving camp. While Blake goes off to do some elephant-feeding studies, I'll have to spend the day alone with the Bayaka.

The Bayaka and I leave camp around eight, cross a stream, head up into the hills, and wander, foraging for wild mushrooms, yams, seasonal fruit, a bark that tastes like garlic, a bark that serves as an antibiotic, a bark containing quinine, an edible vine in the legume family, a sapling that is said to act like Viagra — in short, whatever the forest will provide. With Blake, we follow elephant trails and walk purposefully in single file. With the Bayaka we maintain no consistent direction. My compass becomes useless. I cling to my guides.

My first Bayaka encounter occurred as Blake and I stepped from our pirogue into the waiting crowd at the riverside. A kindly-looking old Bayaka in a torn shirt stepped out from the back of the crowd and headed straight for me. He grasped my hand, stared curiously into my eyes, and wouldn't let go.

"He just wanted to see what kind of a person you are," Blake explained, once I'd pried my hand free.

It was almost as if the old Bayaka recognized me. If he had, it wouldn't have been entirely far-fetched. Douglas Wallace, the geneticist who has made a career reconstructing human migrations around the globe through rates of change in mitochondrial DNA, believes that the Bayaka are descended from a small group of Paleolithic people who once roamed across eastern Africa. Wallace and several others argue that a population genetically very close to the present-day Bayaka were the first modern humans to leave Africa some fifty thousand years ago. "We are looking at the beginning of what we would call *Homo sapiens*," he wrote recently.

In other words, I live in New York, but I'm also the long-lost cousin of the Bayaka, the depigmented descendant of their ancestors who hiked over the horizon and never came back — until now.

Strolling through the forest, I've noticed that my cousins appear to be in a perpetual Wordsworthian idyll; they often gaze dreamily upward, as if contemplating the god that has provided them with such sylvan abundance. At one point, I convey this impression to Blake. He corrects me. "What they're looking for is not divinity but wild honey. Although, for them, it's pretty much the same thing."

Sure enough, my day with the Bayaka devolves into a honey hunt. There are several kinds of wild honey in the forest; one belongs to a stinging bee. Mossimbo doesn't take long to spot what he takes for a stinging-bee hive high overhead, sixty feet up, in a hole in a tree branch. The Bayaka rapidly build a fire and extinguish it. Mossimbo wraps the coals in a bundle of leaves, straps the bundle on his back, grabs a machete, and effortlessly shinnies up a liana along the branchless tree trunk. Soon he's vanished into the foliage, and all we can hear is his machete hacking into a tree branch. Finally he descends with two dry honeycombs.

"*Chef,*" he says, drawing on his minimal French for the first time. "*C'est fini.*"

The hive has been abandoned.

After several more hours of wandering, the Pygmies spot a more accessible stingless sweat-bee hive, climb the tree, and soon revel in honey that tastes watery, smoky. I sample it, but to me it's an offputting soup of bark, twigs, grubs, and dead and dying bees. I leave it to the Pygmies.

After we leave the hive, the sweat bees pursue us vengefully. We're squatting down in front of a pile of bush mangoes, shucking the seeds out of the hardened pits, when I'm suddenly overcome with helplessness. A large part of my frustration comes from the language. Blake is not here to translate my questions. But I'm not just deprived of speech today; I'm also faced with the fact that the forest, which is such a source of bounty to the Bayaka, is, to me, an undifferentiated mass. I don't have the vocabulary to break this environment down into parts. There's nothing I can parse, nothing I can usefully understand. I'm completely at a loss without words. The Pygmies see that I'm wilting.

"Papa," Mossimbo says, affectionately, handing me a mango seed.

By the time we get back to camp, it's thick with tsetse and filaria flies. Tsetse flies carry sleeping sickness. Filaria flies can deposit the larva of parasitic worms in a human's bloodstream. (Blake later comes down with fly-borne elephantiasis.) One of the Bantus slaps a tsetse that is feasting on my back, leaving the dead insect lying in a pool of my blood. I think of what Blake told me when I'd been bitten earlier by a tsetse. "No one can tell me those flies can't transmit AIDS. All you need is a few viral cells. We're in the Congo, after all, and the AIDS problem is huge."

As the afternoon ends, I'm not fit for anything but crawling inside my tent.

The flies disappear at sundown, and I re-emerge for dinner. Smoked fish again. This time it's served with manioc, a cloying flour made from the tuberous root of the cassava plant. After our meal, the Bayaka pull out *djamba* — marijuana — a substance that the Bayaka value only slightly less than wild honey. As they have on many nights, the Bayaka roll the marijuana in forest leaves and inhale deeply. Tonight the ensuing hilarity seems greater than usual. Since all the jokes are in Bayaka or Lingala, I ask Blake for explanations. The Pygmies have asked him if I'm rich, he says. Obligingly, he has told them that I am the richest man in the world.

"You're their new culture hero," he says.

I try to imagine what might have led the Pygmies to speculate about my wealth, and remember that, in addition to the Tevas I wear most days (we're constantly in and out of water), I have two pairs of sneakers, one of which I haven't even worn. Three pairs of shoes! Extravagant, prodigal — *rich.*

I retire to my tent and, crawling in, notice that the ground under the tent floor is blotched with patches of light. I have smoked the *djamba,* and the tent floor looks like a city at night seen from an airplane. Until I figure out that it's a phosphorescent fungus, this vision offers consolation, if only because it reminds me that there is a city out there, somewhere in the world. I fall asleep and have another strange Ndoki dream. A woman appears and teaches me the supernatural art of being in two places at once.

*

We've reached the line of *bais* stretching from north to south that defines the center of the park's elephant life. The word "*bai*" is derived from the French "*baie*," but it has escaped into local usage to describe a miniature savanna maintained by forest elephants in the middle of the forest. "If elephants are lost from an area," Blake says, "*bais* quickly grow over."

One afternoon, Blake and I follow the elephant trails to the Bonye River *bai*. The *bai* is big, the size of three football fields, and it's the first open terrain we've seen since leaving Makao. The afternoon light is soft and golden, playing on the riffling surface of the river as it winds through the clearing. In the water, about seventy-five yards away, are nine forest elephants — four adults and five young, three of them infants. As we watch, an old matriarch ambles out of the forest, followed by two more young and another adult female. The matriarch reaches the riverbed, kneels, drills her trunk into the white sand, and gurgles as she sucks mineral-rich water out of the streambed. When she pulls her trunk up, she sprays river water into her mouth. Upstream, a wading bird picks at the riverbed while three red river hogs browse on the marsh grass, trying to avoid the playful charges of one of the baby elephants. On the far margins a sitatunga, with its distinctive wide, splayed feet, feeds quietly.

During the next hour and a half there is a constant coming and going until we've seen thirty elephants in all. The young ones prance around and engage in mock fights, and the adults spray themselves and their children, as the sunlight flashes in the water droplets. Blake looks blissful. He creeps forward to the edge of the *bai*, quietly sets up a video camera, pulls out his notebook, and begins sketching what are the most distinctive and identifying features of individual elephants: their ears. He'll exchange these later with Andrea Turkalo, a forest-elephant researcher who is studying the social structures of elephant herds in a Dzanga Sangha *bai* across the border in the Central African Republic.

I sit on a fallen tree trunk, relieved, enjoying the light. Elephants are members of the ancient, highly successful order of Proboscidea, which, historically, has contained almost two hundred different trunked and tusked species, including mastodons and mammoths. Beginning fifty million years ago, and as recently as the late Pleistocene, ten thousand or so years ago, proboscideans roamed the globe. Mastodons and mammoths grew up to fifteen feet. But there were also pygmy elephants. (A four-foot-tall elephant, *Elephas falconeri,* survived on the Greek island of Tilos until a little over four thousand years ago. A dwarf mammoth lived on Wrangel Island off Siberia until 1700 B.C.) Then, toward the end of the Ice Age, elephants died off en masse, and today only two species survive — the Asian elephant, *Elephas maximus,* and its bigger cousin, the African elephant, *Loxodonta africana.* Both of these species evolved in Africa, but *Elephas* moved into Asia and then became extinct in its home range. Some argue that only then — about forty thousand years ago — did *Loxodonta africana,* which had been exclusively a forest creature, emerge to seize the open savanna.

The mass proboscidean die-off was part of the mysterious and more general Pleistocene extinctions. Sometime between ten and twenty-five thousand years ago, all mammals weighing more than a ton — as well as many lighter than that — disappeared from Europe, Asia, and the Americas. This is an old story. But the other story is that some elephants survived — as a miracle, emissaries from the prehistoric world.

From Bonye *bai* we head south to Little Bonye *bai,* Mabale *bai,* and, ultimately, Mingingi *bai,* the epicenter of elephant life in the park. Blake points out the various fruit trees associated with elephant trails. The most conspicuous of these, he says, is *Duboscia macrocarpa,* a large tree with an almost gothically fluted trunk. Virtually every duboscia we see stands at the intersection of several elephant trails, gracefully alone in a clearing made by fruiting-season elephant traffic to the tree. Another regular tree along the trails is *Omphalocarpum elatum,* which has fruit growing out of the side of its trunk. The fruit is encased in a heavy, hard-shelled ball — the size of a medicine ball — which the elephants like well enough to dislodge by ramming the tree with their heads.

"The importance of fruit trees for forest elephants has only recently been acknowledged," Blake says. "And that's because almost all elephant research has been based on savanna elephants, which eat very little fruit. In fact, many conclusions drawn from savanna-elephant research are simply not applicable to forest elephants. It's always amazing to me that elephants get lumped in categories the way they do."

As we walk, Blake confesses to me his obsession with the rocker Chrissie Hynde, and in particular with her song "Tattooed Love

Boys." And one evening, after we arrive in camp, Blake spots
Lamba sprawled across his bags. Blake takes his daypack, lifts it
over his head, stands over Lamba as if to hurl it down, and recites:

> Run to the bedroom.
> In the suitcase on the left,
> You'll find my favorite axe.
> Don't look so frightened.
> This is just a passing phase,
> One of my bad days.
> Would you like to watch TV?
> Or get between the sheets?

Lamba is baffled but, with the rest of the Bayaka, laughs nervously. "'One of My Turns,' by Pink Floyd," Blake explains to me.
"You never heard *The Wall* concert they played in Berlin, did you?
There's that whole debate about stadium concerts. I'm not that big
a fan of stadium concerts, but that was a great concert."

As we're ducking under some vines, we see our first snake. It's in
the branches overhead — a big, evil-looking thing nearly five feet
long. Blake can't identify it, but it's not one of the famously poisonous snakes of this region — not a boomslang, not a black mamba,
not one of the several cobras. The Bayaka give us their name for it,
say it's bad, and seem anxious to get away from it. "Can you imagine how many others we haven't seen?" says Blake.

Shortly afterward we scare a leopard off a fresh-killed duiker.
The duiker's entrails are ripped out, but it's still warm. The Bayaka
tie up the duiker and take it along for our dinner.

We're wading in the sandy shallows of the Mabale River when we
discover a dead baby elephant. It's a gruesome and disturbing
sight; the elephant, the size of a pony but stouter, is half submerged, covered in flies, and leaking blood from its trunk.

At this same spot last evening, we saw one of the elephants Blake
had collared two years earlier now standing in the river, still wearing her nonfunctioning transmitter. Considering the size of the
park, this was quite a coincidence. And not only did we see her yes
terday but we saw her with a young elephant following close behind
her; at the time she was collared, she had been pregnant, and this
young elephant looked about a year old — the appropriate age.
Now, it seems, that baby is dead.

"Hell of a thing," says Blake, pacing back and forth. "Hell of a thing." He picks up the baby elephant's trunk, lets it flop back into the water, and examines the tiny tusks and the toenails on each foot. He picks up a stiff leg and turns the little creature over, looking for some telltale sign of what killed it, but he can't find anything except a group of puncture wounds on the animal's chest. With snakes on my mind, I suggest that the wounds might be the result of Gabon-viper bites — and that the elephant may have died of hemolytic bleeding. Blake is unimpressed but seems distressed that he can't come up with an explanation. He frets, hovers, pulls out his notebook and takes notes, gets his video camera and shoots pictures. He is reluctant to leave.

Looking over the little creature, dead of unknown causes, I'm struck again with a sense of being dead — the idea that this lifeless body could be mine. After a quarter of an hour, I persuade Blake to give up his forensics, and we start up a trail — only to turn back ten minutes later. He has decided the puncture wounds are the result of a leopard attack.

"If we could demonstrate that a leopard could kill a baby elephant, it would be quite a thing," he says.

We wade back into the river. Blake pulls out his knife and makes precise incisions along the puncture wounds, two of which go straight through the elephant's chest and into its lungs. A punctured lung could be the source of the bleeding through the trunk. The elephant could have drowned in its own blood. Blake's hypothesis about the leopard suddenly seems plausible.

"Hell of a thing. Hell of a thing," Blake repeats to himself, still agitated, but in much better spirits now that he's arrived at a theory. It occurs to me that science is formidable, and not merely for its accomplishments but because faith in reason leads people to brave treacherous environments like this one.

We camp along the Mingingi River, a mile or so below the *bai*. The day is sultry, buggy. Thunderclaps rumble across the distant forest, and late in the afternoon we're drenched by a brief downpour. But the weather clears overnight, and I awake at three in the morning to gorilla calls echoing up the valley, elephants trumpeting from the *bai* above, and moonlight illuminating the side of my tent.

In the morning we head up to the *bai*. The approach paths are wide and parklike, and the landscape has been designed by elephants. They have dug bathing pools out of the hillsides. The underbrush has been cleared of patches of forest, and tree trunks are swollen to exotic shapes from elephants having picked away their bark. We find a meadow surrounding a highly polished termite nest — an elephant rubbing post surrounded by the marks of heavy traffic and worn down so far that it looks somehow like a public monument.

We creep forward toward the edge of the *bai,* a huge open space of marshy grassland and isolated clumps of trees. A shower has just passed and the mist is lifting off the forest all around. Swallows are dipping in the river. A white palm-nut vulture with its hooked yellow beak is perched on a dead tree limb. A single bull is drinking from a pool.

Just as we're preparing to walk out into the river, nine bongos — large forest antelopes — emerge out of the underbrush and wade into the middle of the *bai,* tails flicking, sides adorned with vertical white stripes, their celestial-looking horns curving gracefully skyward.

Lamba hears what he says is a yellow-backed duiker, the largest of the duikers. We're beyond Mingingi, in the center of the park. We squat while Lamba calls. No response. He calls again. A stick snaps. Silence. Lamba calls a third time. Another stick snaps, off to our right. I wheel around and see two heads duck quickly behind a termite mound. It's a strange, stealthy gesture. The heads are humanlike. We're not the only ones stalking; we're being stalked. Chimpanzees, thinking they're going to find a wounded duiker, have instead found their nearest primate cousins.

"It's just the lads," Blake says, "checking us out."

Along with baboons — and of course humans — chimpanzees are the only primates who regularly kill other mammals. In Nouabalé-Ndoki, chimpanzees set methodical ambushes for the leaf-eating colobus monkeys and even for duikers. They also scavenge other meat — including pigs — and Blake tells me that in the past he has called in chimpanzees by hiding behind tree roots and making duiker calls.

"When they respond to the duiker call, they come for the kill," Blake says. "The males are quite a sight with their hair standing on end. They come whipping around the tree root, see us, and just deflate. They've never seen humans before. I've had one sit and stare at me for five minutes."

In his book *The Third Chimpanzee,* the physiologist Jared Diamond argues that humans are close enough to chimpanzees to properly be thought of as a third chimpanzee species (after chimpanzees and bonobos). The DNA of chimpanzees is 98.4 percent the same as ours, and of the remaining 1.6 percent, most is insignificant. The meaningful genetic differences could be focused in as little as one-tenth of one percent; they account for the genes that lengthened our limbs (allowing us to walk upright and use tools) and, more importantly, altered, as Diamond puts it, "the structure of the larynx, tongue, and associated muscles that give us fine control over spoken sounds." Indeed, a group of scientists have recently isolated a single gene that may underlie the human ability to speak. These scientists are presently trying to determine when this gene evolved. One theory dates it to only fifty thousand years ago — around the time the ancestral Bayaka left Africa and set out to explore the world.

We're in chimpanzee territory now, and after our stalking encounter we find signs of chimps everywhere. We hear them pounding on tree trunks and howling like coyotes out in the forest. We see their skillfully made nests in the trees and the ingenious traps they've set at termite nests, but we don't see the chimps themselves. Noticing that I've become preoccupied with spotting a chimp, Lamba volunteers that the Bayaka make a chimp-hunting charm, but when I ask him about it he averts his eyes. The next day one of the Bantus speaks up. "*Chef,*" he says to Blake, "Lamba was lying. There's no chimp-hunting charm — only a gorilla-hunting charm."

A few nights later, Zonmiputu strips a liana down into fine strands and dries the strands over the fire. ("It's *Manneophyton fulvum,* the liana they use for making hunting nets," Blake explains.) Zonmiputu tosses the mass of shredded vine to Manguso, another of the Bayaka. Taking the mass of vine with him, just at sunset, Manguso climbs into the lower branches of a tree. He makes gentle sounds, gorilla sounds — imploring noises, soft exclamations, sounds of surprise — all the while weaving whatever he's expressing into a rope.

"You do it this way," Zonmiputu explains, "so you can get the gorilla up in a tree."

It's the gorilla-hunting charm.

"Not every Bayaka knows how to make this," Blake says to me. "These people are disappearing as fast as the elephants, and their knowledge is disappearing with them."

Two days later, I'm wearing the charm bandolier-style across my chest when Zonmiputu sees me. He looks alarmed. He's made the gorilla charm for me, but one of the other Bayaka is supposed to wear it. Such things are supposed to be worn only by initiated Bayaka — but we can't, of course, talk to each other, and I only learn about this prohibition later. Zonmiputu sends one of the Bantus to explain that if I come across an elephant, I must take it off. Otherwise the elephant will become mean.

We smell the gorillas before we see them. There's a dusky odor along the trail. The gorillas are just ahead of us, and apparently they smell us. There's a loud crash of tree branches, and a silverback barks, then ignominiously flees. A female with an infant on her back and two juveniles are caught in the trees. For the next ten minutes, they try to muster the nerve to descend and flee. Eventually, the mother, the infant, and one of the juveniles make deathdefying leaps to the ground and run off into the underbrush. The remaining juvenile stays behind, defiantly pounding his little chest until we move along and leave him in peace.

"They're in for a shock when the loggers get here," Blake says.

We're now out of the park and in the Pokola logging concession, which is leased to the German-owned, French-managed company Congolaise Industrielle des Bois (CIB). Blake, who was jubilant while in the forest, now seems depressed.

"Our wilderness walk is over as far as I'm concerned," he says. "We're now in the realm of man."

The prospecting line, however, is only the first sign of what Blake refers to as the park's "biggest land management issue" — industrial logging. CIB now has the rights to two of the three concessions surrounding the park, and over the next twenty years the entire forest surrounding the park will be selectively logged. What this means, Blake says, is that in twenty years the only intact forest in the north of Congo will be Nouabalé-Ndoki.

Logging itself is not the most dangerous threat to wildlife. Loggers in the region generally confine themselves to removing only two species of African mahogany that bring high enough prices on the European market to justify the expense of transporting them. (A single African mahogany log might bring $4,000 on the dock at a European port.) The additional light brought to the forest floor as trees come down may even promote the growth of ground ferns favored by many large mammals, including elephants, and logging may *increase* densities of certain animals. But by building roads, bringing in thousands of foreign workers, and creating a cash economy, logging has invariably led to uncontrolled killing of animals — poaching. CIB is working with the Wildlife Conservation Society and the Congolese government to develop wildlife management within logging concessions and to control poaching, but it remains an ominous situation.

"The big issue," Blake told me, "is for the logging companies to take responsibility for hunting in their concessions. It's not a feasible argument for us to say they shouldn't be here — Congo needs revenue, and we'd be laughed out of the country. Controls on hunting, the prohibition on the export of bush meat, and the importation of beef or some other source of protein are about the extent of our demands on the company."

We descend the Bodingo peninsula, an elevated ridge of land south of the park's border that runs down into the Likouala aux Herbes swamps. We soon discover that more than a prospecting line has been cut through the forest. CIB has surveyed much of the peninsula, marking off the commercially valuable trees with stakes in the ground. The prospectors appear to have been accompanied by a party of Pygmy hunters. We see abandoned snares and places where trapped animals have struggled to free themselves by digging holes in the ground and raking trees with their claws in attempts to escape.

The forest has been cut up in a grid, letting in light, leaving it curiously thin. Taking in the devastation around us, I realize that what's lost when a forest is cut is the weight of evolutionary history, the whole sequence of life, all the voices that the Bayaka can still understand — the voices that existed in nature before we other primates found a way to describe, and circumscribe, the world around us.

Blake is studying an African mahogany that's been marked for harvest. Its dense trunk, which is ten feet in diameter and has oaklike bark, soars upward toward the canopy. "That tree may be nine hundred years old," he says. "Soon it will be gone. Just like that."

We continue down the peninsula and launch off into the swamps. Tsetse flies are in evidence, along with sword grass, thorn forest, army ants. We sprint through the ant columns. We sleep on patches of raised earth, bathe in mud puddles, and drink coffee-colored water out of stagnant pools. One day Lamba finds a green-ish-water-filled excavation — the home, he explains, of an African dwarf crocodile. He squats down and makes a birdlike sound. Soon eight little crocodile heads nervously broach the algae-green surface, their elevated eyes popping up like bubbles.

I am walking behind Zonmiputu when I look up and spy a spider the size of a dessert plate crawling up his back toward his hair and his collar. "Putus!" I shout, using his nickname. Zonmiputu freezes. This is distressing. Zonmiputu is supposed to be invulnerable. I run up behind him, intending to brush the spider off. But the spider has a furrowed, lethal-looking body and strong hairy legs that are tensing as if it is preparing to leap. I grab a stick and whisk the spi-der into the bushes. Zonmiputu turns around, looks at my spider pantomime, grimaces, shudders, and hurries back along the trail.

In Nouabalé-Ndoki there is always the unnerving sensation that something is watching you. A mongoose creeps through the under-brush; a tree snake twirls along a branch. Today, as we scramble over root snarls, plunge thigh-deep through pools of mud, and ap-proach Terre de Kabounga, the end of our walk, we come across the fresh trail of a crocodile and then hit something that really stops us: a human footprint in the mud. It's so fresh that it's still fill-ing with water. Someone has spotted us, and he's hiding.

The Bayaka find the trail and follow it. We hit dry land and soon hear a woman singing, a meandering, flutelike voice. A tall, grace-ful Bantu woman, clad in brightly colored wax-print African fab-rics, her hair in cornrows, is gathering firewood and, though she has seen us, defiantly continues her song. Before long a husband emerges. He's a square-shouldered, handsome man, the school-teacher, he tells us, from the nearby town of Bene. He hasn't been paid in three years, so he closed down the school and left his stu-dents, the future of Africa, to fend for themselves. He moved out into the swamps, along with a good part of the rest of this region's shattered population, to smoke fish and hunt bush meat.

We follow the schoolteacher and his wife to their camp. It's filled with fish and hung with shotguns. Other relatives come out of the forest to stare at us in wonder. They direct us to a path that leads, an hour later, to the cut-over edge of the forest. We emerge onto a red-clay road, blinking and squinting in the harsh, flat light of the open road. The heat, unfiltered by the forest, hits like a blast furnace. We shake hands in a gesture of shared congratulation, but the triumph feels hollow. We've been dreaming of the human world, but now that we've arrived it's disorienting.

We walk for hours. Late that afternoon a big, flatbed Mercedes drives up. The driver is so drunk he can barely stand. The ten of us find space in back among twenty-seven other passengers, sacks of manioc tubers, baskets of smoked fish, mounds of edible leaves, and the carcasses of several dead duikers. Soon we're being carried off toward the logging town of Pokola at such high speeds that at times the big truck seems to go airborne. I offer a silent prayer that, having survived a month in the forest, I won't be killed in a car crash. ‹

A decade ago, Pokola was a tiny fishing village on the Sangha River. It's now a sprawling shantytown built of scrap mahogany. In its busy market, the Bayaka spend their pay outfitting themselves in bright sports clothes until they look, in Blake's words, "like Cameroonian soccer stars." Blake and I drink wine with the French logging managers inside their fenced-off compound. I pull the tick out of my nose. Before I know it, I'm back in New York, where I am treated for schistosomiasis, amoebic dysentery, and whipworms.

Blake's ninth and last "long walk" capped the first phase of his doctoral research and gave him the data to begin writing his thesis. Since our trip he has returned to the interior of Nouabalé-Ndoki several times to collar more elephants and collect data to support his argument that by disseminating the seeds of forest-fruit trees, elephants play a crucial role in the evolution of Central African forests.

But in the interim, civil war has broken out again, and Blake reports that since our trip all of the remaining concessions in the north of Congo have been leased to logging companies. A new sawmill is being built north of the park, and a logging road now runs straight into Makao. Another road cuts across the Bodingo peninsula close to the park's southern border. The place where we saw the gorillas, Blake reports, is already a lacework of logging trails. "The civil war was a disaster for the country," he says. "If there'd never been a civil war, the government might have been more open to conservation. Now development and reconstruction have become the country's highest priority.

"In many ways," he says, "what we saw is already gone."

SCOTT CARRIER

Over There

FROM *Harper's Magazine*

Getting Oriented, Mazar-e-Sharif

IT'S THE END of November and, just in town, I decide to go for a walk. I leave the hotel, cross the street to the mosque, and gaze up at the blue-tiled dome. The instant I stop walking four or five young men also stop, as if they'd just been pretending to be going somewhere. They stand right in front of me. Then quickly there are ten, then thirty, fifty — all boys and men, crowding close together, a hundred eyes looking at me in disbelief.

"Where are you from?" a teenage boy asks.

"America," I say, wondering if this is wise, because we've just bombed their city and their country. But it's the word they want to hear, they want to say it. America . . . America . . . America . . .

"California," I say, wanting to hear it echo. "Mississippi."

Three or four try to speak English. "Hello, how are you?" "Thank you very much." "Okay, good luck, good-bye."

"What do you think about America bombing your country?" I ask the first boy. "Was it a good thing or a bad thing?"

"It was a good thing. When the Taliban here, there was no working, nothing working. Now America comes here. Is it correct? America comes here?"

"You mean will American soldiers come here? I don't know, maybe." He translates this for the crowd, and they start shouting questions, too many to translate. Sort of frustrated, he says, "We want money to make work. We want now the schools."

"I think there might be some money, but I don't know, we might start bombing some other country and forget about Afghanistan."

This makes the yelling get louder. They're not yelling at me, just yelling for the sake of yelling, filling the space with their voices. I look down at a guy in a small cart. One of his legs is missing and the other is very short, like a baby's. He says he needs a new cart, a real wheelchair with bicycle tires like they make in America, and some artificial limbs like they make in America, and he wants to know if I can get him some.

"I don't know how to do that," I say, "but it's possible. I think that's one of the things there will be money for." They just keep pressing in, getting closer and closer, and it's time to get going. So I say, "Okay, good luck, good-bye," and wave and quickly walk back to the hotel.

From the porch on the third floor, I can see 150 soldiers and forty pickup trucks parked outside the gate of the Ministry of Foreign Affairs. Parked inside the courtyard is a black Audi sedan belonging to General Abdul Rashid Dostum, the ethnic Uzbek warlord soon to be named deputy defense minister for the interim government. His men have no uniforms but carry Kalashnikovs and backpacks holding clusters of shoulder-launched grenades, like carnations still in the bud. They wear turbans and black plastic slippers and look half-primitive, like Indians with pickups instead of horses. They're waiting, kicking back. The war is over and they are waiting for the next one to begin.

I climb three more floors to the roof for a view of the whole city. There are a couple of taller buildings in town, but they're blocks away from the center, the mosque. An elaborate piece of turquoise jewelry with two domes and two towers, surrounded by trees and walkways, the mosque is thought to hold the tomb of Ali — cousin and son-in-law of the Prophet Mohammed, and the fourth caliph of Islam — and is said to be Afghanistan's most magnificent. Mazar-e-Sharif, which means "tomb of the saint," is a city of adobe tenements that look ancient, all somewhere in the process of crumbling and collapsing. In the street men pull carts with wooden wheels; other carts are pulled by horses and donkeys, carrying wood and bricks. There are shops with skinned goats hanging upside down out front, shops where chairs and tables are made, shops with material for clothing and drapes. Subtract the cars and the shop where the guy makes satellite dishes from pieces of scrap metal, and ignore the occasional Russian-made proletarian concrete building, and the city would look thirteenth century or even older.

Mazar sits on a long flat barren desert that flanks the northwestern slope of the Hindu Kush. This is where two very old and very important roads converge: the Great Silk Road connecting China and the Middle East, and an intersecting route linking Russia and India. Sixty miles to the north is the Amu Darya, once called the Oxus — a big river with cold, muddy, and fast-moving water. Twenty miles to the south the jagged snow-covered peaks of the Hindu Kush begin to rise. The snow that these mountains pull from the clouds becomes the runoff water that makes living in this desert possible, but a three-year drought has brought thousands of refugees to Mazar, people who were displaced not because of fighting but because their land dried up. I saw some of them as I came into the city — they live in empty lots under pup tents made from blankets and sheets of plastic — or, actually, I just saw the field of little tents. There were no people there. It may have been only the idea of a refugee camp.

Again I go out for a walk, and again I stop, and again four or five men around me immediately also stop, and again a crowd quickly forms. This time I pull out my camera and start taking pictures. They become quiet and still, not afraid or shy of the camera but also not quite sure of its power. I hold it at arm's length down low and they stare straight at the lens and I take their pictures. While I'm doing this I hear a voice, a soft, calm voice next to my ear, say, "Excuse me, are you a journalist?" I turn and see a young man with a shaved head — which is kind of startling — and say, "Sort of." He's wearing a Planet Hollywood T-shirt over a brown turtleneck and checked polyester pants two or three sizes too big and cinched by a belt — kind of a punk look, opposite of the others. And I have this feeling that he might actually be a woman. He has beautiful eyes with long lashes and that soft voice. I look, twice, to see if he has breasts.

"What are you doing?" he asks.

"Just taking pictures," I say. "How old are you?"

"Nineteen. Do you need a translator? I have been studying English in school, but there is no school now — the Taliban sent our teachers back to Turkey. I would very much like to work for you. I will help you in any way that I can, and I will not leave your side. As long as you are here I will be with you."

"What's your name?"

"Najibullah Niazi."

"Najibullah. Why did you shave your head?"

"When the Taliban leave two weeks ago many men shave their beard, but I do not have beard, so I shave my hair," he says, smiling.

"Good one," I say, "but I'm sorry, I don't have very much money and I just can't afford to pay a translator every day."

"For me money is not important. If you have money you can pay me. If you don't have money you don't pay me. When you are finished you can decide."

I know that this is a deal that could go sour very quickly, but I do need a translator and, to a certain degree, I believe him. He's trying to learn to look and act like a Westerner, and probably the best way for him to do it would be to hang out with me. I wonder if his shaved head might frighten the locals, but then he is a local and it's his business, so I let it go.

"Come," he says, "let's go to the hotel and we can talk there." We've attracted a large crowd, some of them spilling into the street, making traffic go around them. "This place is not so good for you."

We walk through the crowd and they go on about their ways, all except for three very dirty little boys who try to stand in front of me and brush my hand, begging for money, but all I have are twenty-dollar bills. Naji saves me by scolding them away.

The Road to Sheberghan

Yesterday Najibullah told me that *Titanic* was such a hit in Mazar that now if you want to say that someone is "with the latest style" you say that he is "titanic." I'd say Najibullah is titanic. I loaned him my sunglasses and hat, and he thinks he looks like a U.S. Special Forces soldier; actually he says that other people think he looks like this, that they can't tell he's an Afghan, and this makes him very happy. He's driving the car — the old chauffeur is relaxing in the passenger seat — pounding the steering wheel to the beat of Afghan disco.

He drives too fast, and he slows down and speeds up too quickly. When passing big trucks on the left, the old chauffeur helps him out by saying whether it's clear — the steering wheel is on the right side, since the car is from Pakistan. And always, when passing, he blows his horn for the entire distance. Everybody does. He swerves around the small potholes but crashes into the big ones. This happens again and again, even though I keep telling him to slow down.

I've been invited to Sheberghan by Dostum. As we leave Mazar, the road is bisected by thirty-five-foot-high walls, three of them, spaced a few miles apart. At each wall three or four young men with Kalashnikovs and walkie-talkies come up and look in the car. Naji speaks to them in English, trying out that Special Forces thing, and when they hear the words "journalist" and "American" they back off and wave us through.

The land here is farmland, but it looks like it's been lying fallow for years. The fields are bordered by trees, and every few miles there's a small village, Hazara houses made from adobe, all cubes topped by a dome. They look biblical, and it feels strange to whip by them at sixty miles an hour. Soon we come to the twenty-six-hundred-year-old town of Balkh, known as "the Mother of All Cities." The prophet Zoroaster is said to have preached and died here, and the mystic poet Rumi was born in a nearby village. The city was taken by Alexander the Great in 329 B.C. and then leveled by Genghis Khan in A.D. 1220. Today Balkh is still a city of walls and fortresses, some nearly completely eroded, others in good condition, with tanks parked on top. Beyond Balkh the farms and fortresses stop and the desert takes over, wiped smooth by wind and sand, barren in a way that makes the basin and range seem lush. In the distance are small caravans of camels and herds of goats, and running along next to the road is a natural gas pipeline: rust-colored, thirty inches wide, resting on small dirt mounds spaced one hundred yards apart.

"Is that a real pipeline?" I ask Naji.

"Yes, it's real. It's the only one in Afghanistan, built by the Russians. The gas comes from the ground near Sheberghan and goes to Mazar, 160 kilometers."

"And it actually works?"

"Yes, for electricity in Mazar. We have one five-megawatt station. My father, he helped in building this, as geology engineer."

Up ahead a teenage boy with a Kalashnikov waves us over. It's not a checkpoint, he just wants a ride, and we have to stop because he has a gun. It's a common form of transportation for the soldiers. But when he comes up to the car the old chauffeur starts yelling at him, "What are you doing? You shouldn't be out here stopping cars on the highway. This man is an American and you should be careful not to upset him or the bombs will find you in your house!"

The kid falls back as if he'd been punched hard. He looks truly frightened.

"He really believed that," I say.

"Yes, they all believe it," Naji says. "And it's true."

"Yeah, but I can't make it happen."

"But he does not know this."

The old man looks at me and smiles.

Xanadu Redux

Dostum's compound in Sheberghan resembles a Soviet Club Med in bad decline. There are two pools, one indoors and one outdoors, both empty and breaking apart. The outdoor pool is deep, with a diving platform, and is surrounded by Astroturf and clusters of streetlights. The indoor pool is housed in the strangest building I've ever seen, made from concrete but fantastical in style, a mixture of Bauhaus and Dr. Seuss. The doors are chained shut, but through the broken windows I can see the pool — long and shallow, perhaps for the women.

In the center of the compound, which is the size of a city block and surrounded by a wall, is Dostum's residence, a modest two-story beach house. Beyond is a garden with long rows of rosebushes and fruit trees, sidewalks and benches, a small mosque in one corner, and a large dry fountain, also made of concrete, in the shape of an opium poppy.

The biggest building in the compound is the guest house — four stories high and running along the northern wall bordering the main street of the town. It has a kitchen and about thirty bedrooms with real beds, and a long conference room on the third floor where Dostum is meeting with more than one hundred local mullahs and commanders. The room is remarkable in that it is clean and has new stuff in it — a red carpet, black felt drapes, chandeliers, new couches and upholstered chairs, and a forty-eight-inch Sony television with a satellite connection. The men are sitting on the couches and the chairs and cross-legged on the floor, wearing turbans on their heads and blankets wrapped around their shoulders — older men with gray beards, ethnic Uzbeks and Aimaqs. Only two weeks before, this city and even this guest house were occupied by the Taliban. (They cut out the heads of the deer in the pastoral murals in the hallways.) For four years these mullahs and commanders have been in hiding in the mountains, while Dostum was in self-imposed exile in Turkey. But now he's back. He's dressed in velour like a medieval monarch — a big man with a round face, black woolly caterpillar eyebrows, and salt-and-pepper hair and beard trimmed short and neat. He looks like a big teddy bear, and I have a strong urge to give him a squeeze, but I don't because I know he's a powerful warlord who is reportedly so strong that he has crushed a man's skull with his bare hands, and so evil that his laugh has frightened men to death, and so cruel that he tied a man to the treads of a tank and then watched as he was crushed. He sided with the Soviets during the 1980s, and during the 1990s, when Afghanistan was torn by civil war, he sided with everyone and no one, making and breaking many promises.

One of the older men, a mullah, stands and tells Dostum that his office in a nearby town has no furniture or carpets left, that the Taliban took everything. "Here you have new things," he says, "but we have nothing left, not even a desk."

Dostum takes this in stride and tells the man that these things will not be a problem but that they will take some time. He has only just now arrived in town. A younger man stands, a commander, and tells Dostum that there are still Taliban soldiers hiding in bunkers outside his village and that they have threatened to die fighting before they surrender. Dostum tells him to tell the Taliban that their resistance is futile — either they surrender or they will be bombed by U.S. planes until there are none of them left.

A man walks to the center of the room holding a sheet of paper in his shaking hands. He stands there and looks at the paper, and then he starts to sing. It's a dirge, with many verses, telling of battles in which brothers and friends fought bravely but were lost. The men in the room are transported, some of them sob, tears falling onto the blankets around their chests. There's something very heavy in the room. I can't see it but I can feel it. These men don't want to fight anymore. Not because they are afraid of fighting, but because they are really very tired of fighting.

The Hotel

The power is off in the hotel, as well as in the entire city of Mazar, but I have a head lamp and a box of wooden matches. The head lamp I brought with me, but the matchbox is from Latvia, and I can't remember how it came to me. Maybe by way of the Moscow bureau chief for the *Boston Globe* who's on the fifth floor. They are fine wooden matches, "Avion," with a picture of an old airplane. The box is also made of wood, and sturdy. It seems very exotic and very much out of place.

There is no power in this hotel and there is no running water in this hotel, and I've been waiting for an hour for a simple dinner to be brought to my room — a four- by eight-foot space with a bed and nothing else. The bed is a steel-mesh hammock with a thin cotton mattress, two dirty sheets, and one blanket. There are better rooms in the hotel, large rooms with windows and kerosene heaters, but I'm trying to save money and this one costs only $10 a night whereas the others go for $35. I don't mind the darkness, and I don't mind the bed, but without running water the communal toilets are filling up and the stink is hard to ignore, but there are no other hotels in town.

I'm hungry. There is a restaurant in town, but even those who've been there don't know where it is. The soundman with a French TV crew said, "You take a taxi and say you want to go to the restaurant. It's around here somewhere, and it's a real restaurant, with tables and tablecloths and enough light so you can see what you are eating. Not bad." But it's night now, and nobody goes out at night. Nobody. The doors are locked and the dogs control the streets.

An hour ago I asked the ten-year-old boy who works here if there was a way I could order something to eat. He speaks English pretty well, sometimes with an attitude if he doesn't like you, but we get along fine because I tip him ten thousand Afghanis (thirty cents) whenever he does something for me.

"Yes," he snaps, "what do you want?"

"Do you have dinner?"

"Dinner?" like he'd never heard the word.

"Yes, dinner, like kabob. Do you have kabob?"

"Kabob, no."

"Rice?"

"Yes, rice."

"And bread?"

"Rice and bread."

"And tea."

"Okay."

"Do you have anything else?"

"What?"

"Is there anything else they can make in the kitchen besides rice and bread and tea?"

"No."

"Okay then. Can you bring it to my room?"

"Yes, yes," and he went off into the darkness and he has not come back. But there are many hungry people in this town, and I roll another cigarette and light it with my exotic matches and listen to the last prayer of the day being sung over a loudspeaker at the mosque.

Love Means Never Having to Say You're Sorry

I am standing outside the Ministry of Foreign Affairs waiting for the young Najibullah to tell the authorities of our plans. He must report in, he says, or they will get rough with him. So I wait. Next to me is a Toyota Tacoma four-door, four-wheel-drive, diesel pickup. Chrome bars over the grill, chrome running boards. In the back bed are three soldiers. The one in the middle is straddling a floor-mounted machine gun with a bore the size of three fingers. The man to his left cradles a machine gun with fold-down stand so that it can be set on the ground or maybe a rock. The other soldier has a Kalashnikov over his shoulder. They're waiting for their commander, who has gone inside the building. The sun is out but it's a cold morning, and two of the soldiers are wearing polar gear dropped from American planes as part of the humanitarian-aid program — thick insulated pants, big coats with big hoods, and black leather lace-up combat boots. It would be really cold riding in the back of a pickup, and these clothes are perfect for the job, so they're styling. It's cool to sit in the back of a pickup with a machine gun. It's cool to be part of the conquering army on a bright and sunny morning.

I ask the men if I can look inside the cab and they say go ahead, getting out and coming around to watch me. The floors and the seats are covered with Afghan carpets that look as if they've just been vacuumed. There's no mud or dirt anywhere, which seems impossible considering that it's been raining for days and there's mud everywhere. On the dash there are red plastic roses, and the front window has little multicolored cotton balls hanging from its border, and there are little stickers around the cassette player of valentine hearts and the word LOVE written in that sixties psychedelic font. I point to the stickers and look at the soldiers and one of them says, "Taliban."

"Taliban?"

"Yes," he says and makes a motion with his hand meaning that the whole truck had belonged to the Taliban.

"Kunduz?" I ask, meaning, Was this truck taken at the surrender of Kunduz?

"Yes, Kunduz," all nodding their heads.

It's strange that Taliban soldiers had decorated the cab this way, like a gay bordello, and it's stranger still that the Northern Alliance soldiers hadn't changed it.

What does this mean?

It means the Taliban were more cool, more hip, than the Northern Alliance.

The Hotel

I've been cold at night so before going to bed I ask for an extra blanket. I find the young man who sweeps the floors and say, "Blanket?" making motions like I'm sleeping and pulling a blanket over my head.

"Blanket?" he asks.

"Yeah, blanket," acting like I'm in bed and shivering.

"Okay, blanket," he says and goes directly to a room just across the hall from mine and pounds on the door. The young man who answers also works in the hotel, also sweeping the floors. My guy tells him that I need his blanket, so hand it over, since I'm a paying guest and all. But the other guy says no way, José, it's cold out tonight. My guy says, listen, you've got to give him your blanket, if you get cold you can go sleep with your friend downstairs. This makes the other guy mad and he grabs my guy at the shoulders and they start wrestling, pushing each other in and out of the room, yelling, knocking stuff over while I'm saying, "I don't want his blanket, stop, listen, there must be another blanket in this hotel somewhere." They stop wrestling and just yell at each other for a few minutes, and then they're not yelling at all but talking quietly, and then they're hugging each other in the doorway and holding hands.

"Blanket?" I say, rather perturbed.
No, they both shake their heads. No.

Fortress of War

The mud in the basement at Qala Jangi is a thick brown mousse, eight inches deep. It makes a sucking noise when I step in it, and then sticks like clay to my boots. It smells of rotting corpses, because that's what's down here, some have been dead for seven days. There are two by the stairs, halfway cemented in the mud, faces swollen, the color of ashes. I walk carefully around them. There are more, a lot more, around the corner, but it's dark in there and I don't have a light and the smell alone is evidence enough.

I back out and go upstairs, neatly avoiding the unexploded mortar shells sunk into the wall. I stand outside the building trying to pick the mud off my boots with sticks from the pine trees shattered by U.S. missiles. When sticks no longer work I try scrubbing it off with snowballs packed from the three inches of snow that had fallen and is still falling, blanketing the battlefield and the rubble, as in photos of the Battle of the Bulge. Workers, including a woman who isn't wearing a burka, are going down in the basement and bringing up coats and shawls, dripping wet. They reek. I reek. I sit on what had been the front porch using a brick to scrape the mud off, and just to my right there's a human foot, smudged and bloody, with a little patch of snow on the heel, snapped clean just above the ankle. Perhaps the body was obliterated with the front door, because there's nothing there but a huge gaping hole.

Qala Jangi, fortress of war. It had been a fuckup from beginning to end. It began with the surrender of four hundred foreign Taliban and ended with a slow massacre, like a Colosseum with air strikes, in which only eighty-five survived. Every mistake along the way had something to do with suicide bombers and the failure to understand suicide bombers. Men with grenades willing to blow themselves up can't really be taken prisoner.

They'd been in Kunduz, where all the Afghan Taliban surrendered by simply driving out of town and switching sides, suffering only hugs and kisses and the loss of their pickup trucks. But for the foreign Taliban the decision was more complicated. General Dostum had a history of deceits and betrayals and it would not have been the first time he slaughtered thousands of men. Still, realistically, there were at least four thousand of them, and it would have been very difficult to slaughter four thousand men on CNN. Also most of them were Pakistani Pashtuns, so it would have been politically difficult to kill them.

On November 24, after a two-week-long standoff involving a lot of negotiations, a group of four hundred foreign Taliban had decided to surrender by driving, in the middle of the night, five hours across the desert to the edge of Mazar-e-Sharif, where they got out and sat down and waited for the Northern Alliance troops.

Dostum's men took a long time disarming the Taliban, and by the end of the day only some had been carefully searched. It was Ramadan, and Dostum's men were hungry and not keen on getting blown up. This is when Dostum said, "Take them to my castle."

Qala Jangi was eight miles away and had the advantage of being enclosed by a mud wall sixty feet tall, four hundred yards on a side, with an elaborate stitch of crenellations, very medieval and huge, surrounded by a moat. Inside were mostly farm fields divided into three compounds separated by more high mud walls. The prisoners were taken to the third compound, a pasture with forty tethered cavalry horses. Also in this compound was a brick building previously used as a military classroom, and underneath this building was an air-raid shelter, a basement, with thick concrete walls, built by the Russians. The plan was to tie the prisoners' arms and then put them in the basement, but before they could do this one of the prisoners blew himself up along with two high-ranking Northern Alliance commanders. Everybody hit the ground, and, to their credit, the other Northern Alliance guards did not start shooting. They pulled out and left the prisoners there for the night. During the night eight more foreign Taliban killed themselves in an explosion. But the next morning, even though the prisoners had been blowing themselves up, two CIA men ("Dave" and "Mike") and two Red Cross directors from Australia and Switzerland went into the third compound. The Red Cross was there to ensure the humane treatment of the prisoners, but the CIA was there to interrogate them. It's not clear what happened — either a prisoner rushed and grabbed Mike in a bear hug and blew both of them up, or a prisoner threw a grenade that killed a bunch of guards, or a soldier threw a rock at a guard, knocking him down and taking his gun and killing him and five others — but something happened and very quickly Mike was dead and Dave was shooting his pistol and a bunch of prisoners were shooting machine guns and the remaining guards fled the compound shutting the gate behind them, leaving Dave and the two Red Cross directors inside.

The three white guys and their associates found a way over the outer wall of the fortress while the Taliban found a huge cache of weapons near the stables. Why the prisoners had been put in an area with an arsenal of weapons is not clear. Some believe that the whole thing was a setup by the Northern Alliance. Others, including the commanding officer of the Northern Alliance, later said that they believed the prisoners could be contained in the basement and that they didn't expect an uprising. But it happened. For the next two days there was intense fighting, the Taliban hiding behind trees and walls of the buildings, and climbing trees to shoot over the walls of the compound, firing rockets and mortars over the walls, screaming God is great and running into open fire and dying. Or just getting obliterated by a series of U.S. air strikes — precision-guided bombs dropped from F-18 fighter jets.

By Wednesday it seemed that all the Taliban were dead, and the Red Cross was allowed into the compound to retrieve, photograph, and bury the bodies. They found 188 Taliban bodies and the bodies of twenty-seven horses, and many of both were in pieces.

Because there were only 188 bodies in the pasture it meant that there must have been close to two hundred other bodies down in the basement. Nobody went down there on Wednesday, but on Thursday some old men were told to start pulling out the bodies, which they did, only to meet with a spraying of bullets. One died and two were wounded; incredibly, there were men down there willing to keep fighting. They'd come out at night and cut pieces of flesh off the horses. They'd drunk water mixed with blood from the floor of the basement. They'd survived the aerial bombardments, and still they would not surrender.

So, first, the Northern Alliance poured gasoline down through a ventilation duct and lit it. Then they poured diesel fuel down there and lit that. Then they dropped rockets and hand grenades, one after another, all afternoon, so many that it became boring. And then they flooded the basement with water, cold water. So much water that dead bodies started floating and the men who were too injured to stand drowned. This was too much for those who were still alive. They began screaming for the Northern Alliance to stop, and then they started coming out, one at a time, until there were eighty-six of them — wounded, wet, filthy, and insane. That was Saturday afternoon, one week after they had been brought there. The smoke from the fires had killed half of them, and then the water had killed half of those who were left, but the rockets and grenades were relatively ineffective because the walls down there were thick concrete, built by the Russians.

Some were treated by the Red Cross, some were given apples and oranges, all were loaded into either an open flatbed or an enclosed container. This is when a correspondent for *Newsweek*, Colin Soloway, discovered that one of the prisoners was an American. He was sitting up, leaning on the tailgate of the open truck. His long black hair and beard were caked with dirt and blood and the skin on his face was dark from soot. Soloway asked him where he was from and he said, "I was born in Washington, D.C."

One of the prisoners died that night in the back of the flatbed, which left eighty-five men alive. If you add eighty-five and 188 and subtract from 400 that means there are still about a hundred bodies in the basement. The smell comes wafting up and rises through the air, and the falling snow does nothing to diminish it. Naji is in the cab, honking the horn. He wants out of here. I leave and go back to the hotel and use my toothbrush, an extra one, to clean every bit of mud off my boots in the bathroom sink. I even take out the laces and wash them in my hands.

The Hotel

The power is out and there are eight of us in the room of the French television producer. She has three kerosene lamps and keeps her kerosene stove so hot that it glows red. She has pâté, and she has vodka, and she has a satellite phone that sits on the floor and is open to anyone who needs it.

There's a knock on the door and she yells, "Come in, don't bother to knock . . . Ah, Damien, you are so beautiful, I was looking for you. Please, take off your shoes."

Damien is an independent cameraman, also French, who's been trying to leave Afghanistan but has no visa to enter any bordering country. It's a complicated story and one that's not uncommon among the journalists here — they came in not worrying about how they were going to get out.

"Damien," she says, "have some pâté, it's very good. I wanted to tell you that we were at the airport today when the French troops arrived, and as it happens I know their commander. He's a very good friend of mine. We were together, years ago, in Congo. Anyway, I mentioned that there were some of us who had no way to get home, and he offered to let us travel on his planes directly to Paris. What do you think of that?"

"Wonderful," he says, "you've solved all my problems *and* given me pâté."

Najibullah is sitting next to me on the floor, transfixed, soaking in everything. This is what he lives for, to hang out with Westerners and study their ways. He knows everyone, and they all like him because he's usually happy and curious and eager to help. He's been offered more money than I am paying him, but he's refused because of his promise to me.

There is another knock on the door and it's the other Najibullah, the number-one translator in town. He's an English teacher and wears a wool suit with a tie, a little stiff for this crowd. He enters and takes off his scarf and hat and says, "I have news. The Black Priest Dadullah, he is in Baaaaallllllllkhhhh." He has a way of torching the last words of certain sentences, either for emphasis or because of a speech impediment. It's hard to tell. The Taliban mullah Dadullah is in the ancient city of Balkh, only twelve miles away. This means there could be trouble, which would be good for business all around.

The situation in Balkh is that there are somewhere between two hundred and three thousand Taliban there who refuse to surrender. Or perhaps there are no Taliban there at all. It's hard to tell. The Black Priest is a hard-line Taliban leader known for his severe punishments. He swore never to surrender, but then he vanished. It was thought that he was in Kandahar or that he was dead, but now he's back — or maybe he isn't. The people of Balkh are mostly Pashtun — which is why Dadullah would take refuge there — and Dostum and his army are mostly Uzbek, and they want not only the Taliban but those who support them. They want their stuff, their money and pickup trucks, and maybe even their land. The advantage of the Pashtuns is that they have governed the region for three hundred years. Dostum's advantage is that he won the war and has an army capable of surrounding the city and then calling in U.S. air strikes.

Every day for the past week there have been at least 150 of
Dostum's soldiers in Balkh. They have three tanks and a couple
dozen pickup trucks with large guns and rockets. The first day they
were there I asked their commander what was going on and he said
they were "cleaning up," going from house to house, disarming the
occupants and looking for Taliban soldiers. I asked him if I could
observe the operation, but he said they only do it at night and so it
would not be possible. A correspondent for National Public Radio
went there a couple of days later and demanded to see the weapons
that had been confiscated and the men who had been taken prisoner, but he was given a long runaround and then told that there
were no guns or prisoners to be seen. On the same day I was
stopped a mile outside of the city because Dostum's men had shot
at a Toyota van and three occupants had been wounded. One guy
had been badly hurt and was taken to the hospital in Mazar, another was hit in the foot and was standing outside the van with a
crutch, bleeding on the road, and the third guy was in the van with
a bandage wrapped around his head, in shock. It's strange. You
look at a man bleeding and it's no big deal, but you look at a man
in shock and you can feel it, the shadows closing in. Everybody was
yelling at me, six or eight men shouting in deep-throated panic, a
step away from spraying the air with bullets.

"Just tell me what happened," I said. "Tell me what happened
and I'll go."

It was a mistake, they said. It was only a mistake caused by someone wearing the wrong color of turban.

That's about as much evidence as we have about what's going on
in Balkh. What needs to be done is for one of us to go there and
stay for the night and go out and see what's happening there — at
night. This would no doubt be very scary and cause a large amount
of pandemonium, and there are no volunteers. We sit in silence,
looking at the kerosene lanterns, wondering if maybe there's still
some more vodka.

The Smaller Minister of Foreign Affairs

I'm running out of money but I want to go to Kabul — just to see it
and the mountains in between. I ask Najibullah how much it will
cost.

"By private car it will take $200, maybe $400."

"That's like a year's wages. There's got to be a cheaper way or no one would ever go."

"Yes, there are local cars, like taxis, and for this it is only $50 for both of us there and back, but we cannot go by local car."

"Why?"

"Because journalists can only go by private car, and sometimes they take a guard with the Kalashnikov."

"But that's not necessary now. Is it? Isn't it safe to go to Kabul now?"

"Yes, it's safe, but we will not get permission to go by local car."

"Then we won't ask for permission, we'll just go."

"But this will be very bad for me." He says this in the most forlorn way, as a sad sigh, as if I am asking him to cut off one of his fingers.

"Then I'll go alone, and that way you won't get in any trouble."

"But I must go with you, I promised you that I would not leave your side, and so I can only go where you go. If you want we can ask to go by local car. Maybe they will say yes."

"But it's late now and the ministry is closed and I'd like to leave tomorrow morning."

"We can ask the man here in the hotel."

"Which man?"

"The man in the office."

"I thought he was the manager of the hotel."

"He works for the Ministry of Foreign Affairs."

"But he's always here."

"Yes, because all foreigners are staying here."

"Then why do you always go across the street to the office to ask permission any time we go somewhere?"

"Because there is another man, a bigger man."

The smaller minister of foreign affairs is in the office sitting next to the woodstove. Najibullah tells him our plans and he asks us to sit down.

"We are asking that all journalists travel to Kabul in private cars with armed guards because we can't be certain of your safety. It is a long way, and out of our district."

I think this is bullshit, just a way to squeeze more money out of me. But I don't say this. "It's very important for my story," I say, "that I travel in a local car."

"Aren't you afraid?"

"No, I'm not. Everyone I've met here has been very friendly and helpful. I haven't had any trouble with anyone, and this is what I would like to write for my magazine, which is read by millions of Americans. I would like to tell them that Afghanistan is a good place and they should come here on vacation, but how can I say this if I travel with an armed guard? I need to take a local car and travel with Afghans."

"But we can't be sure of your safety."

"No, but then who can? My fate is in God's hands, is it not?"

"Yes, certainly. *Insh'allah.*" I had him there.

"*Insh'allah* then. So it's okay?"

"Yes, we will try it this once, but please if you would send word back with the driver, saying that you have made it safely so we do not worry."

A Trip to the Capital City

We leave the hotel just before dawn and take a taxi to the place where the local cars meet. Najibullah tells me to stay in the car while he goes in to buy two tickets. If they see me, he says, they will charge much more for my ticket. He comes back and says, "Okay, let's go, follow me." I get out and all the men who are standing around start yelling at once — *"Khoriji! Khoriji!"* — like they'd never seen a white man.

"Quickly," Najibullah says. "Please, get inside the car."

"What are they saying?" I'm sort of fascinated that my presence can cause such excitement.

"Never mind, just get in the car."

"Tell me what they are saying so I can respond."

He looks at me with a blank stare for a second and then turns and yells at the crowd and they back off and quiet down.

I get in and he tells me that the men were saying that I am a rich man and it's not fair that I buy a regular ticket, and they wanted to take something from me. So he told them that I am a very famous writer and that if they didn't stop bothering me I would tell all Americans that Afghanistan is full of bad men and that nobody should ever come here. It worked. We even have a man with a machine gun standing by the front of the car, on guard, though he's letting a little kid press his face up against my window and stare, only inches away.

The car is a Toyota Corolla sedan. They fill it with three other passengers and the driver, making six — Najibullah sitting in the middle up front with the gearshift between his legs. We drive east out of the city across the flat desert, skirting the foothills of the Hindu Kush. I crack my window because it's steaming up. I look for the mountains, but it's a gray and foggy morning and I can't see a thing except sand dunes.

After fifty miles the fog has lifted and I can see the base of the mountain wall, impenetrable except for a narrow slit, almost like a vagina. We turn and head straight for it — a narrow canyon only fifty feet wide at bottom, room enough for only a river and a road between vertical cliffs of volcanic rock. This place has a very old name, but I don't ask what it is because I want to make up my own. I'm thinking about that when the driver points out the rusted carcass of a Russian helicopter crashed into the cliffs three hundred feet above the road. Then he points out the bomb craters in the road — twenty feet wide and eight feet deep — and the burned-out shells of Toyota pickups off to the side. The Taliban came through here when they fled Mazar and the U.S. planes picked a few of them off, maybe ten trucks and thirty bombs. The driver weaves between the craters and complains that this was a good road before the Americans bombed it, and he wants to know if somebody is going to come and fill in these holes.

"Yes, for sure," I say. "We have special machines for doing this. They're called bulldozers, very big and strong, and we have so many that we don't know what to do with them."

The narrow canyon opens onto a wide, flat valley. It's circular, thirty to forty miles in diameter, surrounded by mountains, and in the center of the circle is a volcanic plug. The surrounding mountains are smooth and barren, sun-baked dirt, like the skin of an elephant. They're either heavily overgrazed or they've never, ever, had anything growing on them, it's hard to tell.

"Is it okay if I smoke?" I ask. I'm hungry and because it's Ramadan there's little chance that we'll be stopping to eat.

"Yes, go ahead," the driver says.

"But is smoking against the rules of Ramadan?"

"Yes, everything is against the rules of Ramadan," he says. "It is forbidden even to smell a flower, or to look at a beautiful little girl. We can have no pleasures during the day, but at night anything is possible."

"But it's okay if I break the rules?"

"For you it is not breaking the rules. You are a Christian and have your own book, and so for you it is not forbidden, am I right?"

"You're right. In fact Jesus smoked hashish."

"No, I think this is not true."

"Well, maybe not, but Mohammed smoked hashish, didn't he?"

"No, sir, I am telling you that this is not true. Where did you hear this?"

"From a Russian." I'm making all this up and realize that I'm bordering on rudeness, but I want to see how he'll react. I grew up with religious fanatics, among the Mormons, and I can't help myself.

"The Russians do not believe in God. You must not listen to what they tell you," he says, and everybody in the car seems to agree on this.

"Well," I say, "what about the deal with women? I haven't seen one woman since I've been here who hasn't been under a burka. Don't you wish you could look at women, you know, just look at them?" And the driver is stunned by this. A *khoriji* speaking of wanting to see Afghan women is too much of an affront. So Najibullah takes over, trying to smooth things out by telling me that perhaps with the Taliban gone the women will someday take off their burkas, perhaps at the university, but that it's not such a good thing because these women might be beaten by their husbands or fathers.

"That's how it used to be," I say, "but don't you think it will change?"

"No," he says, "it will not change, because it's what we believe. The Taliban believed this, but we also believe it, the Pashtun people."

"So have you ever gone on a date?"

"What's a date?"

"Like when you go somewhere with a girl and maybe hold her hand or kiss her."

"No, I've never done this. I've never even spoken with a girl other than my sisters. If I speak with a girl in this way, then our fathers would beat us with a stick."

"What if you actually had sex with a girl?"

"Then we would both be beaten many more times and forced to marry each other."

"What if when you are married, or not you, but someone else is married, and his wife has sex with another man?"

"Then she will be killed with the Kalashnikov."

"Who would kill her?"

"Her father or her brother."

"I don't believe that."

"It's true, believe me."

"You would do this? To your own sister?"

"Yes, I would have to, for my family."

"No," I say, putting my hand on his shoulder. "Naji, I know you, and you wouldn't kill your own sister. I'm sorry, I wasn't really serious before, but this is a serious thing. You wouldn't really kill your own sister."

"Yes, I would. First it is my father's responsibility. If he doesn't do it, then my biggest brother must do it. If not he, then my next smaller brother, and then my next brother, to me, and I'm telling you serious I would do it." To drive home the point he tells the other men what he's saying and they all nod their heads, Yes, she must be killed.

"With a Kalashnikov?" I ask.

"Or by putting the stones on top of her," the driver adds.

The Salang Tunnel

From the plain the road rises over a low pass and then into a broad canyon with pastures and irrigated fields, small villages and the town of Pol-e-Khomri, where there's what appears to be a cement factory and a Soviet army base. Beyond the town is the Hindu Kush — snow-covered sawteeth over fifteen thousand feet high, a natural fortress made from the crashing of India into Asia. Somehow the highway goes up and over these mountains, from the Oxus to the Indus, but it looks impossible.

As it turns out, the ascent is gradual, with switchbacks and avalanche sheds built by the Soviets and marked every mile or so by one of their tanks, parked and abandoned circa 1989, left to rust as monuments. At eight thousand feet there's snow and ice on the road, and our driver gets out and ties on some chains with rope. At nine thousand feet it's snowing. And then the road ends. We're at the Salang Tunnel.

The road ends here because the tunnel was blown up in 1997 by the ethnic Tajik commander Massoud, who was killed in September by Al Qaeda terrorists impersonating television reporters. Massoud's troops had been pushed out of Kabul by the Taliban, and he bombed the tunnel as a defense. Now cars and trucks cannot enter, but you can walk through — a distance of two kilometers — or you can walk over the Salang Pass — two thousand feet higher — the old way, in a blizzard. On the other side it's downhill all the way to Kabul.

At road's end, men and boys — porters — stand in the snow with bare ankles and plastic slippers. All the cargo on this, one of the oldest and most important roads in the world, has to be carried by hand and on the back through the tunnel. They want to carry my pack and I tell them no. They get upset and grab at it — acting like it's a union deal and I don't have a choice in the matter — but I push their arms away and tell them to back off.

"Come quickly," Najibullah says. "And you must walk exactly where I step. There are still land mines here." But it seems that he's exaggerating the risk and maybe freaking out a bit from the alpine conditions.

The north entrance of the tunnel is clear, but inside is a jumble of rebar and slabs of concrete and sections of ventilation ducts, and we have to turn on our head lamps and move carefully so as not to get jabbed or tripped. And then it gets worse, so that we're climbing over and ducking under fallen supports, big slabs of concrete hanging down from the ceiling. There are many other people in here — women with little kids crying, porters with huge boxes on their backs, workers or slaves salvaging scraps of metal and huddling around small fires to stay warm — and the air is so full of dust and smoke that every flashlight makes a distinct cone that fades into darkness. It's creepy, apocalyptic, and bad for your lungs. It takes an hour to get through, moving as fast as we can go without running.

The south portal has been blown apart, so we have to climb over a tall and icy mound of debris, then we're out. It's still snowing, though there's no wind on this side. Just beyond the portal are more taxis and trucks, and another crowd of men. I walk up and they all start yelling, sounding like a swarm of angry bees. They try to surround me, try to block me, but I keep walking. I'm not worried — I'm much larger than they are, and they're wearing those plastic slippers — but I am amazed by the barrage of shouting, they're so excitable. Naji finds a car going to Kabul and tells me to get in.

"What were they saying?" I ask.

"When you came out of the tunnel they were saying that you were a foreigner and that you were alone and that they should take your money and kill you."

"But they didn't have any guns."

"Yes, they have guns. And knives, like this," he says, pulling out a four-inch stiletto. "They hide them."

"Naji," I say, "put that away. No one's going to mess with us."

"Okay, but please stay in the car."

Again there are six of us in a Toyota Corolla and the driver speeds down the mountain, hurrying to get to Kabul before dark. Three times we cross the river at the bottom of the canyon and at each crossing there's a concrete bridge that was blown up by Massoud's troops. In place of the larger concrete bridges smaller bridges have been made down close to the water by piling up big mounds of dirt, sometimes using Russian tanks for buttresses, and spanning the distance with metal planks. Nothing larger than a small truck can pass over these bridges, and at nothing faster than a breathless crawl.

We arrive at the edge of Kabul at dusk. It feels like being in a crater where the bomb exploded a long time ago but the dust still has not settled. The road into the city is lined by shipping containers, side by side, continuous, filled with scraps of metal and firewood and dark dusty stuff like car wheels and motorcycle frames and doors. In front of the containers men stand around and work, pounding metal or cutting wood or fixing horse carts or cutting up empty cans. Our driver is swimming through traffic — honking, stopping, going. I ask Najibullah a question just as the guy on the other side of the back seat says something to me. I say, "Hey, do these people live in those containers?" but Naji chooses to translate for the other guy. "This man thinks you have a very beautiful face and he would like to give his love to you." No one laughs. No one thinks this is funny except for me, and I let the comment fade with the light.

We stay with Najibullah's uncle and his family. They live in a blighted proletarian housing complex, the exterior walls pocked by bullet holes, the stairways fetid with decaying waste, electrical wires rupturing out of circuit boxes like burnt snakes. No running water. But in Kabul this is a good place, a middle-class place. I wait in the stairway while Najibullah goes in to say hello and make sure his aunt is in another room before I come in. His uncle is a very gracious man, thirty-five years old, who tells me, in English, that he's honored to have an American guest in his home. He takes us into the guest room and we sit down on mattresses resting on Afghan carpets.

"Would you like some tea and bread?" he asks, carefully separating each word and rolling the r in bread.

"Yes, thank you."

"In Afghanistan we give our guests everything. While you are in my house whatever you need you have." He's beaming at me like I am a rare jewel, and three of his little children are climbing over one another holding themselves back from petting me like a new puppy.

I've been told that Afghans consider themselves to be the ultimate hosts, that once you are in their home they will die trying to protect you from your enemies. This may be true, but at the same time they won't let you meet or even look at their women.

"What was it like when the U.S. was bombing the city?" I ask. "Did bombs fall close to here?"

"Yes, every night, some only five or six blocks from here. Big bombs, very big bombs. I could not sleep, my children were very afraid."

"Did the bombs kill civilians or did they hit military targets?"

"They hit the military targets, but some civilians were died."

"How many?"

"I think 100 or 150."

"And is that a lot or not that many?"

"I think it is not that many. We are very happy that the Taliban are finished. I am engineer, but I have no work for four years. I work only some days as chauffeur. I want very much to work for my family."

"What do you think America should do to help?"

"America should give peacekeeping force here to take guns.

There are many, many guns, and there are many fighting for Afghan people. If America or United Nations peacekeeping force do not come here then it will be very bad, worse than before the Taliban. But they will come, it is true?"

"I don't know," I say. "Maybe not." I don't want to lie to him.

A Lion in Winter

The next morning another uncle of Najibullah's drives us around the city in his taxicab. We go by the lamppost where the Taliban hung the body of President Najibullah. We drive by the soccer stadium where the Taliban conducted public executions. Then we go to the zoo, which has been bombarded by mortar shells. There are a lot of empty cages with big holes in the walls, but there are still some animals alive — monkeys, hawks and eagles and vultures, and a lion that looks senile or dazed and is missing an eye. In 1993 a mujahedeen soldier jumped into the cage and tried to fight the lion, but the lion killed him. Then the soldier's brother came to the zoo and threw a hand grenade into the cage. The lion bit down on the grenade and it exploded.

Beyond the zoo is the Kabul River, which after three years of drought is not much more than a series of festering pools. Still, there are people using the water — bathing in it, drinking it, and filling buckets to wash taxicabs. We exit the zoo into an entire neighborhood that has been demolished by bombardments — acres and acres of adobe ruins.

"What happened here?" I ask Naji.

"It was the Hazara people who were living here, and Massoud's army shelled them from that hill."

"Why?"

"Because they are Hazara people and Massoud's people are Tajik."

"This was before the Taliban took over?"

"Yes, when the Taliban came they stopped this fighting."

"What a fucking mess," I say. "I'm sorry."

"How long would it take in America to rebuild this place?" Naji asks.

"Oh, shit, in America it might take three years."

"And then it would be as good as Tashkent?"

"Well," I say, "anyplace in America is a lot better than Tashkent. But it's not going to happen like that, I don't think. Maybe America will give Afghanistan some money for rebuilding, but the work will probably have to be done by the Afghan people."

"And how long will that take?"

"I don't know, maybe fifty years."

"But I will be an old man by then."

"Yeah, you would be. My advice to you is to try to find a way to get out of here."

"Where will I go?"

"Anywhere. The world is a big place and there are a lot of things to see. A lot of opportunities."

"But I think this is not possible for me."

I don't know what to tell him. If his family had any money they would have left years ago, along with the rest of the middle class. The only people left in Afghanistan are poor and have few modern skills. It will take a long time, maybe forever, to make this place look even as good as Tashkent, and then it will still suck.

Naji just looks at the ground and kicks a brick and says, "Shit."

PETER CHILSON

The Road from Abalak

FROM *The American Scholar*

EARLY ON Christmas morning I stood with hundreds of people on
a roadside in Abalak, a town in southern central Niger, West Africa,
on the edge of the Sahara. I remember the peculiar fine dust, like
talcum, that arrived on a cool wind and dyed the air a dirty gray.
The harmattan, the Saharan winter wind, had been blowing from
the northeast since November, hard enough to fill the sky with dust
but not strongly enough to carry sand. Fine grit coated everything,
including the fatigues of the soldiers who were running about,
guns slung across their backs, shouting orders and directing traffic.

I was trying to hitch a ride in a supply convoy of civilian vehicles
and heavy trucks that the army escorted twice a week to Agadez,
one of the Sahara's oldest cities and long a center of the trans-Saha-
ran caravan trade. Now the city was under a sort of siege. Agadez
sits in the traditional territory of Berber nomads, the Tuaregs, who
were fighting for a country of their own in the desert. This siege
was not so much physical as psychological, rooted in history and
the suggestion of threat brought on by the dust that veiled so much
— buildings, vehicles, people, even the land itself. In this part of
West Africa, the harmattan signals a season of war, a time when attacks are expected on the Agadez road under cover of dust.

The convoy would travel 150 miles up Niger's National Highway
2 — an asphalt road, six meters wide, obscured for much of the way
by drifting sand. About a hundred vehicles were preparing to depart on this road, and I saw much worth plundering: trucks full of
grain, trucks loaded with onions, petrol tankers, government cars,
private cars, bush taxis. Hausa merchants, women as well as men,

walked about in heavy camel's-hair robes. Scattered among the vehicles was an army escort of six white Toyota Land Cruiser pickups with machine guns mounted on the roofs, and a light tank painted desert khaki.

Abalak is an African road town, part farm village, part military base, and after decades of drought it has also become a refugee camp as well. Hausa farming and merchant families, Arab and Tuareg herders and merchants — unable to understand each other's languages — watched one another here in the streets and from the compounds of their baked-mud houses and goatskin tents, living in uneasy mutual dependence on land fast losing its ability to support them.

Here's a cartographer's technicality. Abalak isn't even in the Sahara, but in the north central Sahel, a narrow belt of arid savanna along the Sahara's southern edge, stretching from Senegal on the west coast to the continent's center. The Sahel, what's left of it, is inland West Africa's agricultural heart and an ecological border region (*Sahel* means border in Arabic) where desert and savanna meet in physical single-mindedness. Heat and wind, the Sahara's greatest exports, drive against a flatness whose colors — the gold and brown of sand, the maroon of laterite rock — clash only with those summer days when the sky is brittle blue and the wind blows softer and hotter.

Here's a reality. As an agricultural region, the Sahelian savanna is nearly irrelevant, having been overpowered by the Sahara. The grasses are mostly gone, and so are the trees. Villagers plant dwarf prosopis, a thorny Sahel native known as mesquite in the American southwest, to shore up eroding washes and to stabilize dunes. Prosopis is often the only visible vegetation. In Abalak it's hard to distinguish desert, the sandy, rocky plains to the north, from the savanna to the south — similar land of only marginal vegetation, where grasses, bushes, acacia, neem, and palm trees are a bit more common. "There's nothing here," wrote a French officer from his post four hundred miles southeast of Abalak in 1944, "but bush and sand."

Across this terrain, wind moves dust and sand with magical power. Sixty years ago in the Libyan Sahara, many hundreds of miles northeast of Niger, German and Allied armies attacked each other under the escort of these storms. And for centuries, West African dust has fallen on Western Europe, in raindrops colored white or red by fine grains of quartz and red jasper that the desert's rare but violent downpours grind off buttes, hillsides, and mountains. Wind does the rest.

Indeed, the wind has done its job so thoroughly that there's little dust left in the Sahara. The light stuff, the actual dust, blew off long ago, leaving 3.5 million square miles of sand and rock laid bare by the wind that blows year-round off the desert onto the Sahel. There the wind picks up half a billion tons of dust a year, the Sahel's remaining topsoil, consuming thousands of square miles as the Sahara marches south: a desert's ecological annexation of a savanna.

For centuries, travelers have struggled to describe the singular ability of these lands to rise and swallow them. This is the English explorer James Richardson's description, written in 1846, of a camel caravan navigating the Sahara a few hundred miles south of Tripoli:

> We followed the tracks of the few of our party who had preceded us . . . But one night of strong wind usually covers up the track, and though the sand does not move in billows, it flies about, first from one side and then the other, and fills up the foot-prints of men and animals. There is no doubt but it requires the most practised eye of the camel-driver to find his way through these regions, and yet, for my life, I could not see that the people experienced difficulty.

Richardson was describing a sandstorm whose heavier particles move in low, dense clouds, usually below the knees, but sometimes at chest level or a bit higher. Sand is too heavy to fly high or stay aloft long. Dust storms are different. They rise to altitudes of fifteen thousand feet, appearing to saturate the atmosphere. A. Starker Leopold, son of the naturalist Aldo Leopold, has clarified the sand-or-dust-storm distinction in his book *The Desert:* "Since dust is so much lighter than sand, the wind can raise huge clouds of it, clouds so dense that in the storm center it is as dark as night."

Harmattan dust blows in on softer, more constant winds, filling the air with a haze for weeks on end. But dense storms of the violence Leopold describes often precede monsoons of the Sahelian summer. Giant cauliflower clouds rumble across the land, churning up sand and dust with a force that makes you think the earth itself is dissolving. Driving rains follow like guerrilla raiders, wiping out crops, filling ravines with rushing water, and then vanishing.

I first experienced such a storm while serving in the Peace Corps in Niger in 1986. From my seat on a bus on Highway 2 near Abalak, I watched dark blue rain clouds form above the brown line of late-afternoon horizon. Then, as if growing fur, the horizon changed to a blurry band, and then to a billowing mass. In open desert, where landmarks are few, African drivers tell direction by reading the color tone of the earth, and by instinct. But dust storms stop even the best drivers. In minutes, the dust overcame our bus and turned afternoon to night. The driver pulled over. When the storm passed, three hours later, real darkness had fallen.

During the nearly five years I spent in Africa, dust became part of my point of view, something to take note of with a glance at the sky throughout each day. After I'd seen just one storm, I couldn't shake that pulsating vision of climate and earth advancing on me like some cosmic army.

I'd hitched a ride into Abalak on a Toyota minibus the day before the supply convoy was to leave. Both sides of the road through town were crowded with vehicles and with men huddling around small fires. I hung around a long time, talking to drivers and looking for a place to sleep. Finally, late in the evening, a man directed me to a "hotel" on the outskirts of town. It turned out to be a bar in a dusty yard surrounded by cinder-block walls. A boy sold bottles of beer from a damp pit covered with wet burlap. The only customer was a truck driver I'd seen hours earlier by the road beside his rig, an eighteen-wheeler carrying onions. He raised his bottle to me as I entered the bar.

"Very nice coat," he said in French, referring to the heavy nylon windbreaker I was wearing. "Will you give it to me?"

I smiled, set my baggage against the wall, and bought two beers from the boy, one for me and one for the driver. I took a seat across from him on one of many straw mats spread on the ground. We sat with our beers cradled in our crossed legs, arms folded against the cold. He wore a battered brown wool sports jacket over several T-shirts; under my windbreaker I had on a sweater. We both wore cotton turbans around our heads to protect against the wind and dust. He was drunk and had trouble keeping his turban wrapped tightly.

We talked about onions and Agadez. I learned that he was Nigerian and was hauling onions from the Kano region. We switched to English, but the conversation kept stalling. He sipped beer and stared at the ground.

"You look worried," I said.

He looked at me and spat in the dirt, wiping his mouth with the back of his hand. "American?"

I nodded.

"You must be a tourist."

I was making this journey with the hope of writing about the Tuareg rebellion, but if I admitted that openly, I might be removed from the convoy and perhaps arrested. The government didn't like the negative publicity of the war. So I smiled at the driver's surmise and did not object.

"I make this trip four times a year," he said, "and now is the worst time to be on this road." He slapped his upper arms with both hands crossed, making a flapping sound and raising a cloud of dust, as if to check whether the stuff were still there. He shook his head. "They hide in the dust. The rebels could be watching us the whole time, traveling behind the convoy, or in the bush beside the road, and we would never even know."

Weeks earlier, he said, a group of Tuaregs in a white Peugeot station wagon had ambushed part of an Agadez convoy on a day thick with dust. In the haze, no one noticed the car climbing onto the road and entering the convoy near the rear, ahead of a half dozen cars and trucks. The Peugeot appeared as if dust had created it. The occupants wore turbans and the uniforms of Niger's army. The car slowed in order to separate the vehicles in the rear from the rest of the convoy. The rebel driver suddenly turned the Peugeot to block the road. The others got out and fired shots in the air and into the lead truck's radiator.

The rebels hurt no one. They stuffed their plunder in the Peugeot and a minibus that they'd commandeered, then disappeared in the dust. They left a few bottles of water for the passengers. An army patrol rescued them hours later.

"How do you know all these details?" I asked.

He glared at me. "How do I know? How?" He touched his chest with the open palm of his hand. "Because that driver is my friend!"

I shrugged. "Sorry. Of course, you know the road well." I paused a moment, remembering that I still had no ride to Agadez. "Do you think you might let me ride with you?" I asked.

He frowned and raised a finger, shaking his head. "No, no! On another road, yes, but here you will be too much trouble. I am sorry, no." He hung his head. I didn't push the matter.

For centuries, Tuaregs have roamed the Sahara, surviving off the trade of camels, goats, slaves, and from piracy. They would appear out of the dust like gritty spirits — men distinguished by their loose robes and tightly wound turbans, often colored indigo blue — to extort their needs from camel caravans and lone travelers. Or, for a price, they would escort a caravan to protect its safety.

Only a few caravans, remnants of the ancient trade between North Africa and the sub-Saharan lands, still cross the Sahara. Traditionally, caravans transported cloth, precious metals, and perfumes to the south, returning with black African slaves and salt. To plunder that traffic outright would have meant killing off a means of support in a land of meager resources: desert suicide. So the Tuaregs have lived by a balance of guerrilla war and petty thievery that gradually bled caravans and other tribes of food and livestock. Outright plunder and murder happened more rarely.

Tuaregs didn't attack openly, preferring instead to mix with their prey in small numbers at first, posing as harmless herdsmen and planting rumors of discontent. They let fear work from within, an ideal tactic for attacking large caravans that customarily spread out into small groups with no coordinated means of defense. This vulnerability exasperated James Richardson, who in 1846 traveled by caravan a third of the way across the Sahara into what is now western Libya. Near the start of the trip, just south of Tripoli, he described in his journal how the caravan was organized. "Each group is its own sovereign master," he wrote, "and will have its own way."

But Tuareg bands also scuttled well-defended French military expeditions, which they attacked aggressively. The French, after all, threatened the nomad way of life through military action and pressure to take up the relatively sedentary work of farming. The Tuaregs challenged France's hold on inland West Africa for fifty years, until they suffered a decisive defeat near Agadez in 1919. They've been warring on and off ever since.

After I left Niger in 1993, several Tuareg groups made peace with the governments of Niger and Mali, but other groups refused to negotiate. The culture of piracy and fear lives on. The U.S. State Department, in a consular information sheet issued last year, warned that the region around Agadez and the Aïr Mountains had "experienced increased criminal activity by armed bandits. In these attacks, groups of foreign travelers, including Americans, have been robbed of vehicles, cash and belongings and left stranded in the remote desert. The government of Nigeria is taking steps to address this problem."

"This is the desert," the driver in the Abalak bar had told me. "Tuaregs will always own this road."

About midnight the truck driver stumbled off to sleep in the cab of his vehicle. The bar owner let me spread my bedroll on a mat in the compound. I lay awake a long time, thinking of James Richardson atop his camel, cursing the wind, dust, and heat, a man well aware of what a fine target his caravan made as it approached the Aïr Mountains northeast of Agadez.

Back on the road early in the morning, I couldn't find the driver and his truck. He'd probably been moved to the rear of the convoy, or had turned back. I tried to buy passage to Agadez in one of the Peugeot station wagons lined up along the road. They were bush taxis, but the drivers wouldn't take my money. A "European passenger," they said, made their cars better targets for the rebels. But the driver of a government bus, a white and orange Mercedes, sold me a seat.

The challenge of getting to Agadez, and my growing worries about rebel Tuaregs, made me feel a sort of kinship with Richardson — another traveler in fear. In March 1850, Richardson was forty-four and newly married when he attempted a second Sahara crossing. He left his wife in Tripoli and set out for the unexplored Lake Chad region, where he hoped to find the "source and causes" of the Arab slave trade so that England might destroy it. Richardson, an evangelical minister, had made the abolition of slavery his life's work. A year and more than a thousand miles later he died, having crossed the desert and reached the Sahel, but not Lake Chad. What killed him, apparently, were heat exhaustion and the climate's gradual wearing on his health. And, I believe, the journey's psychological impact.

Richardson covered much of the distance on camelback in an

Arab merchant caravan. His journals — published by his wife in 1853, under the title *Narrative of a Mission to Central Africa* — include nervous observations of landscape, climate, and Tuaregs, as if he felt it might be perilous to ignore any of them. Not far south of Tripoli, Richardson wrote, "the caravan was in motion fourteen entire hours, over heavy sand, with hot wind breathing fiercely on it." Farther south, he marveled at a "dust devil" — "a column of dust carried into the heavens in a spiral formed by wind, whilst all around was perfect calm." Weeks later he stabbed a thermometer into the sand under blasts of the late summer *gheblee*, called by the Arabs the "hot wind," and measured 130 degrees. He observed how camel drivers found the desert route by looking for camel dung, "which rolls about the surface of the sand." Further on, he wrote of "clouds of sand-dust . . . The fine particles cover and pervade everything, and getting between the skin and the flannel, produce an irritation like the pricking of needles." All the while he watched for Tuaregs, "easily distinguished by their habit of wearing a . . . muffler, with which they conceal their mouths [from dust] and all the lower part of their face. This custom gives them a strangely mysterious appearance."

Richardson thought he'd bought the caravan's security in the Saharan town of Ghāt (now in Libya, on the Algerian border, five hundred miles north of Agadez) by hiring an escort of Kailouee Tuareg tribesmen — only to find the caravan threatened by Tuaregs of other tribes. Small groups tailed them, begging for food as the caravan neared the Aïr Mountains. "Three mysterious Haghars [Tuareg tribesmen] still continued to follow us," Richardson wrote, "declaring that they had no evil intentions, but were merely poor wayfarers . . ." The three disappeared, but were replaced by a different group that kept watch over the caravan. "When it was nearly dusk, five mounted men made their appearance, two of them leading six empty camels . . . I treated them to supper — in fact, I am obliged to feed all strangers . . . During the night these strange fellows disappeared . . . About two in the morning the Kailouees, wishing to start early, began to bustle about in the dark, in order to collect their camels. They could not find any of them."

The camels were gone. The next day Haghar Tuaregs surrounded the caravan and extorted payment under threat of attack.

*

Here's another way to view the land and its problems. Environmental groups and foreign aid workers blame West African dust on the actions of people — a thousand years of deforestation and overgrazing. The United Nations has pinpointed Africa's growing deserts, the Sahara especially, as the continent's gravest environmental threat. The experts have a point, but there's another side to the issue. The Sahara, once a lush plateau, is a natural force at least one hundred thousand years old — there are scientists who believe the Sahara began growing as much as two million years ago — and no one really knows when or how things began to change, or to what extent human activity can fairly be blamed. What we do know is that the soils that the hot Saharan winds rob from the Sahel account for more than half the dust in the global atmosphere. Those fine grains of quartz have settled as far west as New Mexico, sixty-six hundred miles away. Geological Africa mixes with the American West.

A balance of physics and chemistry is at work here, the right combination of vulnerable soils and wind, driven by solar heat — pure airborne energy that helps power the air into a frenzy. Or, as the English meteorologist John G. Lockwood writes in *Causes of Climate,* "The sun drives all the meteorological and climatological wind systems and these continually dissipate energy mainly by friction at the ground surface."

I saw this point demonstrated when I visited Niger's government meteorology center at the national airport in the capital, Niamey. The walls were plastered with ever-changing maps of West Africa, white posterboard with dramatic black arrows that revealed wind direction, temperature, thunderstorm patterns during the monsoon season, and the year-round movement of dust, all measured against the position of the sun.

Hamza Ibrahim, the center's director, bluntly translated the charts for me. "The sun causes these winds," he began. "One energy source we don't lack here in Africa is the sun."

Along Highway 2 from Abalak you can see the evidence of that natural power. The wind shapes dunes in stars and crescents with knife-edge ridges and rounded domes. But all this vanishes in dust that imprisons the landscape behind a shroud, creating open terrain that is much more difficult, if not impossible, to navigate. Dust collects in the wrinkles of your clothes, frosts your hair, coats the inside of your mouth and lungs, disguises your face. To survive, you develop a sense that much is not what it appears to be.

Wind, dust, and heat, in a vast sameness of landscape, are the germs of what the French have called *la Soudanite,* a nervous state that is thought to have afflicted colonial officers in Africa. The French recommended that men serve no more than two years in the West African interior to avoid mental collapse. The ailment, very likely, is what the historian Douglas Porch calls in *Conquest of the Sahara,* his history of the French in the Sahara, a "way to pass off . . . excesses of behavior brought on by the African climate."

I'm talking now about murder, and the complicity of landscape and climate. Some believe that those two factors alone can trigger homicidal mania. In 1900, colonial authorities investigated, posthumously, two French officers who had laid waste to a five-hundred-mile strip of what is now southern Niger. The previous year, captains Paul Voulet and Charles Chanoine had led a force of six hundred African conscripts on what was to have been a geographic expedition. Instead they razed villages and cities. Villagers welcomed them, offering supplies and guides, only to be massacred. In July 1899, the African soldiers mutinied and killed the two officers near a village 180 miles south of Abalak, leaving France with much to explain, both at home and to the African population it had pledged to enlighten.

"Blood was spilled . . . and many villages . . . were burned," wrote an officer who came upon the expedition's swath in May 1899. "I can't understand the causes of such harsh measures."

In his journal, Voulet had complained of wind and dust, lack of water, and fear of Tuareg attack (though none occurred). The closest thing to an explanation finally came with the publication, in 1931, of the journals of two officers sent to arrest the renegade captains. The book's anonymous preface blames "*la biskrite, la Saharite, la Soudanite, l'Africanite* . . . The name is of little importance . . . It is this state of absolute agitation with so many small causes that produces such regrettable effects."

The soldiers marshaling the Abalak supply convoy positioned the government bus ten vehicles from the lead truck. I took the only seat left, just behind the driver. The passengers were mostly civil servants and their families traveling to homes and jobs in Agadez and beyond. I hoped a government bus might be the safest vehicle to ride in, but I could also think of reasons why it might be the most dangerous. Civil servants and merchants, after all, carry money and make good hostages.

As we started to roll, I watched the dust swallow cars and trucks in front of us. It was as if we were driving into a cotton swab. A Land Cruiser escort followed us. Eight soldiers sat in back, legs hanging over the sides of the rear bed, guns poking the air. They had wrapped their heads in turbans. One soldier stood behind the cab, manning a mounted machine gun. Dust blew in sheets across the road, a geological migration that reminded me of the powers bush taxi drivers attribute to dust. They talk of giant swirling dust devils patrolling the roads in hotter weather.

To meteorologists, dust devils sometimes signal that conditions are right for dust storms. The whirlwinds burst from the soil when extremely hot ground heats and fuels the air layer above it so that the air becomes unstable and rises, meeting cooler air above. This cooler, heavier layer of air flows downward to displace more of the hot air. The result is chaotic energy that sucks up dust as the hot air rises. The hotter the patch of ground, the more powerful the dust devil. Some rise to heights of one thousand feet, spinning at sixty miles per hour with the power to pick up and fling small mammals.

A driver once told me he'd seen a vision one windy afternoon on the road to Agadez: a tall, thin woman in flowing white cloth. Her body seemed to extend endlessly into the atmosphere, swaying and twisting in a serpentine way that made him think she was about to lunge and attack, like a sort of spiritual tornado. She was, of course, both spiritual and meteorological: a vengeful being, on the one hand, and a whirling centrifugal column of dust particles, on the other — pressure gradients, sparring drafts of cold and hot air crashing together from above and below and spinning outward in a vortex whose inner workings scientists have never completely understood.

The driver assured me that he'd seen the ghostly woman's face and that her mouth was open in a scream. She didn't attack, but it was weeks before the driver could face the road again.

This is the rarest kind of dust devil, because of its size, and the most dangerous on the road. To drivers the dust devil is psychopathic, an agent of evil that has neither top nor bottom and blinds when it strikes, as if a hand has suddenly gripped the car's entire frame. Bush taxi drivers maneuver wildly to avoid such dust devils. I've been in cars that have struck them, and have felt them grab hold, shake the car with indignant fury, and leave little cracks in the windows from flying pebbles. The Hausa word for wind, *iska*, is the same as the word for ghost. Drivers have a name for sections of road prone to accidents: *hanya mai iska*, which means "road of the wind" or "haunted road."

On the bus I tried to ignore such thoughts by sleeping. At noon the convoy stopped for the midday Muslim prayer. Off the road I stood on a landscape at war, looking off in one direction and then another, hands dug into my pockets as sand broke about my ankles.

I watched travelers, their bodies blurred by dust, spreading prayer rugs on the sand and praying prostrate before Mecca. The men prayed in front and the women behind, while children ran about laughing, and babies watched quizzically from blankets their mothers had laid out beside them. Most of the people in the convoy were Hausa, long-standing enemies of the Tuaregs, lords of the dunes who for centuries had raided Hausa villages to take slaves and foodstuffs.

Miles back, we'd passed three wrecked petrol tankers that rebels had attacked on the road months earlier. Through the dust I could see that explosions had blackened the asphalt. Sand drifts crept up the sides of the metal corpses. As we passed army checkpoints — a common feature on Niger roads in peacetime or war — I felt a tension uncommon farther south, away from the conflict. There were more soldiers up here. They were Niger's best troops, younger and stronger, in smart fatigues and boots. They had automatic rifles, wore field packs, and looked ready to fight.

This was the closest I'd been to war. My awareness of the journey's risk, of the history of the conflict, had made me jumpy and irritable. Now I couldn't even make notes. I thought of Richardson's frustrated declaration against banditry, written in the desert northeast of Agadez: The region, he wrote, "abounds with thieves, and we must now always keep watch."

At the roadside, waiting for prayers to end, a soldier smoked. One stood at the mounted gun. Six others surrounded the bus, staring into the desert with their guns. Then a peculiar event occurred. Down the road a white Peugeot pickup popped out of the haze. The truck raced up the roadbed, across the asphalt, and bounded back into the dust. Dust had almost perfectly camouflaged the truck, but not quite well enough. Soldiers jumped and shouted, and the Land Cruiser took off after the Peugeot so fast the soldiers had to run to get in, their buddies pulling them up by the trousers as if onto a life raft. Passengers cheered. Some shouldered children to watch. "Rebels will die today," a man said. I hoped the pickup's driver was only a farmer hauling wood. Not unusual in Niger, where the few who can afford a vehicle move people and goods at a price and without permits. They would flee at the sight of soldiers — scared soldiers who might shoot before investigating.

In seconds the escort dissolved in the haze. The cheering and talking trailed off, as if everyone realized a decoy had lured away our protection. Behind the bus, I could see nothing in the haze, but I heard voices and the idling motors of the rest of the convoy: sounds suspended in dust.

"You are afraid?" a man asked me in French. He was a big man, tall and heavy, his body protected under a camel's-hair cloak. He wore a white turban and sandals.

"Yes, I am," I said. "Aren't you?"

"Why, no, we are well defended." He laughed. "The rebels would not dare attack us." I stared off and he walked away. I sat in the sand and looked into the dust. We might as well have been sitting in total darkness.

After an hour we heard an engine approach. The escort roared out of the dust and stopped, facing the bus. Our driver had a brief shouted exchange in Hausa with the soldier at the mounted gun. The driver shrugged and waved his arm at the passengers. Time to push on.

On board, I asked the driver what had happened.

"They lost the truck in the dust," he said.

At six P.M. we made Agadez, a city that James Richardson bypassed in his hurry to get to Lake Chad to meet the German explorer Heinrich Barth. But Richardson fell ill and stopped in a village a few days' journey from Lake Chad. He died there in delirium on March 4, 1851. Barth made it to Lake Chad, and learned of Richardson's death weeks after the fact. He traveled to the village to collect the Englishman's journals and carry them to the British consul in Tripoli. "Mr. Richardson could never bear the sun," he wrote to the consul. "I think this to be the chief reason of his death."

In Agadez I stayed at the Hotel Kaosen, named for a fierce Tuareg leader who finally surrendered to the French months after the end of World War I. But I spent most of three days at the police commissariat trying to convince the commandant that I was a harmless traveler, not a white mercenary hired to help the Tuaregs.

The commandant told me to leave the city.

I returned to southern Niger in a much smaller convoy, with two escort vehicles, that left Agadez on a clear, sunny day. "Don't worry," a soldier assured me. "There's no dust for rebels to hide in."

They Shoot Poachers, Don't They?

FROM *National Geographic Adventure*

THE STORY, as I first heard it, had the zing of a Hollywood pitch: Led by a soft-spoken doctor, a band of American conservationists had persuaded the president of the Central African Republic to let them raise a militia and take over the eastern third of the Texas-size country. Their mission was to drive out the marauding gangs of Sudanese poachers who were rapidly wiping out the region's elephants and other animals. Their authority: shoot on sight.

No one had been killed yet when I arrived in Bangui in early March. Throughout the dilapidated capital, signs of a November coup attempt were still fresh: Bullet divots scored the bricks of the Tropicana Club, and a curfew remained in effect. A detachment of Libyan paratroopers hulked in front of the mansion of President Ange-Félix Patassé, who had been bailed out, again, by his friend Muammar Qaddafi.

Most of the fighting had taken place in the northern reaches of town, where the American group, Africa Rainforest and River Conservation (ARRC), had rented a gated compound. As I approached the large whitewashed porch, it struck me that ARRC was well prepared for another flare-up. Scattered among the wicker furniture were several men in fatigues, a couple of AK-47s, a grenade launcher, and a very excited chimpanzee.

Dave Bryant, a forty-nine-year-old South African who had been hired in August to lead the militia, extended his hand. "Welcome to bloody paradise," he said. He introduced a slight, twenty-six-year-old Iowan named Michelle Wieland, who was in charge of ARRC's community-development component, and a thin thirty-five-year-old named Richard Hagen, who had flown up from South Africa to help with security.

"And the little fellow jumping up and down is Commando," said Bryant. "We rescued him from a Sudanese trader, and to show his appreciation he's been crapping all over our floors."

Bryant's face seemed custom-assembled for bad-ass impact. Beneath a clean-shaven scalp, a towering forehead descended into a deep ravine of a scowl line, bridged by wraparound sunglasses. An expansive Fu Manchu mustache arched around a loaded cigarette holder, which dangled expertly from one side of his mouth.

"I guess you've heard that we're in a bit of a cock-up," he said. "We've been stuck in this shit-hole for five months now, trying to get out into the bush to do a reccy [reconnaissance] before the rains hit. We're waiting for gear, we're waiting for money, and we're waiting for vehicles. And we're waiting for people in this zoo they call a government to do something other than put their bloody hands out."

The three were eager to hear about my meeting that day with the American ambassador, Mattie Sharpless. Sharpless had recently arrived in Bangui, and I had asked her what she knew about ARRC.

"The rumor is that they're hiring South African mercenaries and diverting funds into diamond ventures," Sharpless had answered.

Wieland winced when I relayed the quote, but Bryant smiled and leaned back in his chair. "Yes, well. We South Africans don't usually like to use the term 'mercenary.' We prefer to say 'playing at soldiers on a privately employed basis.'"

Bryant had been hired by Dr. Brace Hayse, a Jackson, Wyoming, family physician, conservation activist, and organizer of extreme wilderness trips to improbable, dangerous destinations. Hayse first came to the Central African Republic in 1999, leading an attempt to raft down the eastern CAR's as yet undescended Chinko River.

Hayse was among a minority of Westerners who had even heard of the Central African Republic, a former French colony whose most notorious citizen was a child-slaughtering alleged cannibal named Jean-Bédel Bokassa. Before Bokassa, who ruled from 1966 to 1979, the center of Africa had gained infamy as an abundant source of slaves. Arab raiders, convinced that the dark-skinned infidels south of the Bahr el'Arab River were something less than human, essentially "hunted out" the eastern half of the country, leaving it with only a few thousand permanent inhabitants.

"This is one of the wildest areas left in Africa," says Richard Carroll of the World Wildlife Fund. "Humans were prey, and they learned to stay away. It's sad, but because of this, the animals thrived."

The Chinko region is what ecologists call an ecotone, a zone where two major natural habitats (in this case, forest and savanna) meet, resulting in exceptional biodiversity. Hayse had heard that the region was home to the most impressive herds of the continent — giant elands, lions, leopards, chimpanzees, and especially elephants. He hoped to survey those populations as the team made its descent down the Chinko.

The three-week journey was plagued by food shortages, malaria, and swarms of stinging bees. But to Hayse, the biggest catastrophe was the lack of wildlife. The great herds were gone; beyond the banks of the Chinko — once called the River of Elephants — the forest was empty.

At the mouth of the Chinko, they dragged their rafts onto the banks at the village of Rafaï. It was surely the first time a group of white people had arrived on inflatable rafts. But as Hayse recalls, the villagers greeted them not with curiosity but with relief.

"They said, 'You've come — you've finally come to help us.'"

Subsistence hunting is Africa's oldest endeavor, but in recent years the nature of hunting has changed radically, and a booming market has developed around bush meat. Conservationists say the bush-meat trade is now among the most significant causes of biodiversity loss on the continent. Africans are eating their wildlife into extinction.

In most of Africa, new logging roads aid the bush-meat trade as they cut into fauna-rich habitats. But the eastern CAR has little commercial logging, few passable roads, and few permanent inhabitants. The killing is being done by Sudanese poachers, who began crossing into the CAR in large numbers in the 1970s, when ivory and rhinoceros-horn prices skyrocketed. Skilled horsemen rode into the herds and used spears to cut the elephants' hamstring muscles. They left the fallen animals to die in the sun, then returned to collect the ivory.

By the late 1980s, Sudan's civil war had generated a surplus of cheap guns and trained shooters, and Sudanese merchants saw meat and money on the hooves of just about any animal that roamed in CAR's unpatrolled east. Ivory became a by-product.

Now, each November as the rains abate, columns of up to two hundred well-armed poachers cross the border with horses and camels along the old slave routes. Dividing into smaller groups, the poachers set fires to flush out the animals, then shoot them and smoke the meat.

Until recently, the wildlife around Rafaï had been abundant enough to provide plenty of food for its residents — most of whom are Zande, a Christian-animist tribe — and even employment with French big-game-hunting operations. But with the animals getting scarcer, the poachers had taken to looting Zande villages.

"Sometimes the *braconniers* [poachers] come to trade with us," a villager told me. "But when they cannot find animals to shoot, they come with guns. They make us lie down on our faces. They take everything we cook with. If they find your woman or daughter, they will rape her. They make us smoke their meat, and sometimes they take our people to carry the meat. These people are never seen again."

Hayse spent two days in Rafaï, listening to stories. "The villagers had organized a conservation and self-defense force," he says, "but they had no guns or ammunition. They were saying things like, 'You're doctors; you've got to heal this.'"

Hayse huddled with the other expedition members. Among them were Randy Hayes, the founder of the Rainforest Action Network, and Mike Roselle, who, like Hayse, was a co-founder of Earth First! In the western U.S., the conservation activists had spiked trees and organized rallies; they had blocked loggers from spotted-owl habitats and embarrassed scores of companies and politicians. But none had ever considered the prospect of confronting murderous soldiers in an unstable African country.

"It's fine to float down an unexplored river, doing a first descent and having a great time," says Hayse, "but we came to believe we had an obligation at that point to do something more. A whole ecosystem was going to be lost, just so a few hundred outsiders could make money. But this was a very difficult decision to make, because the poachers weren't going to leave just because we told them to. If we were going to save this place, people would have to be killed."

*

Eighteen years ago, a hunter named Jean Laboureur faced a similar decision as he stood on an overlook in the northern CAR, watching the hillsides ripple as thousands of elephants moved across the savanna.

In the elephants' migration, Laboureur saw innocence and authentic liberty, a freedom unhindered by walls or barbed wire or men with guns. Such freedom was particularly important to him. At the age of sixteen, he had been plucked out of his adolescence in wartime France and thrown into a concentration camp in Germany. Laboureur does not speak of his year in Dachau, except to say that when the camp was liberated, "I left hell and never again had a normal life."

After the war, Laboureur joined the French army and asked to be sent to Congo. After his tour, he was hired to hunt for meat for restaurants in Brazzaville. The job suited Laboureur; it allowed him to disappear into the bush for days at a time. Sometimes, when he saw white men approaching, he would hide, convinced he no longer had anything in common with his fellow Westerners.

"When I met him," says his wife, Claudine, "he was eating one meal a day, communicating mostly with grunts."

In 1965, the couple moved to French Africa's undeveloped reaches, in the northern CAR, They built a luxury hunting camp, Koumbala, and developed a clientele that included French president Valéry Giscard d'Estaing and CAR president Jean-Bédel Bokassa, whom Laboureur had first known as a table boy at the French officers' dining hall in Brazzaville.

Koumbala became the place where Europe's elite came to break trophy-hunting records. But with poachers killing not one elephant at a time but dozens a day, the safe places where the animals could roam were shrinking. Determined to protect the elephants, Laboureur put the majority of the hunting reserve aside for people who wanted to photograph the animals (presaging ecotourism). Hunting would continue in one small area to finance the protection of the rest.

It was Bokassa's predecessor, David Dacko, who had granted the Laboureurs the country's largest safari concession, some forty-six hundred square miles. But it was Bokassa who would often fly in without notice with a hard-drinking entourage to lap up the camp's luxuries. And it was Bokassa who, after declaring himself emperor, nationalized the Laboureurs' reserve in 1977 to rid it of "colonists." The Laboureurs were given just two days to leave. Afterward, the poachers, with no one to fend them off, began swarming across the borders.

After Bokassa was overthrown in a 1979 French-sponsored coup (his excesses had become too embarrassing for Giscard d'Estaing), Laboureur returned to see what was left of Koumbala and its wildlife. The hills that once shook under the weight of thousands of elephants now writhed with vultures, shrieking and circling in the stinking air, tearing at decaying gray-and-red mounds.

Laboureur went back to camp for dinner, which he ate in silence. After dinner, one of his companions remembers, the Frenchman lit a cigarette and sent someone to shut off the generator. As the motor's hum faded, the sounds of the African night came up, and the flywheel spun its last few turns. The light flickered, and then Laboureur's cigarette was the only glow. He stood in the cookhouse doorway, silent, for a long time. Finally, he threw down his cigarette and spat. *"Qu'ils terminent dans les ventres des vautours. Comme nos éléphants."*

"Let them end up in the bellies of the vultures. Like our elephants."

After leaving Rafaï, Hayse spent a week in Bangui, talking to officials. The government was far too broke to pay for a conservation program, they said, but if the Americans could find a way to finance it, they would support it.

Two weeks later, back home, Hayse learned that everyone he had talked to in the CAR had been ousted in a government shakeup. Undeterred, he sent Erik Lindquist, a Jackson-based forest ecologist, to Bangui to make new contacts. Hayse also began seeking funds. Among those he approached was Kathe Henry, who had met the physician in 1992, when he treated her AIDS-stricken son. "Back then," says Henry, "there was a lot of discrimination against people with AIDS. In Jackson, Bruce has a reputation as the doctor who won't turn anyone away."

After her son died, Henry started the Scott Opler Foundation to fund conservation efforts and other causes in his memory. Hayse showed her ARRC's proposal to protect the sixty-thousand-square-mile wilderness through counter-poaching operations, scientific studies, and community-based natural-resource management and development. In addition to recruiting and training an anti-poaching force of four hundred local men, ARRC planned to fix roads, build dispensaries and schools, and teach locals how to exploit their natural resources in a sustainable way. Hayse estimated that the project would need $300,000 to get up and running, and $600,000 per year to keep it going.

"I was a little shook up, because of the possibility of violence," says Henry. "But people say that's the way it's done in Africa; there's no law, there are no jails. It would be a tremendous achievement, the chance to change a country. I thought I could get behind it, so I sent the materials on to the foundation's attorney."

The attorney thought otherwise. In a harshly worded letter, he advised against funding ARRC, citing possible exposure to civil and criminal liability and loss of charitable tax-exempt status. "Charitable activities do not include the creation and training of an offshore, non-governmental military force," he wrote. "The use of deadly force is not a charitable activity."

In the meantime, the search for an experienced antipoaching coordinator had turned up Bryant, who was training game guards at Liwonde National Park in Malawi. His girlfriend, Wieland, was finishing a Peace Corps stint at the park, and she agreed to organize the community-development side of the ARRC program.

By the time Bryant arrived, Lindquist had managed to arrange a meeting with President Patassé. On August 14, 2001, he sent an e-mail to Hayse: "WOOHOOO! We did it! Met with the President today. He gives us full permission to work in the country . . . We basically asked for, and received, the entire Chinko River basin . . . We're celebrating in Bangui tonight . . . at least until 9 when the curfew kicks in. Send case of whiskey . . . urgent."

I went to bed early the night I arrived. In the middle of the night, I heard footsteps treading quietly across the tiled floors outside my room. It was four A.M.; someone was pacing the halls.

It was late morning when I woke again and walked out onto the porch. Commando was stretched out on Bryant's lap with his arms over his head, smiling serenely as Bryant rubbed his tummy. Near the concrete railing, Richard Hagen crouched over two tubes of paint, camouflaging his stove, his tea canister, and his cigarette holder.

I asked Hagen if he had slept well. "Like a slob!" he said, grinning. "But Dave was up early, as usual."

"I like to get up in time to hear the sparrows fart," Bryant said, brushing it off. "Also, it's the best time for an ambush."

The front gate swung open, and ARRC's green pickup rolled through, its bed loaded with four fuel drums and several ammunition boxes. Ange Lesieur, a high-cheekboned Central African member of the Presidential Guard, stepped out and greeted Bryant with a foot-stomping, thigh-slapping salute.

"Ça va, patron?"

Bryant had hired Lesieur from the CAR military to provide security. The army's sporadically paid soldiers make much of their living by stopping vehicles and demanding "coffee money" at gunpoint. (I experienced seven such shakedowns in a single day.) With an officer in the front seat, ARRC personnel could move through roadblocks with minimal hassle — "paying the bribes up front," as Bryant put it.

Three days earlier, Bryant had given several hundred dollars to a local man named Bob Ouinia to acquire essentials — fuel, ammunition, an extra truck, bulletproof vests — for the long-delayed reconnaissance mission. Ouinia had disappeared, and on Bryant's orders Lesieur had tracked him down and brought him in. Judging by the presence of the containers, Ouinia had accomplished his mission.

But when Hagen picked up one of the ammo boxes, it rose far too easily. He thumped one of the fuel barrels; its tone was hollow.

"And the flak jackets?" he asked.

Ouinia responded with the vague "Mmmm" that serves as an answer for just about any question in the CAR. "First, I get containers," he said. Bryant came down off the porch.

"Don't worry, Richard," he said, offering a cigarette. "A sucking chest wound is nature's way of telling you you've been in a firefight."

Bryant is working incognito in the CAR — the name he uses is not his real one — but his disguise has as many holes as a Michigan stop sign, and whiskey drills a few more.

He grew up mostly in England, but moved to South Africa so he could join the army at the age of seventeen. ("I wanted to go to Vietnam to play, but I was underage and my mother wouldn't sign the papers.") After a five-year stint in the army, he fought as a mercenary in the Rhodesian bush war — "the best war I've ever worked in" — and then, in 1993, joined the South African "security" company Executive Outcomes, which had been hired by the South African government to fight in Angola against the Unita rebel movement.

But it was during a 1989 undercover stint in Hong Kong, in which he infiltrated a rhino-horn-smuggling syndicate, that Bryant found his calling. "If I'm good at anything," he said, "I'm good at lying and BS'ing people. Plus, I like animals, and I believe they should have rights."

In southern Africa, the line between paramilitary and conservation work is often blurry, and Bryant moved easily into antipoaching jobs, setting up and training patrols in game parks in South Africa, Mozambique, and Malawi.

Like Bryant, Hagen (who also uses a pseudonym) sought adventure in South Africa, after deciding that the New Zealand army was "too boring." In an obviously long-standing routine, he and Bryant would sit on the porch each evening, cracking sheep and "homo" jokes and waxing nostalgic about guns, hostage rescues, and special-forces runs behind enemy lines.

Hagen is rail-thin, with a Mediterranean complexion and almost-black hair slicked into a pompadour. Beyond his AK-47, ammo, and flares, his war-zone essentials included Brylcreem, English Lapel aftershave, and wet wipes. At thirty-five, Hagen is "too young to have been in any respectable war," said Bryant. But when Bryant invited him to fly north, Hagen said, he jumped at the chance to "have a go at the Sudanese." Bryant laughed and plucked the butt from his cigarette holder. "We needed somebody who was expendable," he said.

In January 2002, Hayse, Lindquist, and some of the Chinko expedition members flew to Washington, D.C., to meet with Olivier Langrand, the director of Conservation International's Africa programs. ARRC had received some small grants, but Hayse was paying for most of its expenses, and he was running short of funds. Hayse hoped that Conservation International, which had just received a pledge for $261 million from Intel co-founder Gordon Moore, could become a long-term funding source.

Langrand had worked in the CAR and was familiar with the poaching issues there. "It was obvious that they knew what they were talking about," he says of the ARRC delegation. "There is probably still enough seed stock in remote pockets that the animals could come back quickly if the poachers were cleared out. We've seen it happen."

But when Hayse described the land Patassé had given them authority over, Langrand was stunned. "This area is four times the size of the Serengeti. Nothing that big has ever been successfully patrolled."

Langrand was also concerned that ARRC had hired an antipoaching expert from South Africa, fearing that Bryant might use methods that "won't work in central Africa, where the culture is different." But his biggest concern was that ARRC would be setting a precedent that might put the conservation community in an awkward position. "This is one of the poorest countries on Earth," he says. "They don't have the resources to enforce the law. We have a group that's willing to do it. But I'm not sure that conservation organizations should be used as a substitute for governments." Langrand encouraged the ARRC team to apply for a grant through CI's Global Conservation Fund. But he told them he wasn't overly optimistic about ARRC's chances for success.

Among Africa-focused conservationists, Langrand included, few would argue against the need for lethal antipoaching enforcement — though most conservation groups are keen to distance themselves from it. "We wouldn't do it," says the World Wildlife Fund's Richard Carroll. "Can you imagine the headlines? 'WWF supporting South African mercenaries to kill Central Africans'? But hopefully [ARRC] can make it happen. It's really a last-ditch effort. I just hope they're understanding what they're getting into."

Carroll had proposed WWF involvement in the area in 1999 but pulled back when he determined that the problems were "well beyond what community conservation could handle."

"It's probably better that the WWF isn't involved," says one mainstream conservationist. "This is the side of conservation that the organizations with the panda-bear logos don't want to deal with. It's dirty, filthy work. And if you want to succeed, you don't put a choirboy in charge."

"You tell those rag-heads they won't get away with this!" Bryant was yelling into the phone about a bounced check written by a Suda-

nese diamond dealer. It wasn't the first time I'd heard such an out-
burst, and each time the subject was obvious — though Bryant
never used the word "diamond."

The decision to get into the gem trade was rooted, at least partly,
in desperation. In the seven months since they had arrived, Bryant
and Wieland had managed to purchase a truck and import an arsenal; they had rented a house and had hired about a dozen locals;
they had made impressive contacts in the Bangui government and
among the missionaries and tribal leaders in the east. The operation seemed on the verge of getting on its feet, but Hayse, who by
then had spent about $130,000, was tapped out. The project, if
it was going to continue, needed a quick and significant infusion
of cash.

"Diamonds looked like a way to develop the project with some
kind of secure financial foundation," says Hayse, "and to provide a
more equable means for the local people to sell the diamonds they
pick up." Diamonds are abundant in the CAR; trading in them is
also one of the dirtiest games in Africa, having been at the center of
everything from virtual slavery in Angola to terror amputations in
Sierra Leone. In a country where foreigners have more than once
posed as do-gooders to cash in on the gems, diamond dealing
could tarnish ARRC's image.

"Of course," says Hayse, "we would be opening ourselves up to
accusations of operating this as a front, but hopefully our results
would be the proof of what we were about."

If Hayse sounds naive, Bryant was bluntly practical: "Michelle
and I hadn't been paid in five months. And the money was just sitting there, lying on the ground."

Erik Lindquist completed a weeklong course in gemology, then
returned to Bangui. He bought several diamonds, following the
advice of Andre Ouinia, Bob's brother. Andre had been recommended by Serge Patassé, the president's son.

Ouinia's appraisals turned out to be ridiculously optimistic, and
the transaction was a loss. Subsequent attempts fared even worse.
In total, Ouinia was given almost $60,000 to buy diamonds. So far
his deals had yielded a net loss of $31,000. Hayse and Lindquist be-
lieve that the problems stemmed from buying bad diamonds —
but Bryant was convinced that Ouinia was cooking the books.

One afternoon, a brand-new Land Cruiser pulled into the compound with Serge Patassé behind the wheel. Bryant yelled toward the kitchen, "Michelle, hide the whiskey!"

As Patassé walked toward the porch, Commando darted behind a potted plant. "Mmmm, those taste so good," Patassé said, glancing toward the furry head peeking out from behind the plant. "But don't wait too long, because the meat gets tougher when they're older."

Patassé announced that he had come to sort out the "misunderstanding" between Bryant and his friend Andre Ouinia.

"This isn't a misunderstanding," Bryant growled. "This is a rip-off. I've tried to be nice and polite, but I'm done. Andre either gets me the money or he gets me the rocks."

Over the next few days, Bryant's frustration grew, and the mood on the porch turned sour. In a pattern repeated over and over, each day of handing out money to various errand-runners — for gear, paperwork, food, beer — was followed by two days of trying to track down the recipients and find out what happened to the cash. The phone stopped working. The power went out. Some nights, we heard automatic gunfire in the distance.

"Curfew-breakers," Serge Patassé said. But in the expatriate community, rumors of another coup attempt were building.

When the telephone started working again, it rang with good news. A third Ouinia brother had found a very rare blue diamond near Bria. "It could be worth $50,000," said Bryant. "Everyone's flying out there to try to buy it. But we financed him and set him up in the business, so he wants to sell it to us. If we get that blue diamond, we're in business."

While Bryant and crew waited for news, I headed to Bangui's bush-meat market with photographer Chris Anderson. We took our time passing through a city once so giddy that French colonists had named it La Coquette. Now, the colonists' meticulously reconstructed image of Europe lay crumbled under layers of dust. Among the few aid workers and other expats who still visit, the bedraggled capital has been rechristened La Marchette — the doormat of Africa.

Much of the city is a field of ruins, and an inadvertent open-air museum to the Bokassa era. We passed under the dictator's crumbling "triumphal arch" and made our way toward his now roofless hillside palace, where his successors are said to have found the body of a schoolteacher hanging on a meat hook near mounds of human flesh prepared for roasting. We walked along the street where a hundred schoolchildren had once dared to stone the presidential car after they were required to wear school uniforms emblazoned with pictures of their leader. Bokassa had ordered the children rounded up, beaten, and executed.

Under Bokassa, the cruelties and injustices of colonialism looked like child's play. French president Giscard d'Estaing indulged the dictator, coveting the country's uranium deposits and diamonds and his beloved hunting reserves. The French government picked up the tab for Bokassa's most outrageous fantasy, the lavish coronation ceremony in which he crowned himself emperor of a renamed Central African Empire. The 1977 event cost about $20 million — nearly the equivalent of the country's annual gross domestic product at the time. Outside the national stadium, the wooden frame of his imperial throne still stands, stripped bare of its jewels.

At the bush-meat market, a woman named Marie-Claire Dogbaide guided us through the species that lay at her feet in hunks, rough-smoked, with a thick black crust. Here was a rib section from a small antelope (about $3). Next to it lay a piece of a python ($2), a buffalo intestine ($1.50), the top and bottom halves of a chimp ($4.50 and $5), and trunk sections from four elephants ($7.50 each). Technically, sales of endangered species are illegal in the CAR, but Forestry Department officials rarely enforce the law.

A truck pulled up to Dogbaide's stall, and the driver unloaded a pile of whole, unsmoked carnage: lizards, monkeys, a porcupine. Dogbaide paid him, then picked up a white-faced monkey by its long tail, which was tied around its neck to make a handle. After showing it to us, she threw the dead monkey back on top of the pile; the animals all seemed to jump a little, animated by the impact.

By the next day, the blue diamond was gone, scooped up by Andre Ouinia. When Bryant heard the news, he walked to the kitchen and returned to the porch with his last bottle of Glenlivet Scotch.

"Looks like it's AWA," he said, taking a long slug from the bottle. "Africa wins again."

Bryant announced that he was "pulling the plug" on ARRC's operation and called his landlady — the president's secretary — to tell her he intended to break the lease. He tried to phone Hayse but couldn't get an international connection.

"I've got to go find another war somewhere," he said. "I can't make a living on my own wars."

Two hours later, the porch was a goat's nest of rifles, beer bottles, and cigarette butts. Bryant, as he worked his way through the Scotch, had hatched half a dozen new schemes — among them a plot to lure Andre Ouinia into the bush and "take him out."

Commando was rolling around, gleefully hugging a bottle of beer he'd swiped and nearly drained. Bryant approached him, and the chimp stumbled backward, tripped over a rifle, and fell into a potted plant. The plant toppled over and the pot broke, spraying dirt across the porch.

"Commando, damn it!"

Bryant rushed at the chimp, his hand drawn back. Cornered, Commando cowered and covered his eyes, shrinking from the expected blow.

When it didn't come, the chimp slowly spread apart two fingers, peeked up at Bryant, and ventured a tentative grin. Bryant's fury faded. Before he walked back to his chair, Bryant shook his fist in a mock "why I oughtta" gesture. Then he sat down and lit a cigarette. When he looked again across the porch, the chimp was standing with one hand curled around the beer bottle and other balled into a fist — which he was shaking, slowly, at Bryant.

The next morning, Bryant awoke with a monstrous hangover — "My mouth feels like I've got a cape-vulture colony nesting in there" — and a seemingly incongruous sense of blustery resolve. "None of the armies I ever worked in taught retreat maneuvers," he said. "We're going east."

The decision seemed to have been catalyzed by early morning radio reports from missionaries all over the eastern CAR. "They are speaking of braconniers everywhere," said Lewis-Alexis Mbolinani, ARRC's liaison with missionaries and self-defense organizations in the region. "They are moving freely along the roads, hundreds of them, and now they have bombed the gendarme's house at Mboki."

Bryant's mission was reconnaissance only, with no plans to actively engage the poachers until ARRC's militia was in place — which couldn't happen until additional funding came in. We hitched a ride in a missionary Cessna, and Bryant sent ARRC's truck east under Lesieur's command. Bryant had told Lesieur to go directly out of town, but Lesieur asked if he could make a stop, for some lard.

"The braconniers have very powerful magic in their gris-gris," said Lesieur. "Regular bullets just bounce off. But because they are Muslims, we can coat our bullets with pig grease to penetrate their magic."

The pilot weighed our luggage before loading the Cessna. "Anything dangerous in here?" he asked.

"Uh, not if you don't pull any pins," Hagen answered with a goofy grin. The pilot chose not to ask any more questions, but he said a prayer just before starting the engines: "Lord, we pray for a safe journey, and we pray for these guys as they seek to help the people and save the animals out there . . ."

"Amen," Bryant said from the copilot's seat. "I'm a big believer in the holy spirit — especially the single-malt variety."

Jean Laboureur's offensive began in the dry season of 1985 and gained momentum quickly. With his son, Matthieu, and ten Central Africans, Laboureur attacked and burned eighty-three poachers' camps that first season, recovering five hundred tusks, killing thirty-seven poachers, and taking no prisoners.

The French media caught wind of the story, and Laboureur quickly became a celebrity in his homeland, the unyielding champion of wildlife in central Africa, the man leading the battle against ivory poaching. Matthieu, who had been raised in the African bush, was nicknamed "Tarzan" by the press.

"He was twenty years old then, a crazy bad-ass," says conservation biologist J. Michael Fay, who arrived at Koumbala at the end of Laboureur's first season back. "He and the old man would go out with a few guys and some old single-shot guns, and they'd take on fifty guys with machine guns and scatter them."

By the second season, Laboureur's team was better armed and making serious progress. By the end of that season, they had reduced poaching by 80 percent, and the next year, the elephants began returning. But one morning three years later, the crusade went terribly wrong.

There are probably a dozen versions of what happened on January 31, 1990. But what is clear is that the Laboureurs were on a family picnic near a river when they stumbled across a group of men they thought were poachers. Shooting broke out, and one man was killed.

But the victim, who had been taking a swim, was not a poacher. He and his companions were Central African game guards who had been hired by a rival European Community–funded anti-poaching program. Jean Laboureur was arrested, charged with murder, and jailed in Bangui.

The controversial case caused a rift between Bangui and Paris, and between Paris and the European Community. Laboureur was eventually released, but the price was high: He left Bangui for southern France with the understanding that he was never to return.

"I love the smell of WD-40 in the morning." It was Hagen's birthday, and to celebrate, he had awakened early, made some tea on his camouflaged stove, and begun cleaning his rifle.

"I certainly hope victory smells better than this," Bryant said.

We had landed the previous afternoon at the Protestant mission in Zemio, run by an energetic American named Wendy Atkins. With the safari companies gone, many of Zemio's residents survive on the hunting, transport, and trade of elephant meat, much of it from the Democratic Republic of the Congo, just across the M'Bomou River. An elephant yields about $250 worth of meat; once smoked, it is brought over the river in baskets and sold at Zemio's market.

Among the shoppers at the market was Karl Amman, a Kenya-based conservationist who was collecting samples of elephant meat for DNA analysis to determine if forest elephants are interbreeding with savanna elephants in the northern DRC.

"It's sad and ironic," Amman told us over dinner, "that it's become easier to buy meat in a village than to collect fecal samples in the field. They've wiped out 80 percent of the elephants within a hundred kilometers of the border. What's next? Buffalo are the next-biggest piece of meat, then antelopes, then it's on down the line to chimps."

Amman is one of the few conservationists who dare to venture into the war-torn DRC's northern region. He is an outspoken critic of "feel-good conservation" in Africa.

"The big organizations pretend they're succeeding, because success brings the money in," he said. "It's 'Just write us a check, and we'll take care of the rest.' But the reality here is a mess."

Amman and Bryant had rendezvoused in Zemio to plan a joint operation in two weeks to arrest eight former Congolese guerrillas living in the CAR who were organizing teams of elephant poachers.

"If I had an accurate idea of where they were crossing," said Bryant, "I could hit them as they came across. We have carte blanche from Patassé; he doesn't care what methods we use. But we have to be careful. We don't want the bleeding-hearts brigade from — what do you call it? — Amnesty International coming down on us."

On our third day in Zemio, Lesieur rolled in with ARRC's truck, its bed stacked high with rifles, rocket launchers, food, and beer. Wendy Atkins, our missionary hostess, looked nervous.

"Patron!" Lesieur greeted Bryant with his foot-stomping, thigh-slapping salute. Lesieur had brought two soldiers. One wore dark glasses, camouflage boots, and an excess of attitude, and Hagen immediately nicknamed him Rambo. Bryant decided that he didn't like either of them. "These aren't soldiers," he said. "They're garden boys with guns."

We had planned to continue east as soon as Lesieur arrived. But only one of the three diesel fuel drums that had been sent ahead made it. If we pushed on, said Bryant, we wouldn't have enough fuel to get back. "Haven't we had enough bloody obstacles?" he yelled. When we left Zemio, we traveled west, toward Rafaï.

Bryant's instructions to his soldiers were cursory: "We've got five hundred rounds between us, a few grenades, and three RPGs. It's not a lot. So I don't want any plinking shots."

I asked Bryant what he planned to do if we were ambushed.

"Don't worry," he said. "Normally when you get Africans in a firefight, it's just a matter of finding cover and waiting until they fire off all their ammo — which is usually about the time it takes to finish off a cigarette. Then you calmly walk toward them and shoot them."

The road west looked like it hadn't been maintained since independence in 1960, and in some places it was nearly impassable. Fending off driving tips from Hagen, Bryant drove through the rising heat, his left arm dangling out the window. His sweaty skin was soon coated with a layer of fine red dust.

At one point, Lesieur cautioned that the road ahead was notorious for hijackings. Bryant put on his chest webbing and checked his gun. "Better feed one up," he told Hagen, glancing in the rearview mirror. "Lesieur's pretty nervous."

As Hagen cocked his AK-47 and clicked off the safety, Bryant stubbed out his cigarette and put the butt in his pocket. (He is possibly the only man in Africa who doesn't throw his butts on the ground.) He wheeled the truck into a tunnel of trees spread over the road.

A few seconds later, shots exploded.

"Bloody hell!" Hagen yelled. He had his gun barrel out the window, sweeping the trees. Then he looked back at the soldiers and saw them sitting at ease, their rifles pointing toward the sky. Bryant guffawed.

"I forgot to tell you," he said. "I told them to fire off warning shots, to scare off anybody who might think we were an easy mark."

In the town of Dembia, Bryant stopped to talk to the gendarme, Christoff Touk Kekke. Kekke told Bryant that if he had fuel and ammunition, he would go after a braconnier named Aboulde who had settled in the area. Aboulde had been guiding other poachers, and he was running raids on nearby villages.

"Our fuel's been stolen," Bryant told him. "But if it hadn't been, we could have a go at him. It might do me good to get some of the frustration out of my system."

Bryant fished a Kalashnikov clip out of his chest webbing and handed it to Kekke — a small gesture that would turn out to be the most consequential action of the entire trip.

We drove all day, sometimes averaging only ten or fifteen miles an hour on the rough roads. By early afternoon, the sky went gauzy, as if it had soaked up the sweat of the trees. In the haze ahead, the road unrolled into distant herds of hills.

Toward evening, the light softened, and the villages along the road began to look more like ephemeral encampments. As the darkness advanced, the villagers moved close to their fires, hud-

dling around the light, warding off the eternity in the shadows of
the trees.

We crested a hill, and Bryant suddenly stomped on the brake
and threw the steering wheel sideways. Hagen was in the front seat,
and as we skidded to a stop, the barrel of his rifle knocked against
the dashboard.

"What the bloody hell is going on?" Hagen said, recovering his
gun.

Bryant nodded ahead, and we got out and walked to the front of
the truck. Illuminated by the headlights, hundreds of tiny blue and
yellow butterflies had alighted atop the red-dirt road, fluttering
wings no bigger than fingernails. I don't know how he ever saw
them.

Finally, we pulled into Rafaï and visited with some of the officials
and local volunteers whom Hayse had first made contact with. Each
had a new report of a robbery, a murder, a rape, a kidnapping.

"If the braconniers think I'm not prepared to use violence,"
Bryant told a representative from the local environmental and self-
defense organization, "I guess I'm going to have to do so to make a
point."

"We are waiting patiently for you to begin," the man said. "We are
ready to help. We will clear the roads for you; we have men ready to
fight alongside you."

Unbeknownst to us, as we were holding our meetings in Rafaï
the gendarme Kekke was leaving Dembia for Derbissaka, armed
with the ammunition clip Bryant had given him. At dawn, he and
his men surprised Aboulde and his two sons at their camp outside
the village. Before the poachers could get to their guns, Kekke captured them.

Next, Kekke apparently marched his prisoners into the nearest
village, where an angry crowd formed, demanding immediate justice.

"He just blew Aboulde away, literally," Bryant later reported. "It
was essentially a public execution. I don't have a moral problem
with it, but we could have the bleeding-hearts brigade saying there
was no due process, despite the fact that hundreds of people had
witnessed the murders and thefts he was doing. But I don't believe
it was necessary to terminate him on the spot."

We hadn't yet heard of the incident as we sat down outside a missionary house in Rafaï to watch the sun set. Bryant called the base in Bangui on a satellite phone, and Wieland told him that Commando was sick. She couldn't find a single veterinarian in the country.

"Maybe one of the MSF [the French acronym for Doctors Without Borders] doctors could look at him," Bryant told her, "owing to the chimp's similarities to a human."

Wieland also reported that talk of ARRC's diamond-dealing had made its way to President Patassé, who couldn't recall having given ARRC permission for such an operation. Apparently, Patassé wasn't happy. Meanwhile, though, rumors of an impending coup attempt were growing.

"I don't know who's going to get thrown out of the country first, us or him," Bryant said.

As we sat drinking warm beer in the fading light, a breeze came up, carrying a spicy-sweet smell. It was the smell of resilience, of optimism — the smell of the color green — and it overwhelmed thoughts of humanity's failures. For a moment, anyway, nature was winning.

When we arrived back in Bangui, Commando was gone. Wieland had found him a home at the Chimfunshi Wildlife Orphanage in Zambia. The missing fuel, meanwhile, had turned up in the supply yard of the MSF compound in Mboki.

Two weeks later, Bryant and Karl Amman would carry out a predawn raid on the Congolese poachers near Dembia. On the CAR side of the M'Bomou River, Bryant's force captured two men immediately. Another five managed to escape across the river — right into the arms of Amman's men. By sunrise, Bryant and Amman had caught seven of the eight ringleaders, and had confiscated elephant meat, ivory, several assault rifles, and ammunition. There were no casualties on either side.

I left the CAR the day after our return to Bangui. At the airport, I noticed blood dripping from some other passengers' boxes. The rainy season was just beginning, and the braconniers would soon begin heading home, with their spoils, along the old slave trails. Come November the rains will cease and the poachers — and ARRC — will return.

*

It takes a long time to get from Bangui to a former convent perched high above a gorge in southern France. It's early spring, and patches of snow still occupy the shady spots; a tough wind blows against the gray-brown vegetation on the mountainsides.

Claudine Laboureur welcomes my wife and me into her sitting room, where yellow firelight warms the thick stone walls. The room is furnished with pelts and African carvings, including a wooden statue of a hippo holding a top hat, the signature souvenir from the Central African Republic.

"He says it's over for us there, that we won't go back," Madame Laboureur says. "But he dreams of Africa every night."

I have heard that Jean Laboureur can be gruff and bitter. But for a man who has experienced the worst of the twentieth century — the Holocaust, the cannibal dictators, the slaughter of Africa's wildlife — he's relatively buoyant when he enters the room. He is balding, and his shoulders are stooped by the weight of his seventy-four years, but his eyes have a roguish glint.

Laboureur takes me through his life in Africa. He turns the pages of photo albums with large, callused hands, and I watch his eyes flicker as he registers each memory: the compound at Koumbala, the heads of state in safari gear, the Land Cruisers and bush planes atop the red-earth landing strip.

"Here is a family photo," he says, pointing to a shot of Matthieu torching a poachers' camp. On the next page, a dead elephant lies on its back in the mud, its body bloated and stripped of its tusks.

"It was only for greed," he sighs. "We tried to stop it. But we lost, always."

When I tell him about the ARRC project, Laboureur perks up. He has spent a long time on the sidelines, thinking through the logistics of such an operation, and his ideas come in extended bursts: They could put GPS-equipped spotters in ultralight airplanes; they could radio the poachers' positions to game guards on motorcycles. Perhaps Matthieu could get involved, and maybe Giscard d'Estaing (now working for the European Community) could find some funding.

"In the right hands," Laboureur says, "you could have some real results. But the world is distracted, and time is getting away from us. In five or six years, this region will be completely empty of animals. That is a loss that humanity will never be able to recover."

Just before dinner, Laboureur switches on the news. The broadcast is filled with scenes of suicide bombings in the Middle East, attacks on refugee camps, rockets, rubble, grief. He mutes the television and turns toward me, as the staggering images carry on in silence, just over his shoulder.

"Listen," he says. "In the past century, all the best minds have been focused on finding more efficient ways to kill. But there are some people who still believe in the possibility of doing something positive for the Earth.

"Perhaps their efforts will end badly, as mine have. But if they should somehow manage to succeed . . . that would be a beautiful thing."

GEOFF DYER

The Despair of Art Deco

FROM *The Threepenny Review*

THE ONLY TIME I have ever seen a dead body was in South Beach, Miami, in the heart of the Art Deco district. It is possible that seeing a dead body there has had an undue influence on my view of Art Deco; but it is also possible that Art Deco has had an undue influence on my view of the dead body. The two are related, I think.

We flew to Miami from boring Nassau and got a bus to South Beach. It was a Sunday, the sidewalks were crammed with visitors, but finding a hotel was not difficult because visitors who had come for the weekend had already checked out of their hotels. We checked in at the Beachcomber, a nice-looking place on Collins in the heart of the Art Deco area. That is a pretty meaningless remark, I know. Art Deco, after all, means nice-looking, or, more exactly, not-as-nice-as-it-looks. Our room at the Beachcomber, for example, did not look quite as nice as the facade of the Beachcomber but it still looked pretty nice. An Art Deco lampshade bathed the Art Deco sheets in an amber Art Deco glow. When we drew back the curtains, the Art Deco spell was broken. The window was cracked, grimy, and the surge of dusty sunlight revealed a damp patch spreading across the carpet from the bathroom wall almost to the center of the room. Then a mouse raced across the marshy carpet and squeezed, with difficulty, under the skirting board of the cramped and moldy bathroom. Dazed stood on a chair and said with — I promise — no trace of emotion, "Eek! A mouse."

"I'll deal with it," I said.

"You mean you'll try to get a discount on the room?"

"Exactly."

I went out to the ponytailed fellow at reception and asked if we could change rooms because there was a mouse in our room, in the room we were in at the moment, and we would prefer a room without a mouse or, if no other room was available —

"Welcome to the tropics," he said. He didn't shrug. There was no need. His voice shrugged. As it happens, we had just come from the tropics where we had not seen a single mouse and so I said, "This is not the tropics." Although the mouse was not a problem for me, I went on, my girlfriend was "freaked out" — I used that exact phrase — by it.

"Whatever," he said, handing me a key to a room on the first floor. "Take a look at that one."

It was nice, I said when I went back down, but it was not made up. Next he offered to upgrade us to a larger room, Room Fifteen, if I remember rightly. That was nice, too, but somebody had been smoking in there, I explained, and it smelled smoky.

"Try Thirteen," he said, handing me another key. I was beginning to wonder if any rooms were occupied. As it happens, Thirteen *was* — by a woman, French, I think, sitting on the toilet. This really baffled him. According to his computer, Room Thirteen was definitely empty, but he suggested I try Six. Six was empty, mouseless, smokeless, made up, unoccupied, actually nicer than where we were. An upgrade was as good as a discount. Fine, I said. In the meantime he had sent someone (who? as far as I could tell he was the only person around) up to Thirteen and there was no one there.

"You must have gone to the wrong room," he said.

"Then how could I have opened the door?" I shot back.

"Some keys work for more than one room."

"Ah." We moved to Six, where we got stoned on this mad skunk. Then we went out, for a walk, to buy smoothies, to experience the Art Deco experience for ourselves. Although we had just booked into an Art Deco hotel, we kept stopping off at other Art Deco hotels to see if we would have been better off in another Art Deco hotel. We compared prices and quality ("the price-quality axis, as it were," I said). There were several other hotels we could have stayed in but, overall, we had quite a good deal.

"We could have got a better deal," I summarized. "But we don't have the worst possible deal. Obviously, we could have paid more and stayed at a better place."

"Or paid less and stayed at a worse place."

"But we haven't found a place that was more expensive and worse."

"And is that really what we're looking for?"

"In a sense, yes. For peace of mind."

"But there's always the chance that in looking for a place that is more expensive and worse we might find a place that is better and cheaper."

"Thereby destroying any chance of ever achieving peace of mind."

"Perhaps we shouldn't look at any more hotels, then."

Except that's what you come to South Beach for: to see hotels. The hotels — the Art Deco hotels — are the attraction. Effectively, the Art Deco experience is the hotel experience. Staying in hotels is a side effect of wanting to see them. In a place with so many hotels, it is the residents who are the tourists, who are not at home. So we continued to look at hotels but we refrained from enquiring about vacancies and rates. Except at the Mermaid Guest House, which was a little more expensive than the Beachcomber but infinitely lovelier. Much of the Art Deco architecture in South Beach is actually a derivative or variant of Art Deco known as Tropical Deco; the Mermaid takes this tendency a little further, away from Deco toward Tropical. We both wished we were staying there — having come from the mouseless tropics, it would have lent a continuity to our trip — but since we had already booked into the Beachcomber there was, Dazed said, "no use crying over spilled milk."

"It's funny, isn't it, people say that, but of course that's exactly what makes you want to cry. The fact that it's spilled. Why would you cry over unspilled milk?"

"You don't like milk, though, do you, darling?"

"I like it in smoothies," I said.

After the Mermaid we didn't ask about vacancies and rates at any other hotels. We didn't enquire at the Victor on Ocean Front Drive because this vast, gleaming white building was unoccupied: utterly vacant, a site of abandoned meaning, in fact, unless the provision of accommodation is considered a side effect of the Art Deco effect, in which case it was a site of purified meaning. With windows boarded up and painted over, it looked, Dazed said, "like Rachel Whiteread's Art Deco sequel to *House*."

"What? Like *Hotel*?"

We were still really blasted from the skunk we had smoked earlier. A little further on, still on Ocean Front, a guy with drive-by shades asked Dazed where she'd got her hair braided. Dazed told him Cat Island. He was asking, really, on behalf of his girlfriend, who was blond and Russian. He was black and Cuban. They were a very modern couple but they were the product also of a long-standing political alliance. They asked us to take their picture in front of the house — mansion, actually — we were standing in front of.

"You know what house this is?" the Cuban said.

"No."

"Versace's house," he said. "This is where he was gunned down."

Dazed handed their camera back and they walked off. I studied the bloodless sidewalk. Dazed said, "This is where he was gunned down."

"Yes," I said. "This is where he was gunned down."

"Do you remember what you were doing on the night he was gunned down?"

"People are always getting gunned down," I said. "No. What were you doing?"

"When?"

"On the night he was gunned down."

"Who?"

"Specifically, Versace, but anyone really. Anyone who was gunned down."

"Malcolm X was gunned down, wasn't he, darling?"

"Yes, although he wasn't nearly so well known as a fashion designer."

"But those glasses he wore have become very fashionable. You see lots of people wearing them. You have a pair, don't you, darling?"

"Yes. And you know the really weird thing?"

"What?"

"They are made by Versace."

"That is *so* creepy."

While we were having this conversation quite a few people were photographed on the spot where Versace was gunned down. I was one of them: Dazed took a picture of me with the disposable camera we had bought in Nassau. Until we had done this we found it difficult to tear ourselves away from the spot, the spot where people were having their pictures taken, the spot where Versace had been gunned down.

It was time, Dazed suggested, to refresh ourselves with a smoothie. We sucked our smoothies — mine had a protein supplement — sitting on a wall by the beach. I made notes for an essay on Art Deco I knew I would never get round to writing.

It is not accurate, I wrote, to say that a shabbiness lurks behind the facade of Art Deco: Art Deco is the facade. Art Deco is the most visible of architectural styles, arranged entirely for the eye — it's in color! — rather than to be inhabited. Art Deco buildings are inhabited, of course, but whereas, from the outside, they look extraordinary, inside, the experience is fairly ordinary. But this is why the Art Deco style is so alluring.

The block of flats where I have lived in Brixton, London, since the early eighties is, essentially, a utilitarian, age of austerity version of Art Deco, without the trappings of Art Deco — without the things that make it Art Deco. These could be added with next to no effort and at minimal expense and the building could be transformed into an Art Deco block, whereupon this area of flats would become as pleasing to the eye as South Beach. The flats themselves would remain the same — but how lovely it would be to feel that we lived in the Art Deco area of Brixton rather than in a shabby block of flats. We could even call it South Beach, Brixton.

Twilight was falling. The sand dulled. We began walking back to our hotel. Pale in the afternoon sunlight, neon — purple, glowing, green — was coming into its own. The sky grew ink-dark.

Back at the Beachcomber, it turned out that we were not the only ones to have changed rooms. The mouse had come too. It was in the wastepaper basket, eating dinner. We preferred to think that it was the same mouse because that was preferable, I said, to admitting that the hotel was actually "a vermin-infested rat-hole."

"You can't call it a rat-hole," said Dazed.

"Why not?"

"Because a mouse is not a rat."

"But a mouse is a vermin, isn't it?"

"I don't know what a vermin is."

"Mice and rats are vermin."

"Are you a vermin, darling?"

"And since rats and mice are vermin, a mouse is, in a sense, a species of rat."

"Am *I* a vermin, darling?"

"So, logically, it is absolutely accurate to call a place infested with mice a rat-hole."

"It is a rat-hole, isn't it, darling?"

That night I woke up several times, hearing rustling and scurrying. In the morning there were mouse droppings on the spare bed and the mouse had chewed through Dazed's make-up bag.

"Look," she said, holding up a copy of our slightly nibbled guide to the Bahamas. "It chewed off more than it could bite."

"D'you think it might eat my computer?" I said.

"I'm worried that it might eat us."

Before going out, we stashed our belongings away on high shelves in the wardrobe, out of harm's way, so it would be harder for the mouse to eat them.

"The mouse is terrorizing us, isn't it?" said Dazed as we locked our room with a key that, in all probability, opened other rooms as well.

"It really is."

"It's gnawing away at our self-esteem."

By the time we had breakfast it was already hot as anything. The sky was a sharp blue. I had a seven-dollar haircut from a Cuban barber who sang while he worked, paying almost no attention to the job in hand. At a spacious bookstore on Lincoln, Dazed bought a copy of *Miami* by Joan Didion. The sun ricocheted off the walls and sidewalk. Even though neither of us is interested in cars, there were lots of interesting cars to look at. Without any warning Dazed asked what I would do if she threw herself in front of one of these cars. I said I didn't know, but my general policy is not to get involved. We went into record stores and clothes stores and picked up flyers for trance parties that had taken place the day before we arrived. Every clothes store played trance but we didn't find any clothes we wanted or any parties we could go to. We just walked around, really, looking at hotels and flyers, buying smoothies, living the Art Deco life, getting stoned on this mad skunk. Then a hustler with wayward hair and unkempt eyes accosted us.

"Do you speak English?" he wanted to know.

"To a very high standard," I said.

"Could you do me a favor?"

"Almost certainly not," I said. For a moment he looked totally crestfallen. Then he went on his way without even saying "Fuck you." In its way it was one of the most satisfying exchanges of my life. He could have been the risen Christ for all we cared.

What else? We watched some beach volleyball and then Dazed borrowed a guy's blades — her feet are quite big — and bladed for a while. She didn't even ask. He *offered*. I sat talking to him, just stuff to say while he swigged semiskimmed milk from a carton and we both watched Dazed gliding and turning on his blades. After blading she wanted to go back to the hotel because it was so hot and the heat was getting to her. I walked with her, back to the Beachcomber, and then strolled on regardless.

In the course of my stroll I became convinced that The Gap, on Collins, was designed to look like an Art Deco whale, some kind of fish anyway. One window served for an eye, three more for teeth. It even had fins and gills. I stared at it for a while, unsure if this was just the skunk talking. Speaking of talking, I wished Dazed had been there so we could have had one of our so-called conversations about the whale, about whether it was a whale or not.

Further on, one side of the street was cordoned off with black and yellow film: POLICE LINE DO NOT CROSS. A crowd, of which I was a part, gathered. Something had happened. You could tell something had happened by the way we were all standing round asking what happened. There was an ambulance, several police cars. A photographer was taking photographs, standing over . . . the body! I say body but I could see only the feet of the body, the grubby white socks. The rest of the body was hidden from view by bushes.

"What happened?" I said to the guy next to me. He had a tattoo of a washing machine on his arm.

"Suicide."

"Oh my."

"A seventy-two-year-old woman. She jumped."

"Shit. Hey, I like the tattoo, by the way."

"Thanks."

"Is it any particular kind of washing machine?"

"Oh, it's like, just a general model, I guess."

"What floor did she jump from?"

"Fourteenth."

I began counting from the ground floor up but soon lost track.

The situation was made more complex by the way that, in America, the first floor is actually the ground floor and the second is the first and so on. The fourteenth was about two-thirds of the way up.

"Happens all the time," the guy with the tattoo of a washing machine on his arm said.

"Does it?"

"It's the heat."

"What?"

"Drives people nuts."

"What does?"

"The heat."

"Yes," I said. "I can imagine." But I was also thinking that Rome is just as hot as Miami and people don't throw themselves off fourteenth-floor balconies there.

"Drives people nuts," he repeated.

"Perhaps Art Deco generates a kind of despair," I said. "Is that possible?"

"Anything's possible," he said. Across the road the photographer was taking photographs of the body. In fact, the whole scene looked like one of those staged photographs of the dead by Nick Waplington. I had never seen a dead body before and now I was seeing one. Or seeing a pair of socks anyway. I was not sure that counted. To really see a dead body, perhaps you have to see the mashed head, the bloody face, but all I could see were the grubby white socks of the dead woman, whose body would soon be zipped up in a body bag.

Back at the hotel Dazed was asleep on the bed and had not been eaten by the mouse, which, I had to concede, was actually the "mice," several of whom scurried away when I entered the room. I took a shower in the shoddy bathroom and then told Dazed about the dead woman. She was very sympathetic, reassuring me that, although I had only seen her socks, it still counted: I could say that I had seen a dead body.

That evening we ate in the same restaurant we had eaten in the night before. In the morning I took Dazed to the spot, the spot where the woman had jumped. Something about South Beach urges you to do this, to visit the spots where people have been gunned down or thrown themselves off balconies.

"It's a place," Dazed said, "with a remarkable capacity to generate sites of instant pilgrimage." I could see now that the old lady had been extremely considerate, jumping into a recess, set back slightly from the sidewalk, so that she would not land on anyone. There was no stain or anything, no dent. Dazed took a picture of me but I was a little nervous standing there in case someone else came down on top of me.

"Hurry up," I said.

"Why?"

"This is a part of the world where people fall through the air at speed," I said. After Dazed had taken the picture we crossed the road and I saw that the balconies on one side of the building were all empty except for chairs on which no one sat. Dazed said that the building was flying at half-mast and I understood what she meant.

We looked at more hotels, enjoyed some more smoothies. Later in the day I saw an old woman hobbling along through the swarming, tanned bodies of the fit and young, the stoned trancers and tattooed bladers, the gay men all pumped up with protein supplements and power boosts, the pierced, slim, salad-eating women for whom Art Deco was an incentive to display and not a source of shoddy despair that could drive you to suicide. I admired the old woman's tenacity, the way she kept going, kept putting one arthritic foot in front of another. She smiled at me and I realized that it was the same woman I had seen yesterday, lying on the sidewalk. I was glad that she had made such a speedy recovery. I knew it was her because of her socks, which were grubby, white, unbloodied.

JACK HANDEY

The Respect of the Men

FROM *Outside*

As LEADER of the expedition, I have come to realize that there is one thing more important than any other — and that is the respect of the men. It is more valuable than your gun, or your knife, or the blue terry-cloth slippers that keep your feet so toasty around the campfire at night.

In fact, the respect of the men can be even more important than the success of the mission itself. So if you're not exactly sure what the mission is, you may not want to ask the men, because you might lose their respect.

You don't get the respect of the men right away. You can try, by getting down in the dirt and begging them for it, or by kissing their boots, or by doing your funny cowboy dance for them. But trust me, these are not going to work.

No, respect is something that has to be earned. And earned slowly, like a fine, respectful wine. You can't try to earn it all at once, maybe by doing something like yelling out "Hey, watch this!" and then rolling all the way down the side of a hill. Even if you explain to the men that there could have been snakes and bees where you rolled, but you didn't care, it won't impress them.

Rather, respect is earned by little things. Let's say you are leading the expedition through the bush, and you announce "I can't go on any farther!" But you do, for about five more hours, until you fall exhausted in the sand. Then you get up and make the men a nice dinner. Things like that.

Or later that night, around the campfire, you are toasting one of your marshmallows, using a stick that you broke off a tree with your bare hands. The marshmallow catches fire, and you wave it around to put it out. Even though it is out, the marshmallow is still smoky-hot, and sparky. But you just pop it straight into your mouth.

Or let's say you are riding your horse over some sharp rocks, so you get off to walk your horse, even though the rocks are really rough on your terry-cloth slippers. The men notice things like that. "You're gonna tear up those house shoes," one of the men might say to you. "I know," you mumble, because your mouth is still sore from the burning marshmallow.

That night you might check outside your tent to see if there is a present from the men, which, if you opened it, would be a new pair of slippers. But there isn't. And you smile to yourself, because you realize that the respect of the men is not the same as the love of the men.

But if it is difficult to gain the men's respect, it is easy to lose it. And the worst part is, you don't even know what it was you did. Was it trying to mash nine burning marshmallows into your mouth at once? Was it telling the men that you laugh at danger, but then not seeing any danger so you laugh at mountains and trees and horse manure? And Curtis's hat? Was it asking them about the hideous howls during the night that sounded like the lost souls of Hades shrieking in agony and torment, and the men not knowing what you're talking about, then having one of the men say, "Maybe it was a tree frog"?

You can never know for sure. But one thing is certain: You can't win back their respect with cheap parlor tricks or, say, a magic trick. Even if you take hours to learn the trick, and you gather the men around the campfire to perform it, and you use a little magic table that you made yourself, and even if the trick, you think, is performed pretty well, this is not going to rekindle the men's respect. You can tell from the looks they give one another, and the lack of applause. You may get a little respect if you get mad and throw the table and the trick parts into the fire, but that's about it. And you may get some respect from the dove for letting him go. But still you are wondering, *What's wrong with these men? Come on, that was a good trick.*

The respect of the men can be a cruel mistress and a harlot. But at other times it can be a nice mistress and a happy slut. You can't think about it too much. But if you ignore it, it can sneak up and coldcock you, like an angry prostitute.

You know it won't be easy, but one day you will again have the respect of the men. You don't know when or how. And you can't help thinking that maybe if you could explain to the men just how difficult the magic trick was, it would go a long way toward getting the whole respect thing going again.

CHRISTOPHER HITCHENS

The Ballad of Route 66

FROM *Vanity Fair*

JOSEPH HELLER'S MASTERPIECE, originally entitled *Catch-18*, was renamed — or should that be renumbered? — by its editor, Robert Gottlieb. Comes the question. Would the novel have had the same pervading influence under its first digits? I can think of at least some reasons to doubt it. First, certain numbers have hieroglyphic power, and repetition has something to do with this quality. Just take the figure six. Consider the mark of the beast and its three sixes. Then, not every number can be made to rhyme with "kicks." Get your jive on Route 55? Not really. Get to heaven on Route 77? Feel free on Route 33? Too insipid. No hint of sexty-sex . . .

Whereas when Bobby Troup's wife leaned over and whispered in his ear as they were speeding toward California in the heady days of postwar liberty in 1946, murmuring, "Get your kicks on Route 66," he knew at once that he had a song right there. (Bob Dylan had to do "Highway 61" twice, or "revisit" it, and still didn't get the same effect.) Sixty-six is three times Heller's 22. Two sixes is a good throw at dice, and always gets a cheer — "Clickety-click, all the sixes, *66*"— at bingo. Nat "King" Cole took the song off Bobby Troup's hands at once, and he sang the refrain as "Route Six Six" with no damage to the lyric. Since then it's been rerecorded or reworked by Dr. Feelgood, Buddy Greco, Depeche Mode, Chuck Berry, Bing Crosby and the Andrews Sisters, Rosemary Clooney, and the Sharks. Mythology says that Jack Kerouac heard the song on a jukebox in 1947 and decided on the spot to take a westward road trip. I first heard it in the great year of '66 itself, when it was belted out by the Rolling Stones. Here are the words, which have become the song lines of America's western destiny:

If you ever plan to motor west, travel my way,
Take the highway that is best
Get your kicks on Route 66!
It winds from Chicago to LA,
More than two thousand miles all the way.
Get your kicks on Route 66!
Now you go through St Looey, Joplin, Missouri
And Oklahoma City is mighty pretty,
You'll see Amarillo, Gallup, New Mexico,
Flagstaff, Arizona. Don't forget Winona,
Kingman, Barstow, San Bernardino.
Won't you get hip to this timely tip:
When you make that California trip,
Get your kicks on Route 66!

When I first bounced to Mick Jagger doing this, I initially heard the fifth line to say, "Forty-two thousand miles all the way," and thought, Jesus, the United States is *big*. And when I lowered myself behind the wheel of a blazing-red Corvette in Chicago in August and pointed myself at the Pacific, the country ahead didn't seem too small, either. From Grant Park on the shore of Lake Michigan — scene of riots at the 1968 Democratic convention — over to the junction of Santa Monica and Ocean.

Just to answer any questions you might have before I roar away: Much local politics is highway politics. After the passage of the Federal Highway Act in 1921, which mandated interstate roads, it was determined that east-west highways would have even numerals, and north-south highways would have odd ones. Roads that cut state lines would be designated by shields, intrastate roads with circular signs. Major highways would carry numbers ending in zero. The Chicago–Los Angeles one was to be called Route 60. Or so the Illinois and Missouri authorities decided. But 60 meant so much to the state officials of Kentucky and Virginia that they were prepared to fight over it. The number 66 was still free when the Illinois, Missouri, and now Oklahoma bureaucrats caved in. So the famous "66" shield was born, and in 1926 marked 800 miles of paved road. It took until 1937 to pave the remaining 1,648 miles of gravel, dirt, and asphalt. In 1977 the route was decommissioned and replaced with a new interstate, which, as if in numerical mimicry of the year

'77 and the number 66, leaves Chicago as Interstate 55, becoming 44 in Missouri before evolving into a banal 40 and an indifferent 15 before hitting L.A, where it peters out in Interstate 10 to the Pacific.

Yet the attachment to the music and mythology of the old road was and is very great, and for long and short and very broken-up stretches you can still leave the main "drag" of interstate-land, with its homogenized gas stations and chain restaurants and franchise motels, and take a spin into a time warp or a parallel universe, where you might have swerved suddenly into *The Last Picture Show* or *Bonnie and Clyde,* or even *The Twilight Zone.* It's all going, and going fast, but then, in my Corvette, so could I.

Perhaps, here, a word about the car. There was a TV series in the early 1960s called *Route 66,* where a couple of lads played by George Maharis and Martin Milner acted as knights of the road on a generic highway, backed by a theme tune from Nelson Riddle and employing a Corvette as a talisman and prop. The ladies among you will not (I hope and trust) be familiar with the sensation of strapping on a huge and empurpled projectile protuberance at about the midsection. But any man who has sat in the driver's seat of a fiery-red Corvette and seen the sweeping and rising hood twanging away in front of him may, as he looks along the barrel, want to make a wild surmise. The song by the artist who was then known as Prince, "Little Red Corvette," just doesn't cover it. Stephen King's mad-car-disease novel, *Christine,* is based on the huge number of songs from the fifties and sixties that personalized automobiles by giving them names, invariably female. My Corvette was too slim and graceful to be a boy, but it wasn't exactly a chick either. I soon got bored with forcing Winnebagos and U-Hauls to dine on my dust, and began to humble ever faster machines, including that of an Illinois state trooper who was fortunately engaged with someone else. The shimmer of Lake Shore Drive and the grime of Al Capone's Cicero fell away behind, and I was even thinking irresponsibly of giving downstate Illinois a miss until conscience pricked me to visit Springfield, home and resting place of Abraham Lincoln.

At once I fell victim to three of the many banes that afflict the modern road warrior in America. Towns that have multiple exits don't tell you which exit will take you to, say, where you want to go.

There is never anybody on the sidewalk to ask. People in cars, if you can catch them as every red light suddenly goes green, usually aren't from here. And when you do find a local, he or she doesn't know the way. It was a Hooters bar that finally helped me to get a fix on Honest Abe; the waitress knew several of the key sites and scrawled them daintily on a napkin and gave me a terrific quesadilla into the bargain. Thus I discovered, following the old brown "66" shields through a shaded part of downtown, that Lincoln may have been reared in a log cabin but it wasn't in Springfield. I also came to the painful realization that was to recur to me times without number. A shiny red Corvette can be a boy magnet, all right. When parked, it drew to my side many garage mechanics and hotel doormen and learned young black men and polite old roadside coots who would inquire after the finer points and details. When in motion it would summon cops from deserted streets and vacant landscapes. But it appeared to leave the female sex quite unmoved. Could it be a fault in the design? Perhaps the silhouette? I began to brood, and in fine brooding country.

Southern Illinois is flat. There is the punctuation of grain silos and elevators (and the elevators now have their own museum, just like every other "66" feature and artifact). This is "the prairie state" and signs along the road announce the restoration of prairie grass, to forestall complaints about unmown roadsides. Some of the 66 byways are explorable, but they are flat, also, and their surfaces are often too rugged for a low-to-the-ground beauty such as I am driving. Then, to the right, there's a sudden sign for the MOTHER JONES MEMORIAL, and I swing to it on impulse as the sky makes a long and leisurely turn from robin's-egg blue to glaring red. Here, just outside the little town of Mount Olive, is the incongruous sight of a cemetery devoted entirely to the union martyrs of the coal industry. And Mary "Mother" Jones, queen of the labor hell-raisers, has her shrine in its precincts. She was born on May 1, 1830, before there even was a May Day, and lived to be a hundred. This region, now so rural in appearance, was once a heartland of King Coal and the proving ground for the great John L. Lewis and his United Mine Workers. The rows — better say the ranks and files — of tombstones almost all bear German and Hungarian and Croatian names, and the dates of half-forgotten massacres on bloody picket lines. It was the coming of the highways that helped break the railroad monopolies in this and other states: another way in which the open road is associated with liberation. I bowed my head at the gate, where it said, THE RESTING PLACE FOR GOOD UNION PEOPLE, and was given a honk and a wave and many high signs by a carload of (entirely) boys as I drove away. Perhaps not many Corvettes are seen making this particular stop. At this stage, I reflected irrelevantly, I was about seven hours from Tulsa.

I crossed the big Mississippi into St. Louis — forever to be mispronounced as a result of Bobby Troup's lyric — as the darkness thickened and the lights picked out the huge arch, gateway to the west, that when finished in 1965 presumably did not make every tourist think consciously or unconsciously of McDonald's and wonder where the twin arch had gone. St. Louis is the city of Charles Lindbergh, pioneer of the aviation industry, which was to supplant both rail and road. It used to be the hub of Trans World Airlines, now deceased, and the TWA symbol was being replaced with the logo of a brokerage on the stadium where the Rams play. ("Flying across the desert on a TWA," as Buddy Holly sang in "Brown-Eyed Handsome Man," "saw a woman walking 'cross the sand." Who will get that line a decade from now?) This is an odd combination of frontier town and respectable town: the birthplace of T. S. Eliot and of Martha Gellhorn, the first of whom fled it because it was too provincial and uncouth and the second because it was too straitlaced. In the heart of music history it occupies a soft spot, as the birthplace of Chuck Berry, the home of the Scott Joplin museum, and the home, if not the native one, of Miles Davis and Tina Turner.

The most striking thing to me, however, was the constant reminder of Middle America's German past. It's not just the prevalence of the Anheuser-Busch and Budweiser ambience. There was a big *Strassenfest,* or street fair, in progress, and in Memorial Park were playing the Dingolfingen Stadtmusikanten Brass Band, Die Spitzbaum, and the Waterloo German Band. Some fifty-eight million Americans tell the census that they are of German origin, even more than say English, and you would never really notice this, perhaps the most effective assimilation in history, any more than you "notice" that the minority leader in the House and the majority leader in the Senate are named Gephardt and Daschle.

In the morning, on an open-air platform of the St. Louis transit system, I fall into conversation with another visitor, named Kevin Honeywood. He wears a nice hat and works for IBM, and he is also looking for a decent place to eat down by the river, so we hunt as a pair. Mr. Honeywood is a boyhood veteran of black South Side Chicago, and as the Big Muddy runs past our equally long and meandering lunch he tells me many things about the old days of "66" as it ran through his neighborhood, things I could never have learned from driving through it. People knew which stretches they weren't allowed to use along Cicero and Cermak and McCormick, but on July 4 they liked to block a section of Ogden Avenue for drag racing. Driving is much easier now for black folks; the rhythm of the road starts to hit me more and more as a variation of upbeat and downbeat, as well as a rapid fluctuation of American geography and history.

In the evening I pay a call on Blueberry Hill, a bar out in the city's "Loop," where Chuck Berry still stops in to play one Wednesday each month. There's a Hollywood-style "walk of fame" on the adjoining sidewalk, with stars and short canned biographies for Tina Turner and the others. The joint itself is a bit tame — ID cards mandatory at the door and that sort of thing — but it has a terrific jukebox and girls playing darts in daring couples and an Elvis Room for events. There's no way to check out the urban-legend rumor that Chuck Berry once had this ladies' room wired for video. I'm beginning to weary of hamburgers already, but the signature version here is highly toothsome and comes with a cheese peculiar to St. Louis, which I failed to write down but mean to check out. Still, the evening needs a round-off and so I favor BB's Jazz, Blues, and Soups, nearer the river, with a drop-by. A convincing rainbow-coalition band with a very strong sax is doing its stuff, and the tourist hour seems to have safely passed, until a terrifying skull-faced blonde detaches herself from a gaggle and whacks me in the features with a star wand. "How ya doin'?" I always think, What kind of a question is that?, and I always reply, "A bit early to tell." She gives me another smack with the wand and holds it up so I can see the number "50" emblazoned at the center. "It's mah *birthday!*" Christ. Does she know about the Corvette?

The next morning I roared past the Mississippi, scattering lesser cars like chickens, and nod to the Gateway Arch while noticing for the first time that gateway is an anagram of "getaway." Then it's down through Missouri and toward the Ozarks. Long ago, when there was an Ozark Airlines, I noticed at airports that that name was "krazo" spelled backassward. The hillbillies have taken enough sneers in their time, and you can tell they don't care, because the landscape is clichéd with revival chapels of obscure denominations, gun shops and gun shows, and liquor stores that say "whisky" or "whiskey" and mean bourbon. This is John Ashcroft country, or was until he lost the Senate race to a deceased person. On the radio, people who are very obviously products of evolution quarrel at the top of their leathery lungs with the verdict. My radio can't shake them for miles, but eventually finds a station that plays Chuck Berry singing the first of his songs that I remember — "No Particular Place to Go." This man's music, remember, is on the twin Voyager space probes, in case there is intelligent life anywhere else.

There are shimmering lakes and grand old steel and iron bridges on the side roads, and the wooded hills make it easy to amble, but I'm sorry I did because by the time I got to Springfield, Missouri, at evening the whole place was shut. It was a Sunday, and most restaurants just don't bother. I finally ran down a steak house, where the automatic raunchiness of the barmaids and waitresses, as they lobbed backchat with the guys, was some consolation for the surrounding Sabbath gloom. Only some consolation, though, because it put me in mind of John Steinbeck's line in *The Grapes of Wrath* about "the smart listless language of the roadsides." Reduced to the TV in my motel, I lucked into a rerun of *Thelma & Louise*, which, while it may not be the best buddy and road movie in history, surely features the best blue jeans. Susan Sarandon and Geena Davis pick up Brad Pitt on the way to Oklahoma City, which I was hoping to hit myself by the next nightfall. Among the soundtrack songs are "Badlands" and "Ballad of Lucy Jordan," which showcases Marianne Faithfull's nineteenth nervous comeback and tells of a girl who never had a ride in a car like mine.

The name Joplin seems to necessitate a stop, like the Bobby Troup line says, and on the way there's a good side stretch of the old Route. On its two-lane pavement, the mirages seem shinier and deeper, and there isn't the eternal nuisance of great swatches of black tire tread, or tire shed, flapping like crows or writhing like snakes under your wheels. For miles I saw no cars in either direction. The town of Albatross was to all outward appearances fast asleep. In Avilla, almost nothing broke the stillness. I tried Bernie's Route 66 bar, with its shanty look and old Pabst Blue Ribbon symbol, but a rail-thin man wearing only jeans and a cowboy hat (and guarding a sign on the fridge that read, FREE BEER TOMORROW) told me they didn't open until late. Following a road of unattended lawn and garage sales, I came to the comparative metropolis of Carthage, where in a slumberous old square there is a marker claiming the town as the site of the first major land battle of the Civil War. On July 5, 1861, it seems, local gallantry fought off "federal dominance" of Missouri in a series of what the polished granite calls "running engagments" (*sic*). That was enough to muse upon until I hit Joplin, which is a wilderness of strip malls and traffic stoplights. "Anything to see or do round here?," I asked the young man in the music store, determined as I was to purchase some independence from the radio stations. "Jack," he replied briefly, knowing from my credit card that this was not my name. Sad to think so of a town that has the same name as Scott and indeed Janis.

There are about a dozen miles of Kansas on Route 66, and if you blink, then, well, you aren't in Kansas anymore. A few of those burgs where, when the wind drops, all the chickens fall over. Kansas City, home of those "hungry little women," is back in Missouri. Best floor it and get to Oklahoma. In Missouri, a distinctive feature is the pull-over pay phone that has been downsized to allow you to call while sitting in your car. In Oklahoma, the keynote is roadside exhortation. Not only is Oklahoma ready to proclaim itself "Native America," but it is also "Cherokee Nation." Regular signs instruct you to KEEP OUR LAND GRAND. It's the boostering and the upbeat that force the downbeat into mind, and not just because of the luckless Cherokee and their "trail of tears." One of the many breezy names for Route 66 is "the mother road," but this phrase was first deployed by Steinbeck (whose centennial is this year) in the following tremendous passage from *The Grapes of Wrath:*

> Highway 66 is the main migrant road. 66 — the long concrete path across the country, waving gently up and down on the map, from Missis-

sippi to Bakersfield — over the red lands and the gray lands, twisting up into the mountains, crossing the Divide and down into the bright and terrible desert, and across the desert to the mountains again, and into the rich California valleys.

Sixty-six is the path of a people in flight, refugees from dust and shrinking land, from the thunder of tractors and shrinking ownership, from the desert's slow northward invasion, from the twisting winds that howl up out of Texas, from the floods that bring no richness to the land and steal what little richness is there. From all of these the people are in flight, and they come into 66 from the tributary side roads, from the wagon tracks and the rutted country roads. Sixty-six is the mother road, *the road of flight.* [My italics.]

The title of his 1939 classic — and just try imagining *that* novel under a different name — comes from the nation's best-loved Civil War anthem. (It was Steinbeck's wife Carol who came up with the refulgent idea.) When first published it carried both the verses of Julia Ward Howe *and* the sheet music on the endpapers in order to fend off accusations of unpatriotic Marxism. But really it succeeded because it contrived to pick up the strain of what Wordsworth called "the still, sad music of humanity." Another subversive, Woody Guthrie, effectively set the novel to music with *Dust Bowl Ballads:* Combine these with the photographs of Dorothea Lange and you have a historic triptych. A song of Guthrie's — "The Will Rogers Highway," another folksy name for 66 — manages to rhyme Los Angeles with both "Cherokees" and "refugees." (Guthrie sounds a bit folksy, too, when you replay him today. But without Woody, never forget, we would have no Bob Dylan and perhaps no Bruce Springsteen.) I remind myself again that this superficially cheery and touristic route was a road of heartbreak for hundreds of thousands of the poor white underclass, who were despised foreigners in their own country.

But black Oklahoma was visited by tribulation far worse and somewhat earlier. (You can revisit part of it in Toni Morrison's Oklahoma novel, *Paradise,* which is the perfect antidote to Rodgers and Hammerstein.) In Tulsa, I made a stop to see the Greenwood memorial, which ought to be better known than it is. The Greenwood quarter of town included in 1921 a thriving business district, known as "the Negro Wall Street." On June 1, 1921, it was torched from end to end in a vicious and jealous pogrom, which burned out most of thirty-five city blocks, incinerating more than twelve hundred homes and businesses as well as at least a half-dozen churches. The forces of law and order either pitched in or stood aside while as many as three hundred citizens were murdered (and planned exhumations may raise that figure). Planes from neighboring airstrips reportedly even dropped explosives into the conflagration. As a symptom of bad conscience, part of the front page of the *Tulsa Tribune* and part of the editorial page were later ripped from the files, and it took a long while before acknowledgment was made, let alone reparations.

It's not an easy part of town to find, and I felt awkward asking directions, but a white receptionist in a motel near the Broken Arrow exit went out of her way to give me slightly too much guidance (and a clip from the local press about the monument), and when I got lost again I was told "follow me and I'll take you there" by a white female motorist. The neighborhood is still surrounded by vacant lots, and somebody has smashed one panel of the memorial, but as I pulled away, Tulsa's nearby Art Deco district seemed friendlier, and I even managed a bleak smile at the signposts to Oral Roberts University, former employer of Anita Hill.

Oklahoma City, miles on through more red-soil country, is not so pretty. (Oh, the sacrifices that songwriters will make for a rhyme.) And some of its inhabitants are a tad bored by its piety. In the joint that I find as evening descends, the bony young barman tells me that locals head for Texas for three things (it's always three things): "Booze, porn, and tattoos." His plump gay colleague, when I ask if there is anything else to look forward to on the road, exhales histrionically and breathes the magic name "*California* . . ." The thin one is an ex-soldier who gives directions by reference to army and airforce bases, and I notice again how much Route 66 has evolved according to military imperatives. It was pulled out of the Depression by the huge traffic of armaments and trainees between the coasts after 1941 — *Oklahoma!* itself was the big musical Broadway hit of the wartime years — then hymned after 1945 by ex-GIs spreading their wings, and finally doomed by President Eisenhower, whose Cold War push for an interstate system had been influenced by the imposing straights and curves of the German autobahns.

A resentful ex-soldier, indeed, was the prompting for my pilgrimage the following morning. On the ruins of the Alfred P. Murrah Federal Building in Oklahoma City is another shrine to the murder of Americans by Americans. A reflecting pool borders a garden with the same number of upright symbols as there were victims of Timothy McVeigh. From a distance these symbols could be anything, but on close inspection they prove to be statuary chairs: rows and rows of stone-and-bronze chairs with straight backs to represent the bureaucratic pursuits of the innocent dead. There are 168 of them; 19 are slightly off-puttingly half-size to mark the murder of the children at the day-care center and elsewhere. The figures 9.01 and 9.03, which confusingly could be dates, are incised in stone to indicate the unforgiving minute that it took for the huge building to slide chaotically into the street. A new whitish concrete statue of Jesus stands with its back to the scene. It's all slightly bland, and the inscription puts the blame on generic "violence" rather than native American Fascism. When this memorial was unveiled, the United States wasn't yet a country that honored the frontline nature of office work. It's clearly a style of commemoration in which we are fated to improve, as the upward curve steepens.

Caring little for booze, porn, or tattoos, I noticed as I dressed to leave Oklahoma City that my white socks, washed together with my red ones, had produced a furtive but somehow flagrant pink. Secure in my own masculinity, and bodyguarded by the sleek Corvette, I decided to make nothing of it and turned the proud prow of the car toward Texas, the resulting unit one potent and seamless weld of man and machine. I stopped on 66 at the town of Clinton, which has the best of the "66" museums, featuring an antique T-Bird and an overloaded Okie truck, and paid a call on the Tradewinds Motor Hotel, now a Best Western, where Elvis Presley used to stop over and sleep on his way to and from Las Vegas. Room 215 is the one his manager always reserved, and the lady at reception, responsive to the name of *Vanity Fair* as well as to my own charisma ("Seen ya on that Fox tee-vee"), gave me and my pink socks a key. The same love seat is still there, with added photographs but — I thought — a bathroom too small for the King's heartbreaking needs. He never showed his face in the daytime, but was once spotted by a room-service maid who went on a Paul Revere ride to alert the whole town. After that, he signed a few autographs, checked out, and, according to at least some accounts, has never been seen in this area again.

*

To rejoin the main drag, one takes old 66 through Erick, a dying dump which used to be home to Roger Miller. I tipped my hat to the singer of "King of the Road," which I consider the best bum-and-hobo ditty since "Big Rock Candy Mountain," and passed on. As I thundered past Elk City, I was listening to Elton John — who, oddly, seemed to be imploring someone, "Don't let your son go down on me" — when I heard and felt an impressive *whomp* somewhere in the rear. The thoroughbred car seemed to shake it off with abandon until, a mile or so later, it nearly threw me by wrenching the steering wheel from my grasp and lurching like a stallion on amyl nitrite. Managing to gain the roadside, I was informed by the screen on the dashboard that the left rear tire had blown and I had experienced "reduced handling." The Corvette has tires which can drive flat for a while, so I limped on, man and machine a single, soggy weld of sagging flesh and soft rubber. Finding a turnoff, I entered the other, parallel world of those who live by vehicular misfortune. Larry's Transmission Shop was mercifully near the exit, and there I whimpered in, with the car (which is able to get in touch with its feminine side) looking suddenly like a brilliantly colored but wounded bird. Larry and Charolett Posey succored me, let me use their phone and their front parlor, refused all money, and summoned another Larry. Indeed, they activated a network — a whole underground railroad — of Larrys. A guy came swiftly with his truck, looked at the tire, briefly pronounced, "She's history," and gave me a ride, with the round and ruined object, back into Elk City. Here, at Larry Belcher's truck and tire center, I was allowed to hang out while strong men frowned at the rare catch. There were no eighteen-inch tires to be had anywhere in Elk City, and the Larrys built me a patch which they wouldn't guarantee would last as far as Amarillo, 140 miles over the horizon. It was, one of the men said, the worst puncture he had seen since he left his army unit in Korea twelve years ago. The damn hole looked as if it had been made by a bullet. (His National Guard unit was being recalled to the colors, and he wasn't that thrilled about it.) It was perhaps at this point, in a world of gruff and tough men who do nothing all day but wrestle with grease and machinery, that it occurred to me that my pink socks were a mistake. Arguably a big mistake. I think I may have sounded unconvincing and even a bit fluting as I bid farewell and decided not to miss my one chance of saying "Is

This the Way to Amarillo?" Tony Christie's simpering seventies hit (he dared to rhyme "pillow" with "willow" while crooning and weeping) plainly hadn't registered with my rescuers, and so I drove on with a fragile tire: man and machine now an uneasy meld of psychological and mechanical anxiety.

However, I had promised myself to risk the byway that reaches the ghost town of Texola, and there was still enough daylight to chance it like a real man. In this part of southwestern Oklahoma, past the rock cuts and bridge spans of the undulant Ozarks, the horizons recede to the utmost, and the red soil shows itself only when there are roadworks. The land flattens out toward the Texas Panhandle, and there Texola lies, desolate down a deserted track. Its position right at the border has meant that it's also been named Texokla and Texoma in its day, before a pre-war vote settled the matter. But the one hundredth meridian has been surveyed seven times, so that the locals had at various periods lived in both Texas and Oklahoma without knowing it, or at any rate without having to move, or care. The point is moot now, because Texola is dead, its barns and shacks boarded up and occasionally adorned with a NO TRESPASSING sign. This is one of the stretches where 66 is still made up of the original white portland-cement concrete squares, which are quaint enough but too quaint for a bulging and patched tire, let alone a bulging and patched driver. I tooled slowly back to the modern world and whispered softly to the Corvette all the way to Amarillo, which with Larry's fine work we reached without incident. On the way, outside the town of Groom, was advertised the largest cross in North America, forcing itself on everybody for miles around, but I deliberately stopped whispering at that point in case anyone thought I was beseeching not just one inanimate object but two.

Why a town should be named "Yellow" I don't know, unless it's after the famous rose of Texas or some long-demolished adobe, but the tones of Amarillo are identical to those of any other town. At this point the society and the landscape begin to vary a bit: You see more horses than cattle — and some noble palominos at that — and begin to hear Spanish on the streets and on the radio, and I was asked to check my unlicensed gun at the door of a restaurant. (I wasn't packing one, so I disobeyed.) But Texas still wasn't as different as it likes to think. You hear a lot about the standardization of America, the sameness and the drabness of the brand names and the roadside clutter, but you have to be exposed to thousands of miles of it to see how obliterating the process really is. The food! The coffee! The newspapers! The radio! These would all disgrace a mediocre one-party state, or a much less prosperous country. Even if you carry Jane and Michael Stern's *Roadfood* guide, you can't always time your stops to it, and if you can't, why, you are at the mercy of the plastic industry and its tasteless junk. The coffee is a mystery as well as an insult: How can it be at once so bitter and so weak? (In "Talking Dust Bowl Blues," Woody Guthrie sings of a stew so thin that you could read a magazine through it; today's percolators contain the ditchwater equivalent. It tastes as if it were sucked up through a thin and soured tube from a central underground lake of stagnant bile.) And talking of reading, what can one say about the local press? It looks like indifferently recycled agency copy from the day before yesterday, relentlessly trivial and illiterate. Happening upon a stray copy of *USA Today* seems like finding Proust in your nightstand drawer instead of a Gideon Bible. And as for the radio — it was a dismal day when the Federal Communications Commission parceled out the airwaves to a rat pack of indistinguishable cheapskates, whose "product" is disseminated with only the tiniest regional variations.

I hear the first curtain-raising show about the twenty-fifth anniversary of Elvis's death as I enter Amarillo, and something in me causes me to lift the phone and send some flowers to my rescuers, Larry and Charolett, back in Elk City. A posy for Ms. Posey. I make it anonymous, except for "the guy in the Corvette." No doubt this will resolve any remaining doubt in her mind about having aided a limp-wristed Brit, but so much the better for the next straggler on that road.

The great Dr. Samuel Johnson had his answer ready when he was asked whether it was worth visiting some piece of scenery. "Worth seeing," he replied, "but not worth going to see." One has to make this snap decision often along Route 66. The Meramec Caverns, supposedly a hideout of Jesse James's and perhaps the site where the first bumper sticker was handed out? No. The Cadillac Ranch outside Amarillo? Yes, all right. In the dirt on the western edge of town ten Caddies, ranging in model from a 1948 Club Coupe to a 1963 Sedan DeVille, have been driven into the ground at what local freaks say is the same angle as the Great Pyramid of Cheops. First rammed home in 1974 by Stanley Marsh, the cars were moved away from the city in 1997 as the sprawl increased, and are now right next to a handy snake farm.

As I trudge across the field toward the half-buried vehicles I am treading where Bruce Springsteen once trod. He later wrote "Cadillac Ranch":

> James Dean in that Mercury '49
> Junior Johnson running through the woods of Caroline
> Even Burt Reynolds in that black Trans Am
> All gonna meet down on the Cadillac Ranch.

Sounds improbable. Spray paint — the very essence of Pop art — had been layered thickly over the exhibits, giving them the look of New York subway cars in pre-Giuliani days. Nobody had written a single thing of interest. I was at first their only visitor, but as I traipsed back across the field I met a man wearing a CHICAGO LAW ENFORCEMENT jacket who said brightly, "Definitely not something you see every day!" No, sir, but if I did see it every day I'd very soon stop noticing it. Nothing goes out of date faster than the ultra-modernistic. Exiting, I see a sign that reads: BATES MOTEL. SHOWERS IN ALL ROOMS. TAXIDERMY. KNIVES SHARPENED. Like a sap, I follow the arrows until I hit a dead end. American kitsch combined with a cheesy false alarm.

Trying to shake a bad mood, I meander over to the ghost town that marks the other frontier of the Texas Panhandle. Here is Glenrio, killed off by the opening of the interstate. Old 66, a pavement which is punctuated in town by a vestigial slab divider, simply peters out into red dirt and potholes. A cemetery for wrecked cars makes a nice counterpoint to a wooden water tower leaning at a drunken angle, downstreet from a wrecked coffee shop. This used to be the site of the celebrated "First and Last Motel in Texas," and some shards of the old sign can still be seen on the abandoned skeleton of the building, which is a dried-out mausoleum preserving the faint redolence of countless cross-border fornications. For additional Larry McMurtry–like eeriness, the spot is so negligible and dilapidated and done-in that my radio "seeker" can't pick up a signal in any direction. A deep calm descends upon me at this discovery, and I just sit listening to the insects until a nearby dog gets up the courage to break the silence. If I roused myself from the enveloping torpor and threw him a stick, it would fall into the next-door state.

This is the New Mexico border, which jauntily announces that I'm now on Mountain time and, as if to press home the point, gradually discloses a handsome mesa hoving into view on my left. At last, some landscape after the flatlands. The mesa also signals the old town of Tucumcari, which is a place of motels, a strip of motels, a grid of motels, a theme town of motels. You could stay in a motel while you looked for a motel room. A motel owners' convention would be a distinct possibility. Queen of the flops is the Blue Swallow Motel, which preserves the old and charming and discreet idea of an individual attached garage, placed like a pigeonhole next to each room. The buildings are pink. The garage doors are blue. Down by the wrong side of the railway tracks, I cheer up further by engulfing two bowls of cheap but gorgeous chili at Lena's Cafe, where Spanish is the tongue and where a flyswatter is placed wordlessly next to my plate. I am politely asked twice, "Are you sure?" The first time is when I ask for a second bowl. The second time is when I leave a three-dollar tip on an eight-dollar check. A large color poster of Jesus Christ is on the outside of the men's-room door: Somehow it's a different Jesus from the one featured in the Protestant highlands and lowlands a few hundred miles back.

The road through Albuquerque mimics an 1849 gold-rush trail, cut in a hurry for those seeking to reach the California diggings from Arkansas and other Dixie territories. Extreme modernity imposes itself at the Kirtland Air Force Base, on the fringe of town, which houses the National Atomic Museum, the nation's principal destination for those who like collectible cards of weapons of mass destruction. I always strive to avoid writing about the "land of contrasts" when I travel, but here in the most ancient settled part of America — there is an Indian pueblo at Acoma which archaeologists theorize has been continuously inhabited since about A.D. 1150 — the nuclear state was born, and its weaponry first designed and tested. Every effort has been made to leach both of these historic dramas out of the roadside scene: The wigwam-shaped tourist

stops and gas stations are parodic and chirpy, and the main re-
minders of the military-industrial world are the long, anonymous
trainloads over to the right, which according to local opinion are
rumbling across their high desert from the huge bases in California. The motels and shops prefer to present this as a relic of the old
Santa Fe Railroad days, when trains had cowcatchers on the front
rather than suspicious materials in the boxcars. There's an extremely short strip of old 66 around here, perhaps the shortest of
all, that preserves the old steel bridge across the Rio Puerco. The
Puerco is a dry gulch, or is at this time of year.

A big rampart of red rock starts to dominate the same right-hand
view, and also begins to look familiar, which, I suddenly realize, it
would to anybody who had viewed an old western movie. (You've
seen it, probably just as a bristling rank of filmic feathered warriors
appears at the summit.) This ridge also marks the Continental Divide, where rainfall — everything hereabouts is decided by water
— makes its decision about whether to flow east or west. The eleva-
tion approaches seven thousand feet and the wind can be fierce. As
I get near to Gallup, a sign on a bridge advises me that GUSTY
WINDS MAY EXIST — a fascinating ontological proposition.
Here, between the Navajo and Zuni lands, is the town that has
some claim to be the capital of Native America. But it too is utterly
buried in an avalanche of kitsch, with more bogus beads and belts
and boots on sale than you can shake a lance at. I find that "folk-
loric" displays of the defeated and subjugated have a marked tendency to induce diarrhea at the best of times, but there is something especially degrading and depressing in the manner of all
this: I prefer the United States of America to the idea of Bronze
Age tribalism, yet surely a decent silence could be observed somewhere, instead of this incessant, raucous, but sentimental battering
of the cash register. On many stretches of road, you can barely see
the primeval hills for billboards and pseudo-tepees. The El Rancho
Hotel in Gallup is actually one of the more restrained evocations of
the oldish days, with only a thin veneer of neon surmounting its basic structure of wooden fittings and weathered exterior. However,
this is more like an outpost of old Hollywood, where the stars of
those movies filmed in and around nearby Red Rock State Park
could get a decent meal and some comfort. The brochure is the

only one I've ever seen that claims both Ronald Reagan and his first wife, Jane Wyman, as guests (it doesn't state whether together or separately), and every room is "starred" with Alan Ladd, Paulette Goddard, and so forth. I'm billeted in the one named for Carl Kempton, whoever he was, right next door to Rita Hayworth. California, which has seemed so far away for so long, suddenly begins to feel attainable. The annual Inter-Tribal Indian Ceremonial, which sounds like the corporate or casino or cable version of a clan gathering, was soon to get under way in the town. One might have expected this to be an occasion for even more cashing in, but all I can tell you is that in Gallup, with its hard and acquisitive glitter and its resolute face to the future, I met with many trivial moments of hostility. Roadside America is always polite, even when the politeness is synthetic, and almost always friendly. But here — and I don't think it was the car — it was the monosyllable and the averted glance, even when I was only asking directions. I couldn't tell whether I was running into a superiority complex, or an inferiority one, but I was glad of a thick skin. I wasn't going to buy anything anyway.

Bleakness stayed with me until I traversed the Arizona border and turned off, near the absurdly named "Meteor City," to view this continent's most astonishing crater. Here, some fifty thousand years ago, a huge piece of iron-and-nickel asteroid slammed into the desert with enough force to transform graphite into diamond. It displaced 175 million tons of limestone and sandstone, and left a beautifully rounded hole, 570 feet deep and 2.4 miles in circumference. We have a silly way of trying to make human scale out of these majestic things, so, okay, if it were a football stadium, I am informed by the "Meteor Crater Enterprises Inc." brochure, it would seat two million spectators for twenty simultaneous games, and include the Washington Monument as a flagpole in the center. I saw, clustered around the telescopes on the rim, the largest concentration of that special tourist species — those who wear shorts and shouldn't — that I have ever witnessed outside Disneyland. The swaying, pachydermatous haunches of my fellow creatures seemed bizarrely transient and vulnerable in the context. Perhaps in reaction, I found it impossible to stand on the edge without looking up rather than down — though down is very impressive — and trying to picture what the last seconds before impact could conceivably have been like. It doesn't take long to give up on the endeavor: Try imagining the apocalypse. NASA trained in this crater for a lunar dress rehearsal. And the moon itself was probably the result of a much more dynamic collision with our planet. The whole solar system is the outcome of similar smashes, as probably was the extirpation of the dinosaurs, whose jokey features are much exhibited locally to capture the kiddie market. It all bears out what I've always said, which is that there can be no progress without head-on confrontation. However, an impact site of this magnitude lends a bit of perspective. Large meteorites or asteroids get through the atmosphere of Earth about every six thousand years or so without burning up, so we are about due for another smack. Go and see Arizona while you can.

On the road into Flagstaff the Corvette gives a slight whinny as it senses a rival. Off to the left is what looks like an old Rolls-Royce, parked outside yet another wigwam-shaped souvenir store. On inspection, it proves to be a beautiful Austin Princess, still with its English license plates, standing aloof in the broiling sun. Inquiries within disclose that it's the property of the store owner, who proudly reveals that he bought it out of a garage in nearby Winslow, where it had been sitting undriven for years. He has no idea how such a vintage masterpiece, with its original ID, came to be hiding in the Arizona desert. Giving Flagstaff a bit of a miss — too metropolitan for my needs — I venture down the hairpin forest road to Sedona, which offers me the most slender and cathedral-like mesa columns as they are noosed in the rays of evening sun. Sedona has become the Aspen of the area, with resort hotels and golf courses and fancy restaurants in phony Spanish courtyards, but the air and light and verdancy are astoundingly refreshing after the high desert.

"Don't forget Winona," urges the song. Winona is put in, I can promise you, only because it rhymes with Arizona. But then, so does Sedona, and you can really find Sedona, whereas you drive straight through Winona without noticing it, and can't even identify it when you turn back. It's become a Flagstaff sub-burg, another featureless location. But the old 66 between Flagstaff and Kingman is one of the best and easiest stretches of the remaining pavement, and it's deliciously quiet and still and untraveled. On one fence post I see a beautiful motionless bird, which to my trained ornithological eye resembles either a very large hawk or a medium-size eagle. It waits imperturbably for a rodent or other small mammal to break cover and make the crossing. It returns my gaze without flinching. Turning away from feral nature, I find this is the only road on which the tradition of the Burma-Shave ad survives. In the interwar years, the makers of that amazingly successful brushless cream evolved the idea of putting a line from a jingle every half-mile or so, thus forcing motorists and their families to keep pace with the rhyme. So you would see, punctuated at intervals, lines such as "If you / Don't know / Whose signs / These are, / You can't have / Driven very far. *Burma-Shave.*" Or "Shaving brushes / You'll soon see 'em / On the shelf / In some / Museum. *Burma-Shave.*" Old-timer accounts of 66 never fail to cite this nostalgic feature. On the road into Seligman, the tradition has revived in the form of a public-service announcement. Over the course of a couple of miles without another car in view, I learn in sequence that: "Proper distance / To him was bunk / They pulled him out / Of some guy's trunk." Can't be too careful.

Seligman itself is one of the smallest and sweetest stops on the Route, and aptly enough its centerpiece is a one-chair barbershop, owned and operated for decades by Angel Delgadillo, a senior citizen with a huge, toothy smile who founded the original Historic Route 66 Association and probably stopped his hometown from going the way Texola and Glenrio did when the road passed them by. These days it's tourism or death, or both. Angel is cutting chunks from the mane of a Christ-bearded hippie type when I walk in, and has the practiced air of an unofficial mayor and ambassador, with a roomful of visitors, so I amble down to the Black Cat Bar and brown-bag store. Here, the friendly Tim tells me that he was moving his truck and his dogs from New Orleans to Washington State about a year ago when he broke down in Seligman and decided to stay. It's nice for the dogs, you can save money, and people are friendly enough, though in a town of fewer than a thousand souls you have to watch out for "the Peyton Place side of things. Everything is everybody's business." All the time I am in Seligman, with its Marilyn Monroe posters and old-style gas pumps, there is a train longer than the town standing at the nearby station.

Kingman is the last major stop before the real desert begins, and here too the old Santa Fe system makes its point with a noble steam engine mounted — like a fish out of water? like a train off the rails? — at the edge of a park. There was a random, decent full-service restaurant as well, named Calico's, where a hauntingly beautiful Spanish waitress had a good sense of the times and distances ahead, fueled me with a rich variety of calories for the ordeal to come, and warned me that the California Highway Patrol was a good deal more picky than the New Mexico and Arizona boys. (The speed limit varies from 75 to 65 as you cross state lines: The limit on the old 66 road is a euphonious 55, and the optimum overall is 77 unless you have a Corvette rearing and plunging under you.)

Steinbeck wrote of his desperate Okies as they left behind "the terrible ramparts of Arizona" and attempted to cross the desert at night because of the appalling glare and heat, and I try to make up time across the anvil of pain that stretches before me. A baby twister gets up outside Kingman and struggles to become menacing. But the turnoff sign to "London Bridge" proves too seductive, and I make the detour to Lake Havasu City, which regularly posts some of the highest temperatures in the continental U.S. I remember reading in my boyhood that some idiot had taken down a bridge over the Thames stone by stone and re-erected it in the desert, and here it all is. On the edge of a lake formed by the Colorado River, an artificial stream has been created, and the old gray span of London Bridge, which had survived fog and drizzle and German bombs between 1825 and 1968, is draped across it. This is the grand scheme of Robert P. McCulloch Sr., a chain-saw and oil and real-estate king who bid on the bridge and got it shipped across the Atlantic, shrapnel scars and all. Apparently he believed that he was getting the spires and drawbridges of Tower Bridge and didn't discover his error until too late. (The one he got was a descendant of the star of the old song "London Bridge is falling down.") But it would be wrong to call this McCulloch's folly, as one is tempted to do. Last year more than one million people made the stop. The howling absurdities of desert-oasis Anglophilia dwarf the collector's-item Austin Princess near Flagstaff as I pass the "Canterbury Estates Gated Community" — gated against what? the Navajos? — and view the Jet Skiers on "Windsor Beach" and the shoppers at "Wimbledon Goldsmiths." Union Jacks hang limply in the heat next to Old Glory. There's a "pub," of course, and some red telephone boxes and a red double-decker London bus. Yet the beer isn't warm enough to be authentic, and while the weathered old stone may last longer in this arid frazzle, it still sags a bit. The genuine fake is starting to become a bit of a theme along here.

Returning to the main road, I pass through Yucca, near Yucca Flat, where the open-air nuclear tests of the 1950s and 1960s had many glowing and electrifying effects, of which the best are captured in the movie *Atomic Cafe*. Which would have been the more impressive and terrifying to see: the landing of the meteor that turned graphite into diamond, or the detonation of man-made devices that could fuse sand into glass? In 1955, John Wayne was playing Genghis Khan, possibly the very worst of his roles, downwind from Yucca Flat during the tests. Of those on the shoot, he was only the most famous one to get lung cancer later on: That location was a culling field. Susan Hayward, Agnes Moorehead, and Dick Powell were also to succumb. Can Wayne have been fatally poisoned by the military he so adored? According to a recent biography, it looks as if that was the way it was. This sinister, worked-over sandscape has a weird antenna on every other hill, and the alien effect persists as the Colorado River cuts again across the wilderness, appearing rather shiny with false modesty after its epic work in designing and forging the Grand Canyon less than a hundred miles upstream. California! Here I come. But right away I am forced to pull in to a state "Inspection Station," as if meeting a frontier in Europe. The boredom and conceit of this — it's the only such barrier in all the eight states of Route 66 — plays to the Californian narcissistic fantasy of being a semi-independent nation, with its own economy. But it also provides a reminder of the cruelty with which the state treated the migrants of the 1930s, tearing up their driver's licenses and turning them back as vagrants, until the courts finally put a stop to it. The gray-haired taxpayer-funded lady at the barrier waves me through after saying she preferred the color of my car to its make. Who the hell asked her?

The Mojave Desert is almost frightening No — it *is* frightening. It's easy to see why the surviving Okies wanted to cross it at night, and not just because of the annihilating heat. In the dark, you wouldn't have to see the grim, dirty hues of the rock and the soil, and the endless, discouraging length of the road stretching ahead forever. There is something infinitely wearying about seeing one summit after another prove to be an illusion, range replacing range with ruthless monotony. The mile markers seem to slow down — *surely* I came farther than that? The sensation, of moving fast but never escaping, is dreamlike and hypnotic but not in a relaxing way, and the knowledge that this is homestretch territory makes me superstitious about a last-minute mishap. Many of the turnoffs on the map are to vanished places that are only names, and the truth is that somewhere along this harsh and lifeless highway the old Route 66 just dies. It disappears into the trackless mess of suburban California as Los Angeles spreads out to embrace and claim it, and the last real stop is in Barstow, where the old road is blocked at the edge of town by a huge Marine base. Here at the El Rancho motel, built out of old railroad ties and festooned with 66 memorabilia, I mentally announced journey's end. The motel is indeed journey's end for a number of other people; in its rear court I was offered crystal meth and the services of a haggard and punctured whore before I could get out of the car. Snarling and shivering figures mingle with those to whom blank, inert amiability has become a signature. Down at the end of lonely street . . .

Bobby Troup's original ditty was better than perhaps he knew. He borrowed from the Homeric tradition by drawing a word-picture treasure map with memorable and rhyming place-names, an *Odyssey*-like mnemonic for the American Dream. And he and Cynthia, who suggested that crucial rhyme in the refrain, were able to buy a house in California within weeks of the release of the song. Postwar optimism drew on freedom of travel, extra dough, and sexual emancipation. Those words and that music touched such a nerve that I don't think I met anybody of any age last summer who, on hearing my plan, failed to respond with something like "Get your kicks, huh?" But try listening to the newer songs that mention the nation's most beloved road trip. On "Lost Causeway," Jason Eklund sings, "Get your kicks on what's left of 66," and says, "So follow state and homespun signs, leading on this historic route / Take a grab at the corporate crapola where history has been rubbed out." (Interestingly, he preserves the eastern pronunciation of "route.") Picking up on the cynicism of the commercialized Indian reservation with its tax-free cigarette bonanzas, he suggests, "Get your *fix* . . ."

The Red Dirt Rangers in their song "Used to Be," which has a tang of Springsteen's "My Home Town," speak of "holes in the roof and weeds by the door" of the trailer where the motor courts once stood, while the Mad Cat Trio intones the words "Get your kicks" with positive sarcasm. The Dusty Chaps, in "Don't Haul Bricks on 66," put their advice — "Route 66 ain't the way to go" — on the same level of obviousness as "Don't go pissing in the wind" and "You know the white hats always win." The music didn't quite die on this road, but it changed from celebration to melancholy and disappointment. Perhaps it all went when the last hitchhiker gave up, or was banned. Larry McMurtry was certainly right, in *Lonesome Dove,* to point out that once something is sold as "the Wild West" it means it's become domesticated. The luminous Robert Crumb registered a similar point in a twelve-frame cartoon, showing the evolution of a roadside scene from a setting with a road to a place where the road was the setting. The old 66 tried to be genuinely different from the new for a while, but it could survive only by selling itself as different, and those very sales tactics meant that it had to become the same. It's another coffee mug, another T-shirt, another line of cheap "Route 66" jeans from Kmart. The living bits of antique 66 are colonies of the new interstate, and the dead bits are, well, dead. I doubt that Texola or Glenrio will still be there if I travel that way again; outside Glenrio, I could already see and hear the earthmovers. In California the fifty-year-old Trails Restaurant, a 66 holdout in Duarte, was demolished almost as I drove by. You never step into the same river twice. All travel is saying farewell. Most voyaging in the United States has become either impossible (by rail) or a misery and a humiliation (by air) or a routine (by roads with no individuality). No poet has yet attempted to say what this defeat means for the American idea. But the melancholy is all around us, transmitted on frequencies that nobody can possess. After one last, brief, yearning sweep along Sunset, I did what I would once have bet I could never do, and roared down Rodeo Drive in a brash Corvette. The window-shoppers barely looked up. The drop-off point for my mettlesome steed was just at the corner of Wilshire. I tethered it, patted it, handed over the keys, and forgot to look back.

EMILY MALONEY

Power Trip

FROM *World Hum*

I LIKE freakish travel destinations. Also, I'm cheap. So when
Naruto University, the rural Japanese school I attend, announced a
free bus trip to a neighboring nuclear power plant, I thought,
Damn, this could be better than last semester's trip to the mayonnaise fac-
tory. I took out my daily planner. As I suspected, it was nearly blank.
I penciled in FREE NUCLEAR POWER PLANT TRIP in capitals.
Then I circled it and waited.

Don't get me wrong, I have no lifelong love affair with mayonnaise, or nuclear power, or any combination of the two for that
matter. It's just that I'm an American at a rural Japanese university,
and the year is turning out to be pretty rural and, frankly, quite Japanese. I have to take my excitement where I can get it. Whether it's
cutting my hair in my dorm's communal shower (last Friday night)
or touring freakish destinations for free, I'm up for it.

When I finally board the tour bus, I am not disappointed. I receive my name tag, a free canned beverage, a pencil, and nuclear
power brochures written in Japanese. I sit by my Korean friends
who also enjoy a good free industrial tour. One leans over and asks,
"They aren't giving us highlighter sets?" She is serious. I say, "Wait.
The tour is just beginning." I am also serious. Sometimes you get
the sets at the end.

The tour begins like any other Japanese tour around the world:
with a tour guide's description of the weather and other obvious
high-pitched pleasantries over a loudspeaker. The Japanese students on the trip, the ones with actual interest in nuclear power,
behave like Japanese on a tour. They promptly fall asleep. The

tour guide is unscathed. Perky, even. She wonders aloud how the weather will affect our viewing of the nuclear power plant. She is hopeful for minutes about this very topic. She describes the view on the right side of the bus. My Korean friend leans over and asks blankly, "Is that woman going to talk the whole trip?" The tour guide, who has clearly heard, tugs up her white gloves, points to a hill on the left side of the bus and says, "A beautiful mountain can be seen on the left side of the bus."

There are, however, brief pauses in the tour guide's chatter for bathroom breaks and three mini-films about nuclear power. From the films I learn about condenser tube leaks and turbine shaft vibration. Pie charts are used. From the bathroom breaks I learn that about every other rest-stop in Japan carries mint chocolate chip ice cream in their vending machines. Old people linger by the toilets and knickknacks at every stop.

Eventually we break for lunch, which, as promised, is free. All the other foreign students, who hoard their university scholarships and resent spending money on the so-called necessity of food, are happy with lunch, or rather its fundamental quality of freeness. I agree with them. I think, *I just saved myself five hundred yen by coming on this trip.* The tour guide, once we re-board the bus, wants to talk about the deliciousness of lunch. "Wasn't the ramen delicious?" she says over the loudspeaker. The Japanese students are already asleep again. On the last leg of the trip, those of us who are conscious are relieved when the tour guide starts the video of *Japan's Funniest Home Videos.*

We arrive first at the nuclear power museum, where we receive a copy of the Yonden company annual report and a pair of 3-D glasses. I'm stoked. I immediately put them on, as do most of the foreign students. We sit through a nuclear power lecture. The tour guide tries to make the lecture fun by using colorful graphs and asking the audience to vote on how large we think the reactor vessel head is. These words are beyond my vocabulary. Sometimes, when I'm tired, I forget the word for Wednesday in Japanese.

Sometimes I forget it in English. My ignorance doesn't prevent me from voting, though. If I have any doubt about, say, what percentage of Shikoku Island's electricity comes from nuclear power, I just vote more than once. I am still wearing my 3-D glasses when we're told to put them on in preparation for the movie.

The movie, which is entitled *A Flying Tour of the Yonden Nuclear Power Facility,* has a cheerful take on nuclear power. It is not at all like the one I saw in high school about Chernobyl, which was downright depressing. This movie has a talking 3-D kangaroo, and shots of the members of the friendly Yonden company "family" engaging in sports day.

I keep my glasses on for the museum tour, where it is explained to us how to get into one of those scary yellow anticontamination suits. My Chinese friend and I lag behind the group to pose obscenely with the mannequins in gas masks. When we reunite with the group the tour guide asks us if we were enjoying the museum on our own. My friend says yes because in our own special way we were.

By the time we finally take the bus to see the power plant in person, there has been an incredible amount of buildup. I fear a letdown. In the movies and brochures, the pictures are of the plant in cherry-blossom season with the blooms framing it in the foreground and an impossibly blue ocean behind it. While it is slightly overcast as the tour guide feared, I am still impressed. This is one mother of a freakish trip. The bus pulls over for photo opportunities, and I get out and take pictures. I hear several Japanese people use the adjective "pretty" to describe the nuclear power plant compound.

Inside the plant it is loud and hot, and because I went to public school and spent my time in the museum pretending to make out with the gas-masked mannequin, that is about all I understand. I feel briefly sorry for the nuclear power workers with their stressful yet boring jobs in their unfortunate green uniforms, and then when the Japanese science students pose for pictures in front of what looks like a big water heater decorated with cartoon characters, I go ahead and do it too. I do not, however, understand that it is a nuclear reactor vessel. Nor do I really care.

Instead, that night's free hotel is the highlight of my tour. All of us students eat a free fish dinner worth ten thousand yen, get drunk on our own convenience-store plum sake, and then at the end of the night go downstairs to take baths. I am drunk and scrubbed once-in-a-lifetime clean when I discover a hot bath on the balcony. My Korean friend and I soak and then, as it starts to rain, we climb up on the metal railing. We see the ocean, the Japanese urban sprawl, and finally right below our warm buck-naked bodies a cemetery crawling out of the darkness. "This was really fun," I say, and then I wonder what the implications of that are. I guess it means I can stand a little Japanese nuclear power propaganda in the name of a free vacation. I guess, disturbingly, it also means I'm beginning to enjoy the freakish propaganda part of my free vacations.

BRUCE McCALL

Winter Cruises Under Ten Dollars

FROM *The New Yorker*

Gdańsk Shipyards Tour: You're skipper of your own vessel as you row, row, row your punt (rental not included) around one of Eastern Europe's most famous shipbuilding basins (permit extra) — but now row lots faster or get swamped by that brand-new freighter sliding stern first down the launching stocks, dead ahead!

Tramp-Steamer Adventure: The world's only tramp steamer entirely crewed by real tramps, the *Dwarf Star* is almost sure to embark from a port to be specified no later than 2002, with a cargo of who knows what bound for who knows where! Specify above- or below-decks accommodations. Pets welcome (ship's doctor's a vet!). Some light deck work and painting required.

Icebreaker Thrills: It's enchanted Lake Winnipesaukee, New Hampshire, in all its winter witchery! You'll zigzag across this frozen water wonderland, with its eerie chorus of cracking sounds, on an unforgettable cruise in the snug comfort of a late-model Buick or other fine car, more waterproof than any boat.

Scientific Expedition: Participate in a unique voyage of discovery. Could ancient man have sailed from Valparaíso, Chile, to St. John's, Newfoundland, in a wicker basket? You'll be the first person on earth to know for sure!

Northern-Lights Arctic Frolic: You get to Baffin Island by New Year's Day, we do the rest: custom-chop your ice floe, point you

south, and shove you off on your way through a nippy eight-month
Arctic winter night. Axe, edible four-color map, polar-bear repel-
lent, and flashlight (batteries not included) provided, with refund-
able deposit.

Dunroamin Mystery Sail: Ted and Tammy invite you and your part-
ner aboard their twenty-four-foot sloop for a weeklong, vodka-and-
Scrabble-filled oceangoing idyll, dedicated to the idea that out on
the high seas there's no taboo that can't be broken!

Hawaii Calls! But then they hang up — so dial the 800 number of
Aden-Ventures, the authorized no-questions-asked booking agent
for all one-way Suez Canal night trips on tugboats, bumboats, and
what have you, in a part of the world known as such a travel bargain
that one local saying is "Your life here isn't worth a dollar."

Channel-Hopping Challenge: Estate in shipshape order? Then
you're a candidate to race from Dover to Calais, God willing, in the
world's first experimental tide-powered midget semi-catamaran,
on its maiden voyage!

Splish-Splash Panama Sun Cruise: No long walk to your cabin, no
noisy parties, no boring lifeboat drills. Floating on your inflatable
raft in the pool at Madame Lazonga's Starlite Motor Court, in the
heart of Panama City's colorful stockyards quarter, means beating
those deluxe-cruise-ship blues — especially when the pool is filled!

Mississippi River Poker Party: If Tom and Huck were compulsive
gamblers, it's a sure bet they'd join Blackie and Doc's nonstop
twenty-four-hour poker game aboard the authentic nineteenth-
century coal scow *Muskrat III*. All you poker novices, welcome
aboard! But remember the scow doesn't dock till the game is finished, and the game isn't finished till they say it is.

DANIEL MENDELSOHN

What Happened to Uncle Shmiel?

FROM *The New York Times Magazine*

Why We Went

WE WENT, my brothers and sister and I, because we wanted to get as close as possible to a terrible crime — to a terrible betrayal. In some of the stories of how our relatives had been killed, after all, they died because they had been betrayed. If you are the grandchild of people who were touched by the Holocaust, if you grew up sneaking furtive glances at the tattoos on your older relatives' forearms, you grew up hearing these stories, and even when I was a child, it seemed clear to me that the betrayal was more terrible, and also more distinctive, than the deaths. (Everyone had died; not everyone had been betrayed.)

It is true that the stories had variations, which, in my private catalogue of them, sounded like the names of obscure chess moves: the Israeli variation (they had been killed right away, according to our Israeli cousins), the Jewish neighbor variation (it was the naive Jewish neighbor who turned them in — did he really expect to get off himself?), the Polish maid variation (it was their own Polish maid who turned them in).

But what all the variations had in common was this: that in the summer of 1941, which was the summer when the Germans rolled into the very small town in what is now Ukraine where most of this story takes place, a town where my mother's family, whose name was Jäger, had lived since the early seventeenth century and where her uncle and aunt and four young cousins continued to live long after everyone else had emigrated to the States, which is why I am here to tell the story — in that summer, when the Germans came to Bolechow, the uncle and aunt and cousins were hiding in a cellar, and the location of this hiding place was revealed by someone close to them. I heard this story so often when I was growing up that I don't actually recall which bits I got from which relative, but I do remember the summer day on which my grandfather told me that the cellar was in the castle of the princes who used to own the town. I remember it because I remember the way he said the word "castle": *kessle*. Very few people I know anymore talk that way. Anyway, that is where they were supposed to have been hiding when they were betrayed, and of course they all died: my grandfather's brother Sam — we knew him by his Yiddish name, Shmiel — and his wife, Ester, and their four girls, Lorka, Frydka, Rochele, and Bronia, the oldest twenty-two, the youngest thirteen.

It was in the hope of learning which variation might be the truth that we went.

We went because we wanted facts rather than legends, details instead of generalizations. Even without the crime, without the war, we would probably have gone back: to have details of sight and smell and sound to flesh out the hard contours of the family stories we had been raised on. But the details we wanted most were those that would help us to imagine the circumstances of the deaths. When I was a teenager, the phrase "killed by the Nazis" became, for me, a kind of Homeric epithet for this uncle and aunt and cousins, summing up everything that needed to be known about them. All my grandfather's relatives came with a tag line. There was the tragic older sister, who Died a Week Before Her Wedding; there were my great-grandmother's mean stepchildren, who Hid Dirty Socks Under the Bed; and there were Sam and Ester and the girls, Killed by the Nazis. This was their official designation. In junior high school, we were asked to bring photographs of family members who had fought in wars, and I brought a picture of Sam in 1916, when he was a private in the Austro-Hungarian Imperial Army. My teacher admired the photograph and turned it over, and on the back I saw that my grandfather had written, in his loping, vaguely foreign script, "Uncle Shmiel, Killed by the Nazis." My teacher clucked her tongue sympathetically and handed it back.

That we could learn anything new about them at all was a recent development. A few years ago, I had made contact, through the

Jewish Genealogy Web site, with a young researcher living in L'viv, the nearest big city to Bolechow. (He called the town, which had at different times in its history been claimed by Poland or Ukraine or Germany or the Soviet Union, by its Ukrainian name, Bolekhiv, which is how it's spelled today, although we, like our grandfather, use the Polish spelling and pronunciation: bo-LEH-khov.) During the course of an increasingly warm exchange of e-mail messages, I had hired this Ukrainian, Alex Dunai, to search the local archives for records of the Jägers. A few months later, I received an elaborately postmarked package containing records of more than one hundred certificates of births and deaths, all of Jägers, all neatly translated on meticulously typed sheets. Until that point, the furthest back I had been able to extrapolate my family's history was to 1867, the year my grandfather's father was born. Alex's researches catapulted us back another century and a half, to 1746.

It occurred to me, then, that other relatives I had given up for "lost" might be retrievable too. I e-mailed Alex, asking if there might be anyone left in Bolechow old enough to have known my family. (This wasn't a given: After virtually all of the town's Jews were killed by Hitler, many of its Ukrainians had been killed by Stalin.) He wrote me back to say he had talked to the mayor of the town, and the answer was yes. The town was tiny, he said; if we came to visit, all we would have to do was walk around and talk to a few people in order to find those who had known them, who might know what really happened.

We went because we, in our thirties and forties, are of the generation of the grandchildren — the last generation that will be touched personally by the Holocaust, the last for whom it will be more than a matter of intellectual or historical interest or of moral inquiry. There is, in our relationship to the event, a strange interweaving of tantalizing proximity and unbridgeable distance. We are the last generation to whom the dead are close enough to touch, yet frustratingly out of reach.

Proximity and distance: My older brother, Andrew, whose Hebrew name is Shmiel, was born twelve years after the end of the war. I can remember meals I had twelve years ago: That is how close they were, Sam and Ester and the girls. Yet that is how far they were too. Once a person has died, it doesn't matter if the space that separates us from knowing them is twelve years or twelve minutes, a second or a century. The closest we can get is to know those, like my grandfather, who were close to them. Then those who were close to them start to die, and we get that much further. Although passing time can sometimes bring us closer too. In the weeks leading up to our departure, the papers were suddenly full of items from Europe about Jewish people being attacked, synagogues destroyed, gravestones defaced. Along with the e-mail messages from travel agents and hotels, there were notes from friends, and sometimes from total strangers, about incidents in England, in France, in Greece, and in Eastern Europe too. As we readied ourselves to retrieve the past, it seemed the past was catching up with us of its own accord.

And so we went. Last August, my sister, Jennifer, my brothers Andrew and Matt (my third brother, busy with work and not so interested in family history, stayed behind), and I boarded a LOT Polish Airlines 767, exactly sixty years after the terrible betrayal supposedly took place, and flew to Poland and met Alex and visited Auschwitz and drove six hours east through what used to be Galicia and came, finally, to the tiny village in Ukraine, the town where my family had lived continuously, in the same house, from the late seventeenth century, when the Jews first arrived, until 1941, when the Germans came.

Whose Terrible Crime?

We went, too, because of the letters, because I feared we might share in the guilt. Apart from a handful of photographs of Sam and his family, what we have of him is a series of letters that he wrote to various family members in 1939. At some point, these letters were collected by my grandfather, who carried them around with him, folded in a large billfold in his breast pocket, until he died in 1980. It would be difficult to say that these letters shed light on the everyday life of Sam and his family, since they are, basically, all concerned with escaping death. But they provided enough information to make me worry whether the betrayal at the heart of this family story wasn't more terrible than had been acknowledged.

The first letter is dated January 16, 1939, a Monday; the last is from August of that year. They can't have been easy to write. In the earlier letters, it is clear that the family business — a meat-shipping concern that he proudly built up after inheriting the butcher shop that had been in his family for two hundred years — is in trouble. One of his trucks has been vandalized; he is subject to anti-Jewish business restrictions; he no longer has easy access to his own money. He asks for money to fix one truck and to pay the exorbitant cost of a permit for another. In subsequent letters, my grandfather's brother wants money not for trucks or repairs but for papers, affidavits and emigration papers for the four daughters, then for two daughters and finally for his eldest daughter, "the dear Lorka." "If it were only possible," he wrote, "to manage an affidavit for the dear Lorka, then this would all be a little easier for me." What makes the letters so particularly difficult to read is, I realize, the second-person address: Since every letter is talking to "you" — as in, "I bid you farewell and kiss you from the bottom of my heart," Sam's favorite valediction — you always feel implicated, always vaguely responsible.

As the requests for money get more agitated, so do the references to the political situation. A letter to my grandfather: "Businesses are frozen, it's a crisis, no one has any business, everything is tense. God grant that Hitler should be torn to bits! Then we'd finally breathe again, after all we've been through." A little later on, in a letter to his younger sister Jeanette and her husband: "From reading the papers you know a little about what the Jews are going through here; but what you know is just one one-hundredth of it: When you go out into the street or drive on the road you're barely 10 percent sure that you'll come back with a whole head or your legs in one piece. Work permits have all been taken away from the Jews, etc. . . ." And this was before the Germans got there; this is just what German hatred had made possible in the Poles, under whose government these Jews of Bolechow were then living, and the Ukrainians, who had forever been their neighbors. The neighbors: "The Germans were bad," my grandfather used to tell me, "the Poles were worse. But the Ukrainians were the worst of all." A month before our journey, I waited for a visa in the stifling lobby of the Ukrainian Consulate on East 49th Street, and as I looked around at the people standing next to me, the line *the Ukrainians were the worst* went through my mind, again and again.

In the later letters, panic erupts; the tension between Sam's vigorous instructions and naive desperation is terrible. "As long as there's some possibility of getting me out of here, do what you can," he wrote to his younger sister. "You should make inquiries, you should write that I'm the only one in your family still in Europe and that I have training as an auto mechanic and that I've already been to America from 1912 to 1913, perhaps that might work . . . For my part, I am going to post a letter, written in English, to Washington, addressed to President Roosevelt" — he spells it "Rosiwelt," which always brings tears to my eyes — "and will write that all my siblings and my entire family are in America . . . perhaps that will work."

We have no way of knowing, of course, how those to whom Sam wrote responded: The only letters that survived are the ones from, not to, Poland. I have read Sam's letters many times, enjoying, each time, their beautifully slanting, slightly old-fashioned script, the archaic turns of phrase, the inserted Yiddishisms, the bold, even aggressive signature, with its gigantic serpentine *S*, and even as I get a curious enjoyment out of all these things, I worry whether the letters' recipients bore some responsibility for the terrible story. Not because of malice, but because of — well, it really wasn't hard to imagine. I was on this trip, after all, with only three of my four siblings. In the 1920s, Sam's six siblings had decided to leave their hometown for either America or Palestine, but Sam decided to stay. "He wanted to be a big fish in a little pond," my grandfather would tell me, with what I once thought was amusement but, I now realize, may have been resentment. My grandfather was vain, too. I think about this, and I wonder whether it was a terrible guilt that drove my grandfather to carry those letters around with him all his life.

The month before my siblings and I left for Ukraine, I convened a conference of my mother and her cousins — the surviving children of Sam's siblings — to ask them what memories they had of that time, when Sam's letters would have been arriving. We sat on my mother's cousin's patio in Chicago, and they reminisced. But they had all been too young at the time to know anything specific. All they could say was that everyone had adored Sam and that everything possible was done for him. "I remember when the news came, after the war, that they'd died," Jeanette's daughter, Marilyn, says in the surprisingly deep southern accent that she acquired during her years away from the Bronx. "There wasn't just crying —

there was screaming." I passed around some Xeroxed translations I had made of Sam's letters, letters to their parents. "No, no, no," my mother said, pushing her copy across the table. "I don't want to read them. It's too sad." Then she made the slightly sibilant, sad clucking noise that she always makes when she's about to utter the Yiddish word *nebech,* which means something like "what a terrible pity."

What We Found

We flew into Kraków and met Alex. We started there because I was eager to travel through what had been Galicia, the province from which so many American Jews spring. Kraków was its westernmost big city; L'viv — or as it was then called, Lemberg — its easternmost. We would be staying in L'viv; Bolechow has no hotels.

We also started there because from Kraków it is only an hour or so to Auschwitz. I had mixed feelings about going. Auschwitz is the gigantic symbol, the gross generalization, the shorthand, for what happened to Europe's Jews; but it had been to rescue my relatives from generalities, symbols, abbreviations, to restore to them their particularity and distinctiveness, that I had come on this trip. Killed by the Nazis — yes; but by whom exactly? The horrible paradox of Auschwitz is that the extent of what it shows you — the rooms full of shaven hair and eyeglasses and artificial limbs taken from victims, the luggage filled with clothes packed for imaginary sojourns — is so great that the corporate and anonymous are constantly asserted at the expense of any sense of individual life. My one personal connection to the place was frustratingly shadowy: My grandfather, something of a roué, married three more times after my grandmother died, and his last wife had been in Auschwitz, where her husband and only daughter were killed. But she never talked about it. It was her new husband, himself the father of an only daughter, who was the teller of stories.

We spent an afternoon there and then headed east to L'viv. Two days later, we drove to Bolechow.

From the top of the little hill just outside the town, Bolechow doesn't look like much: a cluster of houses and streets around a little square, nestled in a depression among some hills. As we stopped to let my brother Matt, a photographer, take pictures, I thought of how vulnerable it looked — how isolated, how easy to enter. We got back in the car and went down and found a handful of people there, each of whom took us a bit closer.

We found Nina first. Alex had parked on the *rynek,* the town square, diagonally across from the onion-domed church, where we could hear services going on, and right in front of the house that stands on what was once my family's property. On the same side of the square as the church was the old town hall, next to which my family's store once stood. Opposite the town hall was the synagogue where my grandfather had been bar mitzvahed; now it was a social club. With everyone in church, the rynek seemed pretty desolate, if peaceful. You wouldn't guess what had happened there.

Suddenly a jolly-looking thickset woman of about fifty passed by, and with a mixture of small-town curiosity and something else, something lighter — the local person's generalized amusement about out-of-towners — asked who we were and what we were doing. Alex explained that we were American Jews who had come back to the town of our origin. While he went on and on, in my mind I kept hearing the phrase *the Ukrainians were the worst.*

The woman cracked a huge smile, and some rapid-fire Ukrainian ensued. "This is Nina," Alex explained. "She is inviting us into her house. She herself was born after the war" — distance, I thought to myself; this is going to go nowhere — "but her neighbor Maria is much older, and she thinks maybe this Maria will remember your family." And so we followed Nina to her cramped flat, in a drab concrete group of buildings behind the old synagogue. As the five of us — four Mendelsohns and Alex — squeezed onto the tiny sofa, Nina uncorked a bottle of champagne bearing a comically ornate label, fetched dusty glasses from a credenza and also made each of us a cup of Nescafé — clearly a great treat. "It is a big honor," Alex told us, smiling.

I wondered what Alex himself was thinking. Alex is a gregarious blond in his mid-thirties with a broad, ready smile, and since the dissolution of the Soviet Union, he has made a career of taking American Jews around the old shtetls of Eastern Europe. Alex was the first Ukrainian I had ever had extensive dealings with, and when we finally met, his warmth and ebullience carried me through the inevitable awkwardnesses of meeting someone in person whom you've only known via e-mail. On the plane to Poland, my siblings and I passed around an excerpt from Jonathan Safran Foer's then-forthcoming novel, *Everything Is Illuminated,* about an American Jew who goes to Ukraine to find out what happened to his relatives; the fictional guide is named Alex. "Great!" our real-life Alex laughed, when we told him. "This will be good for business!" That was in Kraków; during the trip back to L'viv, he had said, a bit guardedly: "I don't tell all friends what it is I do. I don't think they'd understand."

Now Alex was clearly delighted that Nina was rolling out the red carpet. As she did so, my brothers and sister and I exchanged glances, all of us clearly thinking, *Some Ukrainians aren't so bad.* Nina's husband, an affable man who was wearing a bathing suit and flip-flops, banged out tunes on a decrepit piano. "Feelings" was followed swiftly by "Hava Nagilah." We looked at each other again. Then he played "Yesterday."

Maria showed up. She nodded slowly when we mentioned the name Jäger, and I thought perhaps this would be it — the explosion out of generalities into something specific, some hard piece of knowledge. "Yes, yes," Alex told us, translating, "she knows the name. She knows it." I felt, right then, very close to them. This seventy-year-old woman would have been a teenager during the war, and I had a strange impulse to touch her. Then Alex went on. "But she didn't really know them."

Still hoping for something — and sensing, suddenly, how absurd this whole expedition was, how mightily time and space and history were against us — I took out the sheaf of photographs I had brought and showed them to her. Photographs of Sam in his thirties and early forties, wearing a fur-collared overcoat; a studio picture of three of the girls in lace dresses; a photo of the third girl, Rochele, with a broad smile and the same kinky hair that I had as a teenager. Maria shook her head with an apologetic little smile — the kind of smile you can do with your lips framing a frown, as my grandmother used to do. "She doesn't remember them," Alex told us. "She was young, just a child, during the war. She didn't know them herself. It's too bad, because her husband's mother was one hundred years old — she died only three years ago — she would have known." Proximity, distance.

But Alex added that Maria's sister-in-law, Olga, and her husband,

Petro, the oldest people in town, still lived just down the road. Off we went, with Nina in tow; clearly she had adopted us and our cause. As we walked, we asked Maria how the Jews and Ukrainians had got along before the war. "Everyone got along, for the most part," she replied. The children played together; people were friendly. Sure, some people were happy when the Jews were taken away. "There were Ukrainians who helped the Nazis; there were Ukrainians who helped Jews to hide," she said. My ears perked up, and I asked Alex to ask her if there was an old castle nearby, where they might have hidden. Again, the apologetic little smile. Maria turned back, and we continued walking.

At Olga's house, tucked in a sharp curve on the road that leads from the center of town to the old Jewish cemetery, a plump old woman opened the door, peering over Alex's shoulder and looking at us warily through narrowed eyes. Everything about her made me think about food: her face as round as a loaf of bread, her two bright blue eyes peering out between fat cheeks like raisins stuck in dough. Alex started his little speech, and she motioned us in.

Again we filed into a strange living room; again chairs were fetched. Alex was talking, and again I heard the name Jäger, and Olga said something twice. Even before Alex translated, I knew this time would be different, because she was saying, very emphatically, *"Znayu, znayu"*: "I know them; I know them." That much Ukrainian I had picked up. She nodded vigorously and said it again and then started talking animatedly to Alex, who was trying to keep up. "She knew these Jägers very well," he said. "It's not just that she's heard the last name, but she knew this family very well. They had a butchery." She had provided that detail without prompting, he assured us. "She knows," he went on. "She remembers."

My sister and I began to cry. This is how close you can come to the dead: You can be sitting in a living room on a fine summer afternoon, sixty years after they have died, and talk to a doughy old woman who, you realize, is exactly as old now as Sam's oldest daughter would have been, and this old woman can be this far away from you, a yard away, that's how close she is. In that moment, the sixty years didn't seem bigger than the three feet that separated me from the quivering arm of the old woman. I suddenly felt, very intensely, the presence of my grandfather, who before this moment had been the last living person I had talked to who knew them, and suddenly the twenty years since he died seemed to shrink too. And so I sat there, blotting my eyes, thankful that Jennifer was crying as well, and listened to Olga talk. She said the name again and looked at my pictures and kept nodding. Alex went on. "She said that they were very nice, very cultural people. Very nice people."

And then, again, the inevitable distance. "She doesn't know what happened to them, to this particular family. She knows that they, like others, other Jews, they suffered very much."

It is, of course, possible to learn about the sufferings of the Jews of Bolechow without having to go there and track down old women who knew them. You can, for instance, check in the *Encyclopedia Judaica* and learn that the Germans entered the town on July 2, 1941, and that the first *Aktion*, or mass liquidation, took place in October, when a thousand Jews were rounded up and, after being tortured for a day, were brought to a mass grave and shot. You can read that the Jewish population of the town, which had been about three thousand at the beginning of the decade, swelled by thousands who were brought in from neighboring villages. You will learn further that the second Aktion took place a year later, when a few thousand Jews were herded into the town square. Of those, five hundred were murdered on the spot, with the remaining two thousand being deported on freight trains to the camp at Belzec. According to the *Encyclopedia Judaica*, moreover, the majority of the remaining Jews were killed in December 1942, leaving about a thousand by 1943, of whom "only a few" escaped into the nearby forests to join the partisans.

But none of that will satisfy your hunger for details, the hunger I felt twenty-four years ago, when, in my senior year of high school, I wrote to Yad Vashem, the Israeli Holocaust museum, and received that photocopied encyclopedia entry. A Xerox can't tell you what Olga told us that day. I had wondered, for instance, when I was eighteen, what "after being tortured for twenty-four hours" might mean. Olga told us that the Jews had been herded into a community center, where the Germans forced them to stand on one another's shoulders, with the old rabbi on the top, then knocked him down. Apparently this went on for a good many hours.

"Brought to a mass grave and shot"? Olga told us that the sound of the machine-gun fire coming from just up the road was so terrible that her mother finally took down an old sewing machine and ran the treadle continuously, hoping to blot out the horror with innocuous domestic noise. Whenever she described some particularly awful incident, Olga would squeeze her eyes shut and make a downward-thrusting motion with her fat hands, a gesture my mother might have made while saying *nebech*.

Twenty minutes into our talk, Olga's husband, Petro, arrived home from church. A small muscular man of nearly ninety, he, too, immediately recognized the family name. He also told us things: that anyone who tried to help the Jews would be shot, for instance, which we knew — Nina had told us, and Maria had, and Nina had made sure to remind Olga as well, apparently, as we began talking to her. "Some Jews were employed in the local tanneries," the encyclopedia had said. "Later, Jews were employed in lumber work at a special labor camp." What Petro told us was that he had worked at the lumber mill, and that when he tried to fill a wartime quota for new workers with Jews, the Germans threatened him. "Do you really need Jews?" he remembered them saying. "Do you really want trouble?"

As he said this, I was torn between wanting to believe him — wanting to believe that the openness and friendliness that we had experienced on this trip would have been evident in the past as well — and trying to be dispassionate, trying to take with more than a grain of salt everything we heard, since even as we sat across from these people, who had welcomed us so easily into their houses, we remembered what we had been told about the Ukrainians.

Our conversation was coming to a close. Was there a castle nearby? I had asked, and the inevitable answer came again, as I knew it would: that there was no castle, no place to hide. And then, as I realized we would get no closer, we heard a final detail. Brought to a mass grave and shot: Petro recalled very well the Aktion when the Jews were marched to the cemetery and shot in a mass grave.

"Where was the road they walked on?" my brother asked, and Olga jumped up and pointed toward the window and said, "Here!" as Nina clapped a hand to her mouth in, I suppose, horror, as if they were passing by right then. It was that close. According to Petro, as their neighbors the Jews of Bolechow were being marched, nearly naked, on this road, walking two by two, they called out to their neighbors — that is, to Olga, who was still standing and pointing out the window, and to the others — "Stay well," "So long, we will not see each other anymore," "We'll not meet anymore."

The anguished farewells stuck in my mind, but it was only later, after I had returned home, that I realized why: It was the sole detail that connected what we had heard that day to something I remembered from Sam's letters: the self-conscious leave-taking, the unthinkable goodbye entrusted to the air. *I bid you farewell and kiss you from the bottom of my heart.*

This was as close as we would get. We had seen the town we had come from, and we agreed, my brothers and sister and I, that this alone was worth the trip. But as for the other details we wanted, we were too far away. We had found no single piece of information that corroborated the stories we had heard, nor would more be forthcoming: Maria had told us that there was no one left who had been an adult before the war. It seemed clear by now that there had never been a castle; the old couple who had known my family had only the vaguest things to tell us about their lives and couldn't tell us how they had died, couldn't rescue them from *killed by the Nazis*. And in a different way, we hadn't found what we had been looking for in the Ukrainians, either. *The Ukrainians were the worst.* We knew it was true; we had read the books and seen the documentaries. But we found it hard to reconcile with the people we kept meeting. Where was the truth? Which variation was it? The only point of contact between what I already knew and what I learned when we went was a tiny detail that could, only if you wanted it to very much, provide a connection — the detail of the long, terrible farewells, a surface resemblance that was, anyway, wholly accidental.

And then they had nothing more to tell us, and so we said our own goodbyes, and we went. I knew we would not be seeing one another again. As we walked back toward the square, we stopped groups of old people coming back from church. No one remembered the Jägers; none claimed to know anyone who might.

Houses of the Living and the Dead

Just before we left, we stopped in front of the house that stands on the site of Sam's house — our family's house — to take pictures. As we posed, a tall young Ukrainian in his mid-twenties, with the blond crew cut and the long icon's face that so many young Ukrainians have, emerged and asked us, not without a faintly aggressive suspiciousness, what we were doing. Alex answered again, to the same effect: The boy's face split into a bright smile, and he motioned us all inside. "He says it's a big honor," Alex said once more.

And so again we filed into a stranger's house, and the young Ukrainian, whose name was Stefan, begged us to sit in the living room, whose only adornment was a reproduction of *The Last Supper,* and then disappeared into the kitchen for a furious, whispered conversation with his pretty blond wife, Ulyana. "He's inviting you all for a drink," Alex explained, and we all made polite noises of refusal until we saw that to refuse would be rude. So we let him fill our glasses, and we drank. We drank toasts to my grandfather, who was born on the spot we were sitting on; we drank toasts to America and to Ukraine. The high emotion and extreme improbability of the long day was beginning to take its toll: We were all a bit silly. Ulyana bustled in the kitchen, and before long Stefan emerged holding two dried whitefish by the tails, explaining to Alex that he wanted us to take them home with us. He insisted on another round. Stefan said we all looked alike; I told him this would certainly reflect well on the honor of our mother. Laughter, more toasts.

The Ukrainians were the worst. How would Stefan and Ulyana have treated us during the war? It was impossible not to wonder about it. And how would they treat us now, if given a chance — the chance, as we couldn't help thinking, that seemed to be lurking yet again in the resurgence across the continent of the old hatreds? The Ukrainians of Bolechow had lived once before in harmony with the town's Jews, before turning on them. Or before some of them did.

I thought about the long and spacious property outside, which had, just as my grandfather had said, orchards of apple and plum and quince trees, and I asked Alex to ask Stefan how they had come to live in this particular house. I asked because sitting here, enjoying this rather surreal scene, the toasts and jokes and *The Last Supper,* I suddenly felt that I wanted one of these very pleasant local people to be responsible for the fact that it was they, and not us, who were living here. Stefan said the house had belonged to his wife's father, who acquired it after the war. From whom? He spread his hands and smiled the same frowny smile that Maria had given us earlier. "He doesn't know," Alex said.

Well, how would he know? Why should he be responsible for knowing? As we walked outside toward the car, Stefan suddenly rushed up to us with a basket. It was filled with apples, tiny green unripe apples, that he had shaken from one of the trees. "For your mother," he told us through Alex. So she might have fruit from the house that would have been hers.

And then, finally, we went to the cemetery. This wasn't so much to see the mass grave — would we even be able to tell where it was? — but rather the place where members of my family had been buried for three hundred years. The headstones, we knew from Alex's earlier visit, would all be in Hebrew, and there were hundreds and hundreds of them. Another haystack; more needles.

Still, we went. And here again, the unexpected nearness when everything seemed so hopelessly far. As we pulled up alongside the little creek that runs by one side of the ancient cemetery, my brother Matthew started shouting for Alex to stop. "Sima Jäger — Sima Jäger!" he kept saying, and as we looked at where he was pointing, we saw that one solitary headstone, there at the top of the hill, had Roman characters, and on it was written Sima Jäger, the name of my grandfather's great-aunt. "A beloved mother, she was not forgotten by her sons," the inscription said in Hebrew. I did what Jews do when they visit graves and placed a small stone on Sima's headstone and took some rocks from this place to put on the graves of my grandfather and his siblings back home — the least a good grandchild could do.

She was not forgotten: As I stood looking at the forlorn little rock on Sima's huge headstone, I felt, again, what it means to be of the generation of the grandchildren. The rock for Sima — symbolically, a rock for all the Jägers whose headstones I could not find that day or who never got headstones — I placed out of duty: a ritual abstraction. The rock for my grandfather I would place for the sake of love: I knew him. But to my children, the next generation, it is my grandfather who will represent mere duty, who will be too far away.

Over by the edge of the cemetery where the procession of listing stones came suddenly to a halt, blond Ukrainian children were swinging in a rubber tire from the arm of a great old oak. The largish patch of earth over which the tire arced back and forth with its squealing cargo was subtly discolored and very hard, as if it had been tamped down on purpose, long ago.

We went back to Bolechow the next day to take more pictures, but there was no one else to talk to. And then, the day after that, we went back home.

Zeno's Paradox

What we later learned was this:

Rochele Jäger, the third daughter of Sam and Ester Jäger, was arrested in Bolechow during a roundup on September 28, 1941, and shot the next day in the mass grave in the cemetery where her great-great-aunt had been so much more decorously buried. She was sixteen. Her parents, handsome Sam, "the king of the town," as he was called, and his once-beautiful wife, Ester, and their youngest girl, Bronia, were taken in the second Aktion and perished then, although whether they were among the five hundred who perished in the town square or the two thousand gassed at Belzec, we cannot know. Rochele's older sister Frydka kept the accounts in the lumber factory where Petro had worked; she and the oldest, Lorka, the dear Lorka, escaped in 1943 and joined a group of partisans led by a pair of Ukrainian brothers named Babij. By 1943 the ranks of these partisans had swollen to nearly a thousand, and fearing that the Ukrainian group would eventually make contact with the Russians, the Germans launched a huge assault, with tanks, artillery, and air cover, on the forest where the partisans hid out. There were said to be four survivors.

It was only after we returned home that we learned all of this, learned as much as we now know, learned what had happened to them. Six months after our journey, the telephone rang. "Mr. Mendelsohn?" a deep Central European voice said. The line crackled: very long distance. "My name is Jack Greene, and I hear on the grapevine that you're looking for people who knew your Jäger family in Bolechow. You should know that I dated one of Sam's girls, and I'd be happy to talk to you."

And so it was, months later and continents away, that we finally got close to them.

When we returned from Bolechow, we made copies of the videos we had taken there, including those of our interviews with Nina and Maria and Olga, and sent these copies to the remaining Jäger cousins. The two who live in Israel, in turn, had shown the tape to some former Bolechowers they knew. One of them was Shlomo Adler, the leader of the ex-Bolechower community in Israel, who during a flurry of subsequent e-mail messages told us not to believe Petro — he may have convinced himself that he had tried to help the Jews, Adler said, but most likely he did not — and told us not to bother trying to erect a memorial in the mass grave, as we had contemplated doing, because the stones would be vandalized and the construction materials stolen. Most important, he mentioned our trip to Jack Greene, who now lives in Sydney and who dated Rochele Jäger and who knew them and who survived.

I talked to Jack Greene for a long time, and he told me about my family — not only how they died but how they lived. There is no reason to repeat everything he said: After all, how interesting is it that young sweethearts in a small Eastern European shtetl would have watched, say, Wallace Beery movies in the community enter-tainment center, except perhaps that it was in the same entertain-ment center that some of those teenagers would, only a few years later, be forced to entertain their tormentors before being killed?

Jack told me a great many things, specific things. He told me about the meetings of the Zionist organization that he attended in order to see Rochele and about Sam's business ("in Bolechow there were two cars, and one of them belonged to Shmiel Jäger") and about how Bronia "looked like her mother, exactly" and that a friend of his had made his first-ever telephone call on the phone in Sam's house and that the boys and girls would take walks in the park in the evening and that none of Sam's daughters had his showy personality. ("Yeah, he looked it, and he acted the part," Jack said when I told him Sam had always been considered a prince. A big fish in a little pond: Sam had got his wish at a terrible price.) He told me about the soccer games that they would go to after the So-viets took over that part of Galicia in 1939 — the Jews there had two years of relative security, thanks to the Ribbentrop-Molotov pact — and how moviegoing had become unpopular after the the-ater started showing nothing but Soviet propaganda films. I asked him, at the end of our first interview, to tell me in detail what Rochele had been like. He paused, and then he said, "She was a beautiful, wonderful girl."

And he talked, of course, about the war years: about the way that after Sam had been killed and his oldest daughters were making their precarious existences in the little while they still had left to live, Frydka, the second girl, about whose employment prospects Sam had worried in a letter to my grandfather, a letter that I have open before me as I write this — it is that close — had managed to get a job doing accounts in the lumber factory, because the idea was to get yourself into forced labor. "To get yourself a job for the war effort. And that gave you some feeling of security — that they won't take you tomorrow. They might take you in three months, but not tomorrow." It was this girl, he said a little later on, and her older sister, who had escaped in 1943, when it was clear that the end was coming, into the forest with the partisans.

The Babij group, he added, was eventually betrayed by spies. Jews, in fact, who were being blackmailed by the Germans into helping them. That, at any rate, was what he had heard.

It was then that I understood how the stories my family had handed down, the different theories about the betrayal, the chess moves, had come to be. It seemed clear to me, at that moment, that the betrayal of the Babij partisans had got garbled in translation, somewhere between the event itself and the point at which it had been described to my grandfather and his siblings. And in the confusion, the betrayal of many hundreds of people (if indeed it was as Jack Greene had heard) had come to be retold as the betrayal of Sam and his wife and four daughters — and thereafter adopted as my family's narrative, the story my brothers and sister and I had traveled halfway across the world to confirm, because a narrative of greed and naiveté and bad judgment was better than the alternative, which was no narrative at all.

And I saw, then, that my own private suspicions about a closer, more terrible betrayal by my American relatives of their family in Europe was the product of the same desire for a story. I had always thought that my grandfather felt a terrible guilt, but it hadn't occurred to me that what he felt guilty about wasn't that he had betrayed them but that he had no story for them — no way to account for how they had died.

Jack told me something else that night: that, like Sam, his own parents had been hoping to send their children away to safety, but that in 1939 the wait was six years "and by then everyone was already dead." (Jack survived by hiding out in the forest.) It is impossible to say for certain that my grandfather and his siblings did everything they could for Sam and his family, although I now think that they did. What is certain is that nothing they could have done would have saved them.

All during our trip, I had been disappointed because we didn't find anything to confirm the stories I had been told; I had wanted the gripping tales to be true. It was only when I listened to Jack Greene that I realized I had been after the wrong story — the story of how they had died rather than the one of how they had lived. If our instinct is to forsake the everyday and focus on vivid stories when we speak of the dead, it is because of a great distance: From a couple of generations away, you grasp at the legends' broad outlines, because the details are lost — or have been destroyed. The particulars of the lives they led were, inevitably, bland: the kinds of unmemorable things that make up everyone's day-to-day existence. It is only when everyday existence ceases to exist, when knowing that you'll die in three months rather than tomorrow seems like "security," that such lost details seem rare and beautiful.

When we went back, we saw that time is still the terrible enemy: Each year, the details get further away. But we also realized, by going, that we are still just close enough to recover a few more details — to recover something of their lives, as well as of their deaths. At a time when great distance has, paradoxically, brought us very close to the past, when fewer and fewer people think the Holocaust has any remaining relevance yet Jewish gravestones are once again unsafe from vandals, the search for such details may well make a better monument to the lost than the one we had thought about building.

This is why, when Jack Greene told me that what I should really do, instead of talking on the phone for so long, is come to Sydney, I knew that I would go, just as I knew I would probably go wherever my conversations with him might send me: to Long Island to talk to the woman who was one of the four Babij partisans to survive and to Israel, where I can find the old woman who was Lorka's friend, and to wherever else I might find more mundane details. I will go because I see now that there was much more there than I had realized, and although I know that we will never get them back, never quite reach them, there is much of them still out there, enough to tell a little story that could just come close to the truth, and however far away and with every year that passes, I feel I am getting closer.

LAWRENCE MILLMAN

Lost in the Arctic

FROM *National Geographic Adventure*

THE BOAT'S MOTOR had been making curious burbling noises all morning, as if there were a newborn trapped inside it. Then the engine died. My Inuit guides Qungujuq and Zacharias bent over the outboard, trying to figure out what was wrong. Meanwhile, we started drifting southeast.

"Motor very kaput," Qungujuq announced, as if this weren't already obvious. "Must take it apart." It was also obvious that there wasn't any room on the overloaded boat to take apart a wristwatch, much less an eighty-five-horsepower Yamaha outboard.

I confess I wasn't in a particularly jovial frame of mind about our situation, since I knew how unforgiving the Arctic can be. The Inuit have many tales of people going off in boats and disappearing; years later their bones turn up on some distant beach. We continued to drift southeast for the next few hours as Qungujuq examined various motor parts.

"*Qikiqtaq!*" Zacharias shouted. An island.

He pointed to a small patch of land about five miles away, then grabbed our lone oar and began paddling toward it. After a while, Qungujuq took over for him, and then I took over for Qungujuq. I paddled until my arms were ready to fall off, then passed the oar to Zacharias, who was at least five years older than me but much stronger. He paddled the rest of the way, neatly parrying the ice floes that guarded the island. At last a wave thrust the boat onto the gravelly shore with a resounding crunch.

The Arctic had granted us a reprieve, of sorts.

*

In the Canadian North, ice is the final arbiter of human affairs. A few days before washing up on an unknown island, I was biding my time in Sanirajak, an Inuit community on the Melville Peninsula. From there, I planned to travel across Foxe Basin to Prince Charles Island, an uninhabited chunk of land almost as large as Connecticut. It wasn't officially documented until 1948, when a Royal Canadian Air Force pilot taking aerial photographs noticed an unknown landmass in one of his pictures. And even though the low-lying, icebound island has now been charted, it has never been fully explored. But Foxe Basin turned out to be choked with sea ice, so I was stuck in Sanirajak, waiting for a gale to come along and whisk the ice away.

Sanirajak isn't the sort of place where most people would want to spend more than a few hours — maybe not even more than a few minutes. Imagine Appalachia crossbred with a Gypsy encampment, then struck by an earthquake. Imagine residential landscaping that consists of discarded snowmobile treads, fuel drums, cast-off Pampers, bottles, slops, and animal bones. The town's chief attraction, or, perhaps, its chief distraction, is a several-hundred-year-old whale carcass whose odor is still pungent enough to upset the nostrils. I couldn't wait to exchange Sanirajak for the wilds of Foxe Basin.

Each morning, Qungujuq would study the ice with the seriousness of a scholar gazing at a palimpsest, then come to my tent and say, *"Nagga."* ("Not today.") Then he would join me for coffee. He got his caffeine fix by sticking the grounds directly into his mouth like a wad of tobacco, thus avoiding the bland intercession of water.

Sometimes Qungujuq would bring along his father, a barrel-chested elder whose face resembled the contour lines on a topo map. Like a number of other people I'd met in Sanirajak, the old man, Sivulliq, knew only one expression in English: "You're a better man than I am, Gunga Din!" Some years ago, the town's Hudson's Bay Company trader would perform the occasional interment and, instead of reciting a proper burial service, would solemnly intone Rudyard Kipling's "Gunga Din." The poem's famous line had entered the local vernacular as a sort of vaguely reverential sentiment, although no one had the slightest idea what it meant.

Sivulliq said there were Tunit on Prince Charles Island, and he warned me to be very careful: They would attempt to unravel my intestines — a popular Tunit form of entertainment — if I gave them the opportunity.

According to archaeologists, the Tunit, or Dorset people, died out before A.D. 1300. Yet if there was one place in the Arctic where a small band of them might have survived, I figured, that place would be Prince Charles Island. Another thing Sivulliq told me: The weather on Prince Charles Island is awful, and thus it's very easy to get marooned there.

Finally, one morning Qungujuq awakened me by shouting *"Tuavi!* ['Hurry up!'] Ice blown away by big wind." Groggily, I lifted the tent flap and at once saw open water where the night before there had been only an uncompromising sheet of ice.

Within an hour, Qungujuq, his brother-in-law Zacharias, and I had piled our supplies into Qungujuq's twenty-four-foot motorized freighter canoe and were headed east across Foxe Basin. Rather, we tried to head east, but the wind kept shoving us in a more northerly direction. Finally we decided to wait it out, so we put ashore in a cove about twenty-five miles north of Sanirajak. Here we encountered some walrus hunters from Igloolik, a community farther north on the peninsula. One of the hunters had told me that the wind would die down during the night. I asked him how he knew this. Was he observing the flight patterns of certain birds or perhaps using some time-honored native technique to read the weather?

"No," he said. "I heard it on the radio."

The following day, the wind did in fact die down, but it left in its wake a strong lateral swell. Qungujuq and Zacharias took turns trying to keep the boat from being bashed by waves, but despite their expertise as helmsmen, we still got wet. At one point a wave rushed our gunwales and dumped a jellyfish into the boat. Zacharias found this vastly amusing, even though arctic jellyfish can deliver a nasty sting. But Zacharias seemed to find everything vastly amusing, even the albino walrus whoofling at us from an ice pan. An albino walrus, he informed me, means death.

"Death to whom?" I asked.

"Us," he said, grinning.

In spite of the swell, we made good progress, motoring about fifty miles east to Rowley Island, which itself escaped detection until the mid-1930s. Earlier in the day, Qungujuq had shot a ringed seal. After caching most of the meat on Rowley for our return trip, we cooked the flippers and liver. The meal reminded me of the first time I'd eaten seal liver, in Greenland. It was still steaming, having been plucked from a recently killed animal. Whatever hesitation I might have felt about eating it was quickly dispelled by the meat's tangy, iron-rich taste.

"Nattiup tingua mamarijara," I said. ("I like seal liver.")

"Uvanga ijingit mamarniqsaujakka," Qungujuq told me. ("Myself, I prefer the eyes.") Later, he dissected a seal eye and showed me how the clear inner spheroid could be used as a magnifying glass — useful information if you happen to have a seal eye handy.

The next day, the sea was as smooth as blue glass. By early afternoon, we were about twenty-five miles northwest of Prince Charles Island. I was, to put it mildly, excited to be within spitting distance of my goal. That's when the motor conked out.

The island on which we found ourselves stranded looked to be about two miles long and half a mile wide. It didn't appear on my Canadian Geological Survey map; more significantly, neither Qungujuq nor Zacharias knew about its existence. We were lost. Very lost.

"Maybe we've died and gone to heaven," quipped Zacharias.

If this really was heaven, then a lot of clean-living people were going to be very disappointed. There didn't seem to be any pearly gates, only scoured limestone intersected by the occasional quartzite dike. The closest thing I saw to an angel was an ivory gull hovering in the air above us, its stiff wings bright against a high overcast.

The only other winged entities were positively unangelic: mosquitoes. From the instant we landed, they attacked us so aggressively and in such biblical proportions that I figured they hadn't dined on any warm-blooded organisms for a very long time.

Soon Qungujuq had scattered pieces of the motor on the beach. It was ten P.M., but there was still enough light for him to work on our stricken motor. Enough light, too, for me to see a screw that had rolled away and retrieve it for him. But that's almost all I could do: I know less about machines than a dull three-year-old.

The Inuit, on the other hand, seem to have a knack for machines. I once saw an elderly Inuk take apart and repair a helicopter engine, much to the surprise of the Danish pilot, who hadn't been able to repair it himself. When I asked the old man where he had learned about such things, he pointed to his head and tapped it. He'd been born in a realm where you learn to improvise or you don't survive.

Qungujuq was still working on the motor at midnight when Zacharias and I turned in. When I awoke during the night to answer nature's call, there was Qungujuq beside me in the tent, snoring mightily. Zacharias was now on the beach, working in the semi-darkness. In his hand was a tangle of wires that looked like a cat's cradle.

"Think you can fix it?" I said.

"Immaqa," Zacharias replied.

This is by far the most popular word in Inuktitut. It means "perhaps," with an intimation of "probably not." If you're someone who needs straight answers, the Inuit could easily immaqa you to a state of gibbering idiocy.

The next morning Qungujuq and Zacharias were alternately staring at pieces of the motor and swatting at mosquitoes. I tried to gauge from their expressions whether they'd made any headway, and I noticed that neither looked particularly pleased.

"We need a part for the gas line," Qungujuq told me.

"And it will be very hard to order it from here," added Zacharias.

We hadn't brought along a radio or a locator beacon (stupid, yes: In our haste to leave Sanirajak, we'd also forgotten flotation jackets), so I had a hunch we'd be stuck on the island until someone rescued us. Already knowing what he would tell me, I asked Qungujuq whether he thought another boat might pass this way in the not too distant future. He didn't say *"immaqa";* he said *"aakka"* ("no").

"Maybe an airplane?" I said.

Another *"aakka"*: We were nowhere near a flight corridor. Also, our paddle had cracked when Zacharias beached the boat, and it now consisted of two useless pieces. (We'd somehow managed to leave the other one on Rowley Island.) So we were not only lost but marooned as well.

Maybe I was taking my cue from my companions, who weren't at all panicky, or maybe the true nature of our predicament hadn't sunk in yet, but I wasn't overly worried. I told myself: You're not dead until you're dead, and besides, you were the one who had the bright idea to go to a virtually unknown place. Now you've fetched up at just such a place — for God's sake, go out and explore it.

"You need me for anything?" I asked.

Both Qungujuq and Zacharias shook their heads vigorously, as if any attempt to help on my part would only make a sorry situation worse. So I wandered off, accompanied by a full escort of mosquitoes swarming around my bug hat. Qungujuq called me back and gave me his .30-06 rifle, uttering a single word: *"Nanuq."* He was not suggesting that I shoot the hero of the silent movie but that I protect myself against a possible attack from the animal for which Robert Flaherty's hero was named, the polar bear.

Thus armed, I climbed the hogback behind our camp. Several minutes later, I was standing on another hogback — it was probably the highest point on the island — and staring out in every direction over the expanse of Foxe Basin. There was no other land in sight. Indeed, there was nothing at all in sight, since even the ice floes had disappeared during the night. If I'd been standing on the moon, I might have felt a greater sense of solitude, but I doubt it.

I then turned my attention to the island itself. In the sunlight, it was a lot more colorful than it had looked the previous evening. Here and there were delicate arctic wildflowers — purple saxifrage, Lapland rosebay, moss campion, arctic cinquefoil, and buttercups — rising bravely, it would appear, from solid rock. Gossamer tufts of arctic cotton swayed in an imperceptible breeze. A brilliant patch of yellow lichen exploded from its dour limestone host; an equally bright yellow butterfly flitted from flower to flower.

It was so quiet that my steps sounded downright raucous on the gravelly ground. I got the feeling that nothing had changed or even moved on the island since the end of the Ice Age. In every respect, it was a harsh place. Even so, its forlorn beauty took my breath away.

And then I came upon the cairns — half a dozen beehive-shaped structures piled along a gently sloping ridge. Peering through the chinks of one of them, I saw a human skull and several bone fragments; in another, there was a brownish skull fragment, a jawbone with worn teeth, and a scattering of vertebral arches; in a third, a lone skull.

My first thought was: Here's what happened to the last group of people who washed up here when their motor conked out.

But then, in one of the cairns, I noticed a skeleton that had been interred with a large, circular soapstone lamp, which identified the site as dating from the Thule period. The skeleton was curled in a fetal position. Was it possible that these people, who succeeded the Tunit, believed their journey to the afterlife would be less perilous if they left the world in the same posture in which they'd entered it? At any rate, I felt somewhat relieved: The Thule period ended approximately two hundred years before the invention of marine engines.

Still, the graves reminded me of my situation. There was the possibility that this bare speck of land might turn out to be my own final resting place. I imagined my last fragile thoughts drifting away, and then I imagined some archaeologist discovering my bones and wondering what a middle-aged Caucasian was doing so far from his native habitat. For almost the first time since I'd left Sanirajak, I found myself wondering the same thing.

Meanwhile, I was being sucked dry by the mosquitoes, whose persistent probing had helped them locate the holes in my bug net. Not relishing the prospect of death by acupuncture, I quickened my pace. Now only the most aerobically fit of the little bastards could keep up with me. But the island had not been set up as a racecourse, and I tripped over some glacial till and went flying through the air. Don't land on the rifle, I told myself. I didn't land on the rifle. Instead, I landed on my compass, which made a gouge in my chest — possibly the first compass-related injury in human medical history.

I also landed in a boneyard. There were hundreds of ribs, scapulae, and vertebrae scattered around me. The skulls told me the bones were all from walruses, and they indicated why the occupants of the cairns had lived in such an apparently unbountiful place — the charnel pit was only a short distance from the floe edge, home to the paunchy, hulking *aivik*. For the Thule, bounty was determined not by soil but by the object at the end of a harpoon.

Back in camp, Qungujuq and Zacharias were hunched over a checkerboard. They were so intent on their game that neither one noticed me until I was standing beside them. Then Zacharias smiled and said, "We were hoping you would kill a big nanuq for our dinner."

In fact, I was a little concerned about our food supply. We hadn't expected this misadventure, so we had brought only enough for a few weeks. Likewise, we had planned to supplement our diet with meat from seals or a walrus, but we couldn't get within shooting distance without a functioning motor.

That food supply, which now seemed to me incredibly meager, included the following items: a box of expedition-standard oatmeal ("bloatmeal"), five boxes of rice, a bag of dried prunes, a pound of raisins, two bags of pilot biscuits (hardtack), two dozen Snickers bars, eleven packets of freeze-dried fettuccine Alfredo, six packets of freeze-dried chicken cacciatore, four packets of macaroni, a half-empty jar of Cheez Whiz, a small bag of flour, several slabs of *pipsik* (dried fish), a few rubbery pieces of *maktaaq* (narwhal skin), and one slightly moldy apple.

After my companions had finished their game, I asked Zacharias what would happen if we ran out of food.

"We eat each other," he said. He was grinning, but he was also studying me with, I thought, the appreciative gaze of a chef.

During the night the wind accelerated, first baying, then howling, and then shrieking, until it reached a higher decibel level than any wind I'd ever heard. Every hour or so, we would go outside and gather rocks to pile along the tent's guy lines. Were it not for them, I'm convinced, the wind would have picked up the tent — poles, occupants, and all — and deposited it somewhere in the middle of Foxe Basin.

The wind continued to blow the next day, and, except for the occasional rock-collecting mission, we stayed hunkered down inside the tent. Even so, the wind found us, pushing grit under the tent's fly and into our sleeping bags, our clothes, our food, our hair, our Primus stove — everything.

Being trapped in the tent made me even more aware of the degree to which we were imprisoned on the island. But Qungujuq and Zacharias were as composed as Zen Buddhist monks on a retreat, except when they were playing checkers, and then Zacharias — a less accomplished player than Qungujuq — would occasionally shout *"Tuqulirama! Tuqulirama!"* ("I'm dying! I'm dying!")

Ajurnarmat: This is doubtless the second most popular word in Inuktitut. It means something like "Why worry?" or "Hey, what can you do?" In our time together, I came to regard my companions as living, walking, checkers-playing embodiments of ajurnarmat. I envied them this attitude, not to mention their ability to remain unruffled in the face of what I felt was a pretty dire situation.

At one point, they burst into riotous laughter. They were talking about an Anglican minister, a member of the Bible Churchman's Missionary Society, who'd come to Sanirajak fifteen years ago. The man had learned just enough Inuktitut to mistake one word for another. One Sunday, he confused *ijjujut* (Bible) with *igjuuk* and ended up telling his congregation that they should pay more attention to their testicles.

Later, Zacharias recounted a story about a man who'd run out of food during a sledging trip on Baffin Island. The starving man prayed for God's help. All at once he noticed a big slab of meat on the floor of his tent — God had provided! The man flensed the meat, chopped it up, and threw it into his pot. But he died before he could eat it: He had flensed and chopped his own thigh.

My companions thought this story was hilarious. I suspect Zacharias may have told it for my benefit, as a way of saying, "Come on, man, take it easy, or you might end up doing something rash, like eating yourself."

The wind, which I guessed was blowing at sixty-five or seventy knots, showed no sign of relenting. Once, when I ventured outside to pee, I was caught by a gust that was so strong it made my teeth ache. Back in the tent, I occupied myself with my journal: "If I ever get out of this mess, I'm going to adopt a more sedentary lifestyle."

Three days later, with astonishing abruptness, the wind moderated to a mere breeze, as if it had suddenly grown tired after such a prolonged display of power. We could now go outside without being pummeled to jelly and, as it turned out, without being bitten by mosquitoes, which were nowhere in sight. It was early evening, and a sort of ethereal hush had fallen. There was a soft pink marbling in the clouds — solar iridescence. The light had that tentative quality so typical of the Arctic, where every last sunbeam feels as if it's been snatched from the perpetually imminent winter.

Soon Qungujuq and Zacharias were disassembling and reassembling the motor for, it seemed, the hundredth time. I needed to stretch my legs, so I began wandering along the shore. The storm had washed up all kinds of oceanic booty — a golden plover's wing tangled in a matting of seaweed, a dismembered starfish, kelp, fish, and a dead seal. Initially, I thought the seal might be salvageable as food, but, upon closer inspection, I saw that it was scarcely more than a husk, its flesh and organs having already been consumed by crabs, isopods, and other creatures of the sea.

Now I began scavenging the beach in earnest for something that might bolster our rapidly diminishing larder. I wouldn't have turned up my nose at a newly dead fish or bird, but I found only very dead fish and a bundle of feathers so mangled that it was impossible to tell whether it was a bird or the stuffing from a mattress. Then I saw a patch of *Lycoperdon* puffballs on the mossy ground near the shore. I knew that neither Qungujuq nor Zacharias would eat them (the Inuit believe that mushrooms are the shit of shooting stars), but I certainly would.

My foraging was interrupted by the sound of a gunshot. I ran back along the beach. When I got closer, I noticed Zacharias had a bigger than usual grin on his face.

"All fix now," Qungujuq said. The motor was back on the boat and roaring with life.

At that lovely moment, all I could manage to tell him was this: "You're a better man than I am, Gunga Din."

Apparently, the motor's O-ring had been badly chewed up, which meant that the fuel line wasn't getting gas. Qungujuq had replaced the rubber gasket with some kelp, and that had done the trick.

So now the question was, Did I want to continue on to Prince Charles Island? We had enough fuel, Qungujuq told me. Well, maybe enough fuel. And we probably had enough food. If not, we could always shoot a seal or two. The gas might eat through our improvised O-ring, but if that happened, no problem, we'd just use more kelp.

I couldn't tell whether he was in ajurnarmat mode ("Whatever will be, will be") or trying to talk me out of a trip he considered risky. But it didn't matter. I had already decided that it was time to head back to the scuzzy charms of Sanirajak. I had satisfied my desire to explore an island in the back of beyond, an island that had turned out to be even farther off the map than Prince Charles. Also, I didn't want to risk being marooned again. In the Arctic, fate doesn't like to be tempted, much less seduced.

And yet, as we pulled away from the stony beach, I felt a curious sadness. Maybe I'd left part of myself on these obdurate shores, or maybe I just felt sad because I was surrendering a rare privilege — the privilege of solitude. As the island receded in the distance, I thought to myself, There are worse places to which you could bequeath your bones.

The trip back across Foxe Basin was uneventful. We spent another night on Rowley Island and gorged on the seal meat we had stored there. We didn't encounter another albino walrus, which seemed to disappoint Zacharias. Nor did we encounter any ice, except for a few vagrant floes. Most surprising, the only wind was a light breeze from the south, a compass point I hadn't thought about in a long, long time.

At last we came in sight of Sanirajak. Even at sea, I could detect the scent of the dead whale, and it seemed to me the sweetest smell in all the world.

STEVEN RINELLA

Gettin' Jiggy

FROM *Outside*

NIGHTTIME COMES in the form of light rather than darkness when you're hanging around the waterfront in Seattle. Airplanes crisscrossing overhead turn into flashing pinpricks of green and red, and the Space Needle, at the foot of Queen Anne Hill, blazes alive like a desert casino. Soon the lights from ferry terminals, souvenir shops, and clam chowder joints glitter across the surface of Puget Sound, and the waterfront's numbered network of piers becomes a meeting ground for skate punks, panhandlers, yuppies, cops, drunk students, random passersby, and tired tourists dragging their crabby kids.

Sometimes, though, around December, when the solar calendar and the lunar phase align with the earth's rotation just so, an entirely different kind of nighttime meeting occurs here, and all hell breaks loose. Millions of creatures rise out of Puget Sound's depths and look to the emerging lights of Seattle with hungry eyes. Each slimy and voracious predator is armed with ten sucker-bearing appendages, a jet that shoots an inky substance to confuse its enemies, a sharp, pointy beak used to gouge hunks of flesh from prey, and the ability to dodge forward, backward, sideways, or in a 360-degree turn with lightning speed. No anchovy or crustacean is safe from *Loligo opalescens,* otherwise known as the Pacific, or market, squid. And no squid is safe from the Seattle squid jiggers who flock to the docks at dusk and stay into the wee hours of the night, hoping to catch a few.

I first heard about squid jigging from my long-time buddy Matt Drost, a thirty-year-old graduate student and bluegill-fishing midwesterner who's lived in Seattle for five years. His message on my machine — "We're seriously missing out, man; we should be squid jigging" — had the urgency of someone recently hooked into a pyramid scheme. I live in Montana, where fishing becomes nause-ating in its predictability: white people in brown fishing vests, all catching trout. The opportunity to outwit a close cousin of the no-toriously crafty octopus and the vicious giant squid was very tempt-ing. Plus, killing a squid and eating it isn't looked down on like whacking a trout is, probably because trout seem serene and gen-tle, whereas a squid looks like it would kill you if it had the chance.

When Matt, who by now had gotten a taste of jigging himself, phoned again to announce that the peak of squid season would co-incide with his winter break, I bought myself an insulated one-piece mechanic's suit for twenty bucks at a pawnshop, figuring I'd wear it over my styling duds to keep them free of squid ink. I threw it into the trunk of my gray '87 Subaru and took off.

A basic jigging setup involves a standard light rod and reel, a porta-ble floodlight, and a handful of lures known as squid jigs.

Squid-jigging success rests on the jig itself, a five- or six-dollar contraption engineered for cold-blooded simplicity. If you've ever watched a jig bob up and down in the water, you know why its name was derived from the word for a lively dance. The top end of a jig is shaped like a pinkie finger and decorated like a small, flashy fish. The bottom end of a jig sports a profusion of J-shaped needles. A squid doesn't bite the jig and get lip-hooked in the conventional way that fish do. Instead, a squid seizes the jig with its tentacles. The jigger must detect the squid's presence through the rod, then yank on the line to impale the squid on the needles. In winter, when large numbers of squid congregate to spawn, they feed voraciously in the shallow waters at night, gobbling up anything that's smaller than they are. The jig simply has to look alive.

If you ask around on the docks about where to buy a jig, you will wind up with directions to Linc's Tackle. This dusty but well-organized fishing shop lies east of the waterfront, in the Interna-tional District. The shop's founder, Lincoln Beppu, was born in the United States to Japanese parents in 1912 and died in 1992. He opened the corner-store business on Rainier Avenue South and King Street in 1950, about five years after he and his brothers, Monroe, Taft, and Grant, were released from a World War II in-ternment camp for Japanese Americans.

Lincoln Beppu recognized that his neighborhood clientele of Asian immigrants did not have much in the way of disposable income, so he encouraged squid jigging on the grounds that it was cheap and close by, and that you could get a good meal out of it. Lincoln imported many of his jigs from Japan. People have been catching squid in Asia and the Mediterranean for thousands of years, and many centuries ago the Japanese began whittling, from deer antlers, intricate and decorative jigs that look almost exactly like the ones used today. These ancient jiggers lured their quarry with torches instead of halogen lights.

Linc's Tackle is now owned by Lincoln's son, Jerry Beppu, a fifty-seven-year-old man who wears his graying hair slicked back in a way that accidentally appears hip. Jerry's wife, Maria, the daughter of a French-Canadian mother and a Filipino father, helps run the shop. In the window of Linc's Tackle is an old, yellowing sign that says LET'S GO SQUID JIGGING: COME IN FOR ADVICE AND TACKLE.

Matt and I caught Jerry and Maria during their evening rush, which coincides with the setting of the sun. Jerry was peeling a tangerine and Maria was pantomiming back and forth with a man who spoke neither English nor Japanese. She pointed to each available size of jig, which vary in length from a ballpoint pen to a pen's cap, and waited for the customer to nod yes or no. He picked his size. Then she went through the colors, which range widely. Some are plain neon yellow and others are obviously inspired by an appreciation for the psychedelic.

I gazed over the man's shoulder and spotted the squid jig of all squid jigs. It was a beauty: a glow-in-the-dark jobby with a translucent top revealing an internal swirled cat's-eye design. Based on zero experience, I knew this jig would work. It cost me $3.25. I also forked over $23.90 for a one-year out-of-state shellfish license ($8.67 for Washington residents). Matt picked out a handful of trusted jig designs, and we headed for the door. As we stepped outside, Jerry Beppu yelled, "Patience and luck!"

Right about dusk we drove under the Alaska Way Viaduct, near Pioneer Square, a historic district of restaurants and trendy shops a block off the waterfront. We parked between an idling limousine and a man sleeping beneath a blue plastic tarp, walked across Alaska Way, and headed north, "up the Sound," keeping an eye out for anybody who looked like he might be getting ready to jig some squid. It was still a little early and no jiggers were at Pier 63, the most popular gathering spot for jigging, so we decided to try a rogue move and jig Pier 57, a few blocks south behind Fisherman's Restaurant and Bar and a kitschy art gallery called Pirate's Plunder.

I'd pulled the battery out of my Subaru and lugged it along with us. We took two pieces of copper wire with roach clips, ran them from the battery to an AC/DC inverter, and plugged in a big-ass, 2,070-lumen floodlight. When I shone the light on the water, I swore it would parboil any squid that happened along. As we were messing with this outfit, a professional-looking man in his early fifties wearing dress slacks and a trench coat came out of the art gallery.

"What are you doing?" he asked.

I figured he was there to kick us off the pier, but we didn't bother lying. "We were thinking we might try to catch some squid," Matt said.

"You got a light, huh?"

"Hell, yeah," I answered. He went back inside. In a moment he returned with a fishing rod.

It got so windy that I wrapped a bungee cord around my head to hold my hood in place. We drew quite a crowd as it got dark. The art gallery guy's daughter showed up with a fishing pole and her boyfriend. Another guy and girl of about college-freshman age walked up to ask what we were doing. I told them, and they got comfortable leaning against a rail, like they were going to stay until it happened. A man in a red leather jacket walked up. "What you catch?" he asked. He spoke with an Italian accent.

"Squid. You like squid?"

"Yes, I cook many ways," he said. Several other people crowded in close to the light, putting rods together.

I'd never caught a squid, so I wasn't sure what to expect. Puget Sound is also home to the mysterious giant squid, so it was with some trepidation that I lowered my psychedelic jig into the water.

I looked over at Matt. He had his jig in the water about halfway to the bottom, which he said was twenty feet down.

"You want to move the rod up and down," Matt suggested. "Real lightly." Within seconds I became aware that a squid was groping my jig.

I cranked on the reel, and a squid emerged in a fury of squirting ink and grappling tentacles. Even though it was only about eight inches long, an average size, I was struck by the memory of those sea monsters that destroy Tokyo in old Japanese movies. A sea-monster scream seemed so apropos to the squid's emergence that Matt provided one, a habit of his that I adopted as my own. It was a shrill screech, sort of a *gusheegushowee*. As I jacked the squid over the rail, it landed a shot of black ink right on the chest of my coveralls, forming a kick-ass badge. I announced that from now on, I would answer only to Sheriff Squid.

The squid gurgled and changed colors from white to red to brown, like a chameleon wired on speed. At the top of its body a round head with two large eyes formed the base for eight arms and two spindly tentacles. The body, a fleshy cylinder called the mantle, resembled an occupied condom. A thin, cellophane-like shell gave the mantle a slight rigidity. Looking at a squid, you've got to hand it to whoever started eating them. What an open-minded individual! I dropped the squid into my bucket and tried to visualize the legal daily limit of ten pounds.

An aggravating thing about squid is that they'll clear out at any moment, without warning. That's what happened at Pier 57: Just when I was getting my groove and had enough squid to cover the bottom of a five-gallon bucket, we had a squid shutdown. All the folks sharing our light packed up and headed a ten-minute walk north to Pier 63 without so much as a good-bye.

Matt and I followed. Pier 63 was now a big party. A generator powered a large bank of floodlights, and a crowd of fifty people or so was lined up in the glow. People were dropping jigs down into what looked like a docking slip for a large ship.

The generator's owner, a frail old Korean man, was warming his hands in the buzzing machine's exhaust. "I don't jig much myself," he told me. "I just use my lights so my friends and neighbors here can have a good time." I asked him his name, but he wouldn't say, because you're not supposed to use gasoline-powered equipment on public piers. Now and then some pain-in-the-ass type will file a complaint and the cops will be forced to shut him down. "When they do, I cool it for a week and then come back out like nothing happened," he said.

Matt and I thanked him and squeezed into the line. I was standing next to a fifty-two-year-old Cambodian man named Savuth Thach, who was dressed from head to toe in the plastic bags that car dealers send your old tires home in when you buy new ones. He gave us some dried squid. While I chewed, he told me that he'd fled Cambodia in 1975 when the Khmer Rouge took power. He caught squid back in Cambodia by dragging a white rag through the water to lure them up to the surface, where he could net them. "A squid thinks the jig is another squid and wants to mate it, not eat it," Savuth told me. I wasn't going to challenge this theory; Savuth had way more squid in his bucket than I did.

"So do you, like, work the jig in a sexually provocative way?" I asked.

"No, just jiggle and feel," he said, yanking in another squid. "Just jiggle and feel."

Farther along, I met a thirty-year-old Filipino named Rudy, who makes his own jigs out of lead, straight pins, and glow-in-the-dark tape. He used to catch squid in the Philippines by throwing dynamite into the water. The explosion would stun the schools of squid, making them easy to net. These days he gives some squid to friends and uses the rest to make a traditional Philippine dish called adobo, with squid marinated in vinegar, garlic, soy sauce, bay leaves, and crushed peppercorns, then cooked and served with rice. I asked Rudy if he thinks a squid wants to mate with the jig.

"The squid wants to fight the jig," he said, "or maybe mate it."

The mood on the pier suddenly turned serious. Some good schools of squid had moved in, and everyone was concentrating. Matt and I crowded into a gap amid a group of Japanese-American college students. They were fixing to make some ika sansai, a cooked-squid salad. So many squid were getting cranked up over the rail that the pier's surface was slimy with ink. No sooner would you drop your jig down than you were pulling up a squid. Matt and I had been providing sea-monster screams for everybody in our area, but the responsibility had grown too demanding. From then on we screamed only for our own squid.

At one point Matt took a shot of squid ink right in the eye and had to retreat momentarily. The ink is harmless, but it stings a little. As he recoiled, his place was seized by a little old Thai lady in a plastic bonnet who'd been weaving through the crowds searching for primo spots. The woman wanted squid, and she didn't want to stay up all night getting them. She set a small stool down, climbed up so she could reach over the rail, and set into a punishing bout of squid jigging. She'd lower a jig down and stare out over the harbor for a moment. Then, as though she'd been struck by a brilliant idea, she would crank up the lure with a squid attached, give the creature a second to expel its ink away from her clothes, and flick it into her bucket. Several times she pulled up her jig with two squid attached. I couldn't help but let out a double monster scream, which failed to amuse her. She'd jiggle her bucket a bit after every catch, as if assessing the needs of several recipes. After she had a couple pounds, she gathered her things into a basket and left.

The squid kept coming. The fishing motif of "first, biggest, and most" was totally absent. There wasn't a trace of that usual pier-fishing possessiveness about who's standing in what spot. The collective goal was for everyone to get something. Rudy was lending out his homemade jigs left and right. One guy with a hot spot next to a pylon kept waving everyone over. When a woman's jig got caught on the pylon, all activity in her area stopped until it was freed.

The evening's run of squid lasted until about midnight. It was one of those all-consuming, action-packed stretches of time when you can't even think about the things you're supposed to be doing with your life. The catch tapered off until you had to look around for a few minutes to see somebody pull one up. At about one A.M. the gang trickled away. If someone's bucket was low on squid, the folks with good catches poured in a few. And then everyone headed up the hill, back to the lights of the city.

Matt and I caught about ten pounds of squid that night, and it took days to cook them all up. You can eat everything on a squid but the beak, shell, and eyes. We cut the bodies into strips and covered them with pasta sauce. We stuffed them with cheese and mushrooms. We blanched, broiled, and boiled them. But my favorite recipe was the simplest: Squeeze the ink into a pan, add butter, then cook the squid for a minute or two. Squirt with lemon and eat. Then, before the pan cools, suck back the ink. Swish it until your teeth are coated good and black. Then smile at your friends — or, if you're alone, at the mirror. Big smile. You're an American squid jigger.

KIRA SALAK

Mungo Made Me Do It

FROM *National Geographic Adventure*

IN THE BEGINNING, all my journeys feel at best ludicrous, at worst insane. This one is no exception. The idea is to paddle nearly six hundred miles on the Niger River in a kayak, alone, from the town of Old Ségou to Timbuktu. And now, at the very hour I have decided to leave, a thunderstorm bursts open the skies, sending down apocalyptic rain, washing away the ground beneath my feet. It is the rainy season in Mali, for which there can be no comparison in the world. Lightning pierces trees, slices across houses. Thunder wracks the skies and pounds the earth like mortar fire, and every living thing huddles in its tenuous shelter, expecting the world to end. Which it doesn't. At least not this time. So we all give a collective sigh to the salvation from the passing storm as it rumbles east, and I survey the river I'm to depart on this morning. Rain or no rain, today is the day for the journey to begin.

"Let's do it," I say, leaving the shelter of an adobe hut. My guide from town, Modibo, points to the north, to further storms. He says he will pray for me. It's the best he can do. To his knowledge, no man has ever completed such a trip, though a few have tried. And certainly no woman has done such a thing. Earlier this morning he took me aside and told me he thinks I'm crazy, which I understood as concern, and so I thanked him. He told me that the people of Old Ségou think I'm crazy, too, and that only uncanny good luck will keep me safe. What he doesn't know is that the worst thing a person can do is to tell me I can't do something, because then I'll want to do it all the more. It may be a failing of mine.

I carry my inflatable kayak through the labyrinthine alleys of Old

Ségou, past the huts melting in the rain, past the huddling goats and the smoke of cooking fires, past people peering out at me from dark entranceways. Old Ségou must have looked much the same to Scottish explorer Mungo Park, who left here on the first of his two river journeys 206 years ago to the day. It is no coincidence that I've picked this date, July 22, and this spot to begin my journey. Park is my guarantee of sorts. If he could travel down the Niger, then so can I. Of course, Park also died on the river, but so far I've managed to overlook that.

Thunder again. Hobbled donkeys cower under a new onslaught of rain, ears back, necks craned. Naked children dare one another to touch me, and I make it easy for them, stopping and holding out my arm. They stroke my white skin as if it were velvet, using only the pads of their fingers, then stare at their hands, looking for wet paint. I stop on the banks of the river near a centuries-old kapok tree, under which I imagine Park once took shade. I open my bag, spread out my little red kayak, and start to pump it up. A photographer, who will check in on me from time to time in his motorized boat, feverishly snaps pictures. A couple of women nearby, with colorful cloth wraps called *pagnes* tied tightly about their breasts, gaze at me as if to ask: Who are you, and what do you think you're doing? The Niger, in a surly mood, churns and slaps the shore. I don't pretend to know what I'm doing. Just one thing at a time now: kayak inflated, kayak loaded, paddles fitted together. Modibo watches me.

"I'll pray for you," he reminds me.

I balance my gear and get in. Finally, irrevocably, I paddle away.

Before Mungo Park left on his second expedition, he never admitted that he was scared. It is what fascinates me about his journals — his insistence on maintaining that all was well, even as he began a journey that he knew from his first experience could only beget tragedy. Hostile peoples, malarial fevers. Hippos and crocodiles. A giant widening of the Niger called Lake Débo to cross, like being set adrift on an inland sea. It can boggle the mind, what drives some people to risk their lives for the mute promises of success. It boggles my mind, at least, as I suffer from the same affliction. Already I fear the irrationality of my journey. I fear the very stubbornness that drives me forward.

The Niger erupts in a new storm. Torrential rains. Waves higher than my kayak try to capsize me. But my boat is self-bailing, and I stay afloat. The wind slams the current in reverse, tearing and ripping at the shores, sending spray into my face. I paddle madly, crashing ahead inch by inch, or so it seems, arm muscles smarting.

A popping feeling now and a screech of pain. My right arm lurches from a ripped muscle. But this is no time or place for an injury, so I try to ignore the metronome-like pulses of pain. There is only one direction to go: forward. Always forward.

I often wonder what I seek when I embark on these trips. There is the pat answer I tell the people I don't know — that I'm interested in seeing a place, learning about its people. But then the trip begins, and the hardship comes, and hardship is more honest: It tells me that I'm here because I don't have enough patience yet, or humility, or gratitude. So I've told the world that it can do what it wants with me if only, by the end of the trip, I have learned something. A bargain, then. The journey, my teacher.

The Niger has calmed, returning its beauty to me: a river of smoothest glass, a placidity unbroken by wave or eddy, with islands of lush greenery awaiting me like distant Xanadus. Tiny villages dot the shores, each with its own mud mosque sending a minaret to the heavens. The late afternoon sun settles complacently over the hills to the west. Paddling becomes a sort of meditation now, a gentle trespassing over a river that slumbers.

Mungo Park is credited with being the first Westerner to discover the Niger, in 1796, which helped to make his narrative, *Travels in the Interior Districts of Africa,* a bestseller. But I wonder if the sight of his "majestic Niger" was enough reward for the travails he suffered: the loss of his possessions, the brutal confinement by the Moors, the half-starved wanderings in the desert. Before quinine was used to fight malaria, travel to West Africa was a virtual death sentence for Europeans. Colonial powers used only their most expendable soldiers to oversee operations on the coast. It wasn't uncommon for expeditions to lose half their men to fever and dysentery if the natives didn't get them first. So Park's ambitious plan to cross what is now Senegal into Mali, then head down the Niger River to Timbuktu, hasn't a modern-day equivalent. It was beyond gutsy — it was borderline suicidal.

Park wrote that he traveled at the rate of six or seven miles an hour, but I travel at barely one mile an hour, the river preferring —

as I do — to loiter in the sun. I eat turkey jerky and wrap my injured arm, part of which has swelled to the size of a lemon. The Somono fishermen, casting their nets, puzzle over me as I float by.

"*Ça va, madame?*" they yell. How's it going?

Each fisherman brings along a young son to do the paddling. Perched in the back of the pointed canoes, the boys gape at me, transfixed. They have never seen such a thing. A white woman. Alone. In a red, inflatable boat. Using a two-sided paddle. I'm an even greater novelty because Malian women don't paddle: It is a man's job. So there is no good explanation for me, and the people want to understand. They gather on the shore in front of their villages to watch me pass, the kids screaming and jumping in excitement, the men yelling questions in Bambara, which by now I know to mean: "Where did you come from? Where is your husband?" And, of course, they always ask: "Where are you going?"

"Timbuktu!" I call out to the last question. It sounds preposterous to them, because everyone knows that Timbuktu is weeks away and requires paddling across Lake Débo and through rapids and storms. And I am a woman, after all, which makes everything worse.

They shake their heads in disbelief. We wave good-bye, and the whole ritual begins again at the next village. I might be the pope, or someone close. But in between is the peace and silence of the wide river, the sun on me, a breeze licking my toes when I lie back and rest, the current as negligible as a faint breath.

Timbuktu lies somewhere to the northeast, as distant and unimaginable to me as it must have been to Park, who first read about the city in *Geographical Historie of Africa*. Written in 1526 by a Spanish Moor named Leo Africanus, the book described Timbuktu as a veritable El Dorado. The city was indeed a bastion of wealth, the pearl of West Africa's great Songhai Empire, home to a university, one of Africa's largest and grandest mosques, and a population that may have reached fifty thousand. Timbuktu throve off its location as a crossroads of commerce between the great Saharan caravan routes and the Niger River Basin. It was there that men traded Saharan salt for the gold, ivory, and slaves that came from the south. The Arabs gave the Niger the name Neel el Abeed, "River of Slaves." Slavery still exists here, tacitly, though some anthropologists and Malian officials claim the practice was abolished when France colonized Mali in the late 1800s. But I carry two gold coins from home, and if I ever get to Timbuktu, I intend to find out the truth, and then, if possible, free someone with them.

Unbeknownst to Europeans of Park's era, Timbuktu's exalted stature ended in 1591, when a Moroccan army crossed the Sahara with the most sophisticated weaponry of the time — muskets — and sacked the golden city. The raid marked the beginning of a decline from which Timbuktu never recovered. Still, ill-informed Europeans embarked, one after another, for an African El Dorado that no longer existed. There were only two ways to get there: You could risk enslavement or death by trying to cross the Sahara from the north, or brave the malarial jungles of West Africa and then travel up the Niger. Park's first journey ushered in the frantic "Timbuctoo rush" of the early 1800s. The River of Slaves became a highway into a lethal region that was known as the White Man's Grave.

In the middle of the night, I wake with a start: The bear bell on my kayak is ringing — someone has discovered my boat. From inside my tent I hear two men whispering; I can see the beam from their flashlight flickering anxiously about the dark shore. I had hoped that the bell would prove an unnecessary — if not paranoid — precaution, but here we are: the middle of the night, two strange men going through my things, and only a can of Mace and some martial-arts training between me and potential theft and/or bodily harm. But the men don't know that I'm alone. And they don't know that I'm a woman. So I get up, arm myself with a section of a paddle, and burst out of my tent, yelling "Hey!" in a deep voice.

It works. They flee in their canoe. Sighing in relief, I watch in the faint moonlight as they disappear around a bend.

But it's not over yet. About ten minutes later I hear their voices again. And now I see their flashlight beam coming toward me across the savanna. I run to take down my tent and stuff my gear into the kayak. In a matter of minutes, I shove off. I stroke to the middle of the river, then stop paddling. The only sound is the lapping of the quicksilver waters against my boat. No sight of land, no suggestion of people. Just darkness. I'm scared to make a sound. All I can do is float along to wherever the river wants to take me.

I decide not to camp for a while. After a day of paddling, I approach the village of Siraninkoro, inhabited by traditional herders called the Fulani. A few women, large washtubs balanced on their heads, see me and run to alert the rest of the community. Soon everyone who can walk, run, or crawl is awaiting me onshore. I use Park's two-hundred-year-old narratives as my guide and do exactly what he did when he arrived in a new village: I find the chief and give him a generous gift. I sit beside him on his mat and ask if I can spend the night, then accept his calabash full of foaming cow's milk straight from the udder. Things haven't changed much in two hundred years.

The women surround me. They wear large gold disks in their earlobes, and their hair is styled into ornate cornrows. Their skin is light, a dark blue tattoo accentuating the area around their mouths. Here, in this remote village, women wrap brightly patterned pagnes around their waists to cover their legs and buttocks — areas Malians consider sexual — and leave their breasts bare with wonderful nonchalance.

They want to know where my husband is and how many babies I have back home. I try to explain through signs and broken Bambara why I have neither, but it takes some time. We're still discussing it as we eat dinner. I'm afraid we might be discussing it all night, but at last the women declare that it's bedtime. We all lie down side by side on foam mattresses spread outside the huts. Mosquito nets stretched overhead blur the stars. Fleas hop on my skin; chickens jump on us. I fall asleep to the sound of the old folks snoring, goats nibbling at our feet.

Always, at some point in these trips, I suddenly wake up to the reality of what I'm doing. I discover, quite unexpectedly, that I am, say, alone in a little red boat en route to Timbuktu. Somehow this comes as news to me, and I'm forced to pull over and ponder the implications. Timbuktu is so far to the northeast that it hides on another section of my map. My god, I think, but always when it's too late. As is the case now: At least fifty naked children are sprinting over a hill and descending upon my boat. *"Toubabou! Donnez-moi cadeau!"* they scream. Hey, whitey! Give me a gift!

Their excitement turns chaotic. Hands pull and grab at the things in my kayak. I take out a bag of dried pineapple slices and throw them in the air, and the mass of bodies flies toward the treats, kids fighting and tearing at one another. I have never seen anything like it, and I paddle away as if for my life.

I wonder when Mungo Park's moment of realization struck. When he was captured by the Moors and a woman threw urine in his face? When he was so destitute that he was forced to sell locks of his hair as good-luck charms? Or perhaps it didn't come until the second journey, when he found himself in a rotting boat, forty of his forty-four men dead from disease, Park himself afflicted with dysentery. "Though I were myself half-dead," he wrote in one of his final letters, "I would still persevere; and if I could not succeed in the object of my journey, I would at least die on the Niger." Why didn't he turn back? What was wrong with the man?

But I'm beginning to understand Park. Once the journey starts, there's no turning back. The journey kidnaps you, drugs you with images of its end, reached at long last. You picture yourself arriving on that fabled shore. You see everything you promised yourself. For Park, it might have been streets of gold, cool oasis pools, maidens cooing in his ear. For me, it is much simpler: french fries and air conditioning.

And now another storm is coming, a strong wind blowing directly against me. Dark clouds boom and rattle while great Saharan winds churn up the red clay and paint blood trails across the sky. I rush toward shore. The winds get worse, the river sloshing with three-foot-high whitecaps. As I lean forward to secure my bags, a huge wave broadsides my boat, flipping it. I fall out and swim to the surface to see my kayak bottom up and speeding away. I dive for it and grab its tail, turn it over, and retrieve my paddle, only to see my little backpack — the one with my passport, money, journal — starting to sink nearby.

It is as if my worst fears are being realized, one after the next. But by treading water and holding onto the kayak, I'm able to retrieve the backpack. Pulling myself into the boat, I fumble to get oriented in the waves, then paddle toward shore with all my strength. Thunder bellows, lightning flashes. I make it to the bank, rain shooting from the sky with such force that the drops sting my skin. I huddle, shaking from adrenaline, and take a tally of what I have lost: two water bottles and some bags of dried fruit, but, mercifully, nothing else. The Niger has won my submission.

I reach the town of Mopti, everything soaked from my kayak wipeout, and not quite recovered from it myself. I'm wasted. I meet a local man named Assou, a friend of the Peace Corps folks in town.

When I tell him what my trip has been like so far, he says I obviously didn't know about the genies that inhabit the Niger — every Malian knows about them — which explains why I've been having problems. He says it's essential that I enlist these spirits in my cause of reaching Timbuktu, or who knows what tragedies might befall me. At his urging, we head inland to the Bandiagara escarpment to see Yatanu, a Dogon sorceress.

We reach the village of Nini, a collection of mud-brick dwellings and thatched granaries high on a rocky plateau. Dogon women crouch in beehive-shaped menstruation huts in order to protect the village from the devilry of their periods. Assou instructs me to follow the path he takes so as to avoid stepping on taboo ground. Dogon boys gape at me as we pass, their navels protruding from distended bellies like stubby appendages.

We climb the slope to the huts perched above, searching for Yatanu. Assou has never met this woman, but he's heard about her: She's at least seventy years old and is one of the Dogon's most powerful and feared sorceresses. It's hard to get a consultation with her because she doesn't like most people, but I've brought along a village officer to help the cause. Yatanu is unique among her fellow witches. When she was ten, her parents, sorcerers themselves, cut open her left arm and put a scarab beetle into the biceps, then sewed the skin back up. The beetle died, but presumably its spirit remains. Yatanu converses with it to obtain knowledge about people's lives.

Yatanu appears before us: a toothless and wizened woman, breasts lying flat against her chest, a scrappy indigo pagne tied around her bony waist. She stands in the shadow of her hut and stares at me. Assou tells her that I'm here to ask for a consultation — will she grant me one?

She steps forward into the sunlight, sits on her haunches, and studies me. Smiling nervously, I look into her eyes, clouded with cataracts. She says something in Dogon to the village officer, who then translates to Assou, who translates to me: "She likes you."

Sighs of relief all around. I give her a wad of money and ask my question: "Will I get to Timbuktu?"

She puckers her lips and nods as the question is translated. She places her left arm tightly against her chest and speaks to the muscle where the beetle spirit supposedly lives. All at once, the muscle leaps up; a large object seems to strain and lurch beneath the skin.

I've never seen such a thing, nor has Assou. Our mouths drop open.

Yatanu reports her findings: "You'll get to Timbuktu."

Back on the Niger, the days fill with the slow progression of one village after the next, one grove of palm trees after another to break up the monotony of sand and shore. I stay with different groups: the Fulani, the Somono, the Bozo.

All of it takes me to Lake Débo, finally, and the crossing I've been dreading, just as Park dreaded it two centuries before. I see it as the most treacherous part of the journey, where all sight of land will be lost for an entire day. If a storm should catch me, overturn and separate me from my boat, I could drown.

I start the crossing in the early morning, hoping to beat the wind and storms that usually arrive at midday. It's not long before the horizon shows only the meeting of sky and water, the waves sizable and unruly. But perhaps there is something to be said for Yatanu's assistance, because there is no hint of a rising storm.

A river steamer passes me, so loaded with people and baggage that water nearly spills over its gunwales. The ship overshadows me like a giant, her crew cheering and howling, the passengers craning to get a look at me in my tiny boat as I paddle beside their swift vessel. I follow the distant white buoys that guide the boats across, reaching one and then the next, hoping to catch sight of land. The heat becomes intense; my thermometer reads 106 degrees. But I don't stop.

Finally, after seven hours, I'm relieved to see land and the broad channel of the Niger ahead. Hippos peer at me from the shallows, blowing air from their nostrils. Lake Débo barely stirs behind me.

The days become frustrating. I constantly fight the river; its curves and twists seem to take me nowhere. I call it "uphill paddling," the battle against winds that kick up waves and batter me against the high clay banks. But at least my body cooperates; muscles appear on my arms, compensating for my injury.

After another difficult day, I approach a prosperous-looking village to buy a meal and lodging. Stopping at villages is always a crapshoot. What tribe will I get? Will they have food to sell me? Will they like me?

I'm greeted by the usual crowd. Kids swarm around, yelling excitedly. They tell me this village is called Berakousi and that it sits at the spot where the Koula River enters the Niger. I ask what people they are and am told they're Bozo. Fishermen.

As I search for the chief, it quickly becomes evident that I'm not wanted here. I'm particularly troubled by some young men, one sporting a black T-shirt with Osama bin Laden's face printed on it like a rock star's. They harass me in broken French. What man allowed me to travel here by myself? Would I like to have sex with them? I ignore them, but I'm nearly knocked off my feet by the crowd of pushy onlookers.

The chief is in the fields, so I sit on a wicker chair to wait for him, refusing numerous requests from women who want me to breastfeed their babies. I wait and wait. The sun is almost gone. It's too late to go elsewhere, the river too choppy and mercurial along this stretch to make night paddling safe. The villagers are still milling about me when the chief appears. He surveys me, frowning. I give him a wad of money as cadeau, explain as best I can that I'd like to buy a meal and sleep on a patch of ground nearby. He slowly nods. The young men sit around me, demanding money, too. One tells me that he wants the flashlight that I've just removed from my pack. I seem to be the subject of a heated conversation, of which I can understand only the word *toubabou* — whitey.

One of the chief's four wives announces that she has food for me. I thank her and give her some money, and she drops a bowl in front of me. Inside is a rotting fish head, blooms of fungus growing on its skin.

"*Mangez,*" the woman says. She puts her fingers to her lips.

And I'm so hungry and fatigued that I do: I crack open the mottled skin and pull out bits of white meat. Everyone laughs heartily, and I see that this is a joke, feeding me a dog's dinner. When I finish, I notice that Osama and company have requisitioned one of my pens. I decide to let it go. One man sits close to me, his face inches from mine, and speaks threateningly. The chief — my usual benefactor elsewhere — does nothing. When the man wraps his hand about my wrist, I wrench my arm away, holding up a fist.

"Don't touch me," I say.

The villagers laugh. Scolding myself for losing my temper, I get up, put on my backpack, and head to the river. Can I still get out of here tonight? But it's darkness all around, and the Niger churns madly at its confluence with the Koula. I'm stuck.

I sit for hours on the dark shore, slapping mosquitoes, hoping the villagers will get bored and go back to their huts. It feels like a true Mungo Park moment: "I felt myself as if left lonely and friendless amidst the wilds of Africa," he wrote in one of his last letters. When I finally return, the village has cleared out. One of the chief's wives smiles in pity and brings out a foam mattress for me to sleep on. I lie down and wrap myself in my tent's rain fly. It is one of those nights that I know I must simply get through, that promises no sleep.

Each day the land along the shore seems to get drier. Trees have all but vanished, and only scant brush dots the horizon. The people are mostly Songhai now, living in mud-brick homes with ornate windows and doorways and praying in sharp-angled and refined mosques.

I spend a night in a village and wake up with the rooster calls, day only a gray suggestion to the east. My stomach lurches; only two days to my goal, and now this. Some kind of dysentery, though I can't say which — amoebic, bacillary? I'm hoping it's the latter, which is easier to cure. A group of village folk have risen, and they watch me, *tsk*-ing. Poor, sick white woman. The children watch, silent and uncomprehending, as I take down my tent and load up my kayak. I will get to Timbuktu even if I have to crawl.

Back on the river, I alternate between vomiting and paddling; my thermometer already registers 110 degrees. The sun burns in a cloudless sky, and there is no hint of a breeze. The luckier villages have a single scraggly tree to provide shade. I pass village after village, impressed by the tenacity of the Niger as it cuts through the sands, a gloriously stubborn and incongruous river.

I wonder what Park felt on this stretch. His guide, Amadi Fatouma, the lone survivor of the expedition, claimed that Park and his men had to shoot their way through these waters. Which might explain why, at every turn, entire villages gather to yell at me. Gone are the waves of greeting that I experienced at the beginning of my trip. Inexplicably, the entire tone of this country has changed.

*

One more day. I can get to Timbuktu by night, but it's quite a distance on a river so sluggish, with my body so weak.

I start at first light. I have no food left, so I don't eat. Great dunes meet the river on either side, adobe villages half-buried beneath them. I am now in the land of the Tuareg and the Moors. They crouch close to the water and stare at me from their indigo and black wrappings, none returning my waves. Park admitted fearing the Moors most, plagued by nightmares of his captivity among them.

I share Park's trepidation, especially when an island splits the Niger, creating a narrow channel on either side. The narrower the river, the more vulnerable I am. People can reach me more easily; there is less opportunity for escape. And this is the most populated stretch of the river to date. All I can do is paddle hard, the villagers screaming and scolding me as I pass, some swimming after me. I have no way of knowing what their intentions are, so I follow my new guideline: Don't get out of the boat — for *anything*.

When I stop to drink some water, a group of men leap into their canoes and come after me to demand money. With a can of Mace in my lap, I manage to out-paddle them, but more canoes follow their example. It's like a macabre game of tag, and while I can usually see them coming and get a lead, one man is able to reach me and hit my kayak with the bow of his canoe. I know one of us will have to give up, so I pace my strokes as if the pursuit were a long-distance race, and he soon falls behind.

It is more of the same at the next village, and at the next one after that, so that the mere sight of canoes onshore gives me fright. No time to drink water now — to stop is to give them an incentive to come after me. Head aching, I round a bend to see the river widen; I don't see any villages. I stop paddling and float in the middle of the river, nauseous and faint. I squint at the Niger trailing off into distant heat waves, the sands trying to swallow it.

"This river will never end," I say over and over. Still, I must be close. I begin to paddle like a person possessed. The sun falls, burning dark orange in the west, and I see a distant square concrete building. Hardly a tower of gold, hardly an El Dorado, but I'll take it. I paddle straight toward it, ignoring the pains in my body, my raging headache. Timbuktu! Timbuktu! Some Bozo fishermen are watching me. They don't ask for money or cadeaux, yelling instead,

"Ça va, madame?" One man stands and raises his hands in a cheer, urging me on.

I round a sharp curve and approach Timbuktu's port of Korioumé. I pull up beside a great white river steamer named, appropriately, the *Tombouctou.* All at once, I understand that there's no more paddling to be done. I've made it. I can stop now. The familiar throng gathers in the darkness. Slowly I haul my kayak from the river.

People ask where I came from, and I tell them Old Ségou. They can't seem to believe it. I unload my things to the clamor of their questions, but even speaking seems to pain me. Such a long time getting here — three weeks on the river. And was it worth it? Or is it blasphemy to ask that now? I can barely walk; I have a high fever. I haven't eaten anything for more than a day. I would give a great deal right now for silence. For stillness.

We will never know if Mungo Park reached Timbuktu. According to his guide, he was repelled by the locals. In 1827 another Scottish explorer, Hugh Clapperton, heard a tale that Park had made it to the golden city and was received warmly. Regardless, Park ended up dying on the Niger as he had prophesied, getting as far as Bussa, near modern-day New Bussa, Nigeria, before he disappeared.

Timbuktu: the world's greatest anticlimax. Hard to believe that this slapdash latticework of garbage-strewn streets and crumbling dwellings was once the height of worldly sophistication. The pearl of the desert, the African El Dorado is nothing now but a haggard outpost in a plain of scrub brush and sand.

I walk the dusty streets. It is 115 degrees and barely noon. I bow under the weight of the sun, and every action feels ponderous. I pass donkeys scavenging in rubbish heaps and dodge streams of fetid wastewater trailing down alleyways. I visit the former homes of Scottish explorer Gordon Laing and the Frenchman René Caillié, both of whom risked their lives to get here. They must have been just as disappointed. Caillié, the first European to reach Timbuktu, in 1828, and return alive to report on it, wrote that the city and its landscape "present the most monotonous and barren scene I have ever beheld."

Tourists, mostly flown in on package tours, wilt in the sun as they trudge through the streets in search of whatever it is that Timbuktu had promised them. I imagine they, too, are disappointed, though this end of the world knows enough to sell them air-conditioned rooms and faux Tuareg wear at inflated prices. I see that Timbuktu is better left to name and fancy. It is not meant to be found.

History pervades the place, with slavery one of its most secretive and enduring institutions. It occurs among the Bella, a people who are the traditional slaves of the Tuareg. If you mention the idea of slavery in Mali to some experts, though, they say that Mali's constitution prohibits it. They insist that the Bella are now paid workers with civil rights, including freedom of movement. In short, they're not slaves anymore.

Others in Timbuktu tell a completely different story: that the Bella are slaves in fact, if not by law. They are still a form of property that the Tuareg refuse to give up; the Bella are often raped or beaten by their masters and are forced to turn over any money they earn. So is it slavery, then, or is it not?

Before my trip, I was perplexed by a recent human rights bulletin posted on the Web site of the U.S. State Department. It included reports of de facto slavery in Mali. Why had an entire group of people remained the equivalent of slaves in a country that claims slavery no longer exists? Was there no recourse for them? I mulled over the feasibility of actually freeing someone — in itself a controversial act. Some people familiar with the region suggested that I would only be duped by those involved in the negotiations. Others argued that, at least on a psychological and economic level, the Bella would remain hopelessly tied to their Tuareg masters, so that anyone I freed would be left without a means to make a living at all.

But suppose I really could free someone? Just suppose. And then, what if I gave that person enough money to start a business and become self-sufficient? Wouldn't it be preferable to a dehumanizing, often brutal life of servitude? After much soul-searching, I finally concluded that it was worth a try.

So I pay Assou's travel expenses to come up from Mopti and help me with the negotiations, since he grew up in Timbuktu and knows the right people. He won't accept any payment for his assistance: He wants to free someone as badly as I do. Assou is fond of saying that "what you do for others, you do for yourself." Back in Mopti, he told me a secret — though he's Songhai by birth, he was breastfed by his mother's Bella friend. "The Bella are in my blood," he said. "I am one of them." It is a daring admission for him to align himself with this outcast group: Some Malians use the word "Bella" as an insult.

And now a breakthrough: Assou has found a Tuareg master, Iba Zengi (not his real name, we're told), who is willing to sell a Bella or two, but everything must be done in secret, because slavery doesn't officially exist in Mali. Assou will pass on my money and pretend to be the one in charge of the negotiations, or none of this can happen. He has told Zengi that he's freeing the women as part of his college research, and that I'm coming along to help him take notes. Assou has not let on that I'm a writer.

Assou and I arrive at the Bella village, where we sit in the midst of small thatched huts. The people gather around — old and young, children half-clothed, women cradling infants. Assou admits he doesn't know which Bella Zengi will choose to sell. I study each of them and try to imagine what it is like to be them.

There is a brief wait. Zengi lives elsewhere, among his own people; the Bella in this village report each day to him and his family for their work duties. A car arrives, and Zengi steps out. He is cloaked in indigo wrappings, the Tuareg man's traditional desert clothing. I can see only his eyes as he daintily holds the bluish material over his nose and mouth, as if afraid of catching a cold. He sits on a mat before "his Bella," as he calls them. He strokes and pats an older man as one might a favorite pet.

I have Assou ask if these are his slaves.

"Slavery is illegal in Mali," he says calmly.

"But they are 'your Bella.' Are they paid monthly wages?"

He answers that he gives them a place to live, animals to raise, the clothes on their back. When one of them gets married, he provides animals for the bride price. This, I'm to understand, is their "pay."

I turn to a middle-aged woman sitting nearby. "If she wanted to leave and not come back, could she?"

As Assou translates my question, Zengi's veil falls for a moment, revealing a trace of a smirk. "Either I kill her, or she kills me," he says. That is to say, Over my dead body.

I ask Assou to find out who is to be freed and whether my money is sufficient for the purchase of one or two people. They talk for a while. Zengi will free two women, household helpers whom he can spare, since he has three others and enough Bella babies to fill future vacancies. Their price is to be considered a bargain and a sign of Zengi's beneficence: the equivalent of $260, more than the average Malian household income for one year.

He motions to a couple of young women standing at the edge of the crowd. They approach with apprehension. "These are the women," Zengi says. He orders them to take a seat on the mat before me. One holds a sickly-looking baby girl.

I tell Assou, "Ask him if he can include the baby with her mother."

A brief discussion ensues. "He won't," Assou says.

"Then ask him how much the baby is." I can't believe such a sentence has come out of my mouth. Assou asks, but Zengi is shaking his head. Assou leans closer to me. "He's already giving us a favor by selling two people. It's best, when a person gives you a favor, not to ask for more."

Which I take to be a warning. I stare at the little girl and wonder what will become of her, but there is nothing to be done. While I know that her mother can still live in this village and will not be physically separated from her child, the girl will remain bound to a life of servitude for Zengi's family as soon as she is old enough to work. A numbness comes over me. Better not to feel anything. I stand and tell Assou that I'd like to get this over with. Pay Zengi his money. Buy these people already.

Zengi follows us behind a hut — he doesn't want "his Bella" to see him receiving money for their family members. Assou hands him the bundle of bills. The man pockets it and leads me back to the crowd. With a regal wave of his hand, he directs the two women toward Assou and me.

"Go with them," he says. "You belong to them now." The shocked looks on their faces are hardly what I expected. Hell, I don't know what I expected, but definitely not this. The two women obediently follow us as we walk away from the throng. I have no idea what to say to them and ask Assou to tell them that I did this — bought them — so that they'd be free, earn wages, live without having to bow down to anyone.

The women just stand in front of me. Fadimata, who has the sickly baby, is smiling, but the other, Akina, looks like someone has just smacked her in the face. I hand them each a gold coin, worth about $120 apiece, as well as some Malian money. I have Assou tell them that this money is meant to help them start a business, get a footing somehow.

The women nod. Fadimata thanks me, but Akina looks down, silent. I don't understand what's wrong, so I ask if we can go somewhere to be alone. We head into a hut and sit on the sandy floor. The women sneak glances at me; Fadimata holds her — Zengi's — baby.

"So will you start a business now?" I have Assou ask them. Fadimata says she'll buy some millet or rice and try to sell it in the market. Though she'll probably stick around this village to be with her baby, she'll be self-sufficient. Any money she makes from produce that she sells in the market will be hers.

"Did you like working for Zengi?" I ask.

"No," she says immediately. "I want to live my own life and have my own business."

"What do you think about your baby belonging to Zengi?"

"I have no choice." She caresses her daughter's head.

When I ask Akina if she liked working for Zengi's family, she shakes her head, refusing to look at me.

"Did they hurt you?" I ask.

Softly, she says that they beat her. Fadimata nods in agreement: They beat her, too.

I really don't know how to ask the next question, but I feel I must. Did the Tuareg men ever take them . . . rape them?

The women are silent.

I have Assou tell them that they're safe, that I'm their friend.

"It didn't happen to me," Fadimata says. "But it happened to my friend. She told me."

Akina nods in agreement, but she says nothing. I sense that the women are withholding something. Akina looks scared; she fingers her dress, frowning.

I have Assou ask her if she's okay, and she looks into my eyes for the first time. "I feel shame," she says, "about what happened."

And it comes out that she's ashamed that she was sold like some animal. She's ashamed to be sitting in front of me.

"No," I say. "Tell her not to." I reach over and take her hand. She stares at me; we've got tears in our eyes. I keep squeezing her hand. "Tell her not to feel ashamed."

Assou tells her, and her whole countenance relaxes. When I ask her to tell me how the Tuareg have hurt her, she stands and her hands come up and down with an imaginary stick, as if trying to drive it through someone's body. Her expression is one of pure rage, pure hatred. Both women tell me that they were beaten daily, for no reason.

I ask them what guarantee there is — if any — that Zengi won't reclaim them the minute I leave.

"No, he can't," Fadimata says. Akina nods in agreement. "We have his promise. When he told us to go with you, that is a guarantee that means 'You're free.'"

I can only hope they're right. In a society that refuses to acknowledge its slavery, there can be no official papers drawn up, no receipts. If Zengi is honorable, upholds his part of the bargain — as the women assure me he will — then they have nothing to worry about. And the fact that they are already planning their futures, telling me about the millet they will buy, is enough to reassure me. For now. At any rate, perhaps they won't be beaten or humiliated anymore.

When I get up to leave, I shake their hands as they tell me that God will bless me, will take care of me for what I've done. I'm glad to see their happy expressions, though I don't know what to say. Maybe Fadimata can buy her baby from Zengi if she makes enough money? I don't have words.

I go with Assou to the Djinguereber mosque. I want to see the door that, according to local legend, can end the world if opened. This mosque, Mali's oldest, was built by the great Songhai king Mansa Musa in the fourteenth century. It has survived virtually intact and now sits on the edge of town, its spiked minarets reaching skyward, garbage swirling about its walls.

We have the mosque to ourselves; the caretaker is busy with tourists on the roof. Inside it is dim and cool. Faint light trails down from skylights, exposing the clouds of dust kicked up by our feet. It is hugely empty here, where the mud-brick walls reveal the pressing of ancient hands.

The special door is in a wall along the far side of the mosque, hidden behind a simple thatched mat. Assou tells me that no one is shown the door anymore. He doesn't know why. Perhaps it's too dangerous.

"I want to see what it looks like," I say.

Assou laughs nervously. "I never met someone as curious as you."

"I'm serious."

"Then go look." But he is scared.

I creep forward and gently pull back the mat. And here it is: the door that can end the world. It is made of wood, the middle part rotting away. It looks unremarkable, like a piece of faded driftwood. Suddenly, impulsively, I stick out a hand and touch it.

The world doesn't quake. The waters don't part. The Earth continues on its axis, churning out immutable time.

"The world hasn't ended," I declare, my voice echoing off the far walls.

"You must open it," Assou says, laughing.

And I could open it, standing here as I am, the caretaker blithely unaware on the roof. For an insolent moment I pretend I hold the world in my hands. I think of Zengi and the slave women. I think of the Bozo fisherman cheering me on to Timbuktu. It is such a kind yet cruel world. Such a vulnerable world. I'm astounded by it all.

JACOB SILVERSTEIN

The Devil and Ambrose Bierce

FROM *Harper's Magazine*

SATAN, n. One of the Creator's lamentable mistakes, repented in sashcloth and axes. Being instated as an archangel, Satan made himself multifariously objectionable and was finally expelled from Heaven. Halfway in his descent he paused, bent his head in thought a moment and at last went back. "There is one favor that I should like to ask," said he.

"Name it."

"Man, I understand, is about to be created. He will need laws."

"What, wretch! you his appointed adversary, charged from the dawn of eternity with hatred of his soul — you ask for the right to make his laws?"

"Pardon; what I have to ask is that he be permitted to make them himself."

It was so ordered.

— Ambrose Bierce, *The Devil's Dictionary*

"Where is the grave of Ambrose Bierce?"

"It's behind you . . ."

— graffiti in a toilet stall at Big Bend National Park

IN FAR WEST TEXAS, on the side of the highway that runs south from Marfa to Presidio and across the Rio Grande into Ojinaga, Mexico, there is a small green sign that reads, PROFILE OF LINCOLN. Under these words an arrow points west at the jagged foothills of the Chinati Mountains, where you can make out the sixteenth president's profile in the ridges of rock. He lies on his back, forever staring at the sky, his gigantic head inclined gently, as if on a pillow. The short brim of his stovepipe hat has afforded him little shade over the years, and his brow is black from the scorch of the sun. His lips, such as they are, appear cracked and turned down, his forehead wrinkled with worry, his gaze fixed ahead as if in contemplation of some profound bafflement. He seems to wonder, "How in God's name did I end up here?"

The term "Far West Texas" refers to that portion of the state that lies west of the Pecos River. It is a dry and sparsely populated portion. The urban centers are El Paso, a city of 600,000, which recently announced that it may run out of drinking water by the year 2025, and Midland-Odessa, a two-city metropolis of around 180,000. Midland's nickname is The Tall City. It is not tall, but the plains that surround it are flat and empty. Odessa's nickname is The City of Contrasts.

All three cities are located about three hours from Marfa, the little town where this story begins. On the road, you pass through vast cattle ranches, though you do not see many cows. This is the Far West Texas range-cattle business. Since the first boom, in the years after the Civil War, it has been a business in decline. Encouraged by cheap land, and then discouraged by the never-ending drought, Far West Texas cattlemen went about setting up some of the largest and emptiest ranches in the West. As you drive south the situation worsens. Last year some ranchers in Presidio County, where Marfa is located, reported herds as small as one cow per two hundred acres.

The human population throughout the region is as sparse as that of the cow. In five Far West Texas counties that cover as much ground as Massachusetts, Connecticut, and New Jersey combined, there are barely 50,000 people, most of them clustered in small, dusty towns scattered over an emptiness that would be absolute were it not for the occasional thirsting cow. The scout W. B. Parker appraised the area thusly in his 1856 account *Through Unexplored Texas:* "For all purposes of human habitation — except it might be for a penal colony — these wilds are totally unfit."

Parker's appraisal was meant for the human settler, but there was another to whom this desolation appealed. His story is one you will not hear the civic boosters tell, but in the bars and fields you might ask a friend. When he was falling toward earth from heaven, the devil wished to prove a point. He searched the globe for the least heavenly place he could find. Green valleys, cheerful streams, and lush forests did not interest him. With a sneer, he flew over orchards and farms. Too pleasant. Then he came to West Texas. There are numerous topographical features named for him here:

Devils River, Devils Lake, Devil's Backbone, Devil's Ridge, Sierra Diablo, Diablo Plateau, Cerro Diablo. Many of the county's older residents believe that he still lives here, in a mountaintop cave with a nice view of Presidio and Ojinaga.

Four years ago I passed through Marfa as a tourist. I had read an article about an art museum there that sounded interesting. I looked up Marfa on the road atlas — a little speck in the blankness — and made my way there for a one-night stay. A year later, occupied with fantasies of the open range, I headed back. I left my home in California on the day after Halloween, my dashboard covered with leftover candy that melted in Arizona. I arrived in Marfa on a Saturday night. A crowd of girls asked me what I was doing.

"I'm moving here," I announced.

"You'll never make it," one of the girls said. "The boredom will drive you crazy."

I got a job with the *Big Bend Sentinel,* Marfa's weekly newspaper. I covered the school board, the city council, the drought, the Border Patrol, crime, art, rain, the post office, the Amtrak line, the D.A.'s race, and anything noteworthy in Valentine, a flyspeck town nearby. I wrote a long story about a local man who spent six months each year working as a helicopter pilot in Antarctica. "Write that what I miss most is the chile verde at Mando's," he told me.

I found a position as a caretaker on a bygone cattle ranch at the edge of town. The new owners, a couple from Houston, were frequently out of town. It was my job to keep their flowers and fruit trees alive and their paths weeded. I lived in a small adobe building with cold tile floors. Behind my little house was an even littler house, a miniature built by the previous owners for their daughter to play in. It had a miniature broom and a miniature stove. When I watered the pansies around its porch I liked to stick my head in the miniature windows, pretending I was a giant.

About six months after I started working at the *Sentinel* I got a phone call from an old Marfan who wanted me to find an article about him in the newspaper archives. He had been a war hero. He'd misplaced his old clipping, and it was getting yellow besides. He didn't remember the date of the article, but there was a big picture of him on the front page. Could I look for it? This sort of request was common at a newspaper that sometimes felt like a huge community scrapbook, and I had performed the same service many times before. On this day, though, I got sidetracked. In one of the giant archive books, I came across a letter to the editor from the December 20, 1990, edition of the *Sentinel* that contained, after some opening remarks, the following sentences:

> [N]either [Pancho] Villa or his men had any involvement in the disappearance of Ambrose Bierce. Bierce died on the night of January 17, 1914, and was buried in a common grave in Marfa the following morning. In a cemetery then located southwest of the old Blackwell School and across from the Shafter road.

I knew a few things about Bierce — that he had written *The Devil's Dictionary* and *In the Midst of Life,* that he was considered a great misanthrope, that he had disappeared somewhere in northern Mexico, and that his disappearance had never been explained. I read on. The author of the letter was a man named Abelardo Sanchez, from Lancaster, California. He was born in Marfa in 1929 and lived here until he was sixteen, when he joined the air force. In 1957 he was driving from California back to Marfa on a Mexican highway when he picked up an old hitchhiker named Agapito Montoya in San Luis, Sonora. When Montoya found out his driver's destination he piped up, "I been there, during the revolution." Sanchez, who had a keen interest in the history of that war, encouraged his passenger's tale.

As Sanchez's letter explained, Montoya had been a soldier in Antonio Rojas's army, which fell to Villa's at the Battle of Ojinaga in January of 1914. Montoya survived the battle and with four friends began to head south, toward Cuchillo Parado. Along the way they came across an old man who "appeared quite sick from a cold." He was trying to fix a broken wheel on a horse cart.

The old man asked the troops, of which Montoya, at seventeen, was the youngest, if they could help him find Pancho Villa, about whom he intended to write an article. They laughed at him and told him they were trying to get away from Villa. The old man's condition worsened through the night, which the soldiers spent nearby, and in the morning he shifted his aim and asked if they might help him get back across the border and up to Marfa. He offered to pay them twenty pesos apiece. The soldiers agreed.

Sanchez's letter continued:

> During the trip they heard of different books he had written including
> one that my narrator recalled with the word devil in its title he said his
> name in Spanish was Ambrocio. My narrator also recalled that years
> later while visiting in El Paso, he recalled the name of a dairy milk that
> sounded just like Ambrocio's last name. On the second day after cross-
> ing the Rio Grande they were captured by elements of the Third Cavalry
> which was rounding up stragglers who had crossed the border. Bierce by
> this time had pneumonia and could hardly speak, my narrator recalls
> him repeating a doctor's name in Marfa that began with the letter D.

Neither the soldiers, whose English was poor, nor the old man
himself, whom sickness had rendered almost mute, could convince
the troops that he was an American, and he was loaded into a
wagon full of wounded and dying Mexicans. Several days later,
while interned in Marfa, Montoya and his friends found out from a
cavalryman that the old man had died and was buried in a common grave.

I photocopied the letter. Later that night I reread it. It seemed
entirely believable. Why would Sanchez make this story up? The
next day I ran down some of the letter's clues. A Price's Dairy had
existed in El Paso from 1904 until 1970. In 1908 a doctor named
Joseph Calhoun Darracott moved to Marfa from Tyler and opened
a practice.

In the next few weeks I learned more about Bierce. There were
various theories regarding his end. A writer named Sibley Morrill
contended that Bierce had gone into Mexico as a secret agent, dis-
patched by Washington to spy on the Germans and Japanese, who
were plotting a sneak attack with the Mexicans. Joe Nickell argued
that the whole Mexico story was meant to give Bierce the privacy he
needed to go to the Grand Canyon and shoot himself. The most
popular theory had Bierce killed in the Battle of Ojinaga, his body
burned with the other dead to curb an outbreak of typhus. What is
certain is that he departed Washington, D.C., on October 2, 1913,
with northern Mexico as his stated destination. "Don't write," he
wrote to a San Francisco acquaintance on September 30. "I am
leaving in a day or two for Mexico. If I can get in (and out) I shall
go later to South America from some Western port. Doubtless I'm
more likely to get in than out, but all good Gringos go to Heaven

when shot." All his final letters had this macabre tone. He was seventy-one years old, and his health was failing. To his niece he wrote: "Good-bye — if you hear of my being stood up against a Mexican stone wall and shot to rags please know that I think that a pretty good way to depart this life. It beats old age, disease, or falling down the cellar stairs. To be a Gringo in Mexico — ah, that is euthanasia."

In 1861, about two months prior to his nineteenth birthday, Bierce had shipped off with the Ninth Indiana Volunteer Infantry Regiment. During the war he was promoted to second lieutenant and shot in the head by a rebel marksman. Without a doubt the fighting had a profound effect on Bierce, forever tilting his humor toward the dark. Forty-eight years later, along the way from Washington to Mexico, he visited all the battle sites of his youth. He toured Orchard Knob and Missionary Ridge, Chickamauga, Snodgrass Hill, Hell's Half-Acre, Franklin, Nashville, and Corinth. At Shiloh he spent a whole day sitting alone in the sun. In New Orleans he let himself be interviewed by a newspaper reporter, who observed, "Perhaps it was in mourning for the dead over whose battlefields he has been wending his way towards New Orleans that Mr. Bierce was dressed in black. From head to toe he was attired in this color." From New Orleans he made his way across Texas. The final letter to his niece, dated November 6 from Laredo but sent November 5 from San Antonio, said, "I shall not be here long enough to hear from you, and don't know where I shall be next. Guess it doesn't matter much. Adios." For most of November and December he was silent. His last letter was posted from Chihuahua City, Mexico, on December 26, 1913. It was addressed to his secretary and outlined his plan to leave for Ojinaga the following day.

The gloom of Bierce's last letters would not have surprised his friends and readers. Death haunted nearly all of his work, from the war-mangled bodies in his Civil War stories to the mysterious demises in his collection of ghost tales, *Can Such Things Be?* He favored the *coup de foudre*. A man is buried alive, then dug up by two medical students, then bludgeoned to death when he sits up panting in his coffin. An inventor is strangled by his automaton chess player. A killer is pardoned, but the man carrying his pardon can't transmit the message as everyone in the capitol has left to watch the hanging. In "An Occurrence at Owl Creek Bridge," the reader is duped into believing a hanging man's fantasy of escape. In "Chickamauga," a little child wanders out to play in the forest. He comes upon a clearing where a plantation is on fire:

> [S]uddenly the entire plantation, with its enclosing forest, seemed to turn as if upon a pivot. His little world swung half around; the points of the compass were reversed. He recognized the blazing building as his own home!

One of Bierce's many nicknames was "The Laughing Devil."

Sanchez's version of Bierce's end seemed so Biercian. It did not swerve from the expected with quite the velocity of a Bierce story, but it did swerve. Bierce had high hopes for a heroic death before a firing squad or in the heat of battle. Was there not a certain devilish poetry in this unglamorous business with the horse cart and the soldiers, in the confusion of identity, in the common grave?

One morning I called Sanchez at his home. He did not demonstrate much familiarity with Bierce, referring to him repeatedly as "Bryce" and to his masterwork as "*The Devil's Advocate*." He said that before his conversation with Montoya, he "didn't know Ambrose from shinola." Even after that, he had no idea that Bierce's death was an unsolved mystery. What prompted his letter to the *Sentinel* was the 1989 movie *Old Gringo* — starring Gregory Peck as Bierce — based on Carlos Fuentes's novel of the same name. Sanchez told me how his letter was briefly picked up by some local historians and then dropped. "But there is no question in my mind," he said, his voice rising: "Ambrose Bryce, the author of *The Devil's Advocate*, is buried in Marfa."

Archaeologists say the desert is one of the best places to dig for remains. In the arid soil, clothing may remain intact, free of rot and rain, for hundreds of years. The only preferable places for grave digging are the Arctic Circle and Mt. Everest, where even bits of flesh stand a chance against decay.

Sanchez's letter stated that Bierce's grave was southwest of the old Blackwell School and across from the Shafter road, which runs down to Ojinaga. But how far southwest of the school? Past the trailer park? Before Jerry Agan's house? *Under* Jerry Agan's house? And what did "across from the road" mean? A horse pasture that ran along the west side of the old Shafter road looked promising, but my late-night investigation there yielded nothing. Across the road from the horse pasture is a Mexican restaurant without a public rest room called La Carreta, which means The Cart. Was this a clue?

A friend of mine named Michael Roch said that he had heard I was looking for a graveyard near the Shafter road.

"Oliver Cataño took me down there once on horseback," he said, "and I remember my horse stepping over a grave. There wasn't much there. I don't know if I could find it again, but I could try."

We drove down along Alamito Creek and parked the car. Alamito is a dry creek that runs beside the Shafter road. If there has been rain in the Davis Mountains, it gushes a brown torrent for a day or two, but that is a rare occurrence. A few months before, a man had inadvertently drowned his horse in the creek. He had gotten into the habit of staking the animal at various spots along the creek bed where there was something to graze. During that same rain, I saw a telephone pole go flying past on the current, pursued by a live goat.

Michael and I walked down the dry bed. I had thought about carrying my gardener's trowel but decided instead on a wooden stake and some orange surveyor's tape. The desert soil is corky and dense; a trowel will barely scratch your initials. If we found anything, we would need to return with picks and spades and a bar. Michael stopped and scanned the horizon. "It was somewhere down this way," he said, climbing up the east bank of the creek.

We walked through a field of abandoned cars and other weathered artifacts. The junk thinned as we walked. We ducked through a barbed-wire fence and into a large dusty field, then through another fence and into another field. Two horses wandered around listlessly. It was quiet and hot. Discarded bottles had filled up with dust. Michael looked disoriented. "I think this is the spot," he said. We scanned the field before us. It was wide and empty. Michael said, "I guess it could be another field, but this field feels right." We walked up and down, running our eyes over each contour of the ground, each nub of desert grass and greasewood bush. I looked underneath a mesquite tree. Michael snapped a bean pod off a *largonsilla* bush. We looked at each other. "It's strange," he said. "I really thought it was over here."

None of the other Marfans I talked to seemed to know exactly where the old cemetery southwest of Blackwell School was located either. Some of them seemed to think it had been moved.

Talk of graveyards led to talk of devilry. A friend of mine named Frank Quintanar told me about the time, thirty years ago, that a stranger showed up at a Marfa dance. This stranger was handsome and well dressed, and he quickly found a girl to take his arm. Laughing and shrieking, they spun around the floor. As the dance wound down, a boy in the crowd noticed that the stranger had the feet of a rooster. The boy screamed and pointed. The stranger vanished in a puff of smoke. It was the devil.

"And that is why Marfa will never be prosperous," Frank said. We were at the bar.

In another of Frank's stories the devil appeared as a little red demon with horns. He stood outside the kitchen window of one of Frank's friends, steaming. Then he drifted off. Neither of these little episodes seemed very devilish to me, but I was missing the point. This devil was not interested in death and mayhem. He liked to play games with people. He once appeared to a group of Presidio children as a burro with no tail. The children ran to tell their parents. When they returned the burro had vanished. Another time, a woman saw a dancing rabbit with no front legs. She reached for the rabbit, the rabbit disappeared, and she grabbed a cactus. The cactus gave her a minor infection.

It all made a kind of hell-born sense — the Laughing Devil bungling his end, the actual devil laughing. Was not the devil's mountaintop cave said to overlook the very spot where, according to Sanchez, Montoya and his friends found the old gringo fumbling with his broken cart? Would not the devil's trail lead me to Bierce?

To find the devil I went to see Saul Muñoz, a man old enough to know him. Don Saul lived down on the border, in a blink-and-you-miss-it town called Redford. Many people say that Highway 90, which runs east-west through Marfa, is the real border, and that everything south of it might as well be Mexico. Redford would not dissuade you from this notion. I found the small crumbling house perched on a crumbling hill.

Don Saul was born just across the river in El Mulato. Most of his life he was a shepherd. On the mammoth ranches to the north and east, he would spend up to eight months at a time wandering with a herd of sheep. He worked alone, slept in caves, and now and again he would slaughter one of his own flock to feed himself. In later years he was a ranch cook. Around the time I went to see him, he was spending much of his time at home, watching a black-and-white television with a broken contrast knob and smoking pack after pack of Fiesta cigarettes.

He was happy to have the visit, and we sat in his dark, cool kitchen, drinking water from chipped coffee mugs, talking softly in Spanish. Then I brought up the devil.

"What?" he said, surprised.

I repeated my question. Had he ever seen the devil?

"There is no death and no devil," he told me, speaking slowly so I could understand. "We make death and we are the devil."

He started talking about water — how important it is, how to find it, what to do when there isn't any. He rattled off a series of maxims about hydration: "Water brings work." "No water means no life." "When it rains on a man's land, he's got everything."

Why had he been so quick to change the subject? He cursed the drought awhile longer and lamented the slipping away of the old ranch life. What did any of this have to do with my question?

"I was once a cook for thirty men," he sighed. "Those days are over." As he spoke, a polite young man stuck his head in the room. He was tall, with a friendly smile. Don Saul got up to pour him a mug of water. The young man nodded his thanks and sat on the bed in the corner. Don Saul fished another Fiesta from his crumpled pack and sat back down.

"What about animals?" I asked him. There were many folktales in which the devil took the form of an innocent creature. Perhaps I could help him to remember. "Have you ever seen an animal that seemed strange in one way or another?"

He thought about this for a while, burning down his cigarette with long, slow intakes of smoke.

"Owls have their own language," he said, as if he had finally found something that would interest me.

The young man nodded.

I knew that it was common for witches to take the form of owls in local folktales. I asked if he had ever seen one.

"A witch?" he said.

"Yes," I said, glancing sidelong at the young man. Why was he smiling at me?

Don Saul gave me a disappointed look, then launched into a

long argument about how every supposedly extraordinary phenomenon has an ordinary explanation. I could understand only
about half of what he said, since in his eagerness to make me see
his point he had begun to speak more quickly, his hands gesturing
wildly. The last thing he said was, "An owl is just a bird." A silence
fell over the room, and we listened to his dry tobacco crackle. I sat
back in my chair. The young man was still smiling at me. What did
he know?

"A friend of mine did see a witch one time," Don Saul said after a
while, exhaling a large cloud of smoke. "She was flying around in
front of his campfire."

"A real witch?" I asked, sitting up.

"Of course not," he said. "It was his hair hanging in front of his
eye. We are the witch. We trick ourselves."

Don Saul walked me outside into the scorching midafternoon
sun. I thanked him for his time and asked if we might take a photograph. The young man took my camera, lined us up against the remains of an adobe wall, and silently shot two pictures of us squinting into the sun.

I began to look for area historians who might be of some help. It
seemed unlikely that I would have been the first to investigate
Sanchez's letter. I needed the guidance of a trained professional.

After two annoying conversations ("Don't chase fireflies," one
man told me), I found my way to Glenn Willeford, a professor at
the Center for Big Bend Studies at Sul Ross State University in Alpine. He referred to himself as a "Bierce-chaser." I made an ap-
pointment to see him the next day.

Alpine is twenty-six miles from Marfa. Most towns in Far West
Texas are about thirty miles apart, since they were water stops on
the railroad before they were towns. Alpine has a population of
around 5,800, a two-screen movie theater, a lumber store ("We Put
The Pine Back In Alpine"), an Amtrak station, and a state university. The university's mascot is the *lobo*, or wolf, but a cast-iron longhorn with a gigantic rack stood at the campus gate, calling to mind
a passage I had just read from Colonel Richard Irving Dodge's account of life in nineteenth-century Texas:

Every bush had its thorn; every animal, reptile, or insect had its horn
tooth or sting; every male human his revolver; and each was ready to use

his weapon of defense on any unfortunate sojourner, on the smallest, or even without the smallest, provocation.

I parked in the visitor lot. A teenager was picking cigarette butts out of the university's flower beds with a spearlike implement. I tried not to provoke him.

Willeford's office was in the basement of a brick building, in a corner of a large storeroom full of archaeological artifacts and office supplies and boxes of brand-new novels from a westerns series with titles like *Pony Express, Carry My Message,* and *Across the Crevasse.* His desk was wedged between two crates. "No one bothers me down here," he told me. Willeford was first drawn to Bierce by the Civil War stories. "I think his experiences in that war embittered him," he said. "But they made him think about the hereafter, and what men are like, and God. Vietnam did the same thing to me." Willeford had just finished writing a short paper on the Bierce mystery, and one of his central projects had been to refute the Sanchez letter. He handed me a copy. Mortified, I accepted it. Three things became clear in rapid succession: (1) Sanchez's letter was full of holes, some of them serious, some minor; (2) It was unlikely that Ambrose Bierce's bones would ever be found; and (3) I would make a terrible historian. The historian must develop an immunity to the poetry of coincidence. But has he no use for intuition?

I put this question to Willeford, but he dismissed it and proceeded to annotate the errors in my copy of the Sanchez letter: "One week after the battle? Pneumonia kills a lot faster than that." "This was $10 U.S. at the time. Not much inducement." "Unlikely." "Contradictory." "Impossible!"

"I don't think he'll ever be found," he said at last, "but I'm not going to quit looking. You don't know anything until you look."

By the time I left Alpine, night had fallen. Where the road comes down out of Paisano Pass, I pulled over. This is where tourists come from all over the country to watch the sky over Mitchell Flat for the so-called Marfa Mystery Lights. The lights streak across the horizon; they hover in the air; they have, on occasion, approached certain viewers like friendly ghosts ("The Lights of God," Captain Manuel Pedro Vasco called them in 1617). Science has never explained the lights, and many people who have lived in the vicinity their whole lives have never seen them. I sat on the hood of my car.

Some tourists had parked an RV nearby and set up for their all-night vigil. "Do you see anything?" I heard one ask another. I knew that the odds were against them getting any more out of the experience than videotape of the headlights on the Shafter road. Yet every week more tourists came, fooled themselves, slept in their cars with binoculars, bought T-shirts.

The prairie before us was empty and black. Willeford could annotate till dawn; I still believed Sanchez.

It was noon when I arrived in Mexico, and after a quick lunch and some sketchy directions from the woman who had sold me the lunch, I got in my car and drove toward the mountain on which, legend told me, I would find the devil in a cave. I turned right at the decrepit Hotel Ojinaga and rumbled along a terrible road, past the military *campamento* and the *tortillería* and over the railroad tracks. The outskirts of town were a mess of sad old adobe houses, satellite dishes, chickens, and faded political slogans painted on cinderblock walls, with shards of broken glass in place of barbed wire. At the end of the road I could turn either right or left. My lunch lady's directions did not include this fork. The mountain was straight ahead, a small white cross shining from its summit in the fierce sun. I stopped in at a small market called Abarrotes "Nellie."

The butcher in the back of the store was mindlessly working some sort of awful-looking meat product in a huge tub. His arms were bloody up to the elbows. I couldn't take my eyes off him as the woman behind the counter (Nellie?) gave me directions. From the look on the butcher's face, you would have thought he was icing cakes. When a girl walked into the store he raised one gore-encased arm and waved.

Following Nellie's directions, I took the right turn and drove along a road far too wide to be a real road, kicking up a cloud of dust that had completely obscured the store by the time I was a hundred feet beyond it. Past the last house, the road turned left and crossed half-buried train tracks. A small cemetery, overgrown with mesquite trees, marked the beginning of the way to the mountain.

The road began to fork continuously. What looked like flags marking the route to the mountain turned out to be white plastic bags blown into the thorny *ocotillos* along the road, and although their distribution was by no means uniform, one seemed to appear before me each time I thought I'd picked the wrong fork, as if some unseen hand had called together wind, trash, and flora to lead me straight to hell.

I parked at the base of the mountain. The parched prairie spread around me. A breeze blew, but it blew hot and dusty. I started up the trail, which split into two trails, which split into four trails, and although each trail led to the same place, the one I chose always seemed to take the most difficult ascent. I clambered up a steep devil's slide, kicking loose rocks that crashed violently down the mountain to settle in the talus below. I grabbed a root and pulled myself over a small cliff on my stomach. All I could hear was my breath and the wind. I had come alone because I thought these terms would suit my host, but in the emptiness and silence I began to fear that they would suit him too well. When I reached the summit, I sat at the base of the twenty-foot cross and caught my breath. This was a serious cross, designed to protect a lot of people from something very bad. Pieces of cinderblock kept the votive candles around it from falling down the mountain.

The wind picked up. Chinati Peak looked across from the other side of the valley. They say the devil used to string a tightrope between these two summits and prance back and forth, tormenting the villagers below. I gazed down from his perspective. There was the gully where the gringo writer's cart broke; there, the clearing where he found the soldiers, the thicket where they slept; across the river, the hillside where they were captured by the cavalry and loaded into the wagons.

It was all very devilish, but where was the devil? I searched the summit for his cave. The spines on a cactus pointed me in opposite directions. From the dust, an old Fanta bottle cap stared up at me like a dead eye. I did not find the cave.

I got back to Ojinaga just as the stores reopened after siesta and went looking for Bryant Eduardo Holman. Holman was an old mud logger — an oilfield hand — who had moved to Presidio from Roswell, New Mexico, years before, married a Mexican orthodontist, and opened up a native crafts store in Ojinaga called Fausto's. He always kept a close eye on local politics, and I was in the habit of stopping in on him to hear the newest plot he had uncovered; on occasion they held enough water to warrant an article.

"You want to find the cave?" he said. "Sure, no problem."

We took his car, a brown Isuzu Trooper. He drove as fast as he talked, spinning another outlandish tale about municipal corruption and swaggering drug kingpins, and in what seemed like an impossibly short time we were back at the base of the mountain.

"It's just up here," Holman said, waddling up the path.

I had been all wrong to head for the summit. Only a quarter of the way up the mountain, Holman veered off the left side of the path, climbed down a rock to a sandy ledge, and announced, "*This is the cueva del diablo,*" in a spooky voice. He then jumped down inside the cave and launched into a confusing account of the devil legend, which involved Cabeza de Vaca, Pancho Villa, the Aztec god Smoking Mirror, and John Reed, "the father of American journalism." He hopped while speaking.

"To really understand what's going on here," he said, rubbing his hands, "you need to know about the four unlucky days and the powerful syncretism that De Vaca brought to this region. But even then, this is really ancient stuff. It goes back to the Uto-Aztecans and their tales about spiders in caves. Before that even."

The cave was L-shaped, opening out to the valley and up to the sky. It was about ten feet deep and ten feet tall. *Hello? Devil?* Here was the mountain; here was the cave. Where was he? I had come for the devil and found a folk-art dealer. When I turned back to him, Holman was explaining his decision to become a pagan. *Should I check his pant cuffs for chicken feet?*

Down at the Trooper a police truck had pulled up. The road was a dead end, miles and miles from town, but the two fat cops in the cab were not interested in us. They were looking for a stolen Mustang with doors that were a different color from the body.

Several days later I was sitting at home reading a story of Bierce's entitled "The Stranger." In the story, the ghost of an old prospector visits the campfire of a group of "gentleman adventurers." This is in the Arizona desert. The men do not know he is a ghost straightaway. His behavior is strange but they take him for a "harmless lunatic," driven crazy by the solitude of the desert. The narrator observes,

> We were not so new to the country as not to know that the solitary life of many a plainsman had a tendency to develop eccentricities of conduct

and character not always easily distinguishable from mental aberration. A man is like a tree: in a forest of his fellows he will grow as straight as his generic and individual nature permits; alone in the open, he yields to the deforming stresses and tortions that environ him.

Is this what had happened to me? Once I left Marfa would I care where Bierce was buried? Outside my window a work crew from the local nursery was toiling away, installing an automatic irrigation system for my landlords that would fulfill all my watering duties with the flip of a switch and the punch of a code. The sound of their work punctuated Bierce's sentences with clangs and grunts. As I read, I let them supply each grammatical mark — a clang for a comma, a grunt for a period.

Suddenly a cry went up from one of the crew: "Hey! Get over here! Tony hit something!"

I peered through the blinds. The crew gathered around Tony as he pointed at the ground and gestured with his bar. A younger man with a shovel began to dig; the rest stood around with their hands on their hips waiting to see what he would uncover. In no time the young man was standing in a hole that obscured the bottom half of his legs. He dropped out of sight completely, and from the instructions I saw the others giving I understood that he was on his hands and knees, sweeping dirt off something down there. In time he stood up and stepped out of the hole. The whole crew then stood, it seemed, in silence and beheld what he had uncovered. One man crossed himself. Another said something that made the whole group laugh.

It was evening before they left. I had spent the afternoon pacing my room. When the work trucks had finally bounced off the property, gravel crunching beneath their heavy tires, and rolled smoothly onto the blacktop toward town, and when the music from their radios had faded into the night, I stood outside on the open plain.

The wind blew. Along the northern horizon, at intervals, great flashes of silent heat lightning surprised the sky. Swirling over the path, the dried leaves rasped out a greeting. One window of the miniature house had been left open, and the white curtains behind it fluttered softly, hung still, and fluttered once more, like a lady being seated at the theater.

I crossed the yard to the area where the hole had been dug. The practical foreman, blind to the potential historical import of the discovery, had directed his crew to cover it back up. But I had no trouble finding the spot where the digging had been done. In the center of the dirt yard, by a tree stump, a multitude of boot tracks pointed inward, as if the men had stood there for a moment before turning away.

I fell to my knees and began to dig. The dirt had been shoveled already, and once I had broken it up with the trowel it came away easily in my hands. The dirt pile grew at my side. The moonlight brightened. Finally, my fingertips met with that which would not give — a wide, flat stone. I scooped out the dirt to find its edges. It was a large rectangle, made roughly from cement, three feet wide and six feet long. I swept the surface clean with my hands and, bending low, blew down on it, my cheeks filling and emptying with air, the dirt particles flying up off the stone and into my face and hair. I staggered to my feet and stood on the stone. The wind died. The plain was quiet. The stone was blank.

In Far West Texas, on the side of the highway that runs south from Marfa to Presidio and across the Rio Grande into Ojinaga, Mexico, there is a small green sign that reads, PROFILE OF LINCOLN. Under these words an arrow points west at the jagged foothills of the Chinati Mountains, where you can make out the sixteenth president's profile in the ridges of rock. It is not so easy to see — the vast sameness of the landscape's color confuses the eye — and many travelers who stop fail to find the accidental monument. Sometimes I pass them on my way up and down the Shafter road. Their cars are parked along the shoulder, fifty feet past the sign, in positions that testify to the abruptness of the stop; cameras hang idly by their sides; they stare for a while, squinting, furrowing their brows, their lips curling into profoundly baffled grins.

ANDREW SOLOMON

My Dinner in Kabul

FROM *Food & Wine*

I DID NOT go to Afghanistan for the food. In fact, I went there thinking that one bonus of my visit — the primary purpose of which was humanitarian and journalistic — would be the shedding of a few unwanted pounds. Let us be frank: Cuisine is not usually uppermost in the mind of a country devastated by war, hunger, and injustice. I thought that winter rations in Kabul were likely to be grim, and I stuffed my suitcase with high-protein Odwalla bars, a jar of almond butter, and some Scharffen Berger chocolate that a friend gave me for good luck.

This all happened in February, when Kabul was very much a closed shop. You could get there only by taking a United Nations–operated flight from Islamabad. The city had by that time sustained a minor invasion of journalists and government workers, but there were no facilities for tourists, and it was quite a disorienting place to be. The best hotel in town, the Intercontinental, was one of the worst hotels I've ever seen: The ceilings were stained and falling in; the carpeting was threadbare and curiously moist, and seemed to sustain a variety of insect life; there was seldom any electricity and almost never any hot water.

I'd arranged to stay at an old Al Qaeda house that some friends had rented in the fashionable Wazir Akbar Khan area, where we had full-time translators and drivers. (For security reasons, journalists had been told not to go out unescorted.) I had heard that we would have a cook as well, and I mostly felt relieved that I wouldn't have to run around town trying to scrape up food. I had a big meal on my last night in Pakistan, and prepared for the worst.

Dinner my first night in Kabul, however, was a revelation. We had spicy little meatballs in a rich sauce, a wonderful rice dish, crisp fried potato cakes, and delicious fresh Afghan bread. When I expressed astonishment, a friend explained that we had nabbed the best chef in Kabul, and that everyone who came to dinner at our house tried to poach him away. Qudratullah arrived every day at seven A.M. to make us breakfast, produced a hot lunch for us at midday, and prepared dinner for us every night.

One wonder of wintertime Kabul was the markets. In this ruined city, the stalls, surrounded by Taliban-era graffiti on bullet-pocked walls, held a profusion of local foodstuffs: pomegranates and oranges, and all sorts of nuts and dried fruits, and fresh meat (sometimes disorientingly fresh), and spices and grains in sacks, and for some reason a lot of cauliflower, and the largest and most vividly colored carrots I've ever seen (some nearly purple), and eggplants and onions and potatoes, and different kinds of sweets. While the greatest assortment could be found in the food bazaar near the river, I saw rich displays even in the poorest neighborhoods. People had no electricity, no plumbing, no heating, sometimes no roof, but they had food.

Qudratullah was able to get the best ingredients, and when friends would stop by, there was always enough to eat; he had an Afghan capacity to expand meals to accommodate whoever came. So it seemed natural, when a few musicians I'd met volunteered to play a little concert just for me, that I invite them to dinner at our house, where we had not only excellent food but also that rarer Kabul commodity, heat, in this case from a woodstove. The ensemble, they told me, would include eleven musicians; I said they'd all be welcome. They would be playing Afghan classical music on instruments that were forbidden and lost during the Taliban years: the sarinda, the rabab and the richak, as well as Indian drums and the sitar, and always the harmonium.

Then I had a typical Kabul journalist day. I stopped by UNESCO and discovered that my contact there was planning a music festival (but had yet to meet any musicians), so I invited him to our concert. I checked in with Marla, the blond liberal who was staying at the Agence France-Presse house, and I invited her and her translator, who had done a favor for me the day before. I invited all the people who worked at our house — translators, guards, and so on.

Scott from *Newsweek* said he thought Antonia from German TV might like to come, and I was very pleased. And when some people from the *Washington Post* stopped by, we thought it would be a mistake not to include them. I invited a filmmaker I'd interviewed the day before. And so the numbers began to creep up.

When I told the cook we had company coming, he said he'd need some extra money to buy food and some more extra money to buy plates and a bit of further extra money to get someone in to help in the kitchen. I said I thought there would be about thirty of us, and I gave him $200.

My estimate, it turned out, was wildly off. Between the musicians and the house staff and some other people we'd met, we had a good twenty or so Afghans; plus the foreigners all brought friends. By the time we had dinner, at about seven-thirty, there were between fifty and sixty people. Qudratullah, praise be upon him, produced enough food so that all were handsomely fed. We had qabeli pilau, Afghanistan's national dish, a sweet rice pilaf; roast leg of mutton, cooked until it was falling off the bone; roast chicken; borani, a flavorful eggplant dish made with yogurt and garlic; sabzi qorma, an Iranian dish of meat stewed with spinach; salad; and firni, an Afghan pudding made with cornstarch. Of course we had flat Afghan bread. The sweetness of the pilau offset the savory mutton; like many rice dishes, this one offered texture overlaid with flavor, somewhere between rice and rice pudding. The borani was refreshing and pungent, with the heady garlic right up against the sour yogurt, all muted by the rich eggplant. The sabzi qorma was lovely, neither stringy nor tough; the spinach flavor went into the meat and countered its slight gaminess. I was a rapid convert to the firni, though it got its taste mostly from decorative pistachios. The overall effect was a little Middle Eastern and a little Indian, as one might suspect from Afghanistan's location. The most distinctive flavor, in all the meat dishes, was a spice that tasted like coriander — I was never able to get the full details about it.

The musicians played magnificently, and people began dancing. In Afghanistan, women and men don't socialize together; even at a wedding, there are separate halls for women and men. Our Afghan guests, all men, showed us how they dance in a circle. The Westerners joined in, and also showed the Afghans how Western men and women dance together (at the party there were perhaps ten women). The music got more and more exuberant.

"My goodness," said the UNESCO operative. "There *is* music in Afghanistan after all. I will have a festival, I will!"

"Why not eat more? There is more!" said my translator, Farouk. "Let's eat until every plate is clean!"

"Do you think this is getting out of control?" asked Scott from *Newsweek*, who had official responsibility for the house. I had to admit that it was.

At nine, someone showed up with a bottle of whiskey, which in a Muslim country, where the law forbids alcohol, was the equivalent of showing up with pot at an American party. There was a lot of giggling, and a few of the Afghans made rapid progress toward inebriation. The next morning, I was to teach my translator the word *hangover.*

There is a ten P.M. curfew in Kabul, so at nine-thirty we reminded our guests to leave. But the musicians lived too far away to get home in time, so they stayed over. They played and played. As midnight approached, the instruments fell silent, one by one; but the sitar player kept faith by playing his delicate, mesmerizing rhythms on into the small hours. We sat transfixed.

A year ago — even a few months ago — it would have been unthinkable to throw a party in Kabul. The situation was sober and sad. But though the city bears the terrible scars of its recent history, it is full of people longing, at last, for a little bit of pleasure. The Afghans were so pleased that we liked their food and music; it seemed that we were accomplishing a diplomatic purpose simply by eating pilau and borani, by dancing to the sarinda and the rabab and the richak. Afghan hospitality is legendary, and one of the things that was painful to many Afghans about their country's war-torn state was that they had no opportunity to extend their hospitality to foreigners. I went to Afghanistan ready for hardship, and I did see horrible things, but I also felt a warmth, an embrace, and a sense of pride that lay not only in the reform of government, but also in the return to these small satisfactions, so long denied, now so easily and openly and generously shared.

MICHAEL SPECTER

I Am Fashion

FROM *The New Yorker*

THE AIR FRANCE HOSTESS was pleasant but unwilling to compromise. "This flight closes in three minutes," she said. "We don't make exceptions." Chuck Bone, who was sitting in the Concorde's first-class waiting lounge at JFK, reached casually for his cell phone. It was seven-twelve A.M. on a Monday in July. The Concorde was scheduled to depart for Paris at eight, and its passengers generally consider even the briefest delay intolerable. Bone, who was wearing a blue-and-white tracksuit and had a simple diamond stud in one ear, started talking. "Where are you guys? You need to get him here now. They are closing the flight." He listened for a moment and then turned to the woman in charge of the lounge. "He is in the airport," he said. "He'll be at the terminal in five minutes." The hostess, who was now flanked by three colleagues, was unmoved. "Seven-fifteen and we close it," she said. "I am sorry, but Mr. Puff Daddy must come by then, or he will have to take another plane."

Mr. Puff Daddy, the thirty-two-year-old rap impresario, restaurateur, clothing entrepreneur, bon vivant, actor, and Page Six regular — who is also known as P. Diddy, and whose mother calls him Sean John Combs — was expected in Paris within hours. He needed to be on the eight A.M. flight: It was the first day of fashion week, and Donatella Versace had invited him to sit in the front row at her couture show. Versace's shows always attract enormous publicity, usually more for the celebrities in the audience than for the models on the runway. The Concorde was Combs's only hope of making it on time. Jeffrey Tweedy, the vice president of Combs's clothing company, Sean John, was in the lounge looking jumpy. He poured himself a cup of tea and took some valerian. He stared unhappily at the oversized Panerai Luminor watch on his wrist. Seven-thirteen A.M. Two minutes to go.

A few dozen tastefully dressed men and women with chic handbags and understated accessories began boarding the flight. Still no sign of Combs. For the past three days, he had been in Atlanta, at a music-industry event sponsored by Bad Boy Entertainment, the record company he has run for nearly a decade. There had been a party the final night, and Combs didn't leave until around four in the morning. He was driven directly to his chartered Gulfstream G4 jet. By six-thirty A.M., he was on the ground at Teterboro Airport, in suburban New Jersey, but the morning traffic on the George Washington Bridge had begun to build.

By seven-twenty-five, the passengers in the lounge had checked in and most were already on board. The Air France flight attendants were eager to close the door. One was tapping her foot. Everyone in the Combs entourage — Tweedy; Bone, a friend from high school; Mar Sabado, one of Puffy's assistants; her boyfriend, a designer in dreadlocks named Emmett Harrell — was on his or her cell phone or working his or her Motorola two-way pager. Sabado was on the phone with Combs's twenty-eight-year-old chief aide, Norma Augenblick, who was in Paris, making certain that everything was in place for Combs's arrival at the hotel: champagne in ice buckets; a sufficient supply of Puff Daddy's favorite tequila (1800); plenty of Cuban cigars, either Monte Cristo No. 2 or Cohiba. Then, there were the racks of clothing to unpack and organize. Puff Daddy does not travel light, and by the time he reached his hotel suite that evening he expected everything to be in order.

At seven-thirty, a man in a two-piece white terry-cloth outfit appeared at the far end of the terminal. He was wearing white tennis shoes, white socks, a skintight white terry-cloth hat pulled low over his forehead, and a large diamond ring on his right pinkie. He was walking slowly, and talking rapidly into his cell phone. The hostess wheeled around and left when he approached. He looked tired but clearly pleased to see his friends. He embraced the various members of his crew and then shook my hand. "I hope you are ready to seriously hang out in Paris," he said. "Because don't come with us if you can't stay out with us. I fully intend to show Paris the respect it deserves. We are going to rock that place to the ground."

His friends clapped once, the way football players do at the end of a huddle. Then they headed for the plane. It was seven-forty. As Combs turned toward the walkway heading onto the Concorde, a security agent gently put a hand on his shoulder and asked him to step aside; after all, even Al Gore gets searched these days. "Mr. Combs," the guard said. "Would it be possible to get your autograph?" Puff Daddy nodded, pinned his cell phone between his left shoulder and his ear, and, still talking, signed the back of an envelope.

"Thank you, sir," the security guard said. "Have a really nice trip."

Two minutes before takeoff, a stewardess came over and asked, hesitantly, if Combs might be willing to turn off his phone. He apologized, then snapped it shut. Despite his outsized image, Combs is not a big man, and he often speaks in a whisper. When he addressed the stewardess, she had to lean in toward the seat to hear him. "I forget how fast this plane travels," he said. "I was trying to explain it to my son before." "Eet eez zee speed of a boullet," the woman replied. "It eez exactly like we are shot out of zee gun." By the time she had finished describing the velocity of the plane, its cruising altitude, and what happens when the flight breaks the sound barrier, Combs was asleep.

Within moments of touching down in Paris, Combs and his crew were back on their phones. Puffy, now wide awake, seemed to be having trouble with his, so Tweedy, who was sitting one row behind him, offered some advice: "You have to dial 001 to call a New York cell phone, even if the person is in France," he explained. Combs whipped around in his seat. "Yo, Jeff, excuse me," he said, in a low, steady voice. "This is my fourteenth Concorde flight. I'm an international fucking player. I'll tell you how to use a phone."

Combs had come to Paris for fun, but it was fun with a purpose. He considers himself (as do many others) among the most fashionable people in the world, and the business of fashion has become an increasingly central part of his life. Sean John, the clothing company he started three years ago, has emerged as one of the best-selling — and most highly regarded — men's lines in America. Combs's runway show in New York last fall met with praise from even the most skeptical fashion professionals. "It was better than anything in Europe," Kim Hastreiter, the editor of *Paper*, the downtown fashion magazine, told me. "It was perfectly presented, perfectly original American fashion." In 2001, Sean John's sales, which were $30 million in 1999, rose to nearly $250 million.

This year, along with Ralph Lauren and Marc Jacobs, Combs was nominated by the Council of Fashion Designers of America as the menswear designer of the year. He introduced his line with the type of T-shirts and baggy jeans that characterize hip-hop clothing brands like FUBU and Eckō, but he quickly graduated to a more sophisticated look, with a modern, slightly off-kilter approach to classic preppy clothes. This month, he will bring out Blue — a more expensive line of denim directed at older customers. Combs and Tweedy also have ambitious plans to enter the lucrative and complicated world of women's wear, and to open two Sean John stores in New York next year. At a time when many designers are struggling just to stay in business, department stores seem eager for anything Sean John can supply. "Puffy sells second only to Ralph in many of our stores," Kal Ruttenstein, the long-time fashion director of Bloomingdale's, told me. "Some of that is because of his name, of course. But his clothes are actually quite wonderful, and you would be amazed to see how many types of people wear them."

Combs first appeared at the haute couture shows in Paris five years ago. With his hip-hop credentials and his love of the spotlight, not to mention a past that includes highly public moments of violence, Combs provided exactly what the fashion crowd craves: a frisson of danger without much threat of it. He represented the ultimate expression of 1990s style: excessive, ironic, and a tiny bit thuggish. He wore fur and leather and draped himself in enough diamonds to rival Princess Caroline of Monaco. Combs made his first visits to the Louvre and to Versailles, which he described to me as "some awe-inspiring shit." He was escorted to many of the shows by Anna Wintour, the editor of *Vogue*. "Puffy is so wonderfully over the top and flamboyant, and, God, do we need that in our business," Wintour told me. "Fashion goes through severely dull periods and we must have relief. Puff provides it."

Donatella Versace, who knows glitz if she knows anything, was counting on Combs's presence to add some adrenaline to her show. The show was scheduled to begin at eight. At six, Combs was working his way through customs at Charles de Gaulle Airport. The drive into the city would take at least an hour; then he would need to change from his travel clothes into a more fashionable, light-gray, chalk-striped suit, designed by Donatella. He would have to look, in the phrase coined by Andre Harrell, his former boss at Uptown Records, "ghetto fabulous." That meant choosing appropriate accessories: a silver tie, smoke-colored sunglasses, diamond-and-platinum earrings, a bracelet or two; a couple of diamond rings the size of cherry tomatoes, and a watch covered with jewels and worth nearly a million dollars.

There is nothing in fashion more deliciously low than a Versace show. The ambience is one of excess, with security guards stationed along the runway and models regularly spilling out of their tops. The show, which was held at the Palais de Chaillot this year, was delayed. Puffy didn't leave his hotel until eight-thirty. He was with Kim Porter, the mother of one of his two children. (She has another child, whom Combs supports and treats as his own.) By the time they arrived, the bleachers were filled: the Hilton sisters, Nicky and Paris, were there, along with their parents, Rick and Kathy. Two of the Miller sisters — Alexandra von Furstenberg and Princess Marie-Chantal of Greece (along with her exiled husband, Crown Prince Pavlos) — were also in the audience. (They are daughters of Robert Miller, the duty-free billionaire.) These young women are among the dwindling number of people on Earth with the means and the desire to pay twenty thousand dollars for a dress they might wear once.

Combs and Porter, who was dressed elegantly in black and wore a diamond necklace that, next to Puffy's jewels, seemed almost demure, were seated beside the actress Elizabeth Hurley, whose floor-length green evening gown was covered with paisley swirls and glittering stars and cut in a remarkably low V. Hurley wore a silver pendant and pink mules. The front row was a spectacle of preening, with Hurley, George Michael, Rupert Everett, David Furnish (Elton John's lover), the singer Ashanti, and the downtown celebrity actress Chloë Sevigny posing constantly for the cameras. The most photographed guest, by far, was Combs. (*People, Us Weekly,* and about eight European magazines — many of them named *Hello!* in a variety of languages — ran pictures of him with Porter, Hurley, or Donatella Versace. "Wow, Puff Daddeee," the photographers screeched. "Mr. Diddeee, can we see the diamonds?")

The fashion show itself lasted about fifteen minutes. Puffy spent much of that time taking pictures of other celebrities with a tiny camera. As soon as the last girl left the runway, he and his friends, led by three security men, went backstage. Versace was having a party at the Ritz Club later that evening, and Puffy would make an appearance, but he still needed to pay his respects to his host. She was surrounded by her staff, some of whom find Combs an unwelcome addition to their world. ("He is like a mezzo Donatella," one of them said to me. "He's a fashion Mini-Me: half the talent, half the glamour, just as demanding.") Air kisses were exchanged in the dressing area. "It blew me away," Puff said to Versace, about the collection, which included a patchwork coat made from more than eighty types of antique fabric; a short jacket with blue crocodile skin; and a silver ball gown of antique brocade with a silver lamé skirt. Versace beamed. She wore her peroxided hair straight and long, her lipstick was brown, and her skin was a peculiar shade of gray. Puffy embraced her, and then looked at his assistant Norma and nodded. It was after ten o'clock and, as he put it a few minutes later, he was ready to "escalate." Norma passed the word to the security detail, and within minutes the entourage was gone.

Combs moves like a candidate for the presidency. He is always late, he is never alone. (Solitude seems to make him nervous.) Even when he needs to travel a single city block — say, from his Bad Boy offices, in midtown, to the MTV studios, in Times Square — he is loaded into an SUV and driven. This is not purely vanity; Combs has been particularly conscious of security ever since his best friend, the rap star Christopher Wallace, who was better known as the Notorious B.I.G., was gunned down in 1997 in Los Angeles. Combs was with Wallace the night he died, and among his many tattoos there is one on his right wrist, noting B.I.G.'s date of birth and date of death. (The crime, generally attributed to an East Coast–West Coast hip-hop rivalry that also took the life of Tupac Shakur, has never been solved.)

The group was whisked into an underground passage and out a back door. There were scores of kids waiting in the street, and when they saw Combs they started screaming, "Pouf Daddeee, Pouf Daddeee!" and quickly surrounded him, seeking autographs. Combs signed them. (Every time he left a restaurant, hotel, or club

in Paris, he was delayed by honeymooners, tourists, and other people wanting him to sign an autograph or pose with them for pictures. I never saw him refuse.) Combs wanted to go to the hotel for
a drink before heading to Nobu for dinner. After dinner, he went
to Versace's party, and then to another club, where he remained
until dawn. Versace had booked Combs and his entourage into the
Hyatt Regency Paris-Madeleine, and he had a suite on the seventh
floor, with a separate elevator key. It was a nice hotel, well situated
in the center of town. But it was an unusual choice. In Paris, the
beautiful people stay at the Ritz or the Plaza Athénée. Many in the
fashion crowd prefer the intimacy of the Hotel Côstes. Nobody
stays at the Hyatt. (The second night he was in Paris, Puffy visited
Vin Diesel in his suite at the Plaza Athénée — a duplex decorated
in white, with a large terrace off the bedroom — and he quickly
saw what he was missing. "Norma, we need to stay here," Puffy announced. "Time for a change. Get me a room like this." Norma
had anticipated this whim, but the Plaza is always full during fashion week, and there was nothing she could do.)

Not that the Hyatt was a hardship: The suite had a baby grand piano and a large terrace. There were several garment racks in the
living room, with more than a dozen suits, scores of shirts, leather
jackets, what appeared to be twenty or so belts, and twice as many
ties. There were enough shoes to last a lifetime, and enough sneakers to outfit the Knicks. Some of the clothes had been provided by
Versace, but most had been flown over from New York. "Can you
possibly wear all this in four days?" I asked Combs. "All I can do is
try," he replied, with a wink. Sunglasses had been arranged in three
rows on a high table next to a couch in the living room. There were
about ten pairs in each row; each pair was in its original case, with
the top flipped up. It looked like the optical counter at Bergdorf's.
We walked onto the terrace. Montmartre and at least a dozen
church steeples stood out against the pale sky. Despite the hour, it
was still light. A thin wafer of a moon hung above the city. Emmett
and Bone were sitting with Tweedy, sipping wine, taking in the view.

Combs, who often seems uneasy in a crowd unless he is perform-
ing, stood self-consciously on the edge of the terrace. "Before we
get on our way, I just want to say one thing," he said. "We are in
Paris and we are here to learn from one another. We are going to
philosophize and improvise and improve each other's minds. God
gave us the chance to be together in this wonderful place and we

are going to profit from it. I want to drink mimosas at the Eiffel Tower at dawn. I want us to have fun. But we have to be together to do it. You will not leave me and I will not leave you, and we will have the total experience." (Combs never seems still. Even when he's sitting alone in a corner, he pays attention to everything going on around him.) Within minutes, we were off to Nobu, where the Hilton girls and many models, designers, fashion editors, and a few hangers-on were having dinner. After several seating configurations proved untenable, Combs got the waiters to join three tables, and then he ordered approximately two of everything on the menu. When the waiter finished reading back the order, Puffy told him to bring champagne, wine, and two bottles of tequila. "But it has to be 1800 tequila," he said. "And bring it to the table. I want to see the labels."

Dinner ended around twelve-thirty. The Versace party was already under way. By the time we arrived at the Ritz Club, a long line had formed, and the bouncers were on edge. Inside, Chloë Sevigny sat on a bench, posing for photographers, and Liz Hurley was playing blackjack with Versace. Despite their presence, it was an oddly B-list crowd, made up mostly of unknown models, publicists, and Versace's own employees. The Hiltons were there, but they are at every party. At one-thirty, Puffy and his friends packed themselves back into their cars and took off in search of better music and cooler people. They found both. The place, near the Marais, was sweltering and crowded. Waves of hip-hop music rolled across the dance floor. The Nelly song "Hot in Herre" was playing. It was the song of the summer, and, despite the heat, nobody wanted to remain seated. Soon after Combs arrived, the DJ shouted out the obligatory greeting — "P. Diddy's in the house!" — and then played Puffy's No. 1 song "I Need a Girl (Part 1)."

Most people assume that the song is about Combs's relationship with Jennifer Lopez: "Every time I think about your pretty smile, and how we used to drive the whole city wild, damn I wish you would've had my child, a pretty little girl with Diddy's style." Few couples since Richard Burton and Elizabeth Taylor have appeared more often in the gossip columns. While Combs and Lopez were together, it was as if two corporations, AOL and Time Warner, say, had merged; as much as anything else, they were a marketing phenomenon. When I asked whether "I Need a Girl" was, in fact, about

Lopez, Combs laughed ruefully, then shook his head. "It's a fuck-ing song, man. Would you ask a writer if his book is real or fiction? It's just a song."

Gwen Stefani appeared on the edge of the dance floor. In the echo chamber of the fashion world, Stefani is currently among the most adored of celebrities. Puff was thrilled to see her. He grabbed her by the leg and gracefully swung her around so that her head nearly dipped to the floor, then he reached for her foot and slowly caressed it. At that point, he turned to me and started to sort of rap: "I am fashion because I live fashion," he said. It was so hot in the club that it was difficult to breathe, but Puffy was still wearing his suit, and not one button was undone. His tie was so tightly knot-ted it seemed to put a strain on his Adam's apple. A diamond stud was planted in each earlobe. A thick rope of a diamond bracelet — from Jacob, the New York jeweler to the hip-hop elite — adorned his wrist. He said, "From my manicure to my pedicure, from my head to my toe, it's the swagger that I show the world, it's my face, baby. It's my walk, my attitude." He rubbed the wisps of hair on his chin. "Fashion is about leaving on your jacket and tie when other people are too hot to bother." He was also wearing a yellow dia-mond ring, which looked like a piece of rock candy. "Details, baby. It's all about the details. Look at the arm. The ring. The watch. Look at my canary-yellow diamond. Impeccable. Admit it, I am im-peccable." He let out a wolf howl, and dozens of dancers started to cheer. At this point, Norma, who is keenly protective, and who, de-pending on the hour, is a corporate executive, an accountant, a fixer, a party planner, or a high-end concierge, shouted across the floor to me, "This is all off the record, it's off the record!" Combs waved her away. "I don't want this off the record. I've got a lot of shit to say about fashion. It don't really matter what you write about me. Because I'll still be a fashion god, no matter what." Puff walked to a table where his friends were sipping Cristal and eating straw-berries. ("I don't even drink the shit," he told me. "They bring it wherever I am. It's a cliché.") He plunged his arm into a bucket of ice water. Then he waved it in my face. "Look at that ring," he shouted. "Look at the way it glistens. I am a damn fashionable motherfucker, and I'm not ashamed to admit it."

Puff Daddy believes that he inherited some of his fashion sense from his father. "People say we have a similar approach to fashion," he told me one day. "They say he was the fliest man around. But he died when I was three. I saw a couple pictures of him, and that was all." Combs's father, Melvin, spent many years as a limousine driver, and his mother, Janice, told him that his father had died "in his car." That was true, but Melvin Combs didn't die in an accident; he was a drug dealer, and one night in 1972 he was shot dead in his car in Central Park. Combs's mother raised Sean and his younger sister, Keisha, alone, working three jobs — as a school-bus driver, a teacher at a local day-care center, and an attendant for children with cerebral palsy — while her mother watched the children. (Combs and his mother still speak to or see each other several times a week; his sister works for him at Bad Boy, and one of his tattoos is dedicated to his grandmother, who died in 1994.) When Combs was ten, he spent a summer with the Amish in Pennsylvania Dutch country, through the Fresh Air Fund. Not long after that, the family moved to Mount Vernon, where Sean attended Catholic schools. He graduated from Mount St. Michael Academy, in the Bronx.

Even as a boy, Combs was exceptionally driven. Although he has been called the "black Sinatra," his early role models were closer to the president of the 4-H club than to the coolest kid in school. "He came home one day and told me he wanted to start a paper route," his mother recalled when I went to see her at her apartment overlooking the Hudson. "That is how he started. He always wanted to work and make his money. We had a Cadillac car and a house, and he liked life like that," she told me. "Of course, he loves clothes. I do, too. I always made things nice in my house. I'm a fashionable-type person. My husband was a fantastic dresser. It seems to have worn off."

Combs attended Howard University — "the black Harvard," his mother called it. But he was obsessed with music, and was committed to a career as a producer. He begged Andre Harrell, who was then the president of Uptown Records and now runs Motown, for a job as an intern. Harrell didn't have much to lose — interns come free — and he was soon amazed by Puffy's capacity for work. Combs took the train from Washington to New York every week to work for Harrell; before long, he dropped out of Howard, moved into Harrell's house, and became the first (and last) teenage division head at Uptown. "I wanted to get my hustle on," Combs says. His decision to leave school still bothers his mother. "I really was so disappointed about that," Janice told me. "A person works day and night just to educate a kid, and to be able to have a roof over your head and a school uniform. He was a fine student, and when he left college it was hard for me."

Although newspapers like to run pictures of Combs on a jet ski in Saint-Tropez, most of the time if you want to find him you would have better luck calling his office at Bad Boy than checking out the club scene. But no hip-hop musician has successfully positioned himself as a workaholic with a Catholic education who grew up in the suburbs. So Combs found a way to be hipper than anyone as commercial as he is, and to be more commercial than anyone as hip. It has proved to be a remarkably successful formula in music and in clothing. Combs made a name for himself as an energetic club kid who danced in a couple of music videos; by the early nineties, when he was in his twenties, he was a cheerleader for the life of excess that characterized the time. It was an insane era that would see Yahoo! become worth more than General Motors.

From the start, Combs was criticized as a mediocre and derivative rapper. That assessment has not changed, although his 1997 record *No Way Out* sold more than seven million copies and won two Grammys. It is as a talent scout, packager, and creator of deals that he has met with true success. His first act, Jodeci, sold seven million records. Since then, Combs has produced the work of Mary J. Blige, Faith Evans, and many others. More important, though, he discovered Christopher Wallace, a former crack dealer who rapped as the Notorious B.I.G. By 1997, the year B.I.G. was murdered, his albums, *Ready to Die* and *Life After Death,* which drew a chilling, nihilistic portrait of life for an urban black man, had turned him into one of the seminal voices of the decade.

Combs's career has been punctuated by violence. In 1991, he and the rapper Heavy D, among others, promoted an AIDS benefit at City College; too many tickets were sold, there was a stampede, and nine people were crushed to death. In 1999, he and two others were arrested for beating a rival record-company executive in his offices at Interscope Records (with a chair, a telephone, and a champagne bottle). Although Combs was asked only to pay the executive a fine and take a one-day anger-management course, his image suffered badly, street toughs didn't respect him, and his middle-class fans were appalled. Then, just after midnight on December 27, 1999, Combs was involved in an incident at a Manhattan nightclub, in which three people were shot. He fled with Jennifer Lopez in a Lincoln Navigator, but he was arrested and charged with gun possession and attempting to bribe his driver into taking the rap for him. After seven weeks of testimony, covered by New York's press as if it were Watergate, Combs was acquitted of all charges. The verdict was broadcast live on the networks.

The lowest point of Combs's career, though, came after the death of his friend Biggie. Combs was depressed for months, and his mother told me that she had been worried for his life. When I asked Combs whether he felt that he had seen more than his share of violence, he said, "Nearly every black man faces an unacceptable level of violence in this society. I'm not different. Money can shield you; it can protect you. But it doesn't make you white." Eventually, Combs recovered. His tribute to Biggie, "I'll Be Missing You," a remake of an eighties hit by the Police, won a Grammy, and remained at the top of the charts for twenty-eight weeks. It became his signature song. It also helped inaugurate a commercial boom in hip-hop that lasted until the end of the nineties.

That boom is over. Last year, only two of the top twenty-five pop CDs were recorded by rappers: Ja Rule and Nelly. Neither ranked among the top fifteen albums. Hip-hop fashion has, of course, always been tied to the music market. In the early eighties, kids in baggy jeans started listening to Grandmaster Flash and spray-painting their signatures on subway cars. A few years later, in reaction to the emerging marriage of music and fashion, Run-DMC positioned themselves as anti-glamour authentics ("Calvin Klein's no friend of mine / don't want nobody's name on my behind"). Around that time, the clothing line FUBU — "For Us By Us" — was created, so that minority people could wear clothes designed by minorities. By the nineties, though, rappers like the Notorious B.I.G. had embraced the culture of brand names; even their socks bore labels. "I put my hoes in N.Y. onto DKNY, Miami, D.C., prefer Versace," Biggie rapped on "Hypnotize" in 1997. "Every cutie wit a booty want a Coogi."

Early hip-hop clothing lines were not much different from vanity license plates; they were mostly about promoting the image of the star, not about fashion, per se; you can see Russell Simmons's affection for argyle vests, for example, in Phat Farm, or the Wu-Tang

Clan's love of oversized T-shirts in Wu Wear. And, early on, Puffy sent sequins and lots of fur onto the runway. (Puffy loves fur; people still talk about his burgundy ostrich trench coat with the sheared-mink lining.)

If hip-hop music falters in the marketplace, will its fashion also be in danger? Several people told me that Combs was passé. "We don't listen to his music," a white Manhattan teenager who is a particular follower of rap told me. "And nobody I know would buy his clothes." One of New York's best-known fashion editors put it more baldly: "Oh, my God, Puffy is *sooo* two years ago."

But such criticism misses the point. Combs has never really wanted to be the hippest guy in the room; he wants to be the hippest *successful guy* in the room. He told me that his fashion and business idols are Ralph Lauren and Martha Stewart — two self-invented characters whose deft re-creations of America, real and imagined, have made their fortunes. "Those are the templates," he said. "When you look at what they have accomplished, it's magnificent." It is not surprising that he wants to leap out of the world of hip-hop, with its fetishization of Gucci and Fendi, and into the world of Ralph Lauren and Martha Stewart. "Here I think Puffy is very interesting," Kelefa Sanneh, who has written extensively about hip-hop and pop culture, told me. "You can see him shift away from the aspirational approach of the nineties. He is not a great rapper, or even a great producer. But he goes out and scoops up new beats and talent. In clothes, he seems to be doing the same thing. He is a mogul, and he is moving with the market."

Ralph Lauren and Martha Stewart are more than brands; they offer visions of the world. Where Lauren presents an ersatz interpretation of the suburban dream life, Stewart has turned the middle-class hearth and home into an industry. Puffy hopes to dignify the urban life and package it for people who may never have entered a city. He has managed to market his clothes to kids who are tutored for the ERBs and the SATs. He is becoming to the street what Ralph Lauren is to Waspiness and Martha Stewart is to the ideal of the American homemaker. And Combs's empire continues to grow as rapidly as ever. "The thing I love about Puff is that he comes back," his assistant Norma told me. "After B.I.G. died, people thought he would go right down the toilet — then he put out a number-one album. During the trial, Jennifer dumped him, they said his music career was over, he would be going to prison — and even if he got off he would be through. Well, guess what? He has a best-selling record, he's a happy father, his clothing company absolutely rocks. Puffy will always come back. He's like nature."

During his trial, Combs worked on his collection; most nights after court, he sat with Tweedy and the design team and sketched out ideas. He would talk through a notion, and the designers would attempt to translate it into patterns, which he would evaluate. He told me that he founded Sean John because the clothes he saw bored him. "I felt there was a total lack of something," he said. "Fashion was dull, dead. I thought maybe we could bring in some life."

He never saw the clothes he designed as solely an extension of his hip-hop persona; rather, he regards his place in hip-hop culture as a forum for selling clothes. One day not long ago, I walked around the Sean John boutique at Bloomingdale's. I saw clothes simple and sophisticated enough to please Jil Sander. When you first look at them, the clothes seem as if they belonged at Brooks Brothers or Paul Stuart. Then you notice the lavender and mustard cardigans, the shiny mother-of-pearl buttons, and the bold stitching on the coats. Sean John pants are sharply tailored, the textures are rich, and the buyers are often men in their thirties hoping to look cool.

Combs hired Jeffrey Tweedy, a former Ralph Lauren executive, as vice president of his company. Tweedy, a dapper black man who grew up in Washington, D.C., got his first job stocking clothes at Britches of Georgetown. He sees or talks to Combs three or four times a day. "I was a little leery at first," he told me. "I thought, Whoa, what did I need with a celebrity cat who wanted to start yet another label? But the more I talked to him the more I realized he was completely able to do this. He is totally involved, yet willing to let people do their jobs." Sean John is now sold in more than twelve hundred stores. The company, while not yet competitive with Tommy Hilfiger or Ralph Lauren, has easily surpassed its competitors in the urban fashion market, FUBU, Phat Farm, and Eckō.

"We design for a hip young guy," Tweedy told me. "Loves clothing, very stylish, and has a bit of disposable income — not for a teenager but for a man who aspires to wear Gucci one day and

Prada one day and to be able to afford the custom Zegna suits. Now, down the road we will try to develop a lifestyle brand. That's the goal."

As a fashion figure, Combs has transcended hip-hop completely. He has done more: Black fashion has been ripped off and reinterpreted for many years, and Combs has helped take it back from the Tommy Hilfigers of the world. "There is this clear dialectic — it's sort of like jazz," Kim Hastreiter, of *Paper,* told me. "White designers forever would go to 125th Street to see what was happening. That is where they got their inspiration, their cool. Then the blacks turned that upside down. They took the icons of the rich and suburban and blasted them. This is when sweatshirts with the word 'Harvard' printed on them a hundred times emerged; the ghetto was making fun of the suburbs, and if the suburbs were about Mercedeses then the kids in the ghetto would wear a necklace with the word 'Mercedes' in block capitals." After the most recent Sean John runway show, Hastreiter wrote, in *Paper,* "He threw *bling bling* out the window and sent out a low-key, gorgeous ready-to-wear collection. This stuff could stand up to anything, anywhere in the world today."

The company has moved deliberately but with apparent ease in the marketplace. Some fashion veterans are thrilled by its success and the attention it has brought the industry; others find it hard to believe that a man who doesn't know how to sew is considered a successful designer. But the significance of Sean John is no longer questioned. One day while I was in Paris, I ran into Richard Buckley, who is the editor of *Vogue Hommes International.* "I just got an e-mail from this writer who asked me who I thought mattered in men's clothes these days," Buckley told me. "I said the only man who is doing anything important is Puff Daddy. Right now, he is all we got."

The second night of his stay in Paris, Puff Daddy threw a bash at Les Bains Douches, the former municipal bath that has been among Paris's most popular clubs for more than a decade. The party could have been in Saint-Tropez, Newark, L.A., or East Hampton: the crowd, the food, the highly paid, artificially enhanced strippers disrobing on the bar, and the music. (In Paris, some of the women smoked Gauloises instead of Marlboro Lights.)

Men wear gray, and women wear black. They all carry tiny digital cameras and minuscule dual-band cell phones.

The party began around midnight, but there were many stops to make first. Puffy's days in Paris started late — he tended to go to bed about nine A.M. and sleep till early in the afternoon. If there was time, he would work out — he was traveling with a trainer, a stylist, and at least two personal assistants — before beginning to think about the evening's plans. (In New York, he sleeps about four hours a night, and makes only occasional visits to clubs.) This night, Anna Wintour was giving a party to celebrate the publication of a book by Grace Coddington, *Vogue*'s long-time creative director. Afterward, there was to be a dinner at Karl Lagerfeld's eighteenth-century mansion. Oddly, though Puffy had been invited, he was a no-show. I met him and his friends around eleven P.M. at a restaurant down the street from the Plaza Athénée. Usually chatty and solicitous, he was sulking. Norma had somehow marooned him at a restaurant where there was no 1800 tequila. By the time I showed up, she was working two cell phones, trying to repair the damage. She called the Hyatt, but it had none; she struck out at the Ritz, too. It was nearly midnight, and Puff's party was about to begin. Bijou Phillips, who was making a film in Luxembourg with Madeleine Stowe and had arrived in Paris that day, tried to help. "How do you say 'eight' in French?" she asked. "If we could just tell him the number in French, maybe he would have it." Combs had also just been made aware that he had forgotten to attend the Anna Wintour party. "How the fuck could something like that happen?" he asked Norma, who offered no excuses. She put her head in her hands, then ordered roses to be sent to Wintour's hotel. Wintour has been among Combs's most vigorous supporters, and he was beside himself at the notion that he might have offended her. In the middle of dinner, he decided to go to the bar of the Plaza Athénée, down the street, and abruptly got up and left.

The bar was crowded with debutantes, models, actors, and rock stars, most of them transplanted from Manhattan. "I'm with Puffy," Paris Hilton said to her friend Cornelia Guest. You could feel the thrill pass between them. (I had asked Norma if Puffy was, in fact, friendly with the Hilton sisters or the Miller girls. "Not friendly, exactly," she replied. "But there are really only two types of rich people — the ones who go out, and the ones who don't. The Hiltons

go out.") Suddenly, there was a brief confrontation at the bar. Na-
omi Campbell had just arrived, and she and Bijou Phillips were
calling each other names. Phillips bumped into Campbell, and
Campbell wheeled around and screamed, "I could knock you out,
Bijou." The word "bitch" bounced back and forth like a Ping-Pong
ball. There was some suggestion that Campbell, who is even more
unpleasant than she is alluring, had hit on Phillips's fiancé, Sean
Lennon, earlier in the summer. Combs, who has a gift for concilia-
tion that has served him well as a producer, walked over, put his
arm around Phillips, and gently pulled her away.

Black cars were lined up for blocks around Les Bains Douches by
the time Puffy arrived. The party was so crowded that even people
clutching invitations were having trouble getting in; the Hiltons
(accompanied by their parents), the Miller sisters, Ivana Trump,
Tom Ford, Mick Jagger, Eva Herzigova, Vin Diesel, and Bijou Phillips were all there. Jagger, sipping on a Heineken, looked rumpled.
Combs's principal action was to issue whistles to most of the people
in the house and to stand in a corner, stomp his feet, and clap
along with the writhing dancers. He ordered five bottles of Cristal,
four of Veuve Clicquot, two of Absolut, and two of 1800 tequila,
with enough Coke to wash it down. He was dressed casually, in
white linen without a jacket or tie. A diamond crucifix dangled
from his neck. Tom Ford was having a drink at the bar when we
entered. Puff started to walk over to him, then came back and
grabbed me by the wrist and pulled me along. "You got to come
with me for this, dawg," he said. As Combs approached, Ford held
out his hand, but Puff Daddy got down on his knees and started an
"I'm not worthy" wave at him. Ford laughed uncomfortably. "You
are my god," Combs told him. "I worship you."
    Hundreds of people had packed into the narrow old club. Puffy
and his crowd had sequestered themselves in a cordoned-off area
near the entrance. Everyone could see them, but only the chosen
could approach. The group consisted of Puffy, Kim Porter, the rest
of Puffy's visiting friends, Vin Diesel, the Hiltons, and Ivana
Trump. Not long after two A.M., Puff handed a whistle to Ivana, and
she spent much of the next hour blowing it. By that time, the
Hilton girls were on a tabletop, dancing. So was their mother,
Kathy. "I feel so bad for Paris," Bijou Phillips said as she watched

Kathy Hilton wriggling. "Can you imagine how mortified she is watching her own mother acting like that?" The DJ dedicated the Sheila E. song "The Glamorous Life" to Puff. "This is for P. Diddy," he said, using the most current version of his name. (During a particularly searching interview after Combs's trial last year, he announced that from now on he would be referred to not as Puff Daddy but as P. Diddy, which is what Biggie called him. He meant it partly as a joke. The next day, to his astonishment, the news was on the front page of the *Post.*) By four-thirty A.M., the party was winding down. Only the core group remained, dancing to Chaka Khan and some old Prince tunes. At about five, when it looked as though the evening might be over, Combs turned to me and said, "We are going to a strip club, and we are all going together." As soon as he finished speaking and climbed into his car, Norma turned to me and mouthed the words, "Totally off the record." Then we left.

After breezing by two bouncers, we descended through a tunnel with video screens in the floor and walls. Hip-hop music played in the background. Puffy took a seat next to the catwalk where the girls "work." He insisted that I sit next to him. "Let's do an interview," he said. It was five-fifteen A.M. and he finally felt relaxed enough to answer questions. Next to us, there was a spectacularly gifted woman at work. She had started off in a latex cat-woman suit but was now wearing only an elaborate mask, a G-string, and a pair of stilettos. "Look at this woman," Puffy said. "Jesus. Do you think she's French?" (He wanted to tip her, but he rarely carries money. He waved for Norma, but she was across the noisy room.) I reminded him that Norma had decreed that the trip was off the record. "Nothing in my life is off the record," he said. "I wish it was, but it isn't. Never has been." I asked if he enjoys his celebrity. "Of course," he said. "I hate rich people who complain about how tough it is being rich. They are insane. I pay, like, 50 percent taxes and I am very proud of that. I would happily pay more." I asked him if Sean John was as important to him as music, and if he got pleasure out of the clothes. "It's different from music. I don't mix the two. What I do mix is lifestyle. I am making a lifestyle, and it's part of entertainment. This just seems to be an obvious expression of who I am."

"Does the clothing line need to make money for you to be satisfied with it?" I asked.

"Fuck, yes," he said, taken aback by the question. "I want people to know how serious we are and what we are capable of doing. And I want to be known as a businessman who made something better, made my people happy, and had some fun."

It was past dawn, nearly six A.M. "How did you feel about Jennifer Lopez leaving you the way she did?" I asked. Lopez had left him in the midst of the trial after the nightclub shooting, when it seemed as if his musical empire, along with his self-made persona, were about to come crashing down. "Well, you know, I wish her the best in her life. I always have," he said. "But . . ." His voice trailed off. "Look, if she is happy, then I am happy for her." One of his friends had been listening. "Disloyal bitch," the friend said. "She's nothing but a disloyal bitch."

The following night, Puffy was invited to a small gathering at Karl Lagerfeld's mansion. Norma made sure he didn't forget this party. "Go," she told him. "Just get up and go." We were having a late dinner (with Puffy, there is no other kind) in the Buddha Bar, around the corner from the Hotel Crillon, and, as Combs and Porter were leaving, he decided to buy her some Buddha Bar souvenirs. (In recent months, Combs and Porter have spent considerable time together. When I asked him about it, he said, "I don't really know where it will go.") He dropped the souvenirs on the counter and spelled out the name "N-O-R-M-A" to the woman behind the register. Then he placed an international cell-phone call to Norma — who was finishing her dinner about a hundred feet away — and told her to pick up Porter's gifts when she was done. Puffy was in an expansive mood as his limousine sped through the nearly empty streets of Paris. "This city is so fly," he said. "Look at the clocks and the windows and the lights. And those little Smart cars. Even the buses are cool. Can you find a speck of dirt or any garbage on the ground? It's amazing. These people have the food, the clothes, the love. This city is just mad beautiful."

Lagerfeld's home is in the Sixth Arrondissement, a neighborhood inhabited mostly by rich businessmen and diplomats. His house looked as if it could have served as a pied-a-terre for the Sun King. Occupying twenty acres or so, the *hôtel particulier* — as the French call such immense city houses — had been lavishly restored over the previous decade to its pre-Revolutionary opulence. A pe-

tite woman, dressed in Chanel, opened the door onto a grand hall-
way where about a dozen people stood talking and smoking cigarettes. Butlers served champagne. The scene looked like a Ralph
Lauren ad, down to the women in flowing dresses and chignons,
and the sockless men in tuxedos. Pink buds — mainly freesias and
roses — lined the hall and the main salon. The only thing missing
was a golden retriever.

Lagerfeld was completing a late-night fashion shoot. Models
whose clothes were too cumbersome to permit them to move un-
aided were led down a grand marble staircase by walkers, like Thor-
oughbreds being taken to the gate at the Kentucky Derby. The ball
gowns were cut from sheets of silk, lace, and tulle. Several women
wore masks. A chandelier draped in pink silk dominated the salon.
One of the models, in a black hat that was five feet wide, required
two men to guide her, one on each side of the hat. A samba band
played briskly while Lagerfeld snapped pictures; every ten minutes
or so, an assistant would transfer what he had recorded to a powerful computer in the next room. Puff and Kim looked on in amaze-
ment. Lagerfeld seemed pleased to have Puffy in his house — but
wasn't quite sure what to do with him. "Let's take a tour," he said.
And they proceeded to stroll upstairs, where the models were getting dressed. "Good evening, girls," Puffy said politely — before
snapping some Polaroids of himself and Porter in the scene. "I
hope we are not interrupting."

It isn't easy to get Puff Daddy to leave a party, but his friends were
bored, and they weren't mixing with many of the other guests.
Kim grabbed Puffy and dragged him toward the car. The Hiltons
and the Millers and several of their friends needed a ride to the
next stop — a birthday party at a club called Cantina. None of the
women had a car, so they started to pile in with us, and there just
wasn't room. "Wait," Puffy's stylist, a no-nonsense black woman,
yelled. "Them bitches be heiresses. Blond Something von Furstenberg and Hiltons and shit. What are we now, a fucking limo service?
They got to be getting their own damn cars."

Combs had many supporters at the Council of Fashion Designers
of America award ceremonies — the fashion world's equivalent of
the Oscars — this year. Anna Wintour told me that she was rooting
for him, and so did the fashion editors of other magazines. The cer-

emony was held in the Celeste Bartos Forum of the New York Public Library. By seven P.M., limousines had started to pull up to the covered runway on Fifth Avenue. Penélope Cruz accompanied Ralph Lauren; Lauren Hutton came next. Puffy was with his mother, Jeff Tweedy, and several members of the Sean John design team. He was the last nominee to arrive. He was dressed conservatively: a simple diamond earring in each ear, the canary-yellow pinkie ring, and a subtly patterned black suit. His mother was more elaborately attired: She wore black stiletto slippers, diamond hoop earrings, and a variety of amulets. Her blond hair dangled over bare shoulders. They posed together on the red carpet. "Janice, are you proud of your boy?" a television reporter asked. "Yes, I am always proud of Sean," she replied.

By the time they swept into the front hall, it was almost empty. Puff strolled through, working his two-way pager and occasionally taking a phone call. Ralph Lauren came out to say hello and Calvin Klein wandered over to tell Janice how lovely she looked. I asked Puffy if he was nervous. We were standing beneath blowups of Jackie Kennedy, Oleg Cassini, and Audrey Hepburn. "No," he replied. "Why be nervous about what you can't control?"

It wasn't until after eleven P.M. that Alan Rickman presented the award for men's fashion. Puffy stopped sending e-mail and making phone calls. After a brief video display of each man's work, Rickman announced that the award would go to Marc Jacobs. Puffy applauded loudly, smiled at everyone, and then picked up his phone. Tweedy sighed. When we got up to leave, I asked Combs how he felt about losing. He shrugged. "Hey, I didn't lose," he said. "I was nominated. I am just getting started."

HANK STUEVER

Just One Word: Plastic

FROM *The Washington Post Magazine*

DEBT IS SO AMERICAN that even the Pilgrims got here with it. (Someone else's money, someone else's boat.)

Think of their stuff, the things they had to have: the chairs and linens and kettles lashed together in the leaky hull, assembled from some Pier 1 or Bed Bath & Beyond shopping spree of the day. Think of those few dreamers scraping to shore, only to realize they had to send back credit payments, in the form of pelts, which hardly ever made it to the banks, because there were pirates, and no 800 number to call and explain any of this to a customer service rep. Some years later, on a depressing afternoon, I wandered around a J. Crew store and put a brownish gray-flecked ribbed cotton turtleneck on my MBNA America MasterCard, ignoring the faint whispers of a thousand dead Puritans telling me not to. The charge was $55.87.

At that time I was twenty-seven years old and owed, on that card, a total of $2,011 (it would go higher), with no real plan of how to pay it back. "Wow, it's not even payday," a friend remarked. (This was the frugal friend: saver of money and planet, wearer of wool socks with sandals; he who rinsed out used Ziploc bags and hung them out to dry, until his housemates begged him not to.)

I told him I put the sweater on my credit card.

"Do you know how much you'll wind up paying for it by the time you pay it off?" he asked. Not a question so much as a lecture on usury, and not an answer from me so much as a shopaholic credo: "Well, do you know what kind of day I had? Do you know what would happen if I was in a car wreck on the way home, and was lying on the asphalt there, bleeding to death? I'd be mad at myself for not buying the sweater. That's the kind of day I had."

And on some level I believed it, believed in the power of my own consumer disconnect from reality. It's always a slow death on some metaphorical, financial asphalt — the rent, the mortgage, the car payment, the college loans, the doctor, to say nothing of our little wants and desires. The playthings, the pretty things. The Federal Reserve did the math about four years ago, concluding that the national savings rate had slipped below zero, that every penny earned was now owed somewhere, and then some.

But we are collectively deaf to such equations: In late 2001, American households kept an average of six credit cards, carrying a total average balance that one survey calculated at $8,562.

In a rare, horrified examination of the practical, I did my own math last year. By that point, my credit card balances floated around me like dirigibles in some modern dystopian fantasia: $13,774 was the total. Consider that *one* J. Crew sweater: It worked out to about $93, with interest, by the time I wrote all those monthly checks and mailed them away — always to Wilmington, Delaware, a place I regarded only in the abstract.

Wilmington.

Giant post-office boxes in Wilmington.

Here was a no place that to me had become a symbol of all that made us weak and all that made us tick. The monthly cycle of it, the endless spinning of all that revolving debt: revolve, revolve, revolve, and never resolve.

Plastic Paradise

We owe our souls to Wilmington, in the form of monthly credit card bills. To me, Wilmington could have been either Oz or Babylon or neither; it was forty million miles away. Then one day I missed the exit for the New Jersey Turnpike, and realized I'd off-ramped to Plastic Town itself, that Wilmington is in fact a place, and it is only ninety-eight miles away.

I wanted to see the sorting of all those millions of payment envelopes that all those millions of people (you, me, everybody) mail each month to Wilmington, where the credit card giants enjoyed profits last year in the hundreds of millions of dollars, helped by

Delaware's bank-friendly breaks on taxes and a law that removed the limits on how much interest the banks can charge credit card customers. But even with all those interest payments flowing in, almost a third of last year's credit card profits were gained by penalizing customers (sometimes you, sometimes me, always somebody) for not paying their bill on time.

All those stamps licked, and fingers crossed, all that deferring of American dreams — what does it look like on the receiving end? I wanted to see wide grids of gray cubicles, and heaps of envelopes headed through an endless maze, processed day and night, all week, all year; to see how the checks are cashed; to see the granting of momentary waivers of the $35 late fee to customers who call, toll-free, and confess the right kind of sin in the right kind of way. I had a hunch that human beings might be involved in this, which would make the nation's $660 billion in consumer credit debt seem somehow less . . . monstrous.

At MBNA America, the nation's second-largest issuer of credit cards, the walls and floors of its many offices across Wilmington and surrounding New Castle County are emblazoned with the bank's stern variation on the golden rule ("Think of Yourself as a Customer"), and most of the mail is initially read by a machine. It can automatically see through the envelopes and sniff out the account numbers, and is able to render automatic decisions about lateness, down to egregious fractions of a minute.

My efforts to see any of this — much less actual human beings — would mostly be in vain. Each time I called MBNA, First USA, and some of the other larger banks, they were cool to the notion that anyone would want to see how it works. The more follow-up calls I made — some of which I conducted with a happy, childlike curiosity, some of which I conducted with stern business manners, others of which I placed out of a kind of sick determination — the more they ignored me. As weeks dragged on, even my most basic questions about life in Plastic Town were greeted with suspicion or a stony silence.

Still, I kept driving back and forth to Wilmington, where you can feel the presence of the banks in an almost Stepford sense of cheerful convention. It's the same feeling you have listening to the music that plays when the credit card company puts you on hold.

The tallish buildings unmesmerizingly cast shadows on the quiet downtown streets, where less-upwardly-mobile-seeming Wilmingtonians wait at bus stops for buses that seem to rarely come. The banks are bound together along King and Market streets, cool and inert, not unlike my own credit cards, which I had wrapped in foil and again in plastic, then trapped in a block of ice in a Tupperware container sealed with duct tape, and then hid behind a Healthy Choice supreme French bread pizza, all the way at the back of my freezer.

Now I have liberated them — a temporary parole — and brought them to Wilmington.

The banking business is now Delaware's largest industry, employing about thirty-five thousand people. Eight of the nation's ten largest credit card issuers are based in Wilmington, including four of the top five — MBNA, BankOne/First USA, Citibank, and J. P. Morgan Chase. Hundreds of other companies, and nearly 60 percent of Fortune 500 companies, are incorporated — for tax purposes — right here in Wilmington. (It so happens The Washington Post Co. is incorporated in Wilmington, too.)

"A Wilmington address, we've found, is a status symbol in the business world," says the avuncularly candid, hunch-shouldered mayor, James M. Baker. "The opportunity for any business here is just too good to ignore." He is standing in the lobby of the eighty-nine-year-old Hotel du Pont, where the city recently arranged a sort of daylong skirt-hitching in the ornate Gold Ballroom for several dozen business owners considering a relocation to Wilmington.

The afternoon includes much Power Point presenting of Delaware's devotion to good capitalism; tax breaks, especially from the city, abound. There is a touting of the city's effort to resurrect its urban riverfront and make it funky, which thus far has meant some brewpubs, condo lofts in old warehouses, a baseball stadium for the Class A Wilmington Blue Rocks, an outlet mall, and the First USA Riverfront Arts Center. Finally, there is a video of schoolchildren using computers — the business world's universal symbol of progress.

"These companies come and they bring their money," Baker says, and this seems to be the mutual grease that lubricates Wilmington: the constant pursuit of, movement of, management of, rolling in, charging interest upon, issuing court rulings about, drawing up contracts on . . . money. There are rich people any-where, but there aren't many places in America where you can stand still and actually feel as if a Busby Berkeley number is about to break out, a big song and dance about the glory of the dollar. Maybe Wall Street. Maybe here.

A Real Charge

> Mr. du Pont also invited us to come to his house, "Swamp Hall," on Halloween night. He always had a large bag of dimes and nickels and he threw them up in the air and watched us scramble for them . . .
> — From *The Workers' World at Hagley*, oral histories of nineteenth-century life at the DuPont Co.'s gunpowder mills on Brandywine Creek near Wilmington

Along Brandywine Creek, on a late-April afternoon, another sump-tuous Wilmington spring is coming into bloom. Teenagers wave and flash happily bratty smiles from their cars. Traffic sails along through the neighborhoods surrounding the city, past colonial-style homes, many of them actually colonial, or close to it. Parks and golf courses undulate seductively. Even the strip malls seem cute; one, in Greenville, has four bank branches in it.

Wilmington's loyalty to MBNA, BankOne/First USA, J. P. Mor-gan Chase, Citibank, Discover, Juniper, Household, and the other credit card companies exists only in part because the banks have brought the local economy back from the brink, lowered the state income tax, and helped shield residents from both property and sales taxes. There is also a longer tradition of gentle submission to power in the First State.

"It's always been a company town," says Carol Hoffecker, a his-tory professor at the University of Delaware.

"It was a mill town first, then powder with the du Pont family, then chemicals with the DuPont Co. and Hercules and Atlas. Now it's the banks. Just as DuPont saved the city's bacon a century ago, it's the banks that have moved in to take up the slack." The corpo-rations came after the state's passage of the Financial Center Devel-opment Act in 1981, promoted by then-Governor Pierre S. "Pete" du Pont. (Who reflected on it, twenty years later, for the *Wilmington News Journal:* "It's hard to say this was going to change Delaware for-ever. Darned if it didn't work."

The city itself is smallish — about ten miles across at its widest —

and has to it the great middle grade of Eastern Seaboard dullness, a town that is driven through more than driven to. Wilmington is the crucial fork where travelers have to decide: Keep with I-95 to Philly? Or take the Jersey Turnpike to New York?

If you do exit at Wilmington, you are greeted by a cheerful row of patriotic billboards with credit card logos on them, and depending on which way you turn, you will either wind up in corporateville or something a little more gritty and depressed; in one block you come upon the city's bona fide Little Italy, with restaurants, barbers, and pastry shops; in still another block you reflexively lock your doors. If you skip the Delaware Memorial Bridge into New Jersey and stick to I-495, you pass the smokestacks of DuPont and the Port of Wilmington, where everything from European cars and Canadian timber to Indian hemp and Argentine beef is unloaded daily.

Hoffecker wonders if the banks, for all their financial prowess, will ever make the city feel like a city, the way the industries of yesteryear did: "It's been a boost to the heart of the city," she says. "But at the same time they've done things to seal themselves off. You drive to work in one of those places, you park in their facility, at lunch you go eat in their cafeteria, at the end of the day you drive away. You never see anybody around, they're all in those buildings, making their phone calls and adding up their figures and doing whatever else it is that they do in there. They do volunteer work, but they never interact with the community in the old-fashioned sense of walking on the streets. There's a deadness . . . which seems odd, when you think there's so many thousands of workers down there every day."

In many ways, modern Wilmington owes its soul to the company store much as its ancestors relied on the du Ponts. The difference is that the romance of the du Pont days is woven into history, and always on view: The Brandywine mill yards and mansions are now museums and research centers; the hotel is a living monument to a bygone era; the lobby of the DuPont Co. invites visitors in with exhibits extolling the invention of Nylon and Teflon; banners celebrating DuPont's bicentennial currently hang from the city light poles.

The credit card banks, on the other hand, do everything they can to downplay their presence, proffering no narrative of their history, no dynastic family tree, evincing no connective tissue between the financial organs and the rest of the communal body. It's possible to imagine a future Wilmington museum with a bank's name on it — MBNA's chairman, Charles Cawley, has amassed an impressive collection of Wyeths — but hard to imagine a museum that is *about* the banks, explores the story of the state and credit cards. It doesn't seem that anyone will ever know the whole story, or want to tell it. "I doubt if anyone would visit a *museum* about credit cards," laughs Jim Stewart, president of Juniper, a Wilmington-based credit card bank started in 2000.

I have lain awake enough nights worrying about my credit card bills that I would be happy to visit a museum about them. (I think it should include an exhibit of a late-twentieth-century American lying in bed, feeling a buzzing in the bones, a trickle of sweat, a throbbing sense of dread. I think there should be a checkbook, and Chase and First USA payment envelopes spread out on the circa-1996 Pottery Barn night table next to the bed. I think a Sony Dream Machine digital clock should continually flash 3:17 A.M. I think there should also be a bottle of Tylenol PM.)

The lobby of MBNA's headquarters, half a block down from the Hotel du Pont, has a 1932 Duesenberg car parked in the middle of it, but the security guard wouldn't let me in to see it, and I wasn't really clear on what the car meant to the company, or the company meant to the car. It appears to simply symbolize luxury.

The guard did let me crane my neck to look at the Duesenberg through the locked glass lobby door, but only for two minutes. I was squinting, trying to read the MBNA manifesto stenciled on the wall behind the car. I saw all the keywords about customers and trust and success and teamwork. It occurred to me that I am a customer, who once carried a balance of $5,862 on his MBNA card, and had just mailed in a nice little $400 payment toward the $1,063 current balance (at 14.9 percent) three days before the due date, and yet I was not to be trusted to look at the car.

Around town, MBNA is known as "the Firm" or "the brotherhood" by the affectionately jaded, inspiring a happy silence and loyalty in its 10,500 employees, and providing a bounty of conspiracy theories for the so inclined.

Charles Cawley, the company's sixty-one-year-old chairman and CEO, occupies the mythic space in Wilmington once reserved for the descendants of Eleuthère Irénée du Pont: The richest man in town, Cawley is seldom seen by everyday Wilmingtonians.

The rewards of working for the Firm are considerable for the company's executives (there are four MBNA yachts and sport boats — the *Affinity,* the *Impatience,* the *So Far So Good,* and the *Deliverance* — and a company country club west of town, and a corporate jet or two).

"The credit card business grew dramatically in the late 1980s, and it brought with it a lot of highly paid executives, a lot of success, a lot of wealth," says Jim Stewart, the Juniper president, who was an executive vice president at First USA as the industry boomed. "There were two distinct cultures. One . . . was First USA, and I'm biased because I worked there, but I would say it was more informal. We were one of the early companies to go casual, to not take ourselves too too seriously. The other was MBNA, which was very formal. The suits and ties and lapel pins, and people living in lock step — there was a real cultlike image. I lived in a nice neighborhood, and I remember when Cawley renovated his house in a way such as Wilmington had never seen before. Then he moved to a nicer neighborhood and did twenty times the renovation job he'd done before. And other MBNA executives moved there with him. Eventually twenty-five or thirty houses in the same neighborhood were all MBNA."

Fight Club, a broodingly violent 1999 satire by filmmaker David Fincher, appears to take place in MBNA's Wilmington, if you look carefully: The movie's protagonist narrator, played by Edward Norton, works for a monolithic financial company and furnishes his apartment with stylish catalogue furniture that he charges to his plastic. He has a Wilmington Zip Code, and there's a sign near his high-rise apartment that echoes the city's motto: "A Place to Be Somebody." (Those signs have a way of popping up in Wilmington's less-affluent neighborhoods.) He turns to violence when he comes under the spell of Brad Pitt's manic soap salesman, who introduces him to the clandestine Fight Club, where men beat each other senseless as a response to the numbness they feel living in an empty, consumeristic culture.

By the movie's end, the narrator learns that his Fight Club is a hallucination; and as a metaphoric and tragic finale, he blows the skyscrapers of this pseudo-Wilmington to smithereens. It's not a bad movie for anyone who ever had credit card debt and entertained notions of an Armageddon that would set the people free.

"Wilmingtonland"

Wilmington hinges on the great lie that you can have it all.

The lie isn't always bad. It's a benign kind of lie, transmitted all the time, such as the way Monica and Rachel are able to afford and furnish that big Manhattan apartment, when obviously they cannot. ("Why are you in debt?" a counselor asked me once, in therapy, back in the nineties, when everyone told one another about how much money they were making in the stock market. "Friends," I answered, but I meant the TV show.)

Robert D. Manning, a forty-four-year-old economic sociologist at the Rochester Institute of Technology, is the author of *Credit Card Nation: The Consequences of America's Addiction to Credit,* and he is a man so convinced of his role as the bane of the banks that he believes J. P. Morgan Chase keeps tabs on his media appearances, speaking engagements, and testimony before lawmakers. He is only too happy to pinprick the final few bubbles of my plastic sitcom fantasy world.

"In a way, we all live in 'Wilmingtonland,'" Manning says. "Wilmingtonland is that place of a completely different logic. It's the embodiment of the credit card society: Everything's okay, 'Just do it,' don't ask questions, have it now, pay for it later. MBNA has created a wonderful life, where people come to work for them and become completely devoted and compliant to the company. It's an upper-middle-class wonderland, where you never see the Wizard of Oz behind the curtain . . . The banks are charitable, their employees do a lot of volunteer work, they give a lot of money to programs . . . It's very strategic, how the banks leave an imprint on the community, so that no one can be critical of them."

Last year, a group of University of Delaware students began questioning MBNA's "affinity"-card marketing arrangement with the alumni association. (Affinity cards have been a boon to the industry. You can now have a card emblazoned with any allegiance you choose, and a promise of financial support going to your cause for every dollar you charge. There are affinity cards for universities, the National Rifle Association, the Sierra Club. There is a Martina Navratilova card for gay and lesbian causes. There are also affinity cards for Trekkies, rock groups, soda pops.)

When Delaware students protested MBNA's influence on their

campus, Manning says, there was immediate pressure from campus officials to quash the growing vibe of dissent. Two new campus buildings are named after the bank; graduates clamor to work there.

Campus affinity-card agreements, Manning believes, prey on college-age kids who aren't fiscally prepared to have credit cards. The average American undergrad who has a credit card now carries about $2,000 in high-interest debt, he says, usually on a card with the school mascot, which is marketed to him or her at freshman orientation. "There are people in Delaware who think it's okay for college students to have $5,000 or $10,000 in credit card debt by the time they graduate, on top of their college loans," he says. "They say, 'It's good for them to have debt. They're at the beginning of their earning cycle.' I hear this all the time in Wilmingtonland. It's this presumption that debt is good for all of us."

Consumer spending is the last way you can feel like an American with any sway in the national outcome: Every November, consumers are reminded that if we don't spend enough money at Christmas, the economy suffers, and so we rally to the cause. Last year, when the government gave each of us a $300 rebate, the plan came to be seen as a failure because too many people used it to pay off debts, rather than take it to the mall. Spending ourselves into a hole is seen as a path to economic glory.

Wilmingtonians see their communal salvation in the banks. There are perks down-totem, too: Last year, every MBNA employee got an extra week of vacation because profits were so high.

Grousers and crusaders are few, but they exist: "Needless to say, MBNA is a cult, and I loathed my job," griped an anonymous poster to a Web site titled "MBNA Credit Card: Money, Power, Influence and Greed."

"I felt bad calling people and demanding money, being a total jerk on the phone," said the e-mail. "This 'attitude' that I had to have working in collections fell into my regular life outside of work and I just became a total arse. That's horrible. I'm not a mean person, I'm a very caring person, and this, in turn, bummed me out big time. I worked there for about a year . . ."

Ted Keller, who is chairman of the Citizens Coalition for Tax Reform, is a lifelong Delaware resident and spent his career at DuPont, retiring in 1979. He is a strident voice against the tax breaks given to the banks and the power they hold over his community: "They pay a hideously low tax rate," Keller says. "Whenever you try to bring up the issue of fair taxes on these banks, all I hear is, 'Oh, no, because then they'll leave and we'll lose all the jobs.'"

Keller is eighty-one now, and had triple-bypass surgery last year. The Citizens Coalition doesn't seem to have amassed many citizens into much of a coalition. Most of the research and letter-writing is done from Keller's kitchen table, and when he's looking for a certain newspaper clipping he calls out to his wife. The first time I talked to him, he immediately faxed me several pages of Delaware tax law (with his own typewritten marginalia), demonstrating his crusade to change the Financial Center Development Act, which allows banks to pay less than 2 percent in state taxes on most of their profits, and lets them set whatever consumer interest rates they like.

In 1999, for example, MBNA paid — according to Keller's kitchen table, and the company's own reports — $23.6 million in state income taxes, or less than 1.5 percent. Keller thinks it should have been more like 8.7 percent (the initial Delaware tax rate on corporation profits under $20 million), which would have made MBNA's state tax bill in the vicinity of $142 million.

Keller happens to own a few shares of MBNA stock, just so he can attend the annual meeting and politely raise some hell. "People say, oh, that Ted Keller, all he talks about are the banks. Well, when this sort of crap is going on, it's all I can talk about," he acknowledges. "I know a lot of low-income people who are suffering because of this industry. Predatory interest rates are knocking the hell out of us, and it all happens right here in Delaware."

In a stack somewhere, he has a yellowed clipping of an article about the rise of Delaware's tax laws, in which he was interviewed, the only critic. He paws around and looks for it in vain, but he remembers the first line:

"It said, 'Ted Keller is the loneliest man in Delaware.'"

It seems he still is.

The Pit

"The charm of Wilmington," a local told me, "isn't so apparent if you're just seeing it from your car." But for days I drove in it, across it, and around it and found an elusive charm all its own, up and down the hilly routes that snake through New Castle County.

Wilmington proper has a population of just 72,664; the surrounding towns and suburbs, where most of the middle and upper classes live, number half a million. The demographics are plain: 58 percent of the urban residents are black; in the burbs of New Castle, 73 percent are white. "Who lives in all the mansions, is what I want to know," says a waitress at a Howard Johnson's on the Concord Pike. (Answer: bankers, corporate attorneys, scientists.)

Meanwhile, back up, turn around: That's an actual Howard Johnson's, an actual talkative waitress. Already, it's a time-warp heaven. Wilmington continually reveals to me a leftover Tee-Vee America feeling that is hard to resist. Sometimes it's 1946, then 1976, then 1956. Farther down the pike, there's a stereo shop called Hi Fi House, and a Taco Bell so overlooked by the chain's branding police that it still has the Alamo façade, with the old, dancing sombrero logo out front. Certain Delawareans have ancient black-and-white car license plates, which aren't purchased, but inherited from one generation to the next. Certain Delawareans have outdated hair; the mullet count is impressive.

There's the Charcoal Pit restaurant — four locations, but the original 1956 Pit is on the Concord Pike — with its pink neon sign and an *American Graffiti* shabbiness, with desserts on the back page of the menu named after mascots from local high schools: the Hornet, the Spartan, the Bulldog, all of them involving four enormous scoops of ice cream, covered in fruity-chocolate goo. I want to have a date here, with the quarterback and the cheerleader. I want all three of us to share straws. I am lost in an interlude, and the waitress asks me if I'm going to finish my malt in its frosty metal tumbler: "It's melting," she observes.

The Charcoal Pit, and I love the place for this, does not accept credit cards.

Consumption Lessons

Here is Mary Rammel, with her orange-handled scissors.

Rammel is wearing a burgundy pantsuit. She has blond hair flecked with gray, and sympathetic blue eyes, and speaks with the enchanting long *o*'s that denote Delaware: *moast, thoase, hoame.* She is a branch manager of Consumer Credit Counseling Service, a nonprofit agency in the suburbs of Wilmington that tries to help people get out of debt. Her office overlooks a Shell gas station and a busy intersection. The office used to have a staff, but now it's just her, because of budget cuts. (Credit card banks, which used to fund programs like CCCS, have cut their support by more than half in the last three years, while at the same time lobbying Congress to toughen restrictions on Chapter 7 bankruptcy by consumers.)

Rammel sees six or so clients a day, and they're always desperate. "They always ask me, 'Is this the worst debt you've ever seen?'" she says. "I always tell them I've seen worse. And I almost always have."

This morning it was a married couple in their eighties, with a fixed income of about $2,000 a month, a second mortgage, and $62,000 in credit card debt. After hearing their story, and laying out a game plan for them, she took her scissors and cut up their cards, and put them in a large plastic jug where she collects the plastic — enough shards now to start a mosaic in a small basilica — Our Lady of Perpetual Indebtedness. She has filled four jugs. "At first I put them in this little candy jar," she says, pointing to a small glass jar on the windowsill.

That was when she started debt counseling in 1988. Up until then, Rammel had worked at a bank in Dover, approving credit loans. Some applicants looked iffy to her. "Some of these people should not have been given credit. You could just see they wouldn't be able to afford it, but my boss came back to me and said, 'Mary, the form says "pre-approved,"' so I had to approve them."

This is what led her to a job so wildly off-message from the credit card empires of Wilmington that she is reminded of the conflict almost every time she cuts one up.

On her office wall, she has a poster of Norman Rockwell's multiethnic portrayal of the golden rule, but unlike MBNA's motto, it's the actual golden rule — "Do unto others as you would have them do unto you." In the back yard of some of the world's richest banks, Rammel has counseled the poor and the rich. She has seen telemarketers who were broke, and fry cooks, teachers, nurses. Also accountants, lawyers, surgeons.

People have told her that credit cards are good for Wilmington. "You know, it's touchy," she says. "I've thought of this many times — what if everyone paid off the balance on their credit cards? It would be wonderful, and bad for Wilmington. People have said to me, even when they can't pay their bills every month, 'Mary, a little debt is good. It helps all of us.'"

Not infrequently, the people who seek Rammel's help are employed at the credit card banks. They are people whose days are spent talking to the rest of America, trying to collect overdue bills, or processing all those late checks written for the minimum monthly payment on thousands of dollars of outstanding balance. Even then, the message did not sink in: "They come in and tell me how they, of all people, should have known better," she says. "I must say, it's a very humanizing experience for them. It's one thing to know what happens to people who spend more than they can afford. It's another thing to have it happen to you."

A woman came in with her five-year-old daughter, who fidgeted through the one-hour session. The woman proffered her plastic, and Rammel got out the scissors. The little girl, Rammel recalls, "jumped up out her chair, and started screaming, 'Don't you cut up my mommy's credit cards! She won't be able to buy me nothing!'"

She smiles. "Obviously in that case there was some education to be done . . . not only for the consumer, but for her child, too."

A Lot of 'Splaining

On a morning when I wasn't getting anywhere in Wilmington, I pointed the car back toward home, and wound up in the offices of Myvesta, a private debt-counseling firm in a labyrinthine Rockville office park, which helps clients devise a plan and stick to it. It's the Jenny Craig of debt reduction, with a popular series of books, outreach programs, and a weekly syndicated radio show. The office is located a floor above one of those corporations where the human genome is dissected.

Myvesta's co-founder, Steve Rhode, a gentle, wisecracking forty-one-year-old (who reminds me a little of George Costanza from *Seinfeld*), had spent part of his day reading the daily confessions of hopelessly lost credit card citizens. On the company's Web site, Myvesta.org, there is a field where visitors can anonymously "confess" their debt situations. No one ever sees what they type, except Rhode, and he has no way of responding to the confessor.

Myvesta is all about the catharsis of paying off debt. Its programs have a friendly, twelve-step, pop-psychological feel. Rhode and Myvesta's other founder, Mike Kidwell, have nothing against the credit card companies. The problem, according to their message, is us. "No one forces you to take the bank's money," Rhode says. "The first step is always admitting that you got yourself into this mess." He's staged it out, like the grieving process — depression, anger, resolve, etc.

He's been there, too, having stupendously driven himself into bankruptcy in 1990, mostly with credit cards. He emerged a changed man (but a human nonetheless, who still carries plastic). Now he deals with the castaways of consumer culture. One recent client came to him with $1 million in plastic debt.

He has printed out one of the morning's confessions. He won't let me quote from it, but it's depressing. It's from a woman with a shopping problem that she is hiding from her friends and family. She is worried that her teenager will be disgraced because she can't buy him a car. However misaligned her priorities are, Rhode absorbs the hurt she's feeling. "I want to scream," he says, rattling the paper, 'Come in! Come see me! I can help you!'"

He would like to take her for a walk. Just around the office park, out past the golf driving range he can see from the window. Just a breath of fresh air. "So many times I just want to tell people, come walk with me. Let me show you life. Life is free. Life is something you can afford. Everything you're putting on credit cards is something you can't afford."

Leaving Myvesta, I notice that it is Steve Rhode who has started curating that museum to America's credit card problems: In glass cases near the lobby, he has nineteenth-century ledger books of shop owners showing who owed what to whom. He has eighteenth-century documents showing how the Revolutionary War was paid for on credit. (And how one of the men who financed it wound up in debtors' prison.)

He has mid-twentieth-century department store charge plates — "charge-a-cards" — and gasoline cards, and the little jeweled cases that customers carried them around in. The plates are tiny and look like dog tags, the kind Ricky Ricardo used to keep away from Lucy. (The moral was always the same on *I Love Lucy:* If there's trouble to get into, Lucy will. And isn't America much like Lucy, up to its neck in impulse, laughing even as it sobs in exasperation?)

Debt, the Musical

One early evening in the middle of April — near the end of a bizarrely unseasonal 95-degree day, on one of my last trips to Wilmington — I walked all the way around MBNA's four, beigey-blah, interconnected green-awninged buildings, where I saw nothing, and nobody; I looped around the Chase building, too, and then walked seven blocks down toward the Christina River, to ponder First USA's buildings. This is a lot of concrete and empty plazas and walkways. I wished for a skateboard, and the gumption to ride it.

The emptiness here left me wishing I could write a song about credit card problems. We talk about so much as a nation — we talk about war, we talk about politics, we talk a lot about our sex lives. We talk fashion, we talk shopping, we talk frequent flier miles, we talk techno, we talk box-office receipts. Only a real friend will tell you about his debt. Only a real friend would listen.

For everything else, there is MasterCard. (It's become the national prayer.)

And so I want to set the next paragraph to music:

Oh, fair Wilmington, with your seductive corporate tax laws, and your ironclad Court of Chancery rulings on the art of doing business, and your pretty trees, I sing of thee: So many years have I mailed those little envelopes to you, even when I lived thousands of miles away in crappy little apartments, hoping you got them on time, hoping you would keep giving me that which I could never afford. Did you love me back? Tell me now, baby. Tell me you did.

Silence.

Money is, in the end, so very quiet.

My proverbial money ship never came in, but I scraped to the other shore anyhow. Early next year, if things go according to plan (not that things ever go according to plan), I will pay off the last of my plastic debt to Wilmington. This could be it for Wilmington and me, but I doubt it, not so long as its banks fill my mailbox with 2.9 percent introductory come-ons. (So much we've seen together, so many thousands of dollars between us, like a secret affair. I'm not ready to walk away.)

I would like to be able to tell you that in all those thousands of dollars there was a three-week trip to Italy when I was twenty-four, during which I fell madly in love.

Unfortunately, I have to be honest: There was never an Italy.

There was Banana Republic, there was Barnes & Noble, there were new Midas brakes for the car. There was the removal of my wisdom teeth at twenty-four, paid for in part on my Citibank MasterCard, because insurance only covered half. There were motel rooms, and even a few hotel rooms, but they tended to be in places like Yuma, Arizona, and Lexington, Kentucky, and Shreveport, Louisiana, because I have always seemed to be just driving through.

There were enough wedding presents to almost equip the kitchens of people far happier than me. There was something Gucci, but there was so much more Gap. There were disposable contact lenses, so that I could clearly see all that was available to buy, even as I chose not to read the fine print of the terms for buying it. For every nice meal charged to my plastic, there are, I am sad to report, many more charges to what appear to be Chinese takeout joints.

There were glasses of wine that I bought in hotel lobby bars while I waited.

Sometimes I was waiting for someone in particular, and sometimes I was waiting for nothing at all.

(In my twenties, I liked being in hotel lobbies. I liked the idea of lurking over a $9 glass of something in a Napa Valley red and a dish of mixed Brazil and cashew nuts. I took notes for a novel I never wrote.)

So have it, Wilmington. Have what's left of me.

My failure of wallet and willpower leads here. It's a somewhere, even if it is a kind of fat-cat's nowhere. As a bit player in the capitalist drama, I think it's sometimes important to feel small.

In the Hotel du Pont, to escape the heat, I charged a glass of chardonnay to my First USA card — the same one I've carried since my junior year of college, with its obscene 22.9 percent interest rate. I used this card on this evening because I felt naughty, and alive. Later, as the last sunlight dribbled away in a haze, I walked past the glowing office buildings to my car. It was just me and the banks. The footsteps I thought I heard in the warpy heat turned out to be my own.

PATRICK SYMMES

Blood Wood

FROM *Outside*

JUMP GOT HIS NAME because he twitches like the Tasmanian Devil. He is as brown as his father, a Munduruku Indian, but he speaks the slum Portuguese of his mother's home, Altamira, an ugly sawmill boomtown on the Rio Xingu, in Brazil's Pará state. The first time I saw Jump, standing in the trash-strewn mud of Altamira's port, I thought he was drunk, because he was dancing a jig at nine A.M. But he was sober, and concealed his violent spasms, whatever their neurological cause, beneath a repertoire of gestures — suddenly reaching up to comb his hair, or leaping from a chair to point at something. Only in his *voadeira,* the fast aluminum canoe of the Amazon's backwaters, did Jump seem truly at home. He is a good boatman, popular on the river, and since the impulsive shudders of his tiller hand average out, Jump steers true.

High on the Xingu in the wilderness beyond Altamira, Jump takes us straight into the trees, fast, and cuts the engine. At the end of the rainy season, the Xingu runs black and turbulent, drowning its rapids, flooding through the surrounding forest so fiercely that every tree casts a wake. We slide quietly through a slice in the trees, and ground on a spit of red clay. Following Jump, I tramp across the dark space beneath the lush triple canopy. *"A Terra do Meio,"* Jump says: the Middle Land. A chunk of public land the size of Austria, the Middle Land begins here at the confluence of the brown Rio Iriri and the black Rio Xingu. Its pristine stretch of rain forest is itself surrounded by 62,500 square miles of Indian lands — the home of more than twenty tribes, from the Arara and Araweté to the Kayapó, a group renowned for its fierce resistance to outsiders.

Howler monkeys are somewhere up in the trees, lending their bloody-murder screams to a soundtrack of parrot squawks and dripping water. It takes only half an hour to find the place we're looking for, where the chairs, tables, and fine nightstands of the future grow in isolation on slight rises in the jungle, where the soil is rich with minerals and sometimes even dry. Jump pauses to point out various lesser trees, slashing at one with his machete until it drips milky white. *"Borracha,"* he says. Rubber. He points at another — *"Cinchona,"* whose bark is the natural source of quinine — and pantomimes malarial fever. Finally, as we approach the looming trunk of a giant, Jump utters the word I've traveled two hundred river miles to hear: *"Mogno."* Mahogany.

And there before us towers the immense cause of the trouble in this paradise: a lone, regal *Swietenia macrophylla,* a big-leaf mahogany tree rising 130 feet toward the sunlight of the upper canopy, its age, perhaps a century, visible in its gnarled branches, in the alteration of craggy bark and bald spots, in the thick roots that flare out like flying buttresses. Skyward, its small, green crown hardly seems enough to support so much force of life.

The Brazilians like to call mahogany *ouro verde* — green gold. Its wood has become the cocaine of the Amazon, a commodity whose trade thrives on corruption and intimidation, a contraband source of wealth and power jealously guarded by backwoods kingpins. Mahogany is the reason that the head of Greenpeace's Amazon campaign, Paulo Adario, is in hiding, after numerous death threats, disguising himself with an ugly wig and donning a bulletproof vest. Mahogany may be the reason half a dozen Brazilian environmentalists have been gunned down in the last year alone.

If Jump had brought a chain saw, I suppose we could hack into one side of this giant's trunk and bring it down. If we dragged it to the river, we could probably get only about $30 for it, or the equivalent in sugar and gasoline. If we somehow managed to float it seventy-five miles back down the Xingu to Altamira, the price could increase to over $3,000. Maybe more. It's a big tree.

But the real money is always farther downstream. In Pôrto do Moz, near the confluence of the Xingu and the Amazon, we could cut it into thick boards, load it on a ship, and send it steaming out into the Atlantic through the wide delta at Belém, where all the wood from a thousand tributaries must eventually pass. You could get more than a dozen dining-room tables from this monster, each of which could wholesale for $4,000 and retail for much more: In the showrooms on Lexington Avenue back in Manhattan, I've seen table after table of Brazilian mahogany for $15,000 and up. Rough out the math: By the time this tree reaches the furniture markets of America and Europe, the wood could be worth almost a quarter-million dollars.

Our giant is safe, for the moment. Jump aims the machete, waits for a spasm to pass, and makes a shallow slash in the bark to reveal the wood. The first layer is bright red, and fibrous. He strikes again — still a harmless cut, but this time revealing the pale white core. If this mahogany were to float downstream, its heartwood would change. It would dry out, darken. Eventually it would take on a rich red-brown tinge, as though it had been soaked in blood.

In December 1988, when Chico Mendes was shot down by an assassin in the western Amazon village of Xapuri, his murder galvanized a global movement to save the rain forest. Governments protested. Pop stars wrote songs. A thousand T-shirts bloomed. Books and films memorialized the uneducated rubber tapper who died defending the forest.

But the murder of activist Ademir Alfeu Federicci in Altamira in August 2001 echoed barely louder than the gunshot that killed him. Federicci, forty-two, was the leader of a group called the Movement for the Development of the Transamazon and Xingu; he was merely the most visible of countless rural Brazilian activists — social, religious, or labor leaders first, and environmentalists only by necessity, as they fight to preserve the rain forest for the indigenous people and poor farmers who live there. Dema, as Federicci was known, had loudly denounced the crooked middlemen and tree cutters taking mahogany out of the Middle Land, denounced the politicians who abetted them, and denounced the judges who looked the other way. Not long before he was killed, he had denounced the planned construction of a huge hydroelectric dam at the Xingu's Belo Monte falls, a federal boondoggle that would largely benefit sitting politicians, if Brazil's history of massive kickbacks was any guide. Federicci had been denouncing things his entire adult life. He was famous only among his enemies.

On the night of August 25, 2001, Federicci and his wife, Maria, went to bed in their hilltop home in Altamira, near the town's light-ning-rod monument commemorating the arrival of electricity, in 1998. The Federiccis had electricity, but couldn't afford a fan, so they slept with the door open. At one-thirty A.M., two men ap-proached the house; there was a struggle, a shot was fired; Dema Federicci died on the floor, with his wife and children looking on. The police said the killing was a botched attempt to steal the fam-ily's television and VCR, just another robbery gone wrong in vio-lent Brazil. But the Federiccis didn't own a VCR. And a wealthy log-ger had reportedly joked that Dema would soon need some wood himself, for a coffin.

Perhaps you thought the Amazon was no longer a battlefield — it would be easy to assume that the warnings of the eighties and nineties gave way to a lasting solution. We were told that the rain forest was burning, vanishing at up to 3 percent a year, and that forty thousand species would go extinct in a generation. Those fig-ures turned out to be a bit too apocalyptic. More realistic estimates suggest that the rain forest, a vast ecological storehouse encom-passing a Western Europe–size swath of northern Brazil and por-tions of Bolivia, Peru, Colombia, Ecuador, and Venezuela, is shrink-ing at an annual rate of 0.9 percent. The extinction rate, though alarming, is also lower than projected. Still, it's a mistake to suc-cumb to eco-fatigue, to think that media attention made every-thing okay, that Sting and Rainforest Crunch healed all wounds. The majority of the Amazon's 2.3 million square miles — 80 to 85 percent — is still wilderness. But it is disappearing all the same.

The most immediate crisis in the Amazon today is that of vio-lence — violence fueled chiefly by a chain of illegal trade that be-gins with big-leaf mahogany. The tree, which once ranged from southern Mexico to Bolivia, now exists largely in a swath of lonely, slow-growing timber stretching from Brazil into Bolivia and Peru. Its close American cousins were logged out of the Caribbean centu-ries ago, and are nearing commercial extinction in Central Amer-ica; other mahoganies — the African genus *Khaya*, the Philippine *Shorea* — are still found in tropical forests worldwide, but are not as valuable as big-leaf, prized for its color and durability. According to TRAFFIC, a joint program of the World Wildlife Fund and the World Conservation Union, Brazil exports more than half the big-leaf mahogany on the world market — 68,000 cubic meters in

1999, or $70 million worth — much of it from Pará state. Peru and Bolivia split the rest.

Mahogany is merely the wedge that opens the door to a whole cycle of deforestation: The Brazilian government no longer builds roads into the interior, so now poachers ransack the forest for the big trees, because only mahogany brings enough to pay for equipment, or a barge, or a private road. Once a road is built, less valuable woods — cedar, jatoba, and ipe, a rotproof hardwood used for suburban decks — become commercially viable. Plywood makers buy up the soft junk trees. Charcoal makers burn what's left. The roads draw poor farmers, unregistered *extrativistas* who plant yucca, scratching a living from the thin soil. Speculators from elsewhere in Brazil, along with an increasing number of Asian investors, buy up huge tracts, often on Indian or public lands no one has a right to sell. They hire *pistoleiros* to "clean" the land of the farmers who opened it. Cattle ranches and soy plantations follow.

In theory, Brazil does sanction mahogany logging on public lands; companies apply for permits for harvest, transport, and export. But there's been a moratorium on new logging permits since 1996, and an emergency ban on all harvest, transport, and export since October 2001. Despite these safeguards, a massive illegal harvest has taken place under cover of the legitimate one. Legal and contraband logs float downstream together, into the same sawmills and ports. Paperwork is forged, management plans from one forest used to disguise another. Most Brazilian wood ends up in the United States, which, according to TRAFFIC, imported 36,000 cubic meters of Brazilian mahogany in 2001, $44 million worth. Total U.S. big-leaf imports that year were 85,000 cubic meters.

Like any threatened species, big-leaf mahogany is traded under the rules of the Convention on the International Trade of Endangered Species (CITES). And like any illicit trade, it is notoriously difficult to quantify. In 1997, estimates claimed that as much as 80 percent of Brazil's mahogany was illegal. No way, says the country's environmental enforcement agency, the Brazilian Institute for the Environment and Natural Renewable Resources (IBAMA). While mahogany was indeed stolen from Indian lands, the agency says, the vast majority was legal, and today the trade is kaput. But Greenpeace, using IBAMA figures, counters that half the mahogany logged between 1999 and 2001 was taken illegally.

In the future, it should be possible to get more detailed pictures of the problem, thanks to the Amazon Surveillance System (SIVAM), a $1.4 billion project financed largely by the U.S. Export-Import Bank that uses upgraded satellite images and new ground sensors to track illegal activities — including drug smuggling and deforestation — across 1.9 million square miles of the Amazon. But for now, the illegal trade remains a splendid racket, a multimillion-dollar business concentrated in the hands of a few. And as activists like Federicci rise up in the footsteps of Chico Mendes, protesting this racket, they are laid low with dispatch.

The Pastoral Land Commission, a nongovernmental organization linked to the Catholic Church, estimates that in Pará alone, 475 activists have been assassinated since 1985. In 2001, at least 10 Pará social leaders were killed. Most, including Federicci, had signed a letter against government corruption. In October 2001, a list of 24 more Pará leaders who were *"marcados para morrer,"* or marked for death, was published by the Human Rights Commission of Brazil's House of Representatives. It is difficult to track the killings, and dangerous: Leônidas Martins, an Altamira lay worker for the Pastoral Land Commission who collected statistics on Pará killings, was himself threatened with death, as was Zé Geraldo, a political deputy who investigated the crimes.

Meanwhile, the murders get grislier: On July 22, 2002, the body of Bartolemeu Morais da Silva, an activist from the Altamira Rural Workers Union, was discovered beside a highway, with both legs broken and twelve gunshot wounds to the head. It was the second assassination in a month.

In Brazil these deaths have become routine. And in the rest of the world, they have gone unnoticed, as silent as the felling of one more giant in the Middle Land.

Given this climate, an environmentalist has to have a certain defiant disdain for the odds. No one projects this more joyfully than Paulo Adario, the director of Greenpeace Amazonia, a division of Greenpeace International run out of Manaus, the capital of Amazonas state. Led by a Brazilian, and more committed to people than trees, this isn't your usual collection of rainbow warriors. For one thing, in Manaus, saving the rain forest means keeping some serious firepower in the back room.

Greenpeace headquarters sits atop a hill, surveying the sweaty gray buildings and noisy streets along the fat Rio Negro, where it flows into the Amazon. A bricklayer is busy when I arrive in early May, constructing a new guardhouse to go with the new security gate, the new razor wire, and the new electric fence across the roof. There's also a new set of security cameras both outside and inside the whitewashed three-story structure. Greenpeace HQ is starting to look a lot like Fort Apache.

Adario appears on the second-floor balcony, waving at the guard to buzz me in. He is wearing sandals, jeans, and a T-shirt. "This is the opposite of our *projeto,*" he mutters. For Greenpeace, the projeto is supposed to mean openness and transparency, not walls and wire. But after Greenpeace Amazonia released a damning report on illegal mahogany in the fall of 2001, Adario received so many death threats that he and his family moved into the Greenpeace compound. Adario may be too effective for his own good.

Like Chico Mendes, Adario is an inheritor of the *luta,* Brazil's struggle for social justice, and, like Mendes, he uses the environment to fight for larger things. A former journalist from Rio de Janeiro, he spent the 1980s criticizing Brazil's military dictatorship and the corruption of its democratic successor. He joined Greenpeace Brazil when it was founded in 1992, and helped launch Greenpeace Amazonia in 1999. Since becoming director in 2000, Adario has combined international charisma with a homegrown sense of Latin realities, alternating between backwoods bushwhacking in Brazil and lecturing in careful English from Amsterdam to New Haven, where last spring he wowed the green intelligentsia at the Yale School of Forestry. Back home, he borrows freely from the Greenpeace playbook with endless propaganda stunts — sending his young volunteers out to crash forest-industry conferences or rappel down hotels unfurling banners.

"It's not about mahogany!" Adario tells his devoted crew at midnight strategy sessions. "At the end of the day, we are not discussing a tree in the forest! We are discussing democracy!"

A fifty-three-year-old man with curly salt-and-pepper hair, a short beard, and rimless spectacles, Adario fiddles with a can of Copenhagen tobacco as we wander through the building. The top floor has a video production suite, a lunchroom that serves as the main hangout for the dozen or so staff, and a kitchen, but every inch of surplus space is crowded with bunk beds and suitcases. Along with Adario and his family, Phil from England, Dave from Scotland, Merel from Holland, and Marcelo, Agnaldo, and Diego from Brazil have moved into the relative safety of Greenpeace HQ. The place has the fetid, untidy atmosphere of a college dorm during finals.

The second floor looks better. Here, in what Adario calls "the intelligence center," computers are used to crunch data, churn out propaganda, and analyze satellite images from Brazil's federal mapping agency for new roads or freshly cleared ranchland.

Downstairs, in the garage, gear is stacked everywhere: There are two speedboats; two dirt bikes for negotiating rainy-season logging roads; life vests for the *Arctic Sunrise*, the Greenpeace polar vessel that serves as mobile headquarters on investigative forays upriver; an industrial slide projector for throwing slogans onto the walls of banks and other capitalist command posts; an inflatable yellow chain saw the size of a sofa, for mocking sawmill owners; and charts for the floatplane. Tucked in a cabinet, behind some paint cans, is a pistol-grip, high-intensity ultraviolet lantern.

The lantern is the source of Adario's current troubles. Greenpeace launches several long field expeditions each year, and in July 2000 Adario led a four-month investigation up the Xingu. Spotting illegally harvested mahogany logs stacked along the banks on Kayapó lands, Adario and his cohorts generously daubed the logs with invisible ultraviolet paint.

In the next few weeks, the team, accompanied by a film crew, raided several sawmills on the lower Xingu, scanning stacks of mahogany with the ultraviolet lantern. Bingo. The beam illuminated the brilliant purple flash of ultraviolet paint, proving for the cameras that these were the same trees stolen from the Kayapó. They found another large shipment of illegal timber in the yard of COMPENSA, a lumber company partly owned by a Chinese municipal government. When Greenpeace inflated its giant yellow chain saw and picketed the COMPENSA yard, Adario was sued by the company for "invasion of property," a criminal offense with a penalty of up to two years in jail. Adario won the case.

In October 2001, after several more forays up the Xingu, Greenpeace Amazonia released a twenty-page report, *Partners in Mahogany Crime,* that named names all the way down the line, starting with two powerful Pará state businessmen, both connected to top politicians. The report described Moisés Carvalhos Pereira and Osmar Alves Ferreira as "kings of mahogany" who finance illegal logging, broker sales to sawmills, and arrange export through a mafia of shifting front companies. The two men control more than 80 percent of the mahogany that leaves Pará, Greenpeace alleged, and more than half that leaves Brazil. Both are now under federal indictment, and both have used their lawyers to avoid arrest. Moisés — so famous he is referred to by one name, like a soccer star — no longer leaves Redenção, the southeast Pará logging town he basically owns.

Partners in Mahogany Crime got big play on Brazil's dominant television network, TV Globo. It appeared in the midst of a congressional investigation into an Amazon development scheme that had funneled millions into the shell corporations of crooked politicians, and was released as the president of Brazil's senate resigned, under allegations that he was implicated in embezzlement and illegal-logging schemes. In the wake of the report, on October 22, 2001, Brazil announced its blanket mahogany moratorium, leaving the enforcement to IBAMA, an outfit then so broke that it typically deployed just two men to patrol an area the size of California. With helicopter fuel begged from Greenpeace, IBAMA was able to seize $7 million worth of mahogany in ten days.

The Greenpeace report also claimed to have traced illegal mahogany to such well-known furniture makers and retailers as Harrods and, in the U.S., Stickley & Sons, Ethan Allen, and Lane. At the same time, it cautioned that those companies were most likely unwitting consumers and that, unless the wood was certified by the international nonprofit Forest Stewardship Council, "there is no way of knowing whether the mahogany they sell is legal." Still, the report added, "odds are that it is not."

Even Queen Elizabeth II has been caught up in the confusion. In June, the London *Guardian* reported that the new Queen's Gallery at Buckingham Palace had used five kinds of threatened tropical hardwoods, including mahogany, from dubious sources in Africa and Brazil. Like the queen herself, the architects had a policy of buying wood from sustainable forests. But they had hired a contractor, who hired a subcontractor, who hired a supplier, who bought the wood from a middleman, who got it from dealers on the strength of export certificate "details," which are routinely faked.

*

One of the bodyguards brings a paper bag to the Manaus airport. Adario and a half-dozen young volunteers are heading for Belém, the port at the mouth of the Amazon, to crash an industry mahogany conference. Whatever's inside the bag, it looks heavy.

The pudgy guard follows Adario, and I follow him, watching as he puts the bag on the ticket desk with a heavy thud. Airport security looks inside, staples the sack closed, and checks it with the bodyguard's luggage. In Brazil, they do this all the time.

This is Adario's life: a twenty-four-hour security detail. Five days after *Partners in Mahogany Crime* was released, the phone rang at his home in Manaus. A voice said, "You deserve to die, and will die." A few nights later, a dark-colored van pulled slowly past the house, three times; a passerby said that the men inside were holding guns. It was only six weeks after Dema Federicci's murder. Within days, federal police confirmed that there was a price on his head.

When Adario says, "Life in the Amazon costs nothing," he's scarcely exaggerating. Brazil's murder rate has quadrupled since 1980, largely because of organized gangs from urban slums, with names like the Red Commando or the Third Command, who deal drugs and offer assassinations for hire. During my visit, newspaper headlines called one gang the "Exterminators" for blowing away a policeman in Manaus. They don't charge much to kill someone: about $200 to whack José Nobody, a few thousand to eliminate a troublesome judge. This is nothing compared with the losses incurred after the *Partners* report: One wood company, which Adario declined to name, lost $25 million in fines, mahogany, and seized equipment. The math is obvious.

At first Adario declines to specify the size of his particular bounty. ("I don't want to talk about how much," he boasts, "but it's a good price!") Later, over late-night beers with the Manaus staff, he can't resist. The figure he reveals isn't that much, about half the price for killing a judge, or one-third the cost of a mahogany table in New York. It would be a fortune to one of the unemployed assassins living under a tin roof in the back streets of Manaus.

The first thing Adario did was lodge his family in the Manaus Holiday Inn under an assumed name. The federal police were sympathetic and lent him two bodyguards, but eventually Greenpeace had to hire its own. The Adarios moved from hotel to hotel until that got too expensive, and then began shuttling from house to house, friend to friend. In early November, after a fresh round of threats to other members of Greenpeace Amazonia, the Adarios fled to Rio. When they finally returned to Manaus in the spring, Adario took to wearing an Israeli bulletproof vest and disguising himself in a stringy black wig that gave him an eerie resemblance to Ozzy Osbourne.

"My life is all mixed up with Greenpeace," Adario's wife told me one day during a nervous interview at Fort Greenpeace. "It's difficult," she said. "Now I don't feel afraid, but tomorrow, I don't know. If the pressure increases, I don't know . . ."

Adario himself is worried enough about his family members' safety that he asked that names and details about them not be published, but that doesn't mean he's backing down.

"Life is not white and black," he explains. "It is very simple to be an environmentalist in the north. You are a good guy fighting bad guys. Here, bad guys and good guys change sides all the time. It is a chess game, and you have to be a good player."

Adario has consistently confounded those who try to guess his next move: No sooner had Greenpeace fought for the ban on mahogany exports than Adario turned around and started advocating the methods of two logging companies that used low-impact harvesting techniques on private lands. In the long run, keeping the forest intact could generate more revenue than logging it. But so far, aside from a few WWF and Body Shop demonstration projects, sustainable forestry is still only a nice theory when you're talking about a major cash crop like mahogany. Cooperating with (some) loggers, Adario believes, is necessary to move Greenpeace's Amazon campaign away from gringo utopianism and toward Latin American realism. He has forged a relationship, for example, with Cecilio Rego De Almeida, one of the wealthiest land barons in Brazil. Greenpeace doesn't make noise about his 30,000-square-mile claims in the Middle Land, and De Almeida lets Greenpeace use his airstrip to chase off freelance wood poachers. Politics makes for strange hammock mates.

Then again, Adario often won't work with groups that would seem to be his allies, which is why the Greenpeacers have headed to Belém. Adario can't resist a chance for political theater, and a three-day conference on "Sustainable Trade and Management of Mahogany" is the perfect stage.

The sprawling Amazon delta city is being lashed by the tail end of the rainy season, and people duck under colonial eaves and rush, soaking, into the Hilton Hotel, where the lobby is thick with American timber importers in slacks, Brazilian exporters in gold chains, and academics with pocket protectors from both countries. Adario's contingent have put on sport coats, but they don't blend in and are stopped at the door. Greenpeace wasn't invited.

It's not exactly a shoving match. A couple of hotel flacks keep the Greenies at bay while Adario protests — "Why are you afraid of?" — in rare mangled English. Security guards and eventually Pará state police are brought over, and finally Keister Evans, director of the Tropical Forest Foundation, comes out. Evans is a lean, gray-haired American, and his Virginia-based conservation group, which also represents machinery companies like Caterpillar, works with genteel green groups like the Nature Conservancy and the WWF. Familiar duelists, the two begin their usual finger-pointing ritual: Adario claims TFF's politics of compromise clear the way for deforestation; Evans sees blustery Greenpeace as beyond the pale. Adario fulminates about imminent banner-unfurling and street action, and then goes for his ultimate weapon — the media. When a Belém TV crew arrives, Adario bathes in the glow of a camera from TV Liberal, denouncing the "logging mafia" and protesting his exclusion. But Evans calmly surveys the reporters and the microphones, and outfoxes Adario by letting Greenpeace inside. Deprived of the advertised conflict, the journalists leave, and Adario puts on a name tag and takes notes with exaggerated seriousness. "I don't want to win," Adario, clearly frustrated, vents to his staff later. "I want to fight!"

Evans just wants him to go away. His foundation, he says, represents the legitimate players in the timber business, not the millionaire middlemen. "Mahogany," he says wistfully, "has become a lightning rod," at the expense of the legitimate trade. "In Brazil, mahogany is totally out of business. Totally."

"The Amazon has two faces," Adario likes to say. "It's hard to tell what's real and what's mythology."

Out in the small logging towns of the rain forest, the mahogany shutdown is myth; the reality is still in shadows. Greenpeace can't be everywhere, though it helps organize and fund dozens of small local labor, religious, and indigenous-rights groups fighting for land reform. About twenty-five members of these grassroots groups are meeting in Pôrto do Moz, a sawmill town at the mouth of the Xingu, to drum up support for two planned sustainable-forest reserves. Adario suggests that I look them up before the pistoleiros do.

As the turboprop climbs up from the tarmac, the region appears to be in terrible shape, but the slashed clearings soon thin out and the roads disappear. From ten thousand feet, the rain forest looks placid and undisturbed, cut by curving channels that carry one-sixth of the flowing fresh water on Earth. Great flocks of egrets move in V's below the plane, submerged savannas reflect the sky, and the smooth green carpet seems, falsely, like an infinite plain of trees.

The activists gathered in a tin-roofed shed on Pôrto do Moz's dismal main street are mostly fishermen, farmers, and members of a women's cooperative, but there are also three ordained ministers (Catholic, Methodist, and Evangelical, all wearing flip-flops). The only foreigner is Georg Roling, a German development worker with the lean frame of a malaria survivor. Beside him is twenty-nine-year-old Tarcisio Feitosa da Silva, the Amazon's number-one fashion victim, dressed in white from baseball cap to shoes. A former colleague of Federicci's, Tarcisio has taken Dema's place as a thorn in the logging industry's side. There is also a representative from Brazil's leftist Worker's Party, Idalino Nunes de Assis, an older man with the lined face of an activist used to backwoods work. Both Brazilians are in danger: Idalino has received multiple threats, and the federal government has notified Tarcisio that his name is on a death list. By summer's end, both men will be in hiding.

The discussion centers on generating support for the two reserves, which would shut out corporate logging in favor of renewable uses like the harvest of palm fruit, nuts, and a few trees. One would be up in the Middle Land, west of the Xingu. The second would lie just across the river, south of the Trans-Amazon Highway. We set out on a day of forest revivals, spreading the eco-gospel up the Jarauçu, a Xingu tributary running through one proposed reserve. The current is narrow, fast, and brown, and Idalino steers over submerged fields to villages of stilt houses where fat, striped fish are visible through cracks in the floorboards. He regales the villagers with impassioned sermons: "The corporate groups are using you as beasts of burden!"

But many of the extrativistas will have none of Idalino's reserves: They are unregistered with any government; they've heard rumors that they won't be able to plant corn, or keep chickens, that they will be arrested. That night, on a ferry up the Xingu, watching the boat's wake as we rumble upstream to Altamira, Roling laments what he calls "conservation imperialism," the way foreigners' well-meaning solutions — land trusts that buy huge tracts, ice cream companies offering a square inch of forest per pint sold — don't take into account this overwhelming poverty. "Preservation," he says, "doesn't give you anything to eat." (Adario has said the same thing — with twenty million people in the region, "you can't put a bubble over the Amazon.")

Fear of outsiders plays into the hands of logging interests. When parts of the Amazon were declared World Heritage sites in 2000, Brazilian nationalists said foreigners were stealing part of the country. And loggers have circulated a pamphlet that calls Greenpeace the "Vanguard of the Global Monarchy," accusing it of colluding with the British and Dutch royal families to impoverish the Third World.

Black dolphins play in the Xingu after sunset, and we spend a long, surprisingly cold night packed in swaying hammocks, chugging past more than eighty sawmills, before reaching the falls at Belo Monte, where we catch a cab the last twenty-five miles to Altamira. The town where Dema Federicci was murdered is filthy and sprawling, full of trucks, chain-saw dealerships, whorehouses, and pro-logging sentiment. The activists are on eggshells here. Adario won't even visit the city. But posters of Federicci ("DEMA, YOUR WORK IS NOT FORGOTTEN") are everywhere. And Amazon chic has touched even this remote boom town. "You'll never guess who sat right in that seat," a cabdriver told me. "Sting!"

In Altamira more activists greet us, eight of them on death lists of some kind. One is a T-shirted American nun in her seventies, Dorothy Stang from Dayton, Ohio. A member of the Sisters of Notre Dame de Namur, Stang has lived in Brazil since 1966; she's used to the heat, the humidity, and the insects, but not the death threats. "The logging companies work with a threat logic," she says, describing the shadowy magic in which one day a company or rancher will complain about an activist, and the next he'll be gone. "They elaborate a list of leaders, and then a second movement appears to eliminate those people."

Stang says she received her most recent death threat just three days ago, after helping disarm three pistoleiros trying to evict farmers from land claimed by a wealthy rancher. "If I get a stray bullet," the sister says cheerily, "we know exactly who did it."

The last link in this trail of blood and sawdust is up the Xingu in the Middle Land, so I buy 120 liters of gasoline, two blocks of ice, and some food and head for the disgusting Altamira waterfront, where I hire the thrashing, twisting, leaping, jumping, jigging, half-Indian Jump to take me into the rain forest.

Upstream the banks begin to rise up. Clear-cut hills are visible, the trees replaced with cattle. In midafternoon we round an island and come across about a thousand mahogany logs floating patiently in the river. These were chain-sawed from the upper reaches of the Xingu, skinned, cut into twenty-foot lengths, and then started downriver roped into rafts of fifty trunks each. But the shipment was impounded here by IBAMA as illegal, or "precarious," last fall. Two wiry old men, Luciano and Pedro, are living here in a puny houseboat, paid by IBAMA to watch the logs, which are tied to the lee of the island.

"Jump, you devil!" Pedro shouts. *"Tudo bem?"* Everything good?

"Everything legal," Jump replies, and we all shake hands.

We clamber across the blazing tin roof of their boat and hop down onto a forest's worth of mahogany. Barefoot, I pick my way over one cluster, skip to the next, and work my way along the future coffee tables of America until I am hundreds of yards into a sea of mahogany, most of it stolen from land simultaneously claimed by Kayapó and Arara Indians, private landowners, and the government. IBAMA isn't quite sure what to do with it. The middleman who bought the logs and paid to have them rafted downriver has sued to reclaim them. If he wins, this mega-raft will be worth several million dollars.

The trail of blood wood circles back and leads me to Belém. A few days after Brazil's President Henrique Cardoso boasts on the radio about the mahogany moratorium, I take a taxi to the port. I have been inside the front gate only a few seconds when a harried inspector from IBAMA, Senhor Coimbra, happens by, carrying a tape measure. "We just found some mahogany right now," he tells me, dragging me past antique iron sheds that line the docks.

The wood is stacked in plain sight, by the road: 264 pallets of boards, a monstrous display of illegal wood. Coimbra, a small, sunburned, middle-aged man, runs a tape measure over a pallet, does some math, and then swats the wood with a swagger stick of discarded mahogany. "All the measurements are false," he says. The shipping papers describe it as 262 cubic meters; by his calculations, it is 328 cubic meters. I ask if he will impound it.

"We already did," he says. IBAMA discovered this wood months ago in a sawmill up-country and put it under injunction, but a "substitute judge" was miraculously found to release it. Now a forklift closes in, picks up the first pallet, and carries it toward the Amazon, and we watch as load after load is lifted onto a cargo ship named the *Bluarrow*. The wood is plainly marked MOBILE, and is going into the hold alongside cedar equipped with Forest Stewardship Council stickers certifying it as legit. By the time the *Bluarrow* reaches the U.S., it will be hard to tell the shipments apart.

With Latin flourish, Coimbra slaps a big rubber stamp onto the shipping documents. "This export was determined by precarious judicial decision (injunction)," it reads in precarious English. The message is intended for customs inspectors in the United States. One after another, European, British, and now U.S. customs officials have begun impounding suspect mahogany. In a move supported by the White House, the U.S. Department of Agriculture has seized close to $20 million worth of Brazilian mahogany, estimates Greenpeace, at five ports of entry. Five of those twenty-five shipments have since been released, and in July, the U.S. timber industry sued the federal government for the release of sixteen more. Still, there's a chance that Senhor Coimbra's "precarious" mahogany will never reach market.

As we turn to leave, a couple of cops on scooters whiz up. Coimbra looks nervous and signals for me to keep walking, but they cut us off, and a cruiser arrives. We are invited into the back of the police car, taken to the air-conditioned office of the port police captain, and given two cups of coffee and a lecture on interfering with the vital business of loading ships. Despite the fact that Coimbra works in this port every day and is wearing his uniform and badge, the officer leans across the desk and explains that we could be personally liable for the cost of any delays.

There's a picture of him under the glass of his desktop, taken at a customs conference in New York. He's standing in front of the Twin Towers, smiling.

"A terrible tragedy," he says. And then, done humiliating Coimbra and scrutinizing me, he lets us go.

Hours later, a local shipping executive drives up to the port's front gate. A volley of bullets shatters the windshield. He dies in the driver's seat. Somebody owed somebody some money. This is how business is done in the Amazon.

At Fort Greenpeace, in Manaus, yesterday's newspaper is laid out on the table. On the front page is a gory photo of blood mixed with shards of broken glass, another twisted, lifeless body in the background. A couple of assassins botched a job on a street corner just fifty yards from here, trying to get a small-town mayor; his bodyguards got them instead.

After twenty minutes of argument, I convince Adario to let me see what's inside his bodyguard's paper bag. Apparently some of the staff believe it will hurt the group's support if people see Greenpeace with a piece.

The bodyguard goes into the back room, comes back, and, with metallic, practiced gestures, drops out the clip, clears the chamber, and hands me the thing. It is cold and heavy. A snubby little 9mm semiautomatic. Perfect in a close-quarters shootout.

Suddenly there's a commotion. Marcelo, a forestry engineer on staff, rushes into the lunchroom still wearing his bicycle helmet. A new threat has come in. A man has left two messages on the answering machine of Greenpeace's floatplane pilot. In the first message, the man, who sounds drunk, threatens to rape the pilot's daughter and kill his family. In the second, he sounds sober and repeats the threat. The pilot and his family are hiding in one of the safest places in Manaus — the mall.

"This is a bad moment," Marcelo says.

"They're all bad moments," Adario says.

I hand the pistol back to the bodyguard, who reloads it and heads for the truck. Adario prepares to follow.

"Somebody convinced us to save the fucking Amazon," he says, heading for the door. "Now we have to save ourselves." The last time I see him, he's a grainy, black-and-white form on a security monitor, climbing into an armored pickup.

WILLIAM T. VOLLMANN

Where the Ghost Bird Sings
by the Poison Springs

FROM *Outside*

THE WATER'S EDGE at the south end of North Shore — a shut-
tered, graffiti'd, ruined resort town which, as you might have
guessed, lies near the north shore of California's Salton Sea — was
no different than usual, the beach comprising not sand but barna-
cle shells, fish bones, fish scales, fish corpses, and bird corpses,
its accompaniment an almost unbearable ammoniac stench like
rancid urine magnified. Fish carcasses in rows and rows, more sickening stenches, the underfoot crunch of white cheek-plates like
seashells — oh, rows and banks of whiteness, banks of vertebrae;
feathers and vertebrae twitching in the water almost within reach
of the occasional half-mummified bird. Meanwhile, the dock was
crowded with live birds — long-necked white pelicans. Their coex-
istence with the dead birds was jarring, but then so was the broken
concrete, the PRIVATE PROPERTY sign, the half-sunk playground
slide.

It had been worse in other years — seven and a half million
tilapia (African perch) died on a single August day in 1998 — but
this evening it happened to be better. Oh, death was there, but matter had been ground down to submatter, just as on other beaches
coarse sand is gradually ground fine. The same dead scales, the
barnacles licked at by waves of a raw sienna color richly evil in its algal depths, set the tone, let's say: crunch, crunch. Without great
difficulty I spied the black mouth of a dead fish, another black
mouth, barnacles, a dead bird, and then, of all things, another
black mouth.

The far shore remained as beautiful as ever. When each shore is a far shore, then the pseudo-Mediterranean look of the west side as seen from the east side (rugged blue mountains, birds in flight, a few boats) shimmers into full believability. Come closer, and a metallic taste alights upon your stinging lips. Stay awhile, and you might win a sore throat, an aching compression of the chest as if from smog, or honest nausea. I was feeling queasy, but over the charnel a cool breeze played, and a family approached the water's edge, the children running happily, sinking ankle-deep in scales and barnacles, nobody expressing any botheration about the stench or the relics underfoot. Could it be that everything in this world remains so fundamentally pure that nothing can ever be more than half ruined? Expressed in the shimmer on the Salton Sea — sometimes dark blue, sometimes infinitely white, and always pitted with desert light — this purity is particularly undeniable.

Honeymoon paradise and toxic sump. Teeming fishery stinking of dead fish, bird sanctuary where birds die by the thousands. (What choice do the birds have? Ninety-one percent of California's wetlands are gone!) Lovely ugliness — this is the Salton Sea.

If you are confused, so is everybody else. Formed by accident in 1905–1907, when an attempt to divert the Colorado River (and, incidentally, to steal a lot more of Mexico's water) sent a series of floods into the salt-caked basin of California's Imperial Valley, the new sea kept rising, for like all seas it has no outlet. Farms, saltworks, and pieces of towns went under, and by the time the leak was plugged in 1907, the sea covered 500 square miles. Experts predicted evaporation within twenty years. And the water level did go down, at first. But a century later, it still takes up 380 square miles.

In the beginning it was a freshwater realm; trout survived here as late as 1929; a National Wildlife Refuge was established in 1930. Tourists came right away, but the golden age of fishing and waterfowl hunting that old-timers remember started to fade in the 1960s, when the sea began to stink a trifle and the resorts began to board up their windows. Ecologists were already warning that if the salinity — fed by irrigation runoff from the Colorado Desert's salt-rich soils, souvenir of a prehistoric ocean — continued to increase, the sea would become a wasteland. It did rise, of course, and the sea itself crept higher, too; Salton City and Bombay Beach lost houses beneath these strange reddish-brown waters.

Where were those waters coming from? From the Alamo River, fifty-two miles of irrigation runoff in whose bamboo rushes Border Patrol agents now play out their pretend-Vietnam cat-and-mouse exercises; from the rather irrelevant Whitewater River, trickling in from the northwest; and from the New River, with its reputation for filth, gathering sewage, landfill leachate, and industrial waste in the Mexican boom town of Mexicali before turning north to receive fertilizers and pesticides from Imperial Valley fields, meanwhile picking up a little more salt and a little more salt.

The great die-offs began in the 1990s — 150,000 eared grebes in 1992, 15,000 pelicans in 1996, fish by the millions, tilapia and croaker and corvina that had been stocked back in the fifties. Environmentalists raised alarms about the dead birds, the algal blooms, the hypersalinity, and the selenium, a naturally occurring trace element that in high concentrations can be deadly to plants and animals. They studied the sea, but none came to the same conclusions, or they came to no conclusions at all. The only thing everyone agreed on was that the sea was now 25 percent saltier than the ocean itself, and that it would only get saltier until the birds and fishes still surviving there were gone.

They say that as California goes, so goes the nation. And to me the Salton Sea emblematizes California. What can we do about it? What should we do? What does it "mean"? I decided to undertake a course of aquatic exploration. I would ride the New River from its source in Mexico to the Salton Sea, which I'd never heard of anybody doing. How navigable the river was, how dangerous or disgusting, not a soul could tell. My acquaintances in Imperial County said that yes, it did sound like a stupid thing to do, but probably not that unsafe; the worst that would likely happen to me was sickness. The U.S. Border Patrol advised against it, incidentally promising me that should I cross into the United States by means of the New River, I'd infallibly get arrested.

North of the border, the New River curves and jitters for sixty miles in a backward S to a sort of estuary on the southern shore of the Salton Sea, equidistant from the towns of Calipatria and Westmorland. On a map of Imperial County, the towns and road-crossings of its progress are traced in blue, right down to the last demisemiquaver. But immediately south of Calexico's stubby fan palms and pawnshops, there runs a heavy line demarcating the end of California and the beginning of Mexico, and of the state of Baja California. Here the New River becomes the Río Nuevo, and vanishes upstream from all but one of the maps I've ever seen, each time in a different way.

My plan was to cross from Calexico into Mexicali, hire a taxi, and get the driver to take me to the source of the Río Nuevo — wherever that was, but according to most accounts, just a few miles outside of town. Then I would rent a boat and ride downstream. But once I arrived in Mexicali and sought to zero in on the mysterious spot (*excuse me, señor, but where exactly does it start?*), people began to tell me that the river commenced *right here,* in Mexicali itself, in one of the city's industrial parks, where a certain Xochimilco Lagoon was fed by a secret spring. Moreover, the municipal authorities of Mexicali were even now pressing on into the fifth year of a very fine project to entomb and forget the Río Nuevo, sealing it off underground along a concrete channel below the median strip of a new highway, whose name happened to be Boulevard Río Nuevo — a hot white double ribbon of street adorned with dirt and tires, an upended car, broken things. Along its median they'd sunk segments of a long, long concrete tube that lay inconspicuous in a dirt trench; and between some of these segments, where the tube had been buried, were grates. Lifting the grates revealed square pits, with jet-black water flowing below, exuding a fierce sewer stench that could almost be some kind of cheese.

Not far from the border, a yellow pump truck sat roaring as its hose, dangling down into the Río Nuevo, sucked up a measure of the effluvium of Mexicali's 750,000 people. This liquid, called by the locals *aguas negras,* would be used in concrete mixing. What treasures might the river gather here on its way to the United States? Bacteria that could lead to typhoid, hepatitis, amoebic dysentery, perhaps a few other things, says the Environmental Protection Agency. (Well, the kids have respiratory problems just from living here, said one señora who lived a few steps away. They have coughs, she said, and on the skin some pimples and rashes.) Beside the truck were two wise shade-loungers — the temperature was 114 degrees — in white-dusted boots, baseball caps, and sunglasses. I asked what was the most interesting thing they could tell me about the Río Nuevo. They conferred for a while, and finally one of them said that they'd seen a dead body in it last Saturday.

One of the men, José Rigoberto Cruz Córdoba, was a supervisor. He explained that the purpose of this concrete shield was to end the old practice of spewing untreated factory and municipal sewage into the river, and maybe he even believed this; maybe it was even true. My translator, a man who, like most Mexicans, does not pulse with idealism about civic life, interpreted the policy thus: They'll just go to the big polluters — American companies or else Mexican millionaires — and say, "We've closed off your pipe. You can either pay us and we'll make you another opening right now, or else you're going to have to do it yourself with jackhammers and risk a much higher fine." No doubt he was right, and the clandestine pipes would soon be better hidden than ever.

The generator ran and the Río Nuevo stank. The yellow truck was now almost full. Smiling pleasantly, Señor Cruz Córdoba remarked, "I heard that people used to fish and swim and bathe here thirty years ago."

That night, at a taxi stand in sight of the river, the cab drivers sat at picnic tables, and the old-timers told me how it had been twenty-five years ago. They'd always called it the Río Conca, which was short for the Río con Cagada, the River with Shit. The river was lower then, and they used to play soccer here; when they saw turds floating by, they just laughed and jumped over them. The turds had floated like *tortugas,* they said, like turtles; and indeed they used to see real turtles here. Now they saw no animals at all.

For three or four languid days, I sat in the offices of Mexican civil engineers, telephone-queried American irrigation-district officials, and then, in the company of various guides and taxi drivers, went searching for the source of the Río Nuevo. Sometimes the street was fenced off for construction, and sometimes the river ran mysteriously underground — disappearing, say, beneath a wilderness of Pemex gas stations — but we always found it again, smelling it before we could see it. At Xochimilco Lagoon, liquid was flowing out of pipes and foaming into the lagoon's sickly stinking greenness between tamarisk trees.

But the lagoon was not the source, because there was no single source; the Río Nuevo drew its life from a spiderweb of irrigation drains and sewers and springs and lagoons, most of which ultimately derived from the Colorado River. Easing my way past the sentry at a geothermal works, I discovered waters of a lurid neon blue; what had stained them? That water entered the Río Nuevo, and so did this channel and that channel and that channel drawn on the blueprints of the engineers. From a practical point of view, the end came when I peered into the stinking greenness of Xochimilco Lagoon and the taxi driver appropriately said, "The end."

I'd already realized that my plan to raft the Río Nuevo was shot. Early one evening, the heat stinging my nose and forehead deliciously, I had gone to the river, peered down one of the square pits, and wondered whether I would stand a chance if I lowered myself and a raft into it. The current appeared to be extremely strong; there was no predicting where I'd end up. At best I'd drift as far as the border, five miles away, and be arrested. Should there be any underground barrier along the way, my raft would smash into it, and I'd probably capsize and eventually starve, choke, or drown.

While I considered the matter, my latest taxi driver stood on a mound of dirt and recited "El Ruego," by the Chilean poet Gabriela Mistral. Thus Mexico, where the most obscene feculence cannot prevail over art.

It was settled. Since I couldn't spend my own death benefits, I decided to begin my little cruise in the USA.

How many Río Nuevos, how many Salton Seas on this planet already lay poisoned — if they were poisoned — for the long term? The Aral Sea? Love Canal? Lake Baikal? Would their new normality become normative for the rest of us? How bad off is the Salton Sea, really?

"Stories of a polluted Salton Sea are greatly exaggerated," a recent brochure from the Coachella Valley Historical Society informed me. In 1994 the author of the pamphlet, *Salton Sea: California's Overlooked Treasure,* had taken a drive around the sea with her husband and experienced "a wonderful sense of what is right with the world." Five years later, the authors of an alarming and beautifully photographed volume titled *Farewell, Promised Land: Waking from the California Dream* described that same idyllic sea as "a stinking, reddish-brown sump rapidly growing too rancid for even the hardiest ocean fish" and "a death trap for birds." The New River, in particular, "claims the distinction of being the filthiest stream in the nation," the authors wrote. And as Fred Cagle, head of the California Audubon Society's Salton Sea Task Force, told me: "Nine million pounds of pesticides a year on Imperial Valley fields have got to go somewhere!"

There you have it, but according to that confederation of counties and water districts called the Salton Sea Authority, what you have is no more than "Myth #5: The Sea is a Toxic Dump Created by Agriculture." According to the SSA leaflet *Myths and Realities,* "Pesticides are not found at any significant level in the Sea." Moreover, selenium levels are only one-fifth of the federal standard, and (if I may quote from the rebuttal to Myth #4), "Water carried by the New River from Mexico is not a major contributor to the Sea's problems." Still, the leaflet freely if euphemistically confesses the "bird disease outbreaks," "fluctuating surface levels" (which I take to be a tacit reference to the half-buried houses, or to the mostly submerged Torres-Martinez Indian Reservation on the northwest shore), and "nutrient-rich water, algal blooms, and fish kills" (symptoms of what ecologists call eutrophication, which occurs when too much sewage or detergent or fertilizer enters a body of warm water and algae rushes in to exploit, growing like crazy, sucking up all the oxygen, and suffocating the fish). The leaflet acknowledges only one cause for these problems, the one everybody agrees on: salinity. Needless to say, salinity cannot explain algal blooms. As the leaflet reminds us, "We do not know all there is to know about the Sea." There again you have it.

Not that we haven't tried: Is there an agency in the area — international, federal, state, tribal, or local — that has not dipped its sample vials in the waters of the Salton Sea and the New River, looking to discover its secrets? U.S. Fish & Wildlife, the Imperial Irrigation District, the Twentynine Palms Band of Luiseno Mission Indians, the Regional Water Quality Board, the University of California–Davis — all of them and more have monitored selenium levels and nutrient levels and oxygen levels, testing for this and for that. Did their data overlap? No one knows, there was no clearinghouse, they didn't have the funding, that person no longer works here. But in 1998, Congress passed the Salton Sea Reclamation Act, which provided for the Salton Sea Restoration Project, which will conduct more studies. That same year the University of Redlands created the Salton Sea Database Program, whose aim is to collate that lost information and map the environment of the sea. Then will we know?

As for the pelicans, the grebes, and the other birds, they continue their tragic dramas. Whether they get sick from eating the dead fish or from something else entirely nobody knows, but they keep dying — from avian cholera, botulism, and Newcastle's disease. No matter that scientists haven't pinpointed the cause: If you walk the crunching beaches of North Shore, you cannot help but have a feeling that something about the Salton Sea is causing these die-offs, with their increasing if unpredictable frequency.

"We seem to have far too many of these," admits Tom Kirk, the executive director of the Salton Sea Authority. "But keep this in mind, Bill. Twenty thousand birds died at the Salton Sea last year. That's less than 1 percent of the bird population."

José Lopez, an ex-Marine with a cheerful, steady, slightly impersonal can-do attitude, clerked at the motel where I was staying in Calexico. When I told him that nobody seemed willing to take me on the New River or even to rent me a rowboat, he proposed that I go to one of those warehouse-style chain stores which now infested the United States and buy myself an inflatable dinghy. I asked if he would keep me company, and he scarcely hesitated. "Anyway," he said, "it will be something to tell our grandchildren."

The store sold two-person, three-person, and four-person rafts. I got the four-person variety for maximum buoyancy, selected two medium-priced wooden oars, paid $70, and felt good about the bargain. I'd prevailed upon José to bring his father over the border from Mexicali; the old man would drive José's pickup truck and wait for us at each crossing of the road, always going ahead rather than behind, so that if we had to walk in the heat we'd be sure of which direction to go. If we waved one arm at him, he'd know to drive to the next bridge. Two arms would mean we were in trouble.

I worried about two possibilities. The first and most likely but least immediately serious was that we might get poisoned by the New River. The second peril, which seriously concerned me, was dehydration. Should we be forced to abandon the boat in some unlucky spot between widely spaced bridges, it wouldn't take long for the heat to wear us down. It was supposed to be not much over 110 degrees, so it could have been worse.

José was behind his desk at the motel on the eve of our departure, laboriously inflating the dinghy breath by breath whenever the customers gave him a chance. This was the kind of fellow he was: determined, optimistic, ready to do his best with almost nothing.

At seven the next morning, with Imperial County already laying its hot hands on my thighs, the three of us — José, his father, and I — huddled in the parking lot of a supermarket, squinting beneath our caps while José's father stick-sketched in the dirt, making a map of the New River with the various road-crossings that he knew of. We were just north of the spot where the river comes through a gap in a wall that marks the border; across the highway, a white Border Patrol vehicle hunched in the white sand, watching us.

The first place that the old man would be able to wait for us was the bridge at Highway 98, about a mile due north but four miles' worth of river, thanks to a bend to the west-northwest. The next spot he could guarantee was Interstate 8, which looked to be a good ten miles from Highway 98, if one factored in river bends and wriggles.

Sheep-shaped clots of foam, white and woolly, floated down the river. Still, all in all the water didn't smell nearly as foul as in Mexicali. We dragged the dinghy out of the back of the truck, and José, who from somewhere had been able to borrow a tiny battery-powered pump, tautened his previous night's breath work until every last wrinkle disappeared. From the weeds came another old man, evidently a *pollero* — a coyote, or smuggler of illegal immigrants — who laughed at the notion that José and I were going to be literally up Shit Creek.

We dragged our yellow craft down a steep path between briars, and then the stench of the foaming green water was in our nostrils as we stood for one last glum instant on the mucky bank. I slid the dinghy into the river. A fierce current snapped the bow downriver, and I held the boat parallel to the bank as José clambered in. Then, while José's father gripped it by the side rope, I slid myself over the stern and felt José's trapped breath jelly-quivering flaccidly beneath me. I had a bad feeling. The old man pushed us off, and we instantly rushed away, fending off snags as best we could. There was no time to glance back.

Shaded on either side by mesquite trees, paloverdes, tamarisks, bamboo, and grass, the deep green river sped us down its canyon, whose banks were stratified with what appeared to be crusted salt. An occasional tire or scrap of clothing, a tin can or plastic cup wedged between branches, and once what I took to be the corpse of some small animal, then became a fetus, and finally resolved

into a lost doll floating face down between black-smeared roots —
these objects were our companions and guideposts as we whirled
toward the Salton Sea, spinning in circles because José had never
paddled before in his life.

Every now and then I'd see us veering into the clutches of a bamboo thicket or some slimy slobbery tree branches, and I'd drop my
notebook or camera and snatch up my oar, which was now caked
with black matter (shall we be upbeat and call it mud?). Then
woody fingers would seize us, raking muck and water across our
shoulders as we poled ourselves away. The first drops on my skin
seemed to burn a little bit, but no doubt I was imagining things.

José kept spraying me by accident. There was not much to do
about that; certainly I couldn't imagine a gamer or more resolute
companion. He was definitely getting tired now, so I laid down my
notebook between my sodden ankles and began to paddle in earnest. We were passing a secluded lagoon into which a fat pipe
drained what appeared to be clear water. We sped around a bend,
and for no reason I could fathom the stench got much worse —
whiffs of sewage and carrion, as in Mexicali. I vaguely considered
vomiting, but by then we were riding a deeper stretch that merely
smelled like marsh again. The water's green hue gradually became
brown, and the white foam, which occasionally imitated the faux-
marble plastic tabletops in some Mexicali Chinese restaurant, di-
luted itself into bubbles. Everything became very pretty again with
the high bamboos around us, their reflections blocky and murky
on the poisoned water. Occasionally we'd glimpse low warehouses
off to the side.

Another inlet, another pipe (this one gushing brown liquid),
and then we saw a duck swimming quite contentedly. Black-and-
white birds, possibly phoebes, shrieked at us from the trees. I got a
beautiful view of garbage snagged under dead branches.

The heat was getting miserable, and my end of the boat, having
punched into one bamboo thicket too many, hissed sadly under
me, sinking slowly. Since the boat featured several airtight com-
partments, I wasn't too worried, but I didn't really like it, either.
Meanwhile the river had settled deeper into its canyon, and all we
could see on either side were bamboos and saltcedars high above
the bone-dry striated banks. A wild, lonely, beautiful feeling took
possession of me. Not only had the New River become so unfre-

quented over the last few decades that it felt unexplored, but the isolating power of the tree-walls, the knowledge that the adventure might in fact be a little dangerous, and the surprisingly dramatic loveliness of the scenery all made me feel as if José and I were explorers of pre-American California. But it was so weird to experience this sensation here, where a half-mummified duck was hanging a foot above water in a dead tree! What had slain it?

At midmorning the river, now a rich neon lime, split into three channels, all of them impassable due to tires and garbage. Above us, José's father waited at the Highway 98 bridge. I called it quits.

Even after taking a shower my hands kept burning, and the next day José and I still couldn't get the taste out of our mouths. We used up all his breath mints lickety-split; then I went to Mexicali for tequila and spicy tacos. The taste dug itself deeper.

Poor José only got $100. I had to give Ray Garnett, formerly the proprietor of Ray's Salton Sea Guide Service, $500 before he'd consent to take me down the last ten-mile stretch of the New River. Ray had been a fishing guide for decades. Now that he was retired, he still went out on the Sea pretty often, to keep even. He called the Salton Sea the most productive fishery in the world.

"How about the fish, Ray?" I asked.

"I've been eatin' 'em since 1955, and I'm still here, so there's nothin' wrong with 'em," he replied.

As a matter of fact, he thought the Salton Sea must have improved, because he used to get stinging rashes on his fingers when he cleaned too many fish, and that didn't happen anymore.

About the New River, Ray had very little information. He'd never been on it in all his seventy-eight years, and neither had anybody else he knew. That was why he was willing to hazard his $800 aluminum water-skimmer with its $1,200 outboard motor on a cruise. He was even a little excited. He kept saying, "This sure is different."

Ray preferred corvina to tilapia, and he brought some home-smoked corvina along in the cooler. Probably I was imagining the aftertaste.

Stocky, red, hairy-handed, round-faced, Ray did everything slowly and right, his old eyes seeing and sometimes not telling. We put the boat in near Westmorland, and the river curved us around the contours of a cantaloupe field, with whitish spheres in the bright greenness, then the brown of a fallow field, a dirt road, and at last the cocoa brown of the river itself, whirling us away.

The New River's stench was far milder here, the color less alarming; and I remembered how, when I'd asked Tom Kirk of the Salton Sea Authority how much of the Salton Sea's sickness came from the New River, he'd promptly answered, "People point their fingers at Mexico and at farmers. The perception that the Salton Sea is Mexico's toilet is unfair."

Maybe he was right, God knows. Maybe something else was causing the fish deaths and the bird deaths.

"You think there are any fish in this river, Ray?" I asked.

"Flathead catfish. I wouldn't eat 'em. One time we did core samples of the mud in these wetlands. It has just about everything in it."

"Like what?" I asked, but Ray stayed silent.

A little later, he said, "Must be something wrong with this water, 'cause I don't see any bullfrogs. I been watchin' the bank. No turtles, either. Bullfrogs and turtles can live in anything."

Swallows flew down. The river was pleasant, really, wide and coffee-colored, with olive-bleached tamarisk trees on either of its salt-banded banks. We can poison nature and go on poisoning it; something precious always remains. There is always something that our earth has left to give, and we keep right on taking.

Lowering our heads, we passed under a fresh-painted girder bridge that framed a big pipe. There was a sudden faint whiff of sewage, but the river didn't stink a tenth as much as it had at the border, let alone in Mexico. Passing a long straight feeder canal with hardly any trash in it, we found ourselves running between tall green grass and flittering birds. To the northwest, Villager Peak in the Santa Rosa Mountains was a lovely blue ahead of us.

"Have another piece of that corvina," Ray said.

Now there were just hills of bamboo and grass on either side, like the Everglades. Four black-winged pelicans flew together over the grass. The sunken chocolate windings of the New River seemed to get richer and richer. But another smell began to thicken. "The sea's right on the side of these weeds here," Ray was saying.

"What's that smell, Ray?"

"I think it's all the dying fish, and dead fish on the bottom. It forms some kind of a gas. It's just another die-off. It's natural." Was it? Ducks were flitting happily, and we saw dozens of pelicans as we came out into the sea.

"You get away from the smell when you get out here fishin'," Ray said, and he was right. Out on the greenish-brownish waves — "That's algae bloom that made the water turn green. Won't be any fish in here today" — the only odor was ocean.

"They've had studies and what have you ever since the late fifties," Ray sighed. "In 1995 we put 420 hours in and didn't catch a fish. But in '97 and '98 they started coming back. Whether the fish have gotten more tolerant or whether it's something else, I don't know."

Deep in an orangish-green wave, Ray thought it best to turn around. As we approached the river we grounded on a sandbar.

"If you don't mind getting your feet wet," Ray said, "it sure would make things easier."

We pushed. From the shore came a sickening sweet stench of rotting animals, and I soon had a sore throat and my eyes began to sting. When I left him, Ray gave me a kind and gentle smile, and an entire bag of smoked corvina.

"No face which we can give to a matter will stead us so well at last as the truth." That is what Thoreau wrote when he was measuring and meditating upon Walden Pond. "For the most part," he continued, "we are not where we are, but in a false position. Through an infirmity of our natures, we suppose a case, and put ourselves into it, and hence are in two cases at the same time, and it is doubly difficult to get out."

Throughout my researches into the New River and the Salton Sea, I found myself similarly in two cases at the same time. My fault lay in this: I had drunk in a certain doctrine, whose sources are as obscurely ubiquitous and whose substance is as tainted as New River water: that only an "expert" has the right to judge the acceptability of the water of life. The only way I could think of to decide the matter was to abrogate my own judgment and pay technicians to analyze a water sample from the river, and another from the sea. And then I'd know, because a printed report would tell me. But I already knew the truth. The Salton Sea is ghastly. The New River is ghastly.

Squatting over the stinking green water a few steps from the spot where José and I had launched our dinghy, I lowered sterile sample bottles one by one in my latex-gloved hands, standing partly on a fresh human turd to avoid falling in. The chemical odor seemed more dizzying than usual. What was it? I was hoping to find out. I was angling for your basic herbicide-pesticide sweep, including the chlorinateds (EPA method 8151); a CAM-17 for heavy metals; a full method 8260, needless to say, with MTBE and oxygenates; a TPH (that's total petroleum hydrocarbons to you); a surfactant; and a diesel test while I was at it. Originally I'd craved a fecal coliform count so badly I could taste it, but Tom Kirk had told me that the levels of fecal coliform, high at the border, dipped and then rose again at the mouth of the Sea, thanks to all the birds. So to hell with it.

I took my Salton Sea sample up in North Shore. It seemed like a good place because it was far enough away from the New River to reflect the base level of filthiness, so to speak, and it was also good on account of all those fish bones and salt-stiffened feathers. There was only one dead bird on the beach this time, a fluffy little baby. On the pier a man was fishing, perhaps not impressed by the selenium health advisory strongly suggesting that no one eat more than four ounces of Salton Sea fish-meat per two weeks.

I got my two water samples analyzed at California Laboratory Services in Sacramento. Sample one was the New River. Sample two was the Salton Sea.

"On the chlorinated acid herbicides, your 2, 4-dichlorophenoxyacetic acid took a hit on sample one," said the lab man. "On sample two, everything was non-detect. Let's see now, your diesel in the very first sample took a very small hit; the second sample was non-detect. For metals your first sample showed beryllium and zinc, and your second had barium and selenium. Both samples were well below the maximum legal contaminant levels on all that. We ran the 8260 for volatiles plus oxygenates. Both samples were clean."

I inquired how my samples compared to other water they'd tested.

"Relatively clean compared to other wastewater samples," the lab man said. "They're certainly not nearly as nasty as some of our samples from Brazil, Singapore, and China."

I called up the Audubon Society man, Fred Cagle, who'd always struck me as extremely levelheaded and independent. "Do these results surprise you?" I asked him.

"Not at all."

"Well, is the New River the most polluted body of water in North America, or one of the most polluted, or what?"

"It's been getting cleaner," he said. "But it still gets that reputation. It depends on who you talk to. They've found cholera, TB, all that kind of crap."

"What about the metals and organics, from pesticides?"

"It varies tremendously. We've taken hundreds of samples, and they all come out different. The stuff in the sediments may not be soluble; there are just so many variables. Of course you can't figure it out. Scientists can't figure it out."

"And those nine million pounds of agricultural chemicals you mentioned, where do they go?"

"Some of them break down, some of them get oxidized by bacteria. But we don't know that. Scientists get confused too."

"Would you agree that the Salton Sea is the most productive fishery in the world?"

"It's the most productive fishery, but it's also the most limited fishery. All the fish are artificial. We're getting right close to the edge of the salinity window. And why spend $100 million to save a $10 million fishery? Tilapia are an amazing fish. You know, they're a freshwater fish, and in thirty generations they've modified themselves to live in the Salton Sea. But has anybody told you about the parasite levels on those fish? They're enormous. Parasites are in their lungs, everywhere. The people who eat those fish might not enjoy them as much if they knew that."

"I still have a little smoked corvina left," I said. "Maybe I won't send it to you."

"Good idea."

From the mouth of the New River, on the southern edge of the Salton Sea, it's a straight shot halfway up the sea's west coast to Salton City, followed by Salton Sea Beach, then the nearly defunct Sun Dial Beach, and finally Desert Shores, where beside the rickety dock stinking white fishes gaped in the sun, swirling with each algal wave. A couple backed their boat down the boat ramp, the man steering, the woman craning her head with extreme seriousness.

Fish corpses squished beneath their wheels. Meanwhile, Salton City's attractions included a broken motel with drawn-in palm fronds and shattered windows. Emblems of stereotypical cacti and flying fish clung to the motel just as a fool clings to his dying love; its customers were heat, rubble, and cicada song.

The article on California in the eleventh edition of the *Encyclopedia Britannica,* published in 1911, states that irrigation along the Colorado River, which naturally bears only desert vegetation, has made it a true humid-tropical region, growing true tropical fruits. Wasn't that the golden age? Actually, the golden age hasn't ended even now. Looking around me at the Salton Sea's green margins of fields and palm orchards, I spied a lone palm tree far away at the convergence of tan furrows, then lavender mountains glazed with confectioner's sugar; this is the landscape where all is beauty, the aloof desert mountains enriched despite themselves by the spectacle of the fields.

Fertilization, irrigation, runoff, wastewater — the final admixtures of all these quantities flow into the Salton Sea. I couldn't condemn the state of the Sea without rejecting the ring of emerald around it. About the continuing degradation of that sump, José Angel of the Regional Water Quality Board very reasonably said, "It's a natural process because the sea is a closed basin. Pollutants cannot be flushed out. You could be discharging Colorado River water directly into the Salton Sea, or for that matter distilled water into the Salton Sea, and you would end up with a salinity problem, because the ground is full of salt! The regulations do not provide for a solution to this. You have to build some sort of an outlet."

Will they? Are they? The Salton Sea Restoration Project, that congressional marriage of the Salton Sea Authority and the U.S. Bureau of Reclamation, attended by a wedding party of some dozen other agencies, is following the favored bureaucratic course of studying the problem some more, and maybe some of its proposed alternatives will even do something: evaporation ponds, fish harvesting, carcass-skimming barges, wetlands habitats, displacement dikes, diverted Colorado River inflows, desalination ponds. But what about the salt and chemicals rolling in from the fields? "What can you do?" Angel had asked me. "Because fertilizers have a legitimate agricultural use."

I could see that legitimate agricultural use, reflected in the stylized elegance of a palm grove's paragraph of tightly spaced green asterisks and in the ridge-striped fields south of Niland, where sheep and birds intermingled, the cotton balls on their khaki-colored plants so white as to almost glitter. And in a brilliant green square of field, a red square of naked dirt on the left, a double row of palms in between, with their dangling clusters of reddish-yellow fruit. Legitimate use, to be sure, from which I benefited and from which bit by bit the sea was getting saltier and fouler with algae and more selenium-tainted, creating carrion and carrion-stench, which kept seagoers away.

Legitimate use made the half-scorched rubble of the Sundowner Motel, whose rusty lonely staircase used to offer a vantage point across the freeway to Superburger and then out to the sparse pale house-cubes of Salton City. On a clear day one could see right across the Salton Sea from those stairs, but if there was a little dust or haze, the cities on the far side faded into hidden aspects of the Chocolate Mountains' violet blur, and then the stairs too were carried off by the myrmidons of desert time. Meanwhile the Alamo flowed stinking up from Holtville, with its painted water tower, and the Whitewater flowed stinking, and the New River bore its stench of excrement and something bitter like pesticides. And Imperial County flowered and bore fruit. Through that lush and luscious land, whose hay bales are the color of honey and whose alfalfa fields are green skies, water flowed, 90 percent of it not from Mexico at all, carrying consequences out of sight to a 380-square-mile sump.

From a distance it looked lovely: first the hand-lettered sign of MAY'S OASIS, then the Salton Sea's Mediterranean blue seen through a distant line of palms, and then the smell of ocean.

Contributors' Notes

Notable Travel Writing of 2002

Contributors' Notes

Lisa Anne Auerbach is an artist and writer living in Southern California, where she teaches at the University of Southern California and Los Angeles City College. Although her words and pictures have appeared in such legitimate publications as *Outside, Freeze, No Boundaries, Skiing, Bikini, Artforum,* and *Jailbabes,* it's more often the case that she is broadcasting stealthily in her own projects, like *The Casual Observer, American Homebody, The Serious Voyeur,* and the *High Desert Test Sites* publication.

Rebecca Barry is an MFA student at the Ohio State University. Her nonfiction has appeared in *Real Simple, Details, The New York Times Magazine, Travel and Leisure, Glamour,* and *Seventeen,* and her fiction has appeared in *Ploughshares, One Story,* and *Tin House.* She lives in Columbus, Ohio, with her husband and two bad cats and is working on a collection of short stories.

Stephen Benz has published two travel narratives, *Guatemalan Journey* and *Green Dreams.* His travel stories have appeared in journals such as *Grand Tour, River Teeth,* and *TriQuarterly.* He has also written for the *Miami Herald, South Florida Sun-Sentinel,* and *Washington Post.* After stints in Guatemala, Moldova, and Miami, he now lives in Atlanta.

Tom Bissell was born in Escanaba, Michigan, in 1974. He attended Michigan State University, served as an English teacher for the U.S. Peace Corps in Uzbekistan, and worked as a book editor for W. W. Norton and Henry Holt. His fiction and nonfiction have appeared in *Harper's Magazine, Men's Journal, Salon, Esquire, McSweeney's, Agni, BOMB,* and elsewhere. His first book, *Chasing the Sea,* an expansion of "Eternal Winter," was published September 2003, and his short story collection, *Death Defier and Other Stories from Central Asia,* will be published in 2004. He lives in New York City.

Graham Brink graduated from the University of North Carolina in Chapel Hill in 1997. He works as the federal courts reporter for the *St. Petersburg Times* and lives in Tampa, Florida.

Peter Canby is the author of *The Heart of the Sky: Travels Among the Maya.* He runs the fact-checking department at *The New Yorker.*

Scott Carrier is a producer for public radio and HearingVoices.com and the author of *Running After Antelope.*

Peter Chilson is the author of *Riding the Demon: On the Road in West Africa.* His essays and short stories have appeared in the *North American Review, Ascent,* the *American Scholar, Creative Nonfiction,* the *Clackamas Literary Review, Audubon, West Africa Magazine,* and the *North Dakota Quarterly.* He is director of undergraduate creative writing at Washington State University and lives in Moscow, Idaho.

Tom Clynes writes about adventure, conservation issues, culture, and personalities for a wide range of publications and is a contributing editor for *National Geographic Adventure.* As a Pew Fellow in International Journalism, he traveled to Washington, France, and Central Africa to report "They Shoot Poachers, Don't They?" He is the author of *Wild Planet.*

Geoff Dyer's books include *But Beautiful, Out of Sheer Rage* (a finalist for a National Book Critics Circle Award), *Paris Trance,* and most recently *Yoga for People Who Can't Be Bothered to Do It.*

Jack Handey is a former longtime staff writer for *Saturday Night Live,* where, in addition to "Deep Thoughts," he wrote such sketches as "Toonces, the Cat Who Could Drive a Car," "Unfrozen Caveman Lawyer," and "Tonto, Tarzan, and Frankenstein." He is the author of four books, including the bestsellers *Deep Thoughts* and *Fuzzy Memories.* His humor pieces have appeared in *The New Yorker, Playboy, Outside, National Lampoon, Punch,* and elsewhere. He is a winner of two Emmy awards and a Writers Guild of America Award. He is currently working on a comedy pilot for Fox Television. He lives in the Chelsea section of Manhattan with his wife, Marta, and three cats.

Christopher Hitchens is a columnist for *Vanity Fair* and a visiting professor of liberal studies at the New School in New York. His recent books include *Left Hooks, Right Crosses: Highlights from a Decade of Political Brawling, Why Orwell Matters, Letters to a Young Contrarian,* and *The Trial of Henry Kissinger.*

After graduating from the University of Puget Sound, **Emily Maloney** studied in Japan at Naruto University as the 2001–2002 President Miki Memorial Scholar. This year she is traveling in South America. "Power Trip" is her first published article.

Canadian-born **Bruce McCall** is a writer and illustrator whose work appears frequently in *The New Yorker* and other leading publications. He has published three books, and his fourth, *All Meat Looks Like South America,* is forthcoming this fall.

Daniel Mendelsohn is a lecturer in classics at Princeton University. His memoir of sexual identity and family history, *The Elusive Embrace: Desire and the Riddle of Identity,* was named a New York Times Notable Book of the Year and a Los Angeles Times Best Book of the Year. Mendelsohn's articles, essays, reviews, and translations have appeared in *The New Yorker,* the *New York Times,* the *Nation, Esquire,* the *Hudson Review,* the *Paris Review, Travel and Leisure,* and *Food & Wine,* among many others. From 2000 until 2002 he was the weekly book critic for *New York,* for which he won the National Book Critics Circle Award for Excellence in Criticism in 2001. He is currently a regular monthly contributor to the *New York Review of Books.*

Lawrence Millman is the author of eleven books, including *Our Like Will Not Be There Again, A Kayak Full of Ghosts, Last Places, Northern Latitudes,* and *An Evening Among Headhunters.* "Lost in the Arctic" appears in somewhat different form in his recent book of the same title. A fellow of the Explorers Club, he has traveled to the Canadian Arctic fourteen times, Greenland ten times, Iceland seven times, and Paris once (South Paris, Maine, twice). He keeps a post office box in Cambridge, Massachusetts.

Steven Rinella is a correspondent for *Outside* magazine. His essays and reporting have appeared in *DoubleTake, The New Yorker, Nerve, American Heritage,* and many other publications. He is working on a book about the Great Lakes.

Kira Salak is the author of *Four Corners: Into the Heart of New Guinea, One Woman's Solo Journey,* which was selected by the *New York Times* as a Notable Travel Book of the Year. She is a contributing editor for *National Geographic*

Adventure and is pursuing a Ph.D. in English at the University of Missouri at Columbia. Her fiction is featured in *Best New American Voices 2001*.

Jacob Silverstein was born and raised in California and now lives in Austin, Texas. He was formerly a reporter for the *Big Bend Sentinel*, in Marfa, Texas. He is a regular contributor to *Harper's Magazine*.

Andrew Solomon's recently reissued first novel, *A Stone Boat*, was a runner-up for the *Los Angeles Times* first fiction prize and was on the *Village Voice* bestseller list. His best-selling book, *The Noonday Demon: An Atlas of Depression*, won him eleven national awards, including the 2001 National Book Award, and is being published in twenty-one languages. Solomon has lectured on depression around the world, including stints at Princeton, Yale, Stanford, Harvard, and Brown. He is a fellow of Berkeley College at Yale University and is a member of the New York Institute for the Humanities.

Michael Specter has been a staff writer at *The New Yorker* since 1998. He went to *The New Yorker* from the *New York Times*, where he was a roving correspondent based in Rome. Prior to that he was chief of the *Times*'s Moscow bureau. In 2001 he received the Global Health Council's Annual Excellence in Media Award for his piece about AIDS, "India's Plague." He was also awarded the 2002 AAAS Science Journalism Award for "Rethinking the Brain." He lives in New York with his wife and daughter.

Hank Stuever is a staff writer for the style section of the *Washington Post*, where he writes feature stories and essays. He was born and raised in Oklahoma City and has worked as a reporter for the *Albuquerque Tribune* and the *Austin American-Statesman;* he has also written for *L.A. Weekly, The Stranger,* and *Slate*. He lives in Washington, D.C.

Patrick Symmes is a contributing editor at *Harper's* and *Outside* magazines. As a foreign correspondent, he has traveled with Maoist insurgents in Nepal, visited both main guerrilla groups in Colombia, and profiled drug gangs in Brazil. His articles on Cambodia and Colombia have been selected for previous editions of *The Best American Travel Writing*. He is the author of *Chasing Che: A Motorcycle Journey through the Guevara Legend,* an account of a 12,000-mile ride across South America, retracing the journeys and guerrilla campaigns of Che Guevara. He also writes frequently for *GQ* and *Condé Nast Traveler.*

William T. Vollmann was born in California in 1959. His latest work, *Rising Up and Rising Down,* was published this year.

Notable Travel Writing of 2002

SELECTED BY JASON WILSON

JON LEE ANDERSON
  Our New Best Friend. *The New Yorker,* October 7.
  No Place to Hide. *The New Yorker,* November 25.
MAYA ANGELOU
  Raising the Iron Curtain. *Gourmet,* November.
R. W. APPLE, JR.
  Bath. *Town & Country,* August.
LEON ARON
  Restauration. *Harper's Magazine,* May.

RUSSELL BANKS
  The House of Slaves. *Esquire,* October.
PETER BENCHLEY
  Cuba Reefs. *National Geographic,* February.
STEPHEN BENZ
  Soviet Bloc Rock. *TriQuarterly,* Fall/Winter.
TOM BISSELL
  War Zones for Idiots. *World Hum,* October 21.
ROB BUCHANAN
  Across the Great Rift. *Outside,* March.
CHRISTOPHER BUCKLEY
  How Foie Gras Was My Valley. *Forbes FYI.*

TOM CAHILL
  Everybody Loves the Assassins. *Outside,* October.
  The Moonbow Chronicles. *National Geographic Adventure,* May.
MICHAEL CHABON
  The Mysteries of Berkeley. *Gourmet,* March.

BILL DONAHUE
  Wrestling with Democracy. *Washington Post Magazine,* July 7.

FRANCES FITZGERALD
  Silk Robes & Cell Phones. *Smithsonian,* January.
DREW FORSYTH
  Innocent Abroad. *World Hum,* July 13.
IAN FRAZIER
  The Mall of America. *The Atlantic Monthly,* July/August.
DARCY FREY
  George Divoky's Planet. *New York Times Magazine,* January 6.
BOB FRIEL
  Getting to the Bottom of Belize. *Caribbean Travel & Life,* April/May.
  Yo Ho Ho and a Bottle of Merlot. *Caribbean Travel & Life,* March.

MERRILL JOAN GERBER
  The Harpsichord on the Mountain. *The American Scholar,* Summer.
RICHARD GILMAN
  To the Noodle Shop. *The American Scholar,* Summer.
CHARLIE GLASS
  Wild Turkey. *Skiing,* October.
MICHAEL GORRA
  The Peculiarities of German Travel. *The American Scholar,* Summer.
  Travel and Metonymy. *Southwest Review,* Spring.
JEFF GREENWALD
  Technicolor Isles. *Islands,* November.

TOM HAINES
  80 Hours in Guyana. *Boston Globe,* May 12.
  From Seeing to Knowing, from Tourist to Traveler. *Boston Globe,* January 13.
DAVID HALBERSTAM
  Men Without Women. *GQ,* September.
PETER HESSLER
  Beach Summit. *The New Yorker,* September 2.
  The Middleman. *The New Yorker,* October 14 and 21.
CHRISTOPHER HITCHENS
  The Maverick Kingdom. *Vanity Fair,* December.
ANN HOOD
  Bridging the Gap. *Washington Post Magazine,* September 22.

MARK JACOBSON
  This Is the Situation. This Is the Confusion. This Is Angola. *Outside,* September.
MADHUR JAFFREY
  A Passage to Pakistan. *Saveur,* September/October.
MARK JENKINS
  A Modest Proposal. *Outside,* March.

JOE KANE
  The Big Wild. *Condé Nast Traveler,* August.

KATHLEEN LEE
  The Company of Dogs. *Condé Nast Traveler,* May.
MARK LEVINE
  Tuvalu Toodle-oo. *Outside,* December.
MICHAEL LEWIS
  Surfin' Safari. *Gourmet,* May.

ANN MARLOWE
  The Price of Milk (and Sex) in Cuba. *Salon,* February 7.
BUCKY MCMAHON
  The Road to Terlingua. *Esquire,* July.
LAWRENCE MILLMAN
  Beauty and the Beast. *Islands,* March.

ROB NIXON
  Radical Trust on the Road. *New York Times,* August 18.

THE ONION
  FAA Considering Passenger Ban. October 16.
  Frequent Flyer Knows Out-of-the-Way Airport Bar That's Never Crowded.
    December 18.
P. J. O'ROURKE
  Anything Goes. *The Atlantic Monthly,* October.
  Tina's Got a Gun. *Forbes FYI,* Fall.

STEPHANIE PEARSON
  La Ruta Maya. *Outside Travel Guide,* January.
TONY PERROTTET
  Archipelago of Lost Souls. *Islands,* November.
ANDREW X. PHAM
  Gifts. *The American Scholar,* Summer.
ROLF POTTS
  The Last Archipelago. *Condé Nast Traveler,* July.
BRIAN PRESTON
  Baked Lunch. *Transition,* Summer.

ED READICKER-HENDERSON
  Why You're Here Now. *Motionsickness,* November/December.
ALAN RICHMAN
  Auto Gratification. *GQ,* July.
MARK ROTELLA
  Alone at Sunset in a Land Without Singles. *New York Times,* May 26.
RUSS RYMER
  The Oregon Coast and Its Denizens. *The Sophisticated Traveler,* May 12.

KIRA SALAK
  Lost Souls of the Peyote Trail. *National Geographic Adventure,* August.

JOHN BURNHAM SCHWARTZ
  Fear in the Afternoon. *GQ,* July.
BOB SHACOCHIS
  Kingdoms in the Air. *Outside,* October.
BILL SHERWONIT
  Song of the Arctic. *Alaska Magazine,* November.
PAULA K. SPECK
  Almost a Travel Story. *The Literary Review,* Spring.
THOMAS SWICK
  Our Gang in Havana. *South Florida Sun-Sentinel,* March 24–April 7.

PAUL THEROUX
  The Hawaiians. *National Geographic,* December.
CULLEN THOMAS
  The Mark of an American. *New York Times Magazine,* February 3.
LAD TOBIN
  You Virtually Can't Get There from Here. *Fourth Genre,* Fall.
RICHARD TODD
  Lost in the Magic Kingdom. *The Atlantic Monthly,* May.
CALVIN TRILLIN
  Missing Links. *The New Yorker,* January 28.

BILL VAUGHN
  The Snow on the Sweetgrass. *Outside,* October.

SCOTT WALLACE
  Napoleon in Exile. *National Geographic Adventure,* April.
MARCY WEBSTER
  When Time Catches Up with the Traveler. *New York Times,* June 2.
ROBERT WERNICK
  Trouble in Paradise. *Smithsonian,* February.
W. D. WETHERELL
  Vermont on a Dare. *The Sophisticated Traveler,* September 29.

JOE YONAN
  Out on the High Seas. *Boston Globe,* September 22.

THE B·E·S·T AMERICAN SERIES ™

THE BEST AMERICAN SHORT STORIES® 2003
Walter Mosley, guest editor • Katrina Kenison, series editor

"Story for story, readers can't beat the *Best American Short Stories* series" (*Chicago Tribune*). This year's most beloved short fiction anthology is edited by the award-winning author Walter Mosley and includes stories by Dorothy Allison, Mona Simpson, Anthony Doerr, Dan Chaon, and Louise Erdrich, among others.

0-618-19733-8 PA $13.00 / 0-618-19732-X CL $27.50
0-618-19748-6 CASS $26.00 / 0-618-19752-4 CD $35.00

THE BEST AMERICAN ESSAYS® 2003
Anne Fadiman, guest editor • Robert Atwan, series editor

Since 1986, the *Best American Essays* series has gathered the best non-fiction writing of the year and established itself as the best anthology of its kind. Edited by Anne Fadiman, author of *Ex Libris* and editor of the *American Scholar*, this year's volume features writing by Edward Hoagland, Adam Gopnik, Michael Pollan, Susan Sontag, John Edgar Wideman, and others.

0-618-34161-7 PA $13.00 / 0-618-34160-9 CL $27.50

THE BEST AMERICAN MYSTERY STORIES™ 2003
Michael Connelly, guest editor • Otto Penzler, series editor

Our perennially popular anthology is a favorite of mystery buffs and general readers alike. This year's volume is edited by the best-selling author Michael Connelly and offers pieces by Elmore Leonard, Joyce Carol Oates, Brendan DuBois, Walter Mosley, and others.

0-618-32965-X PA $13.00 / 0-618-32966-8 CL $27.50
0-618-39072-3 CD $35.00

THE BEST AMERICAN SPORTS WRITING™ 2003
Buzz Bissinger, guest editor • Glenn Stout, series editor

This series has garnered wide acclaim for its stellar sports writing and top-notch editors. Now Buzz Bissinger, the Pulitzer Prize–winning journalist and author of the classic *Friday Night Lights,* continues that tradition with pieces by Mark Kram Jr., Elizabeth Gilbert, Bill Plaschke, S. L. Price, and others.

0-618-25132-4 PA $13.00 / 0-618-25130-8 CL $27.50

THE B·E·S·T AMERICAN SERIES ™

THE BEST AMERICAN TRAVEL WRITING 2003
Ian Frazier, guest editor • Jason Wilson, series editor

The Best American Travel Writing 2003 is edited by Ian Frazier, the author of *Great Plains* and *On the Rez*. Giving new life to armchair travel this year are William T. Vollmann, Geoff Dyer, Christopher Hitchens, and many others.

0-618-11881-0 PA $13.00 / 0-618-11881-0 CL $27.50
0-618-39074-X CD $35.00

THE BEST AMERICAN SCIENCE AND NATURE WRITING 2003
Richard Dawkins, guest editor • Tim Folger, series editor

This year's edition promises to be another "eclectic, provocative collection" (*Entertainment Weekly*). Edited by Richard Dawkins, the eminent scientist and distinguished author, it features work by Bill McKibben, Steve Olson, Natalie Angier, Steven Pinker, Oliver Sacks, and others.

0-618-17892-9 PA $13.00 / 0-618-17891-0 CL $27.50

THE BEST AMERICAN RECIPES 2003–2004
Edited by Fran McCullough and Molly Stevens

"The cream of the crop . . . McCullough's selections form an eclectic, unfussy mix" (*People*). Offering the very best of what America is cooking, as well as the latest trends, time-saving tips, and techniques, this year's edition includes a foreword by Alan Richman, award-winning columnist for *GQ*.

0-618-27384-0 CL $26.00

THE BEST AMERICAN NONREQUIRED READING 2003
Edited by Dave Eggers • Introduction by Zadie Smith

Edited by Dave Eggers, the author of *A Heartbreaking Work of Staggering Genius* and *You Shall Know Our Velocity*, this genre-busting volume draws the finest, most interesting, and least expected fiction, nonfiction, humor, alternative comics, and more from publications large, small, and on-line. *The Best American Nonrequired Reading 2003* features writing by David Sedaris, ZZ Packer, Jonathan Safran Foer, Andrea Lee, and others.

0-618-24696-7 $13.00 PA / 0-618-24696-7 $27.50 CL
0-618-39073-1 $35.00 CD

HOUGHTON MIFFLIN COMPANY   www.houghtonmifflinbooks.com